LAKEFRONT

LAKEFRONT

Public Trust and Private Rights in Chicago

Joseph D. Kearney and
Thomas W. Merrill

CORNELL UNIVERSITY PRESS ITHACA AND LONDON

First published 2021 by Cornell University Press
Printed in the United States of America

Library of Congress Cataloging-in-Publication Data

Names: Kearney, Joseph D., author. | Merrill, Thomas W., author.
Title: Lakefront : public trust and private rights in Chicago / Joseph D. Kearney and Thomas W. Merrill.
Description: Ithaca [New York] : Cornell University Press, 2021. | Includes bibliographical references and index.
Identifiers: LCCN 2020057771 (print) | LCCN 2020057772 (ebook) | ISBN 9781501754654 (hardcover) | ISBN 9781501754661 (pdf) | ISBN 9781501754678 (epub)
Subjects: LCSH: Lakeshore development—Illinois—Chicago—History. | Lakeshore development—Social aspects—Illinois—Chicago. | Lakeshore development—Economic aspects—Illinois—Chicago. | Lakeshore development—Law and legislation—Illinois—Chicago.
Classification: LCC HD268.C4 .K33 2021 (print) | LCC HD268.C4 (ebook) | DDC 307.1/4160977311—dc23
LC record available at https://lccn.loc.gov/2020057771
LC ebook record available at https://lccn.loc.gov/2020057772

In memory of Edmund W. and Mary Jane Kearney, among whose many gifts to me Chicago was only one —JDK

For the next generation: Jessie, Margaret, and Libby —TWM

Contents

Acknowledgments

This book has been an unusually long time in the making. We began more than twenty years ago, when each of us had been a longtime resident of Chicago. Both of us moved to other cities, one to Milwaukee and the other to New York, where we acquired teaching and administrative responsibilities at different law schools. We found ourselves nevertheless—or, perhaps, all the more—unable to resist the challenge of untangling the history of the Chicago lakefront, which is at once a large puzzle and a kind of miracle. Given our other duties, these efforts were mostly concentrated in the summer months, when it was possible to return to the city. Three articles eventually emerged that are reflected in portions of the book. For example, aspects of chapters 1 and 2 originally appeared in the *University of Chicago Law Review*, and we appreciate its permission to draw on our article, cited in the notes; similarly, for chapters 3 and 4, we rely on our subsequent articles in the *Northwestern University Law Review*. At the same time, we have extensively reworked this material and drawn on further research. The balance of the book, covering most of the twentieth century and the early decades of the twenty-first, is entirely new.

Through the years, we have accumulated an extraordinary number of debts. We have benefited from a variety of excellent collections of archival material in Chicago. The Newberry Library includes in its holdings many of the papers of the Illinois Central Railroad, primarily up to 1906. Given that the railroad was a central player in most of the disputes on the lakefront during this period (to anticipate our story), these were invaluable, especially the onion skin copies of correspondence between the officers of the company. We thank the librarians at the Newberry for helping us locate and decipher these materials.

The Chicago History Museum and the Chicago Public Library were also important sources of primary material. Both have important collections of old Chicago newspapers, many of which are not available online. The Chicago History Museum has an unmatched archive of old photographs, to give only one other of many relevant examples. We wish to thank Lesley Martin, Johanna Russ, and others at these institutions for their assistance in mining their rich and well-curated collections.

The Chicago Park District provided critical assistance, especially in connection with the material in chapters 6 and 7 on the construction of Lake Shore

Drive and associated lakefront parks. We are most indebted to Julia Sniderman Bachrach for giving us access to the park district's extensive archives, without which these chapters could not have been written.

This scarcely exhausts the catalog. Much of the source material for the book comes from court records. We uncovered these in a number of different places, including the Illinois State Archives in Springfield; the Archives Department of the Clerk of the Circuit Court of Cook County; the National Archives and Records Administration at Chicago (with help from Glenn Longacre), at College Park, Maryland, and in Washington, DC; and the library of the Supreme Court of the United States. We gathered legislative materials from the Library of Congress as well as places already mentioned. Additional information came from the records of the US Army Corps of Engineers and the Metropolitan Water Reclamation District of Greater Chicago. We express our appreciation to each of these institutions for its help.

We were fortunate to enlist Dennis McClendon not only in making numerous original maps for the book but in helping sort out various relevant details. We are particularly grateful to him.

The librarians and archivists of the universities with which we have been affiliated or places at which we have presented ourselves also provided invaluable support. In addition to the entities noted above, these include Northwestern University School of Law and the McCormick Library of Special Collections and University Archives at Northwestern; the Evanston Public Library; the libraries of Columbia University, Loyola University Chicago, the University of Chicago, the University of Illinois at Chicago, the University of Illinois at Urbana-Champaign, and the University of Wisconsin Law School; the American Heritage Center at the University of Wyoming; and, last but especially, the Raynor Memorial Libraries and the Eckstein Law Library at Marquette University.

We drew on conversations and support from colleagues and others. James B. Speta and David A. Strifling made a number of helpful contributions to our work. Robert E. Bailey, Gerald A. Danzer, David A. Epstein, Richard A. Epstein, Timothy J. Gilfoyle, Jack Guthman, Richard H. Helmholz, Libby Hill, Ann Durkin Keating, John H. Langbein, Kevin B. Leonard, the late Dawn Clark Netsch, Carl Smith, Henry E. Smith, and John Fabian Witt provided suggestions or counsel at one point or another in this lengthy project. Our families heard and bore much of the lakefront project—and, to be sure, offered encouragement.

We owe our largest debt to our research assistants, whose number the descriptive phrase "army of" would only slightly exaggerate. Some were law students at Northwestern and Columbia. By far the largest number have been students at Marquette Law School. It would be appropriate to acknowledge them individually, but given the long span of time, and the different contributions they have made—some working for part of a summer, others for the school year, and still others for multiple years—the risk of overlooking someone or failing to provide fair credit seems too great. We have thanked them individually, we hope, and we do so again collectively. Without their efforts, there would be no book.

INTRODUCTION

Those flying into Chicago from the east on a sunny day encounter a stunning vista. The first thing they see is a long strip of parkland, rising from the blue waters of Lake Michigan and running almost the entire length of the city from south to north. Immediately behind the parkland, a wall of glass and steel buildings thrusts upward, dramatically reflecting the greenery below. Perhaps most striking to the well-traveled eye, the line dividing the lake from the shore is remarkably free of unsightly vestiges of a rougher, more industrial past, such as rotting docks, abandoned factories and warehouses, or power plants. In this respect, the Chicago lakefront is different from the waterfront of other major cities, such as New York, London, Philadelphia, Cleveland, Detroit, or San Francisco. This book seeks to explain how Chicago came to have such a beautiful, well-tended, and publicly accessible lakefront—the city's most treasured asset.

The path that led to the lakefront of today was by no means direct or inevitable. The history of the lakefront has been one of almost continual social conflict. If the disputes had been resolved differently, the lakefront would look very different today, and more like the waterfronts of other major cities.

Some of the division on the lakefront has pitted the haves against the have-nots. For example, the Potawatomi Indians at various times claimed the filled land along the lakefront, on the ground that their rights to the lakebed had never been validly extinguished. And for many years George Wellington Streeter and his band of squatters did battle with detectives hired by real estate investors over control of the land north of the Chicago River. Streeter was remarkably

FIGURE 0.1. Looking north at Grant Park along the Chicago lakefront, 2018. Dbimages/Alamy Stock Photo.

tenacious, but the wealthy investors eventually prevailed and gave us the high-rise enclave called Streeterville, named in homage to the vanquished contestant. Other conflicts, such as the one over reversing the Chicago River so that it flows out of the lake rather than into it, pitted Chicagoans against the residents of other states.

The dominant form of social conflict on the lakefront, however, has been between different factions within the Chicago elite. To be sure, some of these factions have invoked the interests of the general public in support of their own cause. But the principal actors, and the driving forces behind the disputes, have been groups of wealthy and well-connected citizens who have had different visions about what should be done with the lakefront.

The first of these intramural disputes, which was not fully resolved until after the First World War, pitted the upscale landowners whose property was favored with views of the lake against various interests that wanted to use the lake for commercial development. The initial form of this dispute featured the Michigan Avenue property owners, on one side, and the Illinois Central Railroad, which had been allowed to enter the city along the lakefront, on the other. A related dispute, which involved some of the same actors, pitted the landowners against those who wanted to build an outer harbor in Lake Michigan in order to preserve Chicago's status as a major inland port. Toward the end of the nineteenth century, the Michigan Avenue landowners faced a third challenge, as other wealthy

Chicagoans and influential politicians sought to fill Grant Park, along the lakefront in the center of the city, with monumental buildings, many bearing their names.

Civic antagonism over the lakefront continued into the twentieth and twenty-first centuries, and it again largely took the form of a series of fights between rival factions of the elite. As lakefront parks spread out north and south from the city center, the commissioners of the park districts had to devise ways to overcome the opposition of riparian landowners, who prized their views and access to the lake. And with the emergence of the environmental movement, the lakefront has become the scene of renewed conflict, with those who want to preserve the existing shoreline and open park space versus those who favor using the lakefront for convention centers, expanded universities, museums, recreated football stadiums, and presidential centers. These sorts of fights no doubt will persist into the future. Figure 0.2 provides an overview of the Chicago lakefront and the sites of many of the major conflicts chronicled in the pages that follow.

Because the majority of the social conflicts over the lakefront have been waged by rival elites, the forums in which these disputes have unfolded have been legal ones. The reason is simple: the elites have had the resources to retain lobbyists and lawyers in the hope of enlisting the power of the state on their side. Efforts to influence public opinion have not been ignored, but the critical showdowns have taken place in the city council, the state and federal legislatures, and, perhaps most importantly, the courts; indeed, the lakefront has been the subject of virtually nonstop litigation from the 1850s to the present. We have mined these resources, extracting previously undiscovered or unappreciated information about the contending political forces and personalities involved in the individual disputes. We have tried to describe the legal controversies in such a way that one does not have to be a lawyer to understand the legal context of the disputes in question. But we strongly believe that one cannot fully grasp what was going on without considering the legal processes that shaped and motivated the contesting parties.

Tapping into the legal sources has several unanticipated payoffs. Perhaps most notably, it allows us to draw on a rich source of archival material that has not previously been factored into histories of the lakefront. For another advantage, it reveals certain critical changes in the law—crucial factors, as it turns out, in generating many of the conflicts that emerged over time. One of the most important was a reversal in the understanding about who owns the land under Lake Michigan. Up until about 1860, the legal understanding was that the owners of land on the shore—riparian owners—also owned the submerged land. In the 1890s,

FIGURE 0.2. Major areas along the Chicago lakefront.

it became clear that the State of Illinois owned the submerged land. But in the thirty-some years in between, there was confusion and uncertainty about who owned the lakebed. This, in turn, helps explain much of the private landfilling that occurred during this period, by the Illinois Central Railroad and a forerunner of the US Steel Corporation among others, as well as the shenanigans over control of the area now called Streeterville.

Another legal development of general importance was the slow but inexorable development of new institutions to regulate the lakefront. At the beginning of the period covered by this book, government at all levels was weak, and at the state and local levels was often corrupt. The only way to provide public goods such as wharves, or to preserve open spaces for parks, was through lawsuits invoking the common law. Toward the end of the nineteenth century, the US Army Corps of Engineers and specially created government commissions, such as the sanitary district and the park districts, emerged as major players on the lakefront. Eventually these institutions were able to gain control of the lakefront for public use, and to prevent further illegal landfilling and squatting.

The exploration of legal sources also makes our account broadly relevant to those interested in environmental and urban history. Land that fronts on a major body of water like Lake Michigan is always vexed by tension between public and private rights. But as this book will show, it is not a simple matter to identify what sort of legal regime will strike the right balance between public and private in this context. In some circumstances, private rights—such as the right of private landowners to sue to protect their view of the water—will do more to protect the interests of the general public than will more explicitly public remedies. And defining the public interest in the waters that adjoin land is not easy. Is the public interest served or disserved by filling open water to build parks, museums, convention centers, private universities, and wharves—or railroads and steel mills that employ thousands? And which institution should make these decisions—the legislature, the city, the courts, an administrative agency, or perhaps the people themselves in a referendum?

Focusing more precisely, our history can be seen as an extended case study about one particular legal idea that emerged on the Chicago lakefront and has come to play an important role in American law more generally: the public trust doctrine. Although the outer reaches of this doctrine remain contested, at its core it protects the right of the general public to access navigable waterways. In order to resolve a major controversy over whether the Illinois legislature could grant one thousand acres of submerged land on the lakefront to the Illinois Central Railroad, and then rescind the grant four years later, the US Supreme Court in 1892 decided that such a grant would violate the public trust in which the submerged land was held. The *Lake Front Case* has since been regarded as the leading authority recognizing the public trust doctrine in the United States.*

The public trust doctrine has become intensely controversial. Some would like to see it extended to cover all kinds of resources, from wildlife to the atmosphere to cyberspace. Others see it as a threat to the very existence of private property rights. Our account sheds important light on the circumstances that gave rise to the doctrine on the Chicago lakefront, how the doctrine has performed in its original setting relative to other legal doctrines, how it was transformed in the twentieth century, and how its legacy in protecting public resources has been mixed, in both its original and its transformed versions. We do not suggest that our account answers all the large questions about the public trust doctrine. But it will surely be of interest to those who engage in ongoing debates about it.

Even more broadly, our book can be seen as an examination of the importance of law and, in particular, legal property rights in the long-term development of an important resource like the lakefront. In the short run, the law unquestionably played a significant role in resolving many of the controversies we examine, whether through the adoption of legislation or the resolution of litigation by the courts. In the longer run, we find reason for skepticism. Some legal doctrines emerged to resolve certain controversies, only to be repudiated later on. Others emerged with great force, only to be fatally weakened, or transformed beyond recognition as time passed.

The only dimension of the law that stands out as a strong predictor of the outcome of the struggles on the lakefront is the power of possession. The Illinois Central Railroad engaged in massive landfilling on the lakefront, often (as it turned out) with no legal justification, but was allowed to keep all the improvements it actively possessed, including its former rail yard built on landfill south of the Chicago River, now full of skyscrapers. The wealthy private investors who claimed the made land in Streeterville were allowed to keep it, once they were able to oust Streeter and began developing that land with substantial structures, even if some of the land technically belonged to the state. The construction of Lake Shore Drive was made possible by low-visibility transfers of submerged

* We use the name *Lake Front Case* to refer to the 1888 circuit court decision and the 1892 ruling in the Supreme Court for a number of reasons. It is the popular convention that began in the nineteenth century, from the early days of the case, and has endured. See, e.g., United States v. Illinois Central Railroad Co., 154 U.S. 225, 233 (1894) (noting in a second appeal that this is how the "several cases [were] known and spoken of together" in the trial court). In addition, the Illinois Central and the State of Illinois are such a large part of our story, with so many relevant cases of the era bearing their names, that to refer to *Illinois Central Railroad Co. v. Illinois*, from the caption of the lead case in the 1892 Supreme Court decision, let alone to use some short form of that, would not seem specific enough to be useful in the context of this book.

land to riparian owners, who filled the land and took possession of it without any public protest. The importance of possession was intuitively obvious both to the high-priced lawyers who defended the conduct of the Illinois Central and to the scalawag Streeter, who thought that so long as he remained in possession of some portion of the reclaimed land, someday it would be his. We cannot be sure that this generalization extends beyond riparian land or even beyond the Chicago lakefront. But it suggests that greater attention should be given to possession in considering the potential significance of property rights.

Chicago has been singularly lucky in that the many social conflicts over the lakefront were resolved in the way they were. Massive landfilling of the lake occurred, but it did not ultimately detract from the beauty or value of the lake, in large part because Lake Michigan is so vast. Some structures were built on the fill, but their number was limited, in large part because of the opposition of riparian owners to losing their view of the lake. And once the park districts gained control of much of the lakefront, the structures that were built were largely dedicated to public uses. If the outcome in Chicago was largely fortuitous, part of our motivation in writing this book has been to suggest how a more deliberate mix of policies might produce similar results elsewhere. Conflicting visions and political realities will always frustrate any attempt at comprehensive planning. But understanding how particular choices conspired to produce a generally happy outcome in one particular setting may provide inspiration, or at least some cautionary tales and instructive lessons, for those who aspire to achieve the same ends elsewhere.

1 THE LAKE FRONT STEAL

Our story begins with the construction of the Illinois Central Railroad along the shore of Lake Michigan in Chicago. Today, the railroad has effectively disappeared. Beginning in the 1850s and for more than a century, however, the Illinois Central's massive rail yards and facilities were the lakefront's most prominent feature. The railroad's landfilling to create this empire generated much of the conflict—legal, political, and social—that vexed the lakefront in the ensuing years. It was also responsible for much of the configuration of the lakefront today.

The Illinois Central's facilities stood on what had been Lake Michigan. Whether the railroad had the *right* to construct these facilities turned on who owned the submerged land and whether that owner had the authority to permit such landfilling. Although these questions seemed to trouble no one when the railroad first entered the city in 1852, they soon became important—and the answers increasingly uncertain. These uncertainties would produce, in 1869, what came to be known as "The Lake Front Steal."

The Lay of the Land

The site of Chicago was long thought to be a potentially valuable port. While the south end of Lake Michigan had few natural harbors, the Chicago River was one, at least potentially. The river was also intriguingly close to the watershed of the Mississippi River—suggesting that, with the digging of a canal, the river might connect the Great Lakes to the Mississippi River and thence to New Orleans and the Gulf of Mexico.[1]

The principal impediment to using the Chicago River as a port was Lake Michigan's current. The water in the southern part of the lake tends to circulate counterclockwise. As depicted in figure 1.1, this created a long sandbar, curving south, at the mouth of the Chicago River. The result was that the water at the mouth was often too shallow for shipping.[2]

Soldiers stationed at Fort Dearborn, on the south bank of the river, repeatedly cut a channel through the sandbar, but it always silted in again. In the mid-1830s, army engineers more or less solved the problem by building piers into Lake Michigan from the river's north and south banks. The twin piers functioned like a spout, discharging the river straight into the lake, and thereby reduced the formation of sandbars at the entrance.[3]

It soon became clear that the piers channeling the Chicago River had only redirected the lake's relentless currents. South of the south pier, the lake currents subtracted land by erosion. This area featured Lake Park, running along the lakefront from Randolph Street south to Park Row (a street running eastward

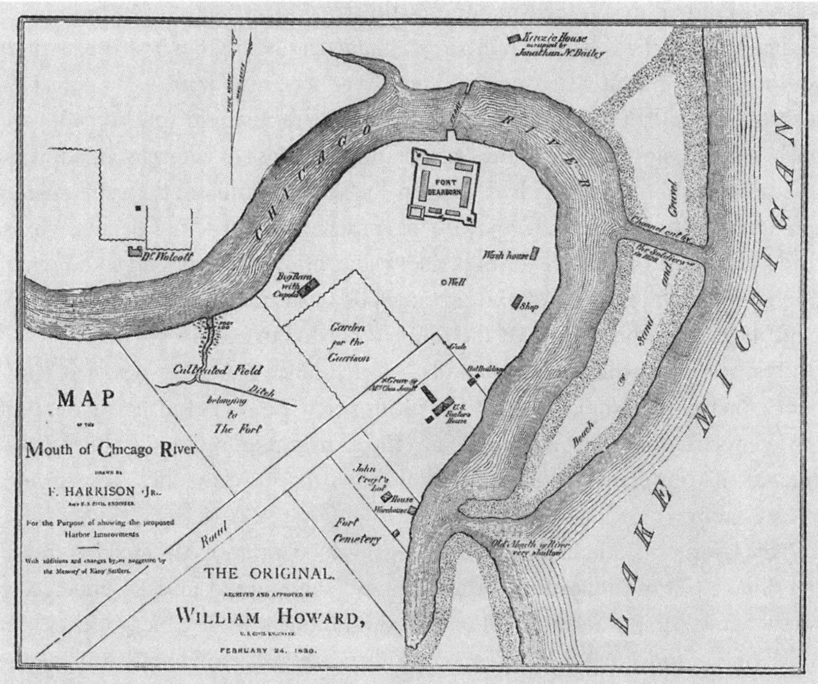

FIGURE 1.1. Mouth of the Chicago River, 1830. Chicago History Museum, ICHi-021558.

from Michigan Avenue, just north of 12th Street). By 1850, some twenty of the park's thirty-five acres had washed away. Across from the park, the west side of Michigan Avenue was lined with residential structures, including an array of fine townhouses called "Terrace Row," where many of the city's elite lived. These properties were in potential jeopardy from the encroaching lake waters. On occasion, residents had to work through the night to prevent Michigan Avenue from collapsing into the lake.[4]

The solution to the erosion problem was assumed to be the construction of an offshore breakwater. Multiple initiatives toward this end in the 1840s and early 1850s were unsuccessful, with disagreement as to whether Michigan Avenue residents or, more generally, the taxpayers of Chicago should pay for it. The matter reached an impasse.[5]

Enter the Illinois Central Railroad. The railroad was the product of coordinated federal and state legislation. In 1850, Congress granted a two-hundred-foot-wide right of way and alternate sections of land on either side, in checkerboard fashion, to the State of Illinois, to support a north–south railroad. The total grant encompassed some 2.5 million acres. The Illinois legislature in 1851 then chartered the Illinois Central Railroad Company and reconveyed the federal lands to the new railroad to subsidize its construction.[6]

The law specified that the railroad would generally follow a *Y* shape, with its southern terminus at Cairo, on the Ohio River. As constructed (see figure 1.2), it would run north to the town of Centralia. There it would split in two, variously heading northwest toward Galena and northeast to Chicago. In addition to regranting the land that had been in the federal domain, the state charter provided, rather imprecisely, that for purposes of constructing depots, shops, yards, and other railroad facilities besides rights of way, the railroad could "enter upon and take possession of and use any lands, streams and materials of every kind" belonging to the state. If the railroad needed to acquire privately owned land, it was given the power to condemn such lands using the power of eminent domain—a compulsory transfer of property in return for the payment of just compensation to the owner. Finally, the charter required that if the railroad entered any municipality, it had to obtain the consent of the local government to its location.[7]

This last provision effectively gave the Chicago Common Council control of the Illinois Central's location within the city. The railroad initially preferred a route that would put its terminal on the south branch of the Chicago River. But much of the land along the route was already possessed by other railroads, so the Illinois Central proposed an approach locating its right of way along the city's lakefront. To accomplish this, and as an inducement to the city, the railroad said that it would build and pay for a breakwater to protect the shore from erosion.[8]

FIGURE 1.2. The Illinois Central Railroad as initially constructed.

Michigan Avenue residents strongly opposed the idea. A railroad would be noisy and smoky. It would also impair their view of the lake, and likely compromise their property values. But the common council was more sympathetic. As Robin Einhorn has written, "If the Michigan Avenue owners would not pay for lake shore protection in cash, they would be forced to pay some other way." On June 14, 1852, over a mayoral veto, Chicago enacted an ordinance permitting the Illinois Central to enter the city along the lakefront. For the next century, the railroad and the Michigan Avenue property owners would be in more or less continual conflict.[9]

The 1852 city ordinance fixed the railroad's location and established its powers in the city. The carrier would enter where the city's southern boundary (then 22nd Street) met the lakeshore. The line would proceed north, first along the lakeshore to 12th Street, then across "the open space known as Lake Park" to Randolph Street, and finally to such grounds between Randolph and the Chicago River as the railroad might obtain to build a terminal. The ordinance gave the railroad a three-hundred-foot right of way from 12th Street to Randolph Street. This was one hundred feet wider than the right of way specified in the federal grant and the state charter. The ordinance did not explain the source of the city's authority to permit this.[10]

Given the erosion that had taken place in Lake Park, the ordinance specified, in effect, that the right of way would run along the shoreline from 22nd Street to 12th Street, but that north of 12th the railroad would be built in the lake—roughly three hundred feet from the shore, by the time it got to Monroe and to Madison.[11]

Some other important particulars concerned the areas south of 12th and north of Randolph. To the north, the ordinance contemplated that the railroad would itself acquire the necessary rights for a terminal and other railroad facilities, through either purchase or condemnation. In addition, the ordinance gave the railroad the authority, starting with whatever riparian lands it acquired in this area, to "extend [its] works and fill out into the lake," to a point four hundred feet west of the east end of the south pier of the Chicago River. In this area would "be located the depot of said railroad within the city, and such other buildings, slips or apparatus, as may be necessary and convenient for the business of said company." The ordinance offered no hint about the source of the city's authority to permit this landfilling. Nor did it authorize any landfills or other improvements south of 12th Street.[12]

For its part, the railroad agreed to erect within three years, and thereafter to maintain, along the eastern edge of its right of way from Randolph south to 22nd Street, a breakwater sufficient "to protect the entire front of [Chicago] . . . from further damage or injury" from the lake waters. In deference to the Michigan Avenue residents, the ordinance prohibited the Illinois Central from constructing any buildings or other improvements to the east of Lake Park that might obstruct views of the lake from the shore. Nor could the railroad allow its locomotives or cars to remain standing on the tracks in this area.[13]

The Illinois Central moved quickly. The railroad drove piles into the lakebed to support a double line of track sitting on trestles. Initially, for both the tracks and the breakwater, it used only two hundred feet of the authorized right of way. North of Randolph Street, the railroad acquired the necessary riparian land and began almost immediately to fill the lake east of this area. Here it constructed its terminal, approximately where the Prudential Insurance Building is located today. Known as Great Central Station, the terminal was the largest building in Chicago when it opened in 1856. The railroad also did some filling south of Lake Park, between 12th and 16th Streets, where it built an engine house and its Weldon repair shops.[14]

It soon became clear that the 1852 ordinance presented operational difficulties. In 1855, the common council permitted the railroad to curve its tracks westward as they approached Randolph Street from the south and to fill in the resulting triangular area. This curve improved access to the terminal building. One year later, the common council similarly permitted the railroad to curve its tracks eastward as they approached Randolph. This gave the railroad better access

FIGURE 1.3. The Chicago lakefront, looking north, ca. 1865. Chicago History Museum, ICHi-062330.

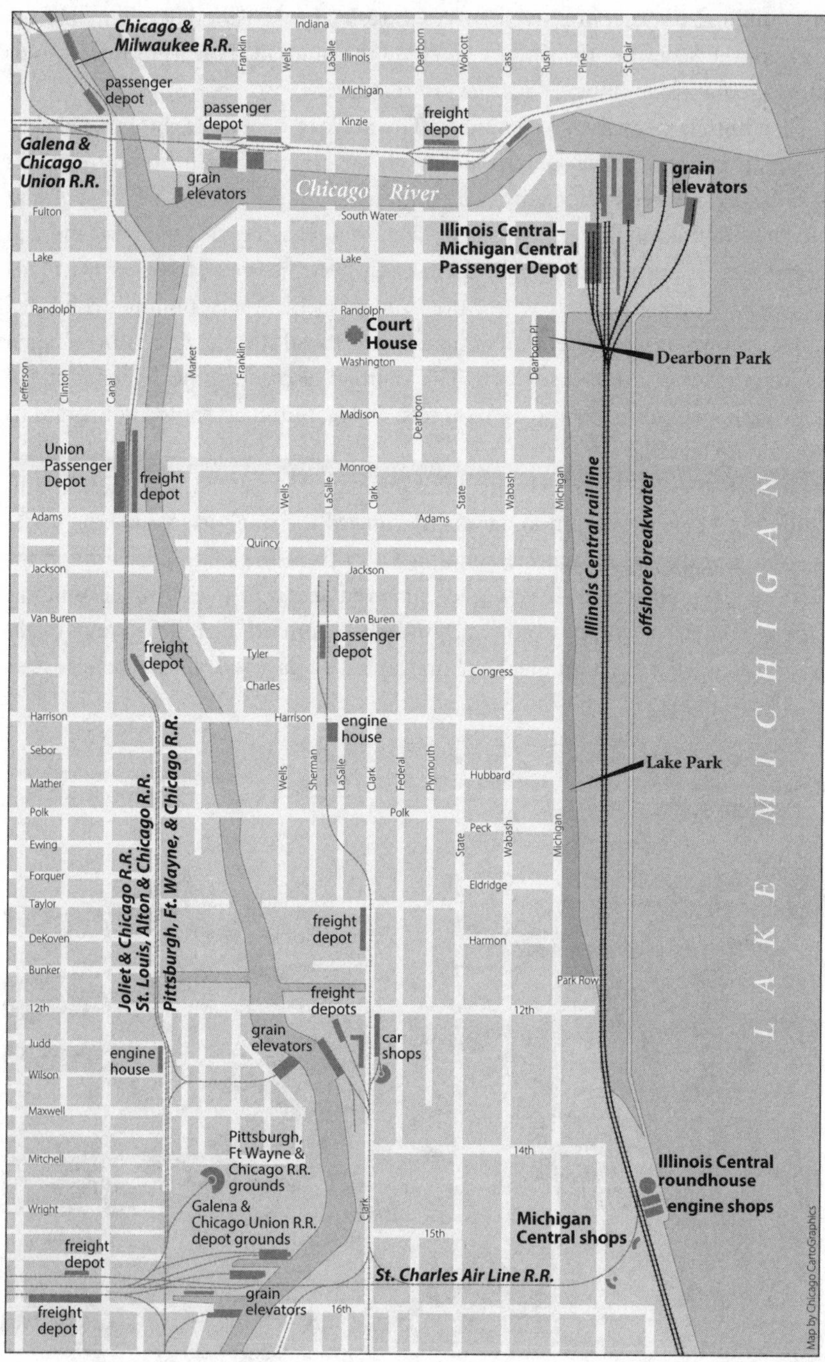

FIGURE 1.4. Major Chicago rail facilities, ca. 1860.

to grain elevators being constructed on further landfill jutting east, along the line of the river's south pier. As with the 1852 ordinance's grant of an extra hundred feet of right of way, neither the 1855 nor the 1856 ordinance explained the city's authority to convey these additional rights to fill and develop the lakebed.[15]

After a lull in further construction but with the end of the Civil War, the lakefront again became the focus of attention. Many called for the construction of an "outer harbor" to the east of the breakwater, to relieve the congestion in the Chicago River from the growing water traffic. Increased passenger traffic on the Illinois Central and affiliated lines gave rise to calls for a larger depot, perhaps in Lake Park between Michigan Avenue and the Illinois Central right of way. To accommodate rising transshipments of grain, lumber, and other commodities, the railroad built new piers and sidings in the landfill area north of Randolph and east of its terminal building. Finally, both Michigan Avenue residents and public advocates, wanting Chicago to follow in the footsteps of eastern cities and create a system of public parks, promoted an improved park along the lakefront.[16]

Figure 1.3 is a photograph of the lakefront taken ca. 1865, looking northward along Michigan Avenue. Terrace Row can be seen at the left. Lake Park, a narrow strip of land, is in the center, with the Illinois Central tracks on the right, standing on piles in the lake and leading to Great Central Station and the railroad's grain elevators, in the distance, north of Randolph. Figure 1.4 shows the configuration of the lakefront and downtown railroad facilities around this time.

Legal Uncertainty over Property Rights in Submerged Lands

We pause in our narrative for an important discussion of a seemingly obscure matter of riparian property rights. This will explain some of the puzzling behavior of the City of Chicago and the Illinois Central in the arrangements allowing the railroad to enter along the lakefront in the 1850s. It also sets the stage for the drama over the lakefront that emerged in the 1860s and produced the "Lake Front Steal."

Under English law, a critical distinction was drawn between the rights in areas of water affected by the ebb and flow of tides and the rights in rivers and lakes not so affected. The king as sovereign owned the submerged land under tidal waters. In contrast, submerged land under rivers and lakes not affected by the tides was subject to private ownership. Absent a grant to the contrary, the titleholder of such nontidal riparian land owned the submerged land to the centerline of the river or lake that the riparian land abutted. Importantly, however, all waters, whether tidal or not, were subject to a general public right of free navigation. Thus, neither the king (as owner of submerged tidal lands) nor private riparians (as owners of submerged nontidal lands) could use their ownership of submerged lands to create obstructions that would block free navigation.[17]

In 1842, the Supreme Court of the United States took an important first step in adapting these understandings to the American context. The court held that the original colonies had succeeded to the English Crown's ownership of submerged lands under navigable waters. Thus, upon independence, title to these lands vested in the state governments. A few years later, under the so-called equal-footing doctrine, the court held that subsequently admitted states created out of federal territory inherited the same ownership rights to submerged lands under navigable waters as the original thirteen.[18]

These decisions involved lands under tidal waters. In England, only tidal waters were officially deemed to be navigable waters. Given its long coastline and short rivers, this understanding did not do great violence to commercial realities. The North American continent, in contrast, contains a large number of waterways that are not tidal but are navigable in fact, including the Great Lakes. By the 1840s, if not before, it was clear that these waterways would play a vital role in the development of American commerce.

The courts of the various states divided over how the Supreme Court's decisions recognizing state ownership of tidal lands should apply to land under waters that were not tidal but were navigable in fact. A majority of states, adhering to English law, held that state ownership was limited to land under tidal waters. A significant minority of states, however, concluded that English law was unsuited to conditions in North America. These courts adopted what can be called the American view: submerged lands under all waters that are navigable in fact, whether tidal or not, are owned by the state as sovereign.[19]

In 1842, in a dispute over the rights to timber on an island in the Mississippi River, the Illinois Supreme Court cast its lot with the traditional English view. The Illinois courts would continue to adhere to this view—at least with respect to land under navigable rivers. To take but one example, the state supreme court in 1868 rejected the City of Chicago's attempt to order the destruction of a wharf built out into the Chicago River. The court said that "the rule is well settled, that the title of a riparian owner extends to the middle thread of the stream if it is called for as a boundary."[20]

If this were all of the law bearing on the question of ownership of the lakefront in Chicago, then the relevant legal principle would seem clear. Lake Michigan is not regarded as tidal water. Hence, the owner of riparian land bordering on Lake Michigan would own the submerged land to the centerline of the lake. There would be only one question: who owns the land on the shore? Considerable evidence suggests that this was in fact the assumed legal rule about ownership of the bed of Lake Michigan up through the 1850s.[21]

Illinois's acceptance of the English view of riparian rights in submerged lands explains why the Chicago Common Council believed that it could convey a three-hundred-foot right of way to the railroad for its operations in the lake. The city evidently assumed that it was the owner of Lake Park. Hence, under the English view, the city also owned the bed of Lake Michigan off Lake Park and could convey an interest in this lakebed to the railroad (provided that it did not interfere with the public right of navigation). The same assumption explains the city's grant of authority to the railroad to engage in extensive landfilling north of Randolph Street and to curve its tracks outside the three-hundred-foot right of way south of Randolph. Likewise, we can understand why the Illinois Central, as the owner of riparian lands along this segment of the lakeshore, felt free to engage in aggressive landfilling south of 12th Street without any official blessing of the common council. Under the English view, the railroad as riparian owner could engage in fills and improvements of adjacent submerged lands, provided that it did not impair the public right of free navigation on the lake.

Soon, however, discordant themes began to emerge in the law that would eventually undermine any confidence about the ownership of submerged lands beneath Lake Michigan. One came in 1852, when the Supreme Court of the United States, in *The Propeller Genesee Chief v. Fitzhugh*, overruled earlier precedent and held that the admiralty jurisdiction of the federal courts was not limited to tidal waters but extended to all waters that are navigable in fact, including the Great Lakes. The court cited many of the same factors, including the greater importance of inland rivers and lakes to commerce in North America, that had convinced some state courts to reject the English definition of navigability in disputes over the ownership of submerged lands. The court cautioned that its decision involved only admiralty jurisdiction, not property rights, but in retrospect *The Genesee Chief* undoubtedly tipped the balance in favor of the American view regarding ownership of submerged lands, at least in those jurisdictions and circumstances where the issue was open.[22]

Another discordant element concerned a rule of boundary construction. Early in the nineteenth century, it was well established that when a deed specified a river or stream as the boundary of property, courts would presume that the property extended to the centerline of the watercourse. Gradually, however, American courts began to differentiate between the rules applicable to rivers or streams, on the one hand, and ponds or lakes, on the other. By 1850 a leading treatise declared that "[t]he law of boundary, as applied to rivers, is without doubt inapplicable to the *lakes* and other large natural collections of fresh water in this country." The author suggested that when a deed describes a lake as a boundary, the riparian landowner is presumed to own only to the shore or edge of the lake—and thus *not* to own the submerged land to the centerline.[23]

In 1860, the Illinois Supreme Court embraced the new rule of construction for large lakes. In a decision called *Seaman v. Smith*, the court held that a deed referring to "Lake Michigan" meant the shoreline, not the centerline of the lake. The "circular shape" of most lakes, the court said, militated in favor of the shoreline as the correct boundary. Although no question was presented in *Seaman* about who in fact owned the bed of Lake Michigan, after 1860 a careful Illinois lawyer would have reason to doubt whether the English view of riparian rights in submerged lands, faithfully followed by the Illinois courts with respect to rivers, would necessarily be extended to riparian lands abutting Lake Michigan. Authoritative word on the subject nevertheless did not come until the lakefront litigation and the 1890s—far in the future.[24]

The identity of the riparian owner of the land known as Lake Park was even less clear than the rule determining ownership of the bed of Lake Michigan. This is revealed by a remarkable editorial and follow-on letters published by the *Chicago Tribune* in 1867. The editorial, headlined "Who Owns Lake Park?," suggested that although "[i]t has been supposed that the city of Chicago had an unquestionable title to this important piece of property," a closer examination of the subject disclosed arguments to be made that the park was owned, instead, by the state, by the commissioners of the Illinois and Michigan Canal (whom we shall meet hereafter), or by the United States government. Believing the last of these to have the best possible claim adverse to the city, the *Tribune* encouraged the city to seek congressional legislation ceding the federal government's rights and title to the city.[25]

The editorial elicited some legally sophisticated responses. One writer concluded that the canal commissioners owned not only the park "but also, all beyond to a distance of a nautical league from the shore." At the end of this letter, the editor of the *Tribune* appended the following comment: "Query.—Where does our correspondent find any authority for the assumption that the title to the bottom of the lake . . . is vested in the riparian owner?" The answer (not stated in the paper) was, of course, that the Illinois Supreme Court's doctrine about the ownership of riverbeds provided the authority. But by 1867, at least for newspaper editors, this answer was too implausible to be taken seriously with respect to Lake Michigan.[26]

In short, by 1867 the legal title to the Chicago lakefront was deeply vexed—from the ownership of the strip of land known as Lake Park to the applicability of the English or American rule to the lands under Lake Michigan. If the American rule applied, then the state owned the submerged lands, subject to whatever rights the Illinois Central had acquired through its charter from the state in 1851. (The rights the railroad had obtained from the city would be of no value, unless the state had first granted its rights to the city, which it had not done.)

If the English rule applied, then the submerged lands were owned by whoever was determined to be the owner of Lake Park, subject to whatever rights the railroad had acquired from this party. It was a fine mess.

1867: The Lakefront in Play

The uncertainties about the legal status of Lake Park and the submerged land of Lake Michigan involved relatively esoteric questions about property rights. Some lawyers thought they could predict the answers. A few of the more confident tried to exploit these predictions to seize all or part of the lakefront for themselves.

The first concerted effort emerged in the 1867 session of the Illinois legislature. The General Assembly at that time met in odd-numbered years. As the session was about to commence, the Illinois Central's president, John M. Douglas, in Chicago, wrote to William H. Osborn, chairman of the executive committee of the company's board of directors in New York City, that he did "not believe this Company has any enemies in the legislature or out of it."[27]

Douglas was badly mistaken. In early February 1867, a bill was introduced to incorporate a private company, "the Chicago Harbor, Pier and Dock Company." It would have the power to construct a new outer harbor for Chicago and to "connect the same by roadways across railroad tracks, body of water or land," using the power of eminent domain if necessary. The named promoters included a number of Chicago's leading citizens, lawyers being especially prominent. These included Jonathan Young Scammon, who had interests in Michigan Avenue real estate, and Melville W. Fuller, the future chief justice of the United States. The bill's sponsor in the state house was Henry M. Shepard, Fuller's law partner.[28]

Reaction in the Chicago newspapers was fierce. The *Chicago Tribune*, employing an early use of the word "steal" in connection with lakefront legislation, asserted that "a bolder or more infamous attempt to steal a vast property belonging to the public has never been attempted." The proposed grant would give the company the right "to build a city with water privileges upon the site belonging to Chicago, and not render any compensation therefor." The *Chicago Times* speculated that the scheme's object was to obtain the submerged land and then resell it to the city.[29]

The bill's sponsor, Henry M. Shepard, was a busy man during the legislative session. He also introduced and obtained lower-house passage of another bill, which became known as the Skating Park Bill. One unfavorable review characterized this as "giving the Michigan Park basin in the city in fee to a company of private speculators, under the pretence of cutting ice, skating, yachting, and other festive employments." The *Chicago Times* characterized the bill as the "Michigan Park Steal."[30]

The Illinois Central was understandably alarmed by these efforts to wrest control of the lakefront via legislative grants. Its primary concern was that its physical improvements and its right to use the lakefront not be imperiled by a grant of the submerged land to some other entity. On February 16, 1867, the railroad's president, Douglas, instructed the company's Springfield representative, "Devote yourself entirely to lake matter.... Better stay and see that nothing goes through surreptitiously—Make the city keep a strong delegation there till the close of the session and see it out." He expected "a hard fight." To fend off the efforts to secure a legislative grant of the lakebed for a private corporation, the railroad threw its support behind an effort to secure greater control over the lakefront, including any harbor, for the City of Chicago.[31]

Intrigue over the lakefront continued throughout the 1867 legislative session. In the end, however, despite the efforts of Shepard and others, none of the bills became law. The railroad breathed a sigh of relief.[32]

1868: Debating the Future of the Lakefront

The 1867 legislative session stimulated a wider-ranging public debate about the future of the lakefront. It will be useful to refer to the areas depicted in figure 1.5. "North Lake Park" (sometimes called "the three blocks") refers to the solid parkland from Randolph Street south to Monroe Street, together with the submerged land out to the Illinois Central right of way. "South Lake Park" refers to the solid parkland from Monroe Street to the south, together with the submerged land out to the railroad's right of way. "Proposed outer harbor" refers to the area east of the right of way, extending an indefinite distance into the water, where a new outer harbor might be built.

The primary concern in 1868 was how to prevent future giveaways by the General Assembly, either of Lake Park or of the site for an outer harbor. In an editorial titled "The Future Harbor of Chicago," the *Tribune* again urged the city to make "[a]n application to Congress for a grant of the title to all land lying east of the present frontage of the city." The newspaper gave this explanation:

> It has not been more than a year since a bill transferring all the land east of Michigan avenue, and for one mile eastward into the lake, and lying between Madison and Twenty-second streets, to half a dozen private persons . . . was introduced into the Legislature of Illinois, and failed to pass only because this journal sounded the alarm in time. But there is not a day while the Legislature is in session when such a bill may not be pushed through corruptly, and it will then be too late to take those proper precautionary steps which ought to be taken now. The city of

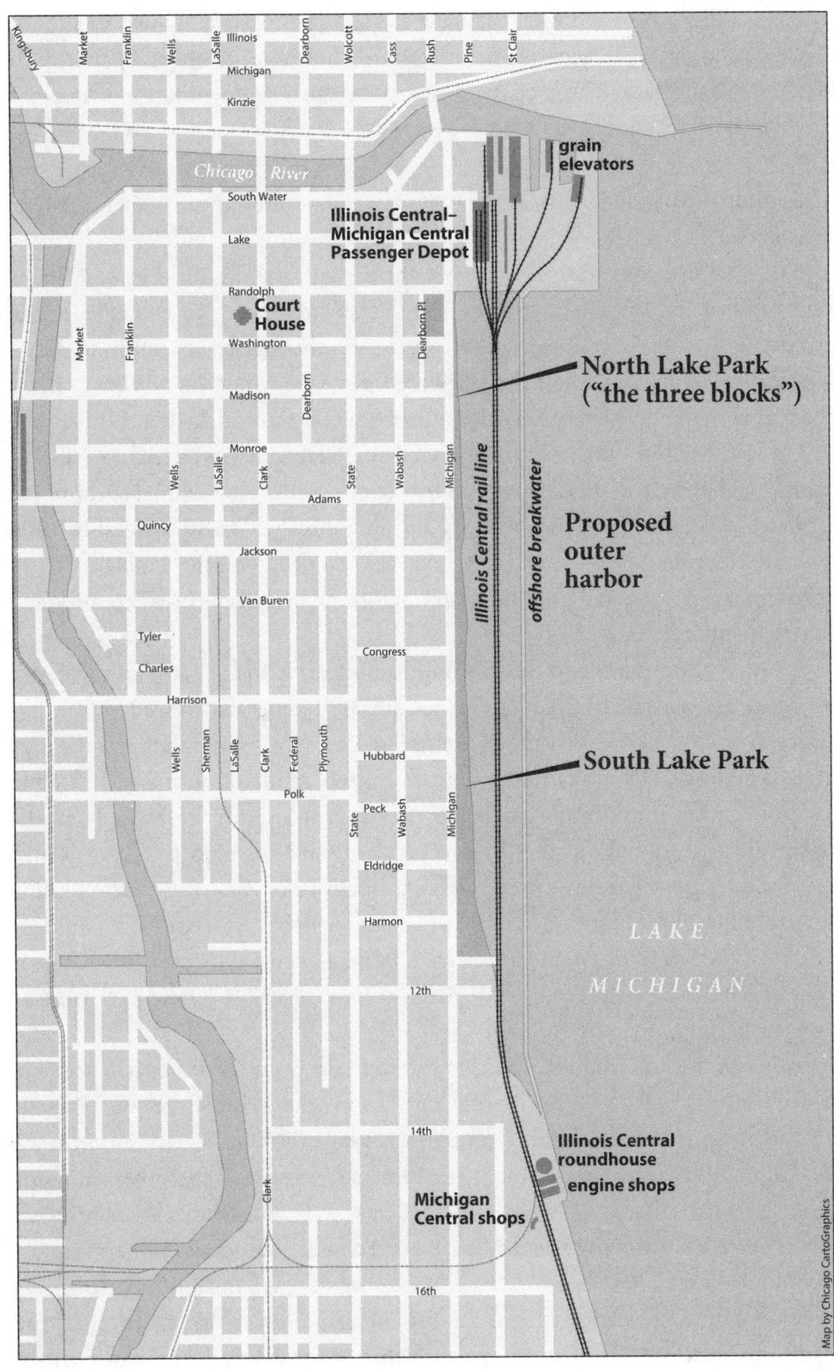

FIGURE 1.5. Locations of north Lake Park, south Lake Park, and proposed outer harbor.

> Chicago has too much at stake to submit to have a city two miles long and one mile wide planted between it and Lake Michigan, particularly when that city will be the property of a private corporation, having an irrepealable charter.

The editorial concluded with the first of many pleas throughout 1868 for federal legislation.[33]

The legal understanding underlying these pleas was muddled at best. If the problem was that title to Lake Park and the lakebed remained with the federal government, then federal legislation would clear the matter up. But in that case a purported grant of the land by the state legislature would be no threat. If, on the contrary, the problem was that, under the equal-footing doctrine, title to the bed of Lake Michigan had been conveyed from the federal government to Illinois upon statehood in 1818, then federal legislation could provide no solution: the United States would have no authority left, and only the General Assembly could give the city title. For most of 1868, however, the debaters showed little sign of agreeing on or even grasping the exact nature of the property-rights problem that they intuited.

Another issue coming to the fore and complicating the debate was the desire for more parks. According to one source, it was "a generally conceded fact that Chicago is remarkably destitute of breathing places for its population." The biggest stumbling block was money, both to acquire land and to make it suitable for public recreation. Many saw Lake Park as a solution. Interestingly, north Lake Park was thought at the time to be unsuitable for park purposes. Thus, the *Tribune*, among others, proposed that north Lake Park, out to the Illinois Central right of way, be sold and the proceeds (which it was assumed would go to the city) used to augment south Lake Park. This would "net a magnificent sum which would amply suffice to give Chicago the finest public park west of New York."[34]

This was not idle chatter. The city entered into negotiations over a possible sale of north Lake Park to the Illinois Central and other railroads for the purpose of constructing a new passenger depot. In January 1868, a special committee of the common council reported that the Illinois Central and the other railroads collectively had offered $800,000 for north Lake Park. The committee's reaction was positive but carefully hedged: it supported a sale but would not commit to recommending a price.[35]

Soon a bidding war broke out among the same forces that had sought the lakefront in the 1867 legislative session. Henry M. Shepard, Fuller's law partner, publicly offered $1,000,000 for north Lake Park. Two weeks later, another lawyer upped the ante, offering $1,250,000.[36]

Others dissented. A group of leading citizens, including many Michigan Avenue owners, opposed any sale of north Lake Park. Their remonstrance to the common council included perhaps the first invocation of the idea of a public trust with respect to the lakefront: public grounds of the city "ought to be held forever sacred as the property of the public in *trust* for the enjoyment and use of all conditions and classes of poor, as well as the rich, among our people."[37]

At the end of 1868, the common council moved toward adopting the committee's recommendation to seek a sale of north Lake Park to the Illinois Central. Like the committee, however, the council deferred addressing the matter of price. To resolve the property-rights issue, the council resolved to seek both federal and state legislation transferring the relevant rights to the city. As the first step, the city prepared to send to Springfield a deputation, headed by Alderman Joshua Knickerbocker, also a member of the Illinois House of Representatives, to seek the desired legislation in the upcoming session.[38]

The failure of the common council to reach an agreement on price with the Illinois Central for the rights to north Lake Park, combined with the unsettling prospect of a bidding war, undoubtedly caused the railroad to rethink its situation along the lakefront. The *Tribune* warned the city's political leaders that their failure to nail down an agreement with the railroad might induce the latter to turn to Springfield, not as an ally but as a competitor. The warning was prescient.[39]

1869: Chicago and the Illinois Central Go to Springfield

Before turning to the critical events of 1869, we offer some preliminary observations about the institution in which they transpired. The members of the Illinois General Assembly in this era would descend on the state capitol, in Springfield, every other year, conducting all business in a matter of months. Many served in the legislature only once. Upon their arrival, the legislators took up lodgings in boarding houses or at the Leland Hotel. During the day, they would run into lobbyists at nearly every turn. In the evenings, they found liquor flowing freely, and cigars consumed with equal gusto, in the hotel's dining room and bar. The consumables—and perhaps a few other vices as well—were almost certainly underwritten by the lobbyists.

How much influence did the lobbyists wield? Consider an account in an 1867 *Chicago Tribune* story written during a pitched battle over regulating warehouses. This account portrayed the legislators as "merely men, mostly poor—generally living on their wits; a majority of them lawyers, whose profession and practice require them to receive fees for advocating and defending wrongs as well as

FIGURE 1.6. Illustration of the Leland Hotel (before 1899). Courtesy of the Sangamon Valley Collection, Lincoln Library, Springfield, Illinois.

rights." As to whether one could "buy the vote of any member"—"Are there no diamonds among them?"—the article quoted a lobbyist who said, "Yes. We can purchase *any* member's vote; but there are some who are like the diamond, and to buy them costs far more than their votes are worth." Of course, to say that a "cheap vote" would be as useful in a roll-call vote as a "*dear* vote" was not to deny that "it is necessary to secure the services of some shrewd, sharp, experienced rascals, like Senator—, (you know who I mean,) to pilot our bills, amendments, motions and parliamentary manoeuvres; else the whole craft might be shipwrecked and go to the bottom."[40]

The unnamed senator undoubtedly was Alonzo W. Mack. A native Vermonter who had moved west in stages, Mack arrived in Illinois after completing medical studies. He became involved in Republican politics and took up the practice of law. In 1862, Mack helped organize at Kankakee a regiment of volunteers for participation in the Civil War. Commissioned a colonel, he served as commander until early 1863. After the war, he helped establish the *Chicago Republican* newspaper.[41]

Mack was elected to the Illinois House in 1858 and then to the state senate in 1860 and again in 1864. During the 1867 legislative session, Mack played a central role in blocking railroad regulation. He was sufficiently impressive and influential that he received extraordinary committee assignments. His chairmanship of the committee on railroads was especially concerning to the Democratic *Chicago Times*, which regarded a majority of that committee's members as "[m]en who, on account of a plentiful lack of brains, will interpose no argumentative obstacles which Doctor Alonzo W. Mack will not find the way to overcome." Yet that was not the extent of it: "In fact, Mack is on all the committees where there is any selling or trading to be done, or any money to be made."[42]

In 1869, Mack was no longer a senator, but the Illinois Central retained him to represent its interests with respect to the Chicago lakefront. He set up shop at the capitol during the day and residence at the Leland Hotel at night. One newspaper's correspondent described the latter scene at some length, emphasizing that "there is no jumbling and mixing up of people at the Leland House dinner-tables." Apart from "a couple of tables for the ladies,"

> [a]t others sit strangers, chance visitors; at others, men who have business—legitimate business—with the Legislature; at another, members who claim to be honest; at another, members who are in the market. Of course, there is no sign out, but it is understood that "every article at this table is unconditionally offered for sale." Then there is another for special lobbymen, at which presides—*sicut inter ignes, Luna minores*—Dr. Mack. When a person leaves the "honest men's" table and goes over to that of the "corruptibles," it is an intimation that he is ready to listen to proposals.[43]

This description is of particular interest because it is set forth in the context of discussing Senator Irus Coy, from Kendall County, whom the newspaper denounced for supporting the lakefront bill. The newspaper account said more about Coy: "The business of the session commenced, and I began to see more clearly the course pursued by my man. The Lake Front bill came up, and he supported it, supported it zealously, for he had enjoyed the privilege of dining at Dr. Mack's table, and of learning from that person, just precisely how things stood. He was one of the first recruits—no eleventh hour convert, but an early believer in the doctrine of the poet: 'Heaven sent us here to vote and trade.'"[44]

The City of Chicago made the opening bid for control of the lakefront in 1869. On January 13, Knickerbocker introduced legislation designed to transfer to the city whatever rights the state held in Lake Park and the submerged land east of Lake Park. The bill also specifically authorized the city, after consulting with the federal government, to arrange for the construction of "docks, piers, breakwaters or other works," so as "to enlarge the harbor of said city, and promote and encourage the commerce upon, and the navigation of the said lake." The city was forbidden to alienate the harbor lands, east of the Illinois Central's right of way (although certain types of leases up to ninety-nine years would be permitted). Finally, the bill permitted the city publicly to sell all or part of the park, between Michigan Avenue and the railroad, so long as three-fourths of its aldermen concurred.[45]

Within days, legislators serving areas outside Chicago began to oppose the bill. No doubt tracking arguments made by Mack, "downstate" members questioned why such a valuable resource as the future harbor of Chicago should be reserved for the city.* The state's rights to the Chicago harbor, in the words of a Springfield newspaper, "ought to be made a source of revenue to the State."[46]

During the early legislative maneuverings, the Illinois Central carefully concealed its hand. But by its internal account (and soon enough by an external one), it was "hard at work." Fomenting opposition to the city's bill was only Mack's first move for the railroad.[47]

In late January, a substitute bill drafted in great secrecy—and essentially constituting the Lake Front Act as finally enacted—was introduced. The substitute largely tracked the structure of the Knickerbocker bill, with four major exceptions. First, the substitute conveyed the land outside the breakwater, for the construction of a new harbor, not to the city but to the Illinois Central; this area extended one mile into the lake and would be later characterized as "something more than a thousand acres." Second, the substitute effectively directed the city to convey any interest in north Lake Park to the railroads, upon payment by the railroads to the city of $800,000 in four installments. Third, the substitute "confirmed" the rights of the Illinois Central to operate along the lakefront in accordance with its original charter and to maintain the various lakefront facilities constructed in accordance with its riparian ownership. Finally, in a provision to attract downstate legislators, the substitute provided that the Illinois Central was to remit to the state treasury 7 percent of the gross receipts from all leases or improvements to Lake Park or the submerged lands, in perpetuity, just as its charter required for its other operations in the state.[48]

The Illinois Central quickly gained the upper hand in the struggle. To the extent that Mack required direction, Douglas was calling the shots from Chicago. In early February, he reported to Osborn in New York of "this lake shore business" that "a thing more complicated with diverse interests I was never engaged in": "Individuals, City, State—and it is perhaps our good fortune that these

* We follow the local convention of using "downstate" to refer to anything outside the northeastern corner of Illinois—i.e., beyond Chicago and the surrounding six-county area of Cook, DuPage, Kane, Lake, McHenry, and Will Counties.

interests are antagonistical, and that they are unable to unite against us." Though a cautious man, Douglas expressed confidence in the outcome.[49]

Douglas assessed the prospects correctly. The House Committee on Municipal Affairs and Insurance agreed to report the substitute bill to the full lower chamber. It would wait a day or two so that Knickerbocker might prepare a minority report. On February 10, the house voted (by a margin of forty-nine to twenty-nine) to adopt the substitute bill, and by a similar vote (fifty to thirty) to set the bill for a required third reading.[50]

The opponents did not capitulate. On February 16, with the legislature temporarily adjourned, a call went out for a "GREAT MASS MEETING!" of "citizens of Chicago who are opposed to giving away the Lake front." Yet this rally, held at downtown's Farwell Hall, did not quite provide the hoped-for spark. One newspaper suggested that the rally "has greatly strengthened the chances of the success of the bill, as it demonstrated conclusively that the feeling of opposition to it in Chicago is neither so intense nor wide-spread as Little Knickerbocker has endeavored to make the legislature believe."[51]

On February 20, the railroad's bill passed the house by a vote of fifty-two to thirty. The *Tribune* correspondent expressed grudging admiration for Mack for the closeness of the actual vote to his prediction a month earlier, when the bill scarcely had been seen by any legislator.[52]

The house had not yet finished with the lakefront. One of the substitute bill's opponents, William Strawn, introduced a startling resolution demanding the appointment of a joint committee of the house and senate to investigate "supposed corruption of members of this General Assembly." In particular, the committee would determine "whether any improper influence, pecuniary or otherwise, has been used or offered directly or indirectly to any member of this General Assembly to induce them or any of them to vote for or against any bill, resolution or measure, pending or heretofore pending before this General Assembly."[53]

Views about the resolution varied predictably. "[F]riends of the Lake Front bill" had no doubt that the resolution's "object is not to investigate, but to delay and interfere with, the passage of the bill in the Senate." One newspaper, hostile to the Lake Front Act, reported "a general belief here, in the lobby and in the House, that a large amount of money has been successfully used for the passage of the bill." Notwithstanding the rancor it generated, the resolution passed the house without any recorded dissent.[54]

When the senate took up the matter, its first act was unanimously to approve the house resolution to appoint a joint committee to investigate corruption. Although both houses had thus concurred in the investigation measure, it is unclear whether such a committee ever met. In any event, the matter of a legislative investigation of corruption quickly dropped from sight.[55]

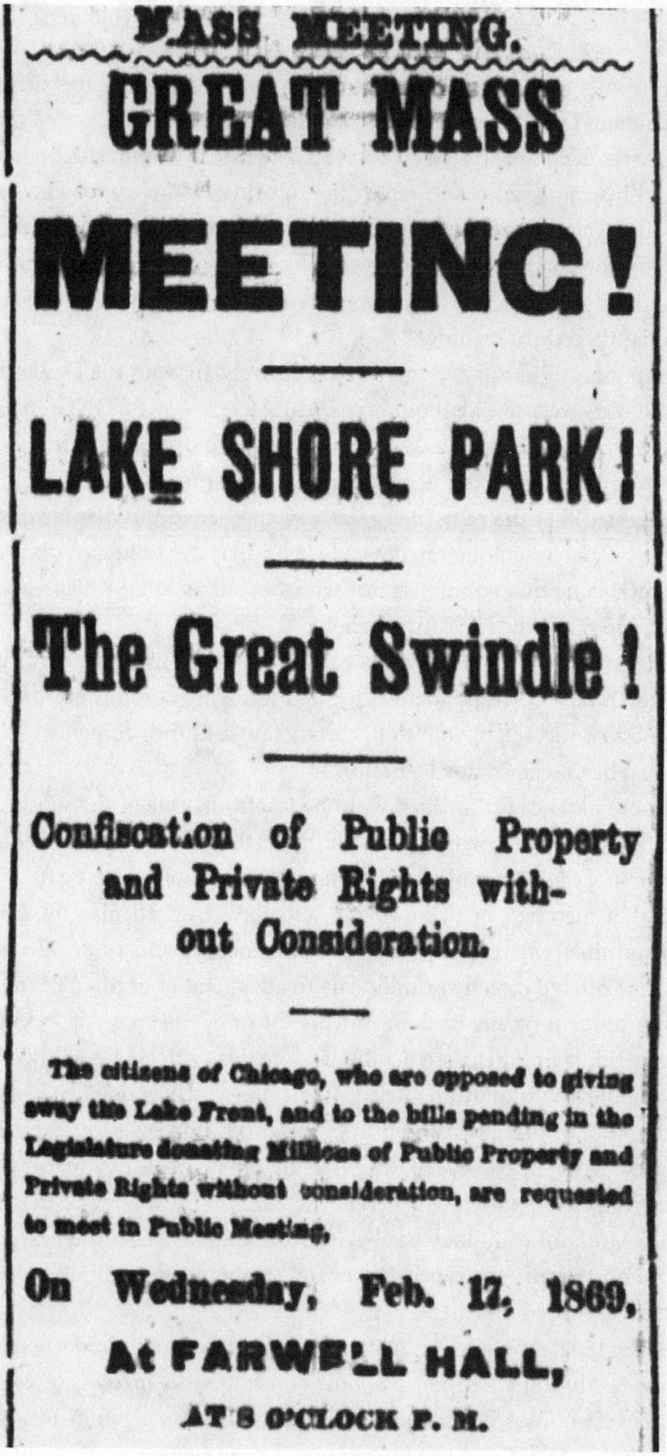

MASS MEETING.

GREAT MASS

MEETING!

LAKE SHORE PARK!

The Great Swindle!

Confiscation of Public Property and Private Rights without Consideration.

The citizens of Chicago, who are opposed to giving away the Lake Front, and to the bills pending in the Legislature donating Millions of Public Property and Private Rights without consideration, are requested to meet in Public Meeting,

On Wednesday, Feb. 17, 1869,

At FARWELL HALL,

AT 8 O'CLOCK P. M.

FIGURE 1.7. Notice for the Farwell Hall rally. *Chicago Evening Journal*, February 16, 1869. Courtesy of the Serial and Government Publications Division of the Library of Congress, Washington, DC.

When the senate turned to the lakefront bill itself, "Captain Mack moved his headquarters to the Senate chamber . . . and maintained it from early morn to dewy eve." The senate determined in short order, by a vote of fifteen to ten, to order the bill to a second reading. A reporter could not resist noting that fifteen was the number of senate votes Mack had said, earlier in the session, that he had secured. The bill was read for the second time and referred to the Committee on the Judiciary, despite a concern that its chairman, Senator Jasper D. Ward of Chicago, was known to be opposed.[56]

On February 26, the Judiciary Committee, by a single vote (five to four), recommended passage of the bill. A vigorous effort to secure passage the next day was unsuccessful. A special dispatch to the *Tribune* reported that Mack had been on the floor of the senate, "running frantically between the seats" of supporters, until he was reminded of a rule prohibiting former legislators from coming within the bar of the senate. Despite the result of this particular skirmish, even the *Tribune* correspondent thought the bill still likely to pass: "Captain Mack is at his post, and is as vigilant as ever. He will be a clever man that can out trick him."[57]

On March 8, the senate approved the house's lakefront bill by a vote of fourteen to eleven. Yet the battle was not over. In reporting the senate vote, the *Tribune* noted that "there seems to be a feeling creeping over the people here that Governor Palmer will veto this Lake Front bill." Indeed, "Dr. Mack does not feel that he is safely out of the woods."[58]

During the wait for the governor's decision, there emerged certain arguments resembling the public trust doctrine that the Supreme Court would adopt in the *Lake Front Case* almost a quarter-century later. A writer to the *Chicago Tribune* developed this theory, conceding the state's ownership of the submerged lands but denying its right to dispose of them. The letter pointed out that the Supreme Court had never determined whether the state's ownership was "a proprietary right or sovereign right." The unidentified writer concluded that "navigable waters and rivers are never the subject of sale, but are inseparable from sovereignty." The *Chicago Republican* endorsed a similar analysis.[59]

The new claim that the lakebed could never be sold was unquestionably a change of strategy by opponents of the lakefront bill. One writer to the *Republican* wryly observed that the newspaper's article, titled "No Right in the State to Sell or Grant Away the Navigation," has "set me to wondering who could have been its author":

> It could not have been one of the aldermen, nor even our worthy Mayor. . . . Did not the city formerly ask of the State a grant of this right?
>
> . . .
>
> Lastly, I am positive that the article does not reflect the view of the eminent legal gentlemen of our city—Hon. J.Y. Scammon, Hon.

> Thomas Hoyne, or Hon. Melville W. Fuller, who, with their associates, set their signatures to the contract to construct the private outside harbor for themselves IF THEY COULD GET THE RIGHT FROM THE STATE. Well, they did not get it; and that was probably the milk in the recent Farwell Hall cocoanut.[60]

After weeks of speculation, Governor John M. Palmer vetoed the lakefront bill on April 14, 1869. The governor's veto message did not go to fundamental questions of the state's title to the submerged lands or its authority to alienate them. Nor did he deny "that this property must be improved and prepared to subserve the purposes of commerce," or that it was correct "to say that neither the State of Illinois nor the city of Chicago will undertake the work of improvement." Rather, Palmer focused on "[t]he pecuniary value of the public property which it is proposed to dispose of by this bill, and the grave questions of policy and good faith, on the part of the State, that underlie it"—the latter seemingly a veiled reference to the allegations of corruption surrounding the bill.[61]

The matter seemed ripe for a compromise. In fact, there appear to have been efforts at reaching one, at least on the part of the city. And the *Tribune* reported that even if they overrode the veto, the railroad's supporters "will then present a supplemental bill" responding to Palmer's objections.[62]

Under the Illinois Constitution at the time, the legislature could override a veto by a simple majority vote in both houses—and it did. The lower chamber acted on Thursday, April 15, 1869. The next day, hastening to adjourn, the senate voted for the bill by the same margin as before—fourteen to eleven. The *Tribune* reporter noted that this was one vote short of Mack's prediction and allowed that "[o]ne senator must have deceived him." There was no formal effort to consider any supplemental bill. The reporter observed, "The introduction of such a bill was, probably, never contemplated by the friends of the lake front, and it was talked over as a sort of soothing syrup to certain enemies of the measure to quiet them."[63]

The Illinois Central, in the words of Osborn's response to Douglas's telegram from Springfield, was "much rejoiced at your final success." For Douglas, there was a sense of relief that this "very difficult" matter had been satisfactorily concluded. Osborn, upon seeing the final law, reiterated his pleasure, noting that "after all the delay and difficulty attending its final passage—it is so much simpler and more comprehensive than I supposed it possible for you to obtain."[64]

The railroad's euphoria was short lived. In retrospect, the Illinois Central probably committed a fatal error in turning its back on the city's overtures for a compromise after the governor's veto. If the railroad had moved even partway toward meeting the city's concerns, most likely it would have proceeded to build its new depot and probably also some kind of outer harbor, and the

Chicago lakefront would look a good deal different today. But as often happens, the victorious party succumbed to hubris at the moment of its triumph, thereby sowing the seeds of destruction of what it had gained. Consider that, in large part because of the enmity of the city, no depot was ever built in north Lake Park, no significant outer harbor was ever constructed, litigation dragged on into the twentieth century, and the Supreme Court of the United States adopted the public trust doctrine to legitimize the undoing of the railroad's victory.

The Motives of the Illinois Central

What more can be gleaned specifically about the motives of the railroad in seeking enactment of the substitute bill?

We have already seen how the *Tribune*, in late 1868, speculated that the Chicago Common Council's reluctance to commit to selling north Lake Park to the Illinois Central might force the railroad to go directly to the legislature. Newspaper commentaries from early 1869 continued and confirm this theme. The *Chicago Times*, for example, attributed the lakefront controversy to the "illiberal action of the common council, in refusing to consent to the use of a small portion of the land involved, for necessary depot purposes." That paper was sympathetic to the railroad's substitute bill, observing that the Illinois Central "stands in constant peril of some legislative grant to a private corporation, which, if sustained by the courts, would divest it of its riparian rights in this property,—some three separate attempts having been already made, at different sessions of the legislature, to procure a grant of this property to a private corporation."[65]

These accounts suggest that many outside observers saw the Illinois Central's motives as largely defensive—to protect its extensive investments along the lakefront against a potential legislative grab made possible by the uncertain status of property rights in submerged lands. On this view, the railroad concluded that it was necessary to secure a transfer of rights directly from the legislature, rather than from the city, because it could no longer trust the city to protect its existing lakefront interests.

Even more instructive on the Illinois Central's reasons are two letters written by Osborn, the chairman in New York, to European investors, who dominated ownership of the railroad. The first was written shortly after the governor's veto was overridden. Its predominant theme, even in the flush of victory, emphasized the defensive objective. Osborn stressed the problem of title security, and the need to harmonize the various permissions obtained from the city with the understanding (which was relatively new, a point Osborn did not make) that the state held title to the submerged land. He emphasized that the act "would confirm the title to that which we have hitherto acquired" and that it would "authorize the Company to take possession of so large a surface from the shore of the Lake that any other individuals or corporations would be prevented from getting possession of this key to the outer harbor." Only in a second paragraph did Osborn turn to the prospect that the grant would be "very remunerative," comparing the outer harbor to the "splendid docks" of London. But even here he remained vague and cautious.[66]

The second letter, sent in early June, was evidently prompted by concerns that European stockholders had expressed after reading accounts of the lakefront controversy in newspaper clippings sent to them by American correspondents. Now, Osborn described the justification for the Lake Front Act almost exclusively in defensive terms. The objective was to defeat efforts by rivals, including those "professing to represent the City of Chicago," to grab the submerged land east of the Illinois Central's operations, which would thwart the railroad's ability to continue to function and to grow in the future. Only as a minor afterthought did Osborn mention the potential future value of the grant to the company, ending the letter as follows: "What we were determined to prevent was the taking possession by anyone else of the Lake outside of us. In view of the present and future commerce of Chicago the grant is of very great value."[67]

In short, the available evidence suggests that the Illinois Central's principal motive was to protect and defend its existing investments on the lakefront. Only as a secondary matter, when the Illinois Central officers began to contemplate the significance of their success, did they begin to muse about the possible future profits to be earned from control of the outer harbor. The picture of the Illinois Central as a grasping plutocratic corporation, such as emerges in Justice Stephen Field's opinion in the *Lake Front Case* and is carried forward by implication in modern public trust accounts, is thus a caricature of what happened in 1869. The adage that fear is a more powerful motivator than greed in explaining economic behavior would seem to be fully applicable to the Illinois Central in that year.[68]

The Public Interest

We are also interested in the question whether participants in the legislative debates perceived any public-interest rationale for the Lake Front Act. Two preliminary observations are in order.

First, it is frequently assumed today that the Lake Front Act gave the Illinois Central monopoly control over the entire Chicago harbor. This is wrong. The northern limit of the grant was "the south line of the south pier extended eastwardly" of the Chicago River. Consequently, the railroad would have no control over the entrance to the river and hence no control over access to the extensive existing harbor facilities located along the river. The practical effect of the Lake Front Act, in this regard, was to authorize the creation of a large, privately owned harbor facility in the lake that would act as a supplement to the existing harbor facilities along the river. These existing facilities, from all accounts, formed a reasonably competitive market, as any riparian owner along the river could construct a pier or dock, provided that it did not obstruct navigation. Thus, the Lake Front Act did not create a giant monopoly; it was more analogous to a bill authorizing a private toll road to be built on a route parallel to an existing (if congested) public highway.[69]

Second, although later commentators could discern "no reason to believe that private ownership would have provided incentives for needed developments," it was in fact assumed by all in 1869 that a new outer harbor could be built only with private capital. No one in the debates suggested that the State of Illinois could or would undertake such a project itself—a point that Governor Palmer explicitly acknowledged in his veto message. The skeletal state government lacked both the resources and the engineering and administrative capacity for any kind of major public works project. The city of course wanted a grant of the submerged land in order to assume control of the project. But it was widely understood that, in practice, this would mean long-term leases to private entrepreneurs (such as the Shepard/Fuller group), who in turn would raise the money and do the actual construction work, remitting rents to the city for the right of occupancy. Nor was there any suggestion that the federal government could undertake construction of a new harbor. As we shall see, Congress would shortly appropriate money for a new breakwater in Chicago in the early 1870s. But no one at the time thought that the federal government had the authority to construct wharves and docks, as opposed to a breakwater. Private enterprise would have to do the job.[70]

Given these shared assumptions, the debates make it abundantly clear that many and perhaps most of those voting for the Lake Front Act sincerely perceived it to be in the general interest. The argument reduced to a simple choice between the only two realistic candidates for development of an outer harbor: the City of Chicago and the Illinois Central. The Chicago proposal would enrich the aldermen—they would determine who would be awarded the leases and contracts—but it would provide no direct financial benefits for persons living outside Chicago. The Illinois Central proposal, in contrast, would result in expanded Illinois Central operations, which would be subject to a 7 percent gross receipts tax, with all of these revenues going into the state's coffers to be used for projects throughout the state. For the typical downstate legislator, the choice was easy.

The sentiments of supporters were reinforced by the perception that opposition to the Lake Front Act was centered among wealthy Chicagoans anxious to protect their investments in Michigan Avenue property. One supportive legislator was reported to remark along these lines: "The private gentlemen who remonstrated against the bill may shed a tear at parting with their splendid residences. He sympathized with them. But the House could not say to the great State of Illinois, you shall stand still because Mr. Scammon wants to catch a breeze from Lake Michigan."[71]

The Lake Front Act was, then, an early example of a phenomenon that would become familiar in later years: a fight between Chicago and downstate interests, here won by the latter. The pattern of voting on the bill in each house confirms the city-downstate dichotomy. More than three-quarters of Cook County legislators opposed the railroad's substitute bill, and the other legislators from northeastern Illinois also voted against it, though by a narrower majority. By contrast, two-thirds of all other legislators *supported* the substitute bill. This is consistent with the divide in the debates and commentary over the public justification for the two bills.[72]

The Question of Corruption

A final question is whether the Lake Front Act was facilitated by bribery or other corrupt action of the Illinois Central or its agents. In sorting through the evidence here, it is first necessary to distinguish between the frequent charges of "fraud," "swindle," and "steal"—used as colorful expressions for legislation—and actual charges of corruption. Allegations in the former category were plentiful—on both sides. Knickerbocker attacked the Illinois Central bill as "a stupendous fraud." Representative E. S. Taylor, a supporter of the measure, responded that "[t]he only scheme that [he] had seen that looked like a fraud, was the scheme by which it was proposed to give to thirty-two aldermen in the city of Chicago the unprecedented privilege of inaugurating a ten or fifteen million dollar dock system, with its attendant schemes of plunder and robbery." In short, if "corruption" means lust for gain, there was ample basis to hurl the charge at partisans on all sides.[73]

Allegations of actual bribery were far fewer. These tended to appear later in the legislative process, after it was clear that the Illinois Central bill would pass in the house. Although this timing perhaps suggests that embittered Chicago forces manufactured the charges, it is also possible, of course, that the charges emerged only once the railroad's illicit acts became known.

And what are we to make of the enactment, immediately after passage of the lakefront bill by the house, of a joint resolution to create a committee to investigate "whether any improper influence, pecuniary or otherwise," had been brought to bear on any bill? Surely, one would think, such an extraordinary measure lends inferential support to the proposition that the Lake Front Act involved some kind of foul play. Yet the resolution passed both the house and senate unanimously. This is perhaps not what one would expect if members of either body had in fact taken bribes and were afraid of an investigation.

The *Tribune*, however, offered an alternative explanation consistent with corruption: "The lobby never pay their money until a job is perfected. It must go through both houses and over the Governor's veto before the greenbacks change hands. No cure no pay, is the rule of those astute gentlemen who practice before committees and among legislators." This suggested that payoffs would be made later in the spring—after the measure became law—and that it was thus riskless for the proponents of the bill to support the investigation resolution. The paper did not explain how legislators could ensure payment in those circumstances.[74]

The *Chicago Times* had a different take on the resolution, suggesting that its purpose was "solely to frighten timid senators into voting against the lake-front bill, for fear their motives might be misconstrued if they supported it." Its reporter expressed doubt that any money had in fact exchanged hands in the house, noting that if it had, it was at most a "very small" amount. "The liberal support the bill has received," he suggested instead, "is due to the merits of the bill itself."[75]

A potentially more reliable source of information is the correspondence of the officers of the Illinois Central. Two passages, both in letters by Douglas to Osborn in 1869, provide some inferential support for the proposition that the railroad used illicit means to procure the Lake Front Act. The first is from mid-January:

> In case we get through with our business on the lake to our satisfaction, it may require more money than contemplated in the resolution passed by the Board.
>
> However I shall proceed as economically as possible in the matter, accepting success at almost any reasonable expense if we can't do better.

The first sentence, standing alone, could be explained on innocent grounds. If Douglas had decided to seek a legislative grant of the outer harbor as well as the depot site, this clearly would "require more money" than merely building a new depot. The second sentence is more damning. It suggests that Douglas is referring to additional expenditures that must be incurred, without delay, based on his own discretionary authority. Constructing a new outer harbor obviously could await the board's approval of additional funding. The "reasonable expense" in connection with "our business on the lake" therefore refers to something else. The most likely supposition is that it refers to expenses to be incurred in procuring the legislation itself.[76]

The second passage is from a letter of February 3. Douglas wrote there, "My great trouble has been to keep quiet about this—not to overstate its importance—not to let these people know prematurely the estimate we place upon it, *and above all to confine within our own knowledge the steps taken to secure it*" (emphasis added). Conceivably, the italicized phrase could refer simply to some of the tactics employed by Mack, such as stimulating downstate opposition to the Chicago bill and then springing the substitute bill. But the revelation of any such tactics would be at most mildly embarrassing. This would not be a disclosure against which the railroad must guard "above all." It is more plausible that the "steps taken to secure" passage of the bill were ones entailing some illegality or immorality, and thus whose publication would be deeply damaging to the reputation of the Illinois Central (and its officers).[77]

In the end, although it cannot be said definitely that the Illinois Central used corrupt means to secure the Lake Front Act, the documentary record clearly leans in that direction. We will return to the issue in chapter 2, after considering evidence from the 1873 legislative session.

After the Act

Once the Lake Front Act became law, the Illinois Central began immediately to plan for expansion of its facilities and development of the outer harbor. Its enthusiasm was quickly tempered, however. On the last day of May 1869, Douglas wrote Osborn with the news that "the City is preparing for litigation on a large scale, which will probably be commenced within a few days." He conceded, "This I did not look for so soon." Douglas recommended letting "the excitement originating in the passage of the law subside," deferring any development of the outer harbor "for a time."[78]

The first suit came from an unexpected source—not the city but Cyrus H. McCormick. The industrialist and Michigan Avenue resident sought an injunction against the city, the Illinois Central, and two affiliated railroads "to prevent the occupation of the three blocks intended for depot purposes" (that is, north Lake Park). Though concerned, Douglas emphasized to the railroad's chairman that "[t]his proceeding . . . has nothing to do with what lies East of the breakwater."[79]

Meanwhile, the railroad focused on its upcoming payment to the city. The Lake Front Act required the three railroads to proffer four staggered payments of $200,000 for north Lake Park. The city comptroller was willing to accept the initial check from the railroads, with a reservation of rights, but an indignant common council would pass a resolution stating that his action did not bind the city and that it would not receive any money from the railroads "until forced to do so by the courts." The comptroller placed the money in a special-deposit account in a bank (where it remained until the railroads finally asked that it be returned several years later).[80]

Several days after receipt of the check, in the summer of 1869, the mayor and two aldermen called on Douglas. The railroad's president privately characterized them as inquiring about "fair terms" to settle "the matter of the three blocks." From New York, Osborn advised that, so long as Douglas could get another railroad involved, he should "commence by substituting $900,000 for $800,000 and dicker with them [the city] for some time." Osborn opined that "they will take a million—and be glad to get it." Douglas shared his confidence that summer: there would be a bump or two in the road, "as there is about everything of any importance in this world," but the matter was proceeding "as well [as] or better than I expected."[81]

Then, unexpectedly, the local US attorney, J.O. Glover, filed a new lawsuit in federal court on behalf of the United States. Like the McCormick action in state court, this action sought an injunction barring the Illinois Central from any construction in north Lake Park. The theory was that the federal government was still the owner of this portion of Lake Park, that the plat opening the nearby land for sale contained a dedication requiring that the park remain forever free of buildings, and that the United States, either as owner of the land or as trustee for the public beneficiaries of the dedication, had standing to seek an injunction against violation of the dedication's terms.[82]

District Judge Thomas Drummond quickly granted the injunction in August 1869, issuing a substantial opinion. He reasoned that the plat language did not create a "statutory dedication" under Illinois law, but was a valid common-law dedication. The consequence, the judge concluded, was that the federal government "hold[s] the title in fee to the land subject to the dedication which had been affixed to it." In short, the railroad could not take north Lake Park without overcoming the federal government's property rights.[83]

The Drummond injunction had the effect of freezing plans to construct a new depot on the north Lake Park site—as things turned out, for all time. The Illinois Central did not appeal, and the preliminary injunction would be made permanent in the summer of 1871. Perhaps the railroad determined to put off a new depot and to concentrate on preserving the grant of the outer harbor. Osborn had written to European investors in June 1869 that the railroad could get by with Great Central Station for another ten or fifteen years. The benefits and costs of preserving the grant of the submerged land—that is, the area for the outer harbor—may have appeared more auspicious.[84]

In any event, the Illinois Central shifted its attention to solidifying its claim to the submerged land. The path toward achieving secure property rights in this outer harbor area may have seemed more straightforward. Osborn's correspondence indicates that the railroad was now wholly convinced that the American view of ownership of nontidal submerged land would be applied to Lake Michigan, meaning that the state owned the land. If this was so, then the possible ownership by the United States of north Lake Park would not affect the state's ownership of the submerged lands or its power to convey them to the railroad. Moreover, the vested-rights doctrine, which the Supreme Court had developed under the contracts clause of the Constitution, seemed to say that so long as the Illinois Central accepted the grant of the outer harbor, and especially if it took steps in reliance on that grant, the courts would not permit the legislature to repeal the grant. Finally, the outer harbor was, without doubt, the bigger prize, in terms of both protecting the railroad's investments along the lakefront from some future grant to another corporation and enabling future revenue growth.[85]

Preserving the grant to build an outer harbor thus became the priority. For example, in his settlement negotiations, Douglas was careful not to treat the outer harbor as part of the north Lake Park discussions. "[O]f course," Douglas noted to Osborn about the harbor, "we cannot relinquish one foot, and can never listen to any negotiations proceeding upon such a basis."[86]

One step taken by the railroad to fortify its claim to the outer harbor was to undertake additional construction outside the existing breakwater, including both groundwork for new piers north of Randolph and construction of a new breakwater from Park Row to a point about two blocks south. Management emphasized moving forward with these investments in 1870, even in economic conditions that Douglas found increasingly "alarm[ing]." Thus, New York headquarters issued a general directive to operations in Chicago "to cut your Construction expenses right down," but this was "with the exception of the Lake Shore protection, which must be prosecuted." One possible motivation was to establish that the railroad had acted in reliance on the grant of rights to the outer harbor under the 1869 act.[87]

There is also the curious matter of the Illinois Central's "acceptance" of the Lake Front Act in a formal resolution by its board of directors on July 6, 1870. The act did not require this. The delayed acceptance (and the further delay in communicating it until November 1870) may have been prompted by a perceived need to come within a provision of the new Illinois Constitution adopted in 1870. As subsequently summarized, the resolution "direct[ed] the President of the company to give notice to the State of such acceptance, and [of the fact] that the company had commenced work upon the shore of the lake at Chicago under the grants referred to." The formal acceptance may have been intended to buttress the railroad's claim of vested rights under the 1869 grant.[88]

The Illinois Central had good reason to be apprehensive about the status of the legislative grant of the submerged land. In the winter of 1871, Senator Willard Woodard of Cook County introduced a bill that would have repealed the Lake Front Act outright. Senator Thomas A. Boyd, a downstater who had championed the act in 1869, reported unfavorably on the bill on behalf of the Judiciary Committee. The committee's view was that "rights had actually accrued under that law which made it wrong to attempt to repeal it," and the bill failed. Nonetheless, opposition to the railroad's development of the outer harbor clearly persisted.[89]

Soon, that opposition appeared as additional litigation. In July 1871, US Attorney Glover brought another civil action against the railroad—this time concerning the outer harbor. The theory was that the railroad's construction work was threatening navigation in the lake, a matter of exclusive federal authority. The action seems to have been precipitated, in part, by an appropriation of $150,000 by Congress in 1870 for "enlargement of harbor facilities at Chicago, Illinois." This appropriation, the first of many over the years to come, essentially injected a federal actor—the US Army Corps of Engineers—into the imbroglio over the outer harbor. According to Glover, the US Army had exclusive authority under the legislation to establish the lines of the outer harbor, and the railroad was filling part of the harbor with earth. The government further alleged that the company intended to continue the filling to a point at least six hundred feet east of the land it had already made, and that this would obstruct the navigation of the lake and damage the new outer harbor. The Illinois Central evidently agreed to the entry of a preliminary injunction. As we will see in the next chapter, it eventually agreed to a settlement severely restricting its ability to engage in further construction of harbor facilities without the consent of the federal government.[90]

We have seen in this chapter how the emergence of uncertainty about property rights can lead to great political and legal struggle. Who owns the bed of a body of water? Most people probably never give any sustained thought to the question and consequently have only the most imprecise opinion about the answer. Yet the question of title to submerged land becomes critical when issues such as building a railroad in the lake, expanding a park along the lakeshore, constructing a new depot on landfill, or building an outer harbor in the lake come to the fore. When lawyers begin to sense that the common assumption that A owns the resource may be wrong, and that the courts will eventually hold that B holds the right, all sorts of machinations are likely to break out in order to take advantage of the reallocation of rights in favor of B. This is especially true if B—the putative new owner—is a relatively weak and easily manipulated institution, such as the Illinois General Assembly in the latter half of the nineteenth century. This is a critical part of the explanation for the conflict that emerged on the Chicago lakefront in the 1860s and produced the "Lake Front Steal." As we will see, it also provides a vital clue to various critical developments on the lakefront well into the twentieth century.

2

THE LAKE FRONT CASE

The stalemate on the lakefront produced by the hostility to the Lake Front Act and by Judge Drummond's 1869 injunction was soon disrupted. On October 8, 1871, fire broke out on the city's southwest side. The flames devastated a large portion of Chicago, including the residences of almost one-third of the city's population and most of the downtown area. After devouring Terrace Row on Michigan Avenue, the fire reduced Great Central Station, north of Randolph Street, to a mere shell. The main line of the Illinois Central tracks was spared—an unanticipated benefit of a railroad in the lake.[1]

After the Fire

For the lakefront, what happened after the fire was of greater significance. Leaders of the city—whose mayor, Roswell B. Mason, was a former chief engineer of the Illinois Central—decided to use the massive debris from the fire to fill in Lake Michigan in the area between Lake Park and the Illinois Central breakwater. It did not occur to anyone to ask the state's permission. In any event, the Lake Front Act—then the law—made the Illinois Central the owner of the submerged land, and it readily agreed to landfilling by citizen volunteers. "Slowly the water area west of the tracks, which had been extensive enough to provide sailing room for small craft, was filled in," the leading modern historian of the Illinois Central has recounted. "Within a few months the trestle work was completely filled in, and the tracks of the railroad were on solid ground."[2]

This unexpected event presumably changed the calculus about the need for a new passenger depot. Not only was the existing depot destroyed, but the costs of constructing a new one in north Lake Park had been significantly reduced, given the landfilling. The immediate problem was that the time had long passed to appeal Drummond's 1869 injunction against building in "the three blocks." Yet if Drummond was right that the United States remained the owner of north Lake Park, it is hard to see how overturning the injunction would have resolved the title problem. Injunction or no injunction, the United States would have to release its claim to the land. And getting Congress to enact legislation releasing the federal government's supposed title would be a heavy lift.[3]

In the meantime, the Illinois Central and affiliated lines had to make do without using the three blocks for a new depot. In 1872, the railroad built wooden sheds in front of the old stone walls of the original depot, Great Central Station,

FIGURE 2.1. Illinois Central depot, north of Randolph Street, with a wall of the original Great Central Station still standing in 1893, twenty-two years after the Chicago fire. Courtesy of the Newberry Library, Chicago, IC Photos-3-Box 3-Folder 65.

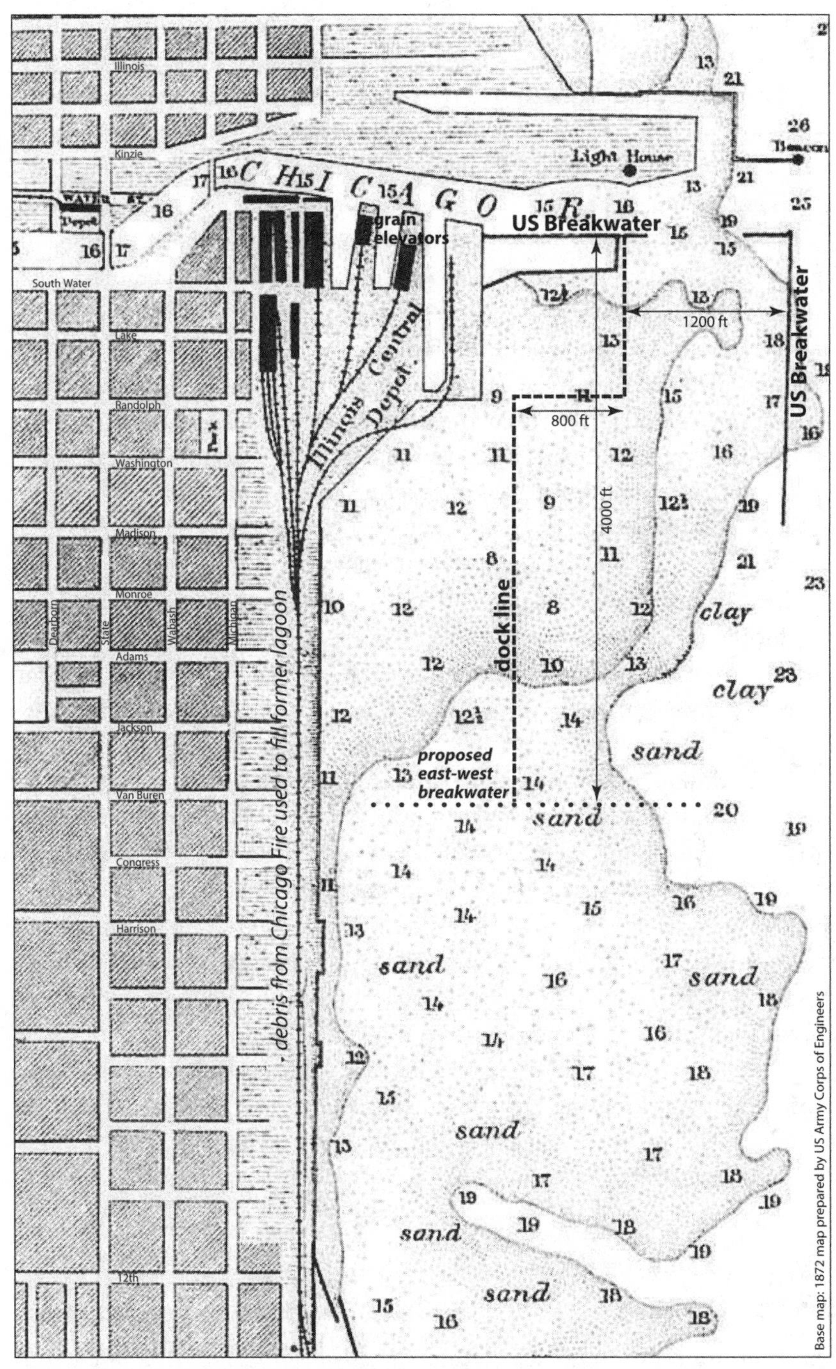

FIGURE 2.2. Map showing location of 1872 dock line.

north of Randolph Street. This makeshift depot, hemmed in by limited space, was deemed inadequate by the Illinois Central's affiliated lines, with the result that some of them employed a variety of temporary stations of dubious legality south of Randolph Street during the 1870s and into the 1880s. In 1878, the city permitted the Illinois Central to build a small brick passenger depot in Lake Park at Van Buren Street. This, too, was of doubtful legality. But no one challenged it.[4]

The second action that US Attorney J. O. Glover had brought, challenging the authority of the Illinois Central to construct any harbor facilities in the lake without the approval of the federal government, was settled in January 1872. We can only conjecture about the railroad's motivations for agreeing to the settlement. The immediate need to rebuild facilities after the fire undoubtedly consumed the carrier's capital. And it is likely that the railroad did not perceive the US Army as hostile to its long-range plans. The army engineers were dedicated to expanding opportunities for commercial navigation, so acquiescing in the army's insistence on approving any future design of an outer harbor may have been perceived as posing no great threat to the railroad's aspirations.[5]

The settlement drew an imaginary dock line, as shown in figure 2.2. Inside this line, the Illinois Central was permitted to construct docks and wharves provided that it followed federal construction guidelines. Outside the line, it could not undertake any construction without the express, further consent of the United States.[6]

The dock-line settlement greatly reduced the scope of rights conferred by the Lake Front Act. Although discussions of the act to this day emphasize the extraordinary scope of the grant in the original act—more than one thousand acres in total—the settlement with the federal government effectively trimmed the area under Illinois Central control back to a modest curtilage around the railroad's existing improvements. Combined with the impasse about building a depot in north Lake Park, the practical import of the Lake Front Act was now but a shadow of what it had seemed in 1869.

During 1872 and the following year, the railroad resumed at least some of its construction activities within the now-reduced outer harbor. The carrier later maintained that between 1869 and 1873 it had expended some $230,000 in developing various facilities in this area.[7]

1873: Repeal

The 1870s were a period of great economic distress in the rural Midwest. This produced the Granger Movement, a form of rural populism with railroads a particular focus of agitation. Illinois was the epicenter of the movement, and the Illinois Central was the object of particular scrutiny.[8]

Although it is hard to imagine that the Illinois Central was unconcerned with what might transpire in the 1873 legislative session, no direct evidence of the railroad's attitude exists. The railroad's president, John M. Douglas, had suffered what is described in company histories as a "physical breakdown," and resigned the position in spring 1871. His successor, John Newell, an engineer, was much less given to confiding about political matters in correspondence with William H. Osborn, the chairman in New York City. The railroad also had to muddle through without its master lobbyist, Alonzo Mack, who had died in early 1871.[9]

When the legislature convened, Senator Joseph Reynolds quickly introduced a bill to repeal the Lake Front Act. Led by its three Cook County members, the senate Committee on Municipalities voted unanimously to recommend repeal.[10]

The tenor of the legislative deliberations in 1873 was very different from those in 1869. Whatever corrupt inducements may have facilitated passage of the Lake Front Act, the thrust of the debates in 1869 was largely pragmatic, the focus being how best to assure a new passenger depot and a new outer harbor for Chicago. In 1873, there was no discussion about how to obtain these public goods. The deliberations were negative and recriminatory. Probably because of the state of the economy, all participants tacitly recognized that there would be no new depot or outer harbor in the foreseeable future. The sole question was whether to punish the Illinois Central and its supporters for their presumed venality in 1869.

In this climate, the Illinois Central focused on arguing that repeal would be unconstitutional. It retained John N. Jewett, a former state senator and constitutional law expert, who appeared before the senate committee and took up what one skeptical newspaper described as "that old familiar strain about the Dartmouth college, and the other worn-out tune about 'vested rights.'" He sowed some doubt. Thus, notwithstanding an initial unanimous vote to back the bill, the committee now deferred final action.[11]

Under pressure from Reynolds, in mid-March, the senate committee finally discharged the bill—but without any recommendation. The *Chicago Times* reported that "the committee appeared to be very glad to get rid of it in any way." A few days later, Jewett's brother-in-law, a member of the lower chamber, where a repealer had also been introduced, requested a deferral so that Jewett could return to Springfield to testify before the body's Committee on Railroads and Warehouses. The house committee agreed.[12]

Around this time, a representative "caused a little excitement" by introducing a bill for the appointment of a joint committee, with full subpoena powers, to investigate "the means used to secure the passage of . . . the Lake-Front bill" through the legislature of 1869. The motivation behind the investigation bill, as four years earlier, was unclear. On the one hand, it is plausible that the investigation was devised by the proponents of repeal as an *in terrorem* device to induce the railroad to drop its opposition to repeal, in exchange for dropping the investigation. On the other hand, the bill may have served as a delaying tactic by opponents of repeal, given that the mandated inquiries would not have been completed until after the legislative session. Thus, one newspaper charged that the investigation bill was a smokescreen "under cover of which the repealing bill may be fatally stabbed."[13]

It soon became clear that the railroad would be hard pressed to stave off repeal. By the time Jewett arrived to address the house committee, it was too late: the committee had reported the repeal bill favorably. The railroad refocused its attention on the senate. The vested-rights argument was expected to get a more favorable reception there because of the number of lawyers in the upper body. The railroad accordingly sought a referral to the Judiciary Committee. One of the Illinois Central's lobbyists (perhaps a military veteran) sent word to the railroad's president that "you should send *all the forces at your command* to Springfield at once—for it will require an immense influence to make a successful fight in an open field." Changing metaphors, the lobbyist was "strongly inclined to think we can smother the Bill if we can get it to the Judiciary Com[mittee]."[14]

The *Tribune* grew alarmed, fearing that, in the event of such a referral, "Mr. Jewett's arguments will overwhelm his legal brethren." Others thought that something apart from the quality of the Illinois Central's legal arguments was causing movement among the senators. The *Chicago Evening Journal* contended that, "by-and-by, when a vote is reached, if ever, we may ascertain how many of the Senate's twenty-five lawyers are the paid attorneys of the railroads." It concluded, "The bill will pass the House, but not the Senate, for there are too many lawyers there. Mark the prediction."[15]

The prediction was very nearly correct. In late March, the house voted overwhelmingly (127 to 5) to repeal the Lake Front Act. In the senate, as the *Tribune* reported, "[t]he fight waxe[d] warm." Allegations of corruption in 1869 abounded, with one senator recalling of the Lake Front Act, "Iniquity presided over the conception of the scheme, fraud was present at its birth, and honesty would rejoice at its death. This was worse than Credit Mobilier, salary steal, and all the iniquities perpetrated by Congress." The ultimate vote was close: nineteen senators voted in favor of referring the repeal bill to the Judiciary Committee, and twenty-two against. A swing of two votes—prompting a referral—very likely would have meant the repeal bill's defeat. Now, most observers anticipated its passage.[16]

The railroad appears at this point to have concentrated on defeating the investigation bill. The essential argument against investigation was that the legislature "should not take up the time and money of the State to go back four years to wash the dirty linen of a preceding Legislature." It was also suggested that "[t]hose who wanted investigation were disappointed in stealing the land themselves."[17]

To be sure, the investigation bill had proponents, some of whom saw more value in it than just exposing to "public scorn" the "men who were bought like steers in the market." One legislator maintained that determining whether the Lake Front Act had been procured by fraud would have practical importance, even if the repeal bill passed. The railroad argued "vested rights" associated with a contract with the state, he noted, but "fraud" would support setting a contract aside. The motion to defeat the investigation bill resulted in a rare tie and thus failed to carry the house by a single vote out of the eighty-eight cast. Nevertheless, it was clear that if repeal passed, the investigation bill would quietly die.[18]

The railroad made a final effort against the repeal bill. Jewett returned and, along with other former senators, worked against it. Their efforts were unavailing. The senate voted thirty-one to eleven in favor of repeal. On April 15—one day shy of four years after it had been enacted over a predecessor's veto—Governor John L. Beveridge signed the bill repealing the Lake Front Act.[19]

The course of proceedings in 1873 reinforces the judgment, advanced more tentatively in chapter 1, that the Illinois Central used corrupt means in 1869. Serious proposals were made in two separate legislative sessions to launch a formal investigation of corruption in connection with the Lake Front Act. We can imagine how such a proposal might be used strategically once, for intimidation or delay. But it is hard to imagine its use as a trick twice. More likely, the idea did not die because the proponents of an investigation had genuine reasons to suspect misconduct. It is also significant that the Illinois Central in 1873 was deeply concerned about a formal investigation, and fought to defeat it. This, too, suggests that the railroad had something to hide. Finally, the allegations about the exact nature of the corruption—such as one former representative's claims of hush money paid to newspapers and of cash payments ranging as high as $20,000 to legislators—became more specific after 1869.[20]

Confusion Compounded

The immediate effect of the repeal was negligible. The 1869 Drummond injunction had frozen construction of a new depot in north Lake Park. The 1872 settlement had restricted development of the outer harbor. It is true that, beginning in 1870 and continuing to 1875, Congress appropriated modest sums of money for the army to construct a new breakwater outside the one built by the Illinois Central in the 1850s. This was designed to facilitate the construction of an outer harbor. But the army was not authorized to build piers and wharves—this was universally regarded to be a local function. With no resolution of the question of which entity, if any, was entitled to develop an outer harbor, the breakwater served as a refuge for vessels waiting to enter the Chicago River, and nothing more.[21]

The repeal was largely symbolic legislation: a rebuke of railroads for all they did that was resented, including charging high rates for the transport of grain and livestock to market and generally high-handed behavior. The legislation did not offer any alternative vision as to how to create the public goods that the 1869 act, however imperfectly, had sought to bring forth—an outer harbor, a new depot, and more and better parks.

Indeed, the primary contribution of the 1873 repeal was to further muddy an already convoluted legal picture. By its terms, the repeal nullified any confirmation of rights decreed in 1869, and returned matters to where they had stood before the Lake Front Act. As we have seen in chapter 1, this status quo ante was a confusing mélange of arguments over whether the English rule or the American rule applied to ownership of land underneath Lake Michigan, combined with at least four different theories as to the owner of the now-enlarged Lake Park. To this, the repeal added a new argument about whether the legislature could constitutionally abrogate whatever rights the Illinois Central had obtained in 1869.

In retrospect, it seems surprising that a decade would elapse before litigation erupted. Part of the explanation is the economic collapse in the early 1870s. In the first five years of the decade, the Illinois Central was fully preoccupied with rebuilding its terminal facilities after the fire and trying to cover its dividend. Revenues declined by 10 percent, and the carrier added no new miles of track. Another part of the explanation is the substantial completion of the new breakwater by the army outside the railroad's original breakwater. This allowed ships to shelter at anchor until space opened up along the river; it thus relieved river congestion to a degree. But the primary explanation is the sheer intractability of the legal issues.[22]

Renewed Conflict

Eventually the economy recovered, commercial traffic grew, and the Illinois Central, like other regional railroads, began adding new miles of track. Congestion became an irritant not only in the river but also within the rail yards and operations of the Illinois Central in Chicago. The issues that gave rise to the Lake Front

Act of 1869—the need for a new passenger depot and the desire for an outer harbor in the lake—returned with greater force than before. Other issues joined them, such as growing demand to preserve and improve Lake Park. Negotiated solutions were sought but repeatedly fell apart, as we shall see, under the weight of the number of parties with conflicting claims and, especially, the confusing picture about property rights.[23]

As rail traffic on the lakefront lines grew, and with the expansion of passenger service to south suburban communities such as Hyde Park and Kensington, public frustration with the makeshift passenger terminal north of Randolph Street mounted. Among other defects, the crude depot had no train shed, which meant that passengers were forced to stand in rain or snow getting on and off trains.[24]

Chicago politicians responded by reviving the proposal to sell north Lake Park to the railroads for a new passenger depot. In 1880, Mayor Carter H. Harrison Sr. and the railroads discussed a sale of the three blocks, now augmented by the debris from the fire, with the city receiving slightly less than the $800,000 that,

FIGURE 2.3. Congestion at the mouth of the Chicago River, ca. 1869. Chicago History Museum, ICHi-039380A; J. Carbutt, photographer.

with theatrical flourish, it had rejected as inadequate under the 1869 act. The immediate stumbling block was Judge Drummond's 1869 decision holding that the United States had legal title to north Lake Park. To pave the way for the sale, legislation was introduced in Congress to relinquish to Chicago any claim by the federal government. It passed the Senate but died in the House of Representatives. Disagreement also persisted over whether a sale of north Lake Park would be linked to the Illinois Central's relinquishing any claim to the outer harbor. By early 1881 the idea of building a new depot in north Lake Park had died a second death.[25]

Proposals to sell north Lake Park to the railroad for a new depot would be revived in 1885 and again in 1889, but negotiations always foundered on the same point: the city wanted the railroad to relinquish its claims to the outer harbor, and the railroad refused, expecting the courts to vindicate its claim of vested rights under the original Lake Front Act.[26]

In the early 1880s, the Illinois Central gradually took the matter of an outer harbor into its own hands. While careful to avoid constructing any wharves or piers in front of Lake Park—which arguably would have violated the ordinance allowing it to enter the city and unquestionably would have enraged the Michigan Avenue owners—the railroad undertook major expansions of its facilities north of Randolph and south of 12th Street.

North of Randolph, the Illinois Central embarked on an aggressive expansion program beginning in 1880. Large new wharves jutting into the lake were constructed in 1880 and 1881; they were called Piers 2 and 3, joining Pier 1 from almost a decade earlier. Unlike previous piers, these three were accessible directly from the lake, a departure made possible by the army's new breakwater. In a very real sense, Piers 1, 2, and 3 constituted an "outer harbor," though on a much less grandiose scale than that contemplated by the Lake Front Act.[27]

The piers offered particular advantages to the thriving lumber industry. Chicago's lumber trade was at its peak; schooners carrying boards from mills in Michigan and Wisconsin to wholesalers in Chicago accounted for a large percentage of the commercial traffic on the Chicago River. The railroad's new piers reduced the delays experienced by lumber wholesalers in receiving their consignments. They also somewhat alleviated the irritation of pedestrians and wagon drivers who had to wait for swing bridges to open and close as schooners shipped lumber up the river. And, of course, the Illinois Central perceived a great advantage for itself: it could capture a large share of the lumber business before it entered the Chicago River, at the expense of railroads with terminals on the river's south branch.[28]

The city effectively endorsed the new piers, authorizing in 1880 an extension of Randolph Street by viaduct over the existing Illinois Central track.

FIGURE 2.4. Illinois Central lumber docks on the south bank of the mouth of the Chicago River (undated, likely late 1880s). Courtesy of the Newberry Library, Chicago, Midwest MS 129.

It was to be paid for by the railroad, but this would be a public street, allowing wagons to reach the new piers. For its part, the army approved construction of the new piers, even though they extended eight hundred feet beyond the dock line established by the settlement agreement of 1872. The State of Illinois was not consulted.[29]

It is unclear why the Illinois Central thought it had the authority to extend its facilities into the lake without the state's consent. Most likely, the railroad remained convinced that the legislature's grant of the submerged land in 1869 was a vested right, making its revocation in 1873 a nullity. As a fallback, the railroad could claim that its original state charter of 1851, which provided that the railroad could take any of the state's "lands" or "streams" for the purpose of constructing stations and other facilities, provided the necessary permission. There was no suggestion, at this time, that the railroad thought that its construction of piers was justified by the common-law privilege of riparian owners to "wharf out," without regard to ownership of the lakebed, to reach the navigable portion of a watercourse.[30]

The Illinois Central was equally aggressive in the early 1880s on the other end of Lake Park—to the south. This was perilous territory. After the fire of 1871, much of the Chicago elite had decided to relocate to Prairie and Calumet Avenues on the South Side, just west of the Illinois Central tracks. This area, beginning near 16th Street and proceeding south more or less parallel to the lakeshore, was soon filled with stately mansions. Prairie Avenue, in particular, would come by the end of the century to be described as "the most expensive street in America west of Fifth Avenue."[31]

The Illinois Central's initial efforts south of Lake Park did not directly threaten these interests. Apart from building a breakwater between 25th and 27th Streets in 1882, the railroad focused on the area north of 16th Street. The same year, it extended the pier it had previously built off 12th Street, in a southerly direction to the middle of 16th Street. This would incidentally help protect the railroad's Weldon shops, originally built in 1853–57, but its primary purpose was to create a slip or basin for "vessels loaded with materials for the company, or having freight to be handled." In 1885, the carrier constructed a massive new pier at the foot of 13th Street. This was designed in part to substitute for completion of the government's breakwater on the south side of the harbor of refuge, but was also intended "for receiving and discharging vessel cargoes . . . that cannot be handled in the freight yard down-town on account of insufficiency of room and busy times." All this entailed new landfilling, but the army found no interference with navigation.[32]

The new piers constructed north of Randolph Street and between 12th and 16th Streets meant that the Illinois Central—without building anything in front of Lake Park—had moved some way toward constructing a de facto outer harbor under its exclusive control. Figure 2.5, the so-called Morehouse map from the *Lake Front Case*, shows the Illinois Central operations and improvements on the lakefront as of the mid-1880s.

The issue that finally precipitated a lawsuit concerned the original line of track in Lake Park. The railroad had used only two hundred feet of the three hundred feet of right of way that the 1852 city ordinance granted. This narrow funnel of track was the sole link connecting the burgeoning terminal facilities north of Randolph Street with the main line south out of Chicago. By 1880, the track was used by numerous railroads, including the Illinois Central, one of its original partners (the Michigan Central), and the Baltimore & Ohio Railroad. All together, up to 170 "regular trains," 90 "transfer trains," and scores of locomotives and switch engines used this segment every day.[33]

Frustrated by operational delays, in 1881 the Illinois Central began driving rows of piles parallel to, and outside, the railroad's existing tracks and original breakwater, in order to begin filling an additional one hundred feet of right of

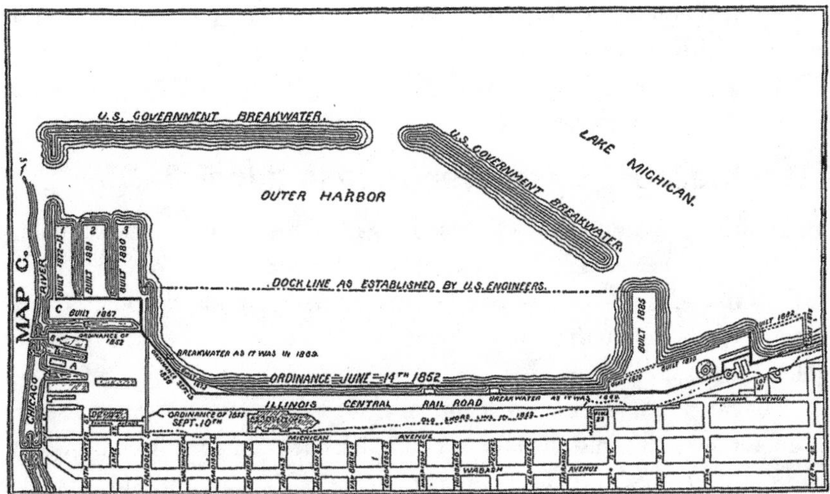

FIGURE 2.5. Morehouse map. *Lake Front Case*, 146 U.S. 387, 413 (1892) (statement of the case).

way for more lines of track. Within hours, the army engineer in charge of the Chicago harbor, one Major G. J. Lydecker, ordered a halt.[34]

There ensued a yearlong federal process to determine whether the Illinois Central would be allowed to fill the additional one hundred feet. The secretary of war, Robert Todd Lincoln, son of the late president, asked the US attorney general for his legal opinion. Attorney General Benjamin H. Brewster advised that the question of title to the lake bottom was of no concern to the United States. The critical question, he said, was one of fact for the War Department: whether the new construction "will obstruct, encroach upon, or interfere with the harbor improvement, and thus injuriously affect its usefulness in the interest of navigation." Lincoln thereupon appointed a formal board of inquiry, consisting of three generals. After holding hearings in Chicago, the board reported in June 1882, outlining a plan that would have allowed additional landfilling both to expand the Illinois Central's existing right of way and to construct more piers in a new outer harbor. Lincoln, however, disapproved the report, finding that it would require the War Department to impose conditions beyond its authority and that it presupposed the railroad to have title to the submerged land, which was in dispute.[35]

Secretary Lincoln's decision obviously disappointed the Illinois Central and other advocates of a new outer harbor. Expansion of Chicago's harbor facilities was perceived to be more imperative than ever. Yet given the legal imbroglio over title to the lakebed, it was impossible for the Illinois Central—or anyone else—to move ahead with development of an outer harbor in the contested area. Litigation was widely seen as the only answer.[36]

"The Greatest Case Ever Tried in Illinois"

And, finally, litigation came. On March 1, 1883, the attorney general of Illinois filed suit against the Illinois Central, naming also the City of Chicago as a defendant. The railroad answered and included claims against the other parties. It removed the case to the federal circuit court, on the grounds of the presence of federal questions.[37]

Though also named as a defendant, the United States initially refused to enter an appearance. This frustrated the Michigan Avenue and Prairie Avenue owners, who had achieved significant success persuading local US attorneys to sue in the name of the United States to block expansion by the railroad. The owners tried mightily to persuade the federal government to join in the fray, based on the claim that the United States retained title to Lake Park. The Illinois Central was entirely opposed to federal intervention. The agitation over federal participation eventually generated congressional attention and an elaborate appeal to the US attorney general, who finally relented and authorized a suit in the name of the United States against the railroads. To the disappointment of the property owners, the federal government's entry came too late to allow the US attorney to participate in developing the trial record or even in oral argument. The circuit court nevertheless held that the rights of the United States would be determined together with those of the other parties. In the end, the prolonged effort to enlist the participation of the federal government contributed to a four-year delay before the trial finally started, in 1887.[38]

In the meantime, the level of rancor between the principal antagonists—the Illinois Central and lakefront property owners—rose to an ever-higher pitch. A "citizens' committee" agitated against the railroad and chastised Mayor Harrison for complicity in the railroad's expansionism. Newspapers were filled with stories about the legislature's alleged corruption in 1869. B. F. Ayer, the railroad's general counsel, would later suggest in open court that the newspapers had been paid by wealthy property owners to spread propaganda. The landowners demanded that the railroad stop filling along the lakefront south of 13th Street. The railroad claimed that the city's health department was doing the filling. The mayor ordered the railroad to stop. The filling stopped, but the railroad proceeded to drive piles in the lake, claiming that this was different from filling. In the midst of all this, the state filed a "quo warranto" proceeding in state court, challenging the Illinois Central's actions in the lake as going beyond its authority as a railroad corporation. The railroad responded by removing the new action to federal court. And on and on it went.[39]

The main show in the federal circuit court, when it finally got underway, was before Supreme Court Justice John Marshall Harlan, sitting as circuit justice, and District Judge Henry W. Blodgett. Evidence was taken before a master in chancery of the court, between April 8 and May 31, 1887. Considerable legal talent was on display. In addition to the state attorney general, George Hunt, the state had the services of two prominent law firms, Williams & Thompson and McCagg & Culver, both of whose fees likely were paid by the property owners. The Illinois Central was represented by B. F. Ayer, its general counsel; Lyman Trumbull, a former US senator; and John N. Jewett, its longtime constitutional law expert. The citizens' committee complained bitterly that the city was being out-lawyered. It raised money to augment the city's legal effort, which led (by an unspecified route) to the city's appropriating $5,000 to procure the services of Melville W. Fuller, who the next year would be appointed chief justice of the United States.[40]

The evidence was extensive. Jonathan Young Scammon and Fernando Jones testified in their capacities as the oldest inhabitants of Chicago with personal knowledge of the development of the lakefront stretching back to the 1830s. The Illinois Central also introduced extensive evidence about the many improvements that it had made after 1869 in reliance on the Lake Front Act and about the severe congestion in its facilities from rising volumes of traffic.[41]

Oral argument before Justice Harlan and Judge Blodgett lasted more than a week, from July 5 to July 13, 1887. Each of the parties set forth sweeping claims to support its control and authority over the lakefront. The state claimed that it owned the submerged land and that the grant to the railroad had been validly repealed in 1873. Thus, any landfilling by the Illinois Central beyond that necessary for railroad purposes as authorized in its 1851 charter was unlawful and should be enjoined. The city claimed that it was the owner of Lake Park and thus, as riparian owner, enjoyed various rights and privileges with respect to the lake offshore from the park. Hence, the city controlled development of the harbor. The Illinois Central claimed that the 1869 Lake Front Act validly transferred the state's property rights in the submerged land and that, under the vested-rights doctrine, the state was powerless in 1873 to repeal it. Thus, the railroad owned the submerged land and controlled the harbor.

Justice Harlan Rules

In 1888, Justice Harlan ruled. His approach was to settle as many issues as possible, giving something of value to each contending party. The state got title to

FIGURE 2.6. Justice John Marshall Harlan, ca. 1890. Library of Congress, Prints and Photographs Division, LC-USZ62-40292.

the submerged lands. The city received title to the augmented Lake Park. The railroad could keep all of its existing tracks, facilities, piers, and wharves on the lakefront. The United States' authority to regulate navigation in the harbor was affirmed, but it was held to have no remaining property rights in north Lake Park.

Harlan confirmed the state's ownership of the submerged lands in a single sentence followed by the citation of several Supreme Court decisions, none quite on point, involving tidal lands and rivers. The question of who owned the lakebed lay at the heart of the legal uncertainty vexing the lakefront. One might think that it deserved a more thorough analysis. But none of the parties had disputed the state's ownership. The state of course endorsed its own ownership, as did the Illinois Central—in order to establish the state's right to sell the submerged land. The city was in no position to dispute it, having itself sought a grant of the submerged land from the state in 1869. The United States took no position on the issue.[42]

The city's title to Lake Park followed from the court's conclusion that the United States, in subdividing the land on the original shore, had fully and legally conveyed to the city all of the federal government's rights to streets, parks, and common areas. Judge Drummond's decision of 1869, to the effect that only a "common law" dedication had been made, leaving title in the United States, was thus repudiated. The city was also held to own the land created by debris from the fire. This was on the dubious ground that the city's charter authorized it to create a breakwater, and if the city instead of the Illinois Central had done so, and if it had then filled the land between the breakwater and the original shore, "it could not be doubted that it would have become the owner of all the ground thus reclaimed and occupied." Justice Harlan did not explain how authority to build a breakwater created an implied right to engage in landfilling inside the breakwater. Judge Blodgett agreed with this general analysis of the city's rights, but offered the qualification (in a short opinion labeled a dissent) that the state and city did not control the two hundred feet on which the railroad had established its right of way. A right of perpetual use, he reasoned, had been granted by the state directly to the railroad in its charter, the only condition being that the city had to consent to the location of the right of way, which it had done.[43]

The railroad's right to keep all of its existing improvements, including the de facto outer harbor it had only recently constructed north of Randolph and south of 12th Street, was justified on two grounds. One was the railroad's status as a riparian landowner in these areas. Citing another string of Supreme Court opinions, Harlan observed that riparian owners had been held to have a common-law right to build a wharf to connect their land to the navigable portion of the abutting body of water. "It was in the exercise of these riparian rights," he asserted, that the railroad had acted in "the shallow water east of the shore line."[44]

The second justification came from the language of the Illinois Central's original charter from the state. Paraphrasing the charter, the court noted that the state—now held to be the owner of the lakebed—had "expressly authorized the railroad company to enter upon, take possession of, and use any lands, waters, or materials" belonging to the state, for the location of facilities necessary for constructing or maintaining the railroad. Given these charter provisions, "the right of the railroad company, so far as the state and city were concerned, to fill in the lake, to the extent prescribed by [the 1852 ordinance], and to use the ground thereby made, was placed beyond question."[45]

Harlan devoted the most attention to the question whether the state had the authority to repeal the Lake Front Act in 1873. He began by considering a number of arguments by the state to the effect that the Lake Front Act of 1869 had not been duly enacted, including the claims that the bill was not read three times in the senate and that the grant of the land was not accompanied by the seal of the state. The justice patiently rejected all of these contentions. The great contest over the outer harbor was not going to be decided on a legal technicality.[46]

With respect to the railroad's critical vested-rights argument, Harlan drew a sharp distinction between the provision of the Lake Front Act confirming the existing rights of the Illinois Central and the one granting a thousand acres of submerged land for a new outer harbor. The rights that had been confirmed, he held, were fully vested. If the railroad's existing improvements had been expressly authorized by statute, they could not have been taken away except on payment of compensation—that is, by eminent domain. "But," he reasoned, "subsequent legislative ratification or confirmation of what was done is equivalent to original authority." The state had no power by legislation to revoke the confirmation.[47]

By contrast, Harlan concluded, the state could revoke the grant of submerged land to build an outer harbor. He construed the Lake Front Act as having given the Illinois Central only a discretionary power to construct an outer harbor. Because the railroad had not begun to construct such a harbor before 1873—Harlan regarded the improvements the company cited as being essentially de minimis—the state was free to revoke this power. The legislature in 1869 had conveyed, "in effect, only [a] license" to the Illinois Central to develop the harbor, and it is inherent in the nature of a license that it can be revoked at any time. This construction flew in the face of the language of the 1869 act conveying the harbor to the railroad in "fee," an awkwardness not pointed out by Harlan.[48]

In keeping with his construction of the Lake Front Act as granting only discretionary powers to the railroad, Harlan concluded that the rescission of the grant of the three blocks for purposes of constructing a new passenger depot was also permissible. Once the railroad asked for the return of the initial $200,000 payment, the situation returned to what it had been before 1869. So the title remained in the city.[49]

All in all, Harlan's decision was an exercise in pragmatic accommodation. No one went away empty handed. The dominant theme was ratification of the status quo—and, in particular, ratification of the existing possessory rights of the respective parties. The railroad got to keep all its track, terminals, yards, wharves, and piers, over which it exercised active control. All it lost was future development rights. The city got to keep all of Lake Park, over which it episodically exercised control. All it lost was the power to oust the railroad from the lakefront. The federal government got to keep its breakwater and to continue to exercise a veto power over new facilities in the harbor. All it lost was its abstract claim to north Lake Park, over which it had long ago relinquished control. The only party given nothing but abstract rights was the state, which was declared to be the owner of the submerged land—over which it had never exercised effective control. As we shall see, the inability of the state to prevent encroachments on the submerged land would continue to vex the lakefront for many years to come.

The Illinois Central initially regarded the Harlan decision as a victory—with good reason. The ruling secured the railroad's claim to all of its improvements along the lakefront, including the de facto outer harbor that it had been aggressively assembling in the 1880s. Even as to the loss of the grant of submerged land, Harlan's rationale did not rule out the possibility that the railroad could return to the legislature and obtain similar privileges in the future.[50]

Stuyvesant Fish, the railroad's new president, nevertheless asked each of his lawyers whether the railroad should appeal to the Supreme Court. The lawyers all opined, unsurprisingly, that the railroad would achieve even greater success if they were allowed to pitch the vested-rights argument to the higher court. Thus, nearly two and a half years after the Harlan decision was announced, the Illinois Central appealed.[51]

The World's Fair

During the interlude between the circuit court decision and the Supreme Court ruling, another event emerged that permanently transformed the lakefront. In the late 1880s, momentum began building for a world's fair celebrating the four hundredth anniversary of Christopher Columbus's voyage to the Western Hemisphere. Chicago raised very substantial monies and showed more enthusiasm than rival cities, and in 1890 Congress selected Chicago as the site for the World's Columbian Exposition. President Benjamin Harrison fixed May 1, 1893, as the opening day.[52]

Although much has been written about the fair, and its impact on Chicago and the imagination of the nation at large, no one has offered a detailed explanation of why the fair was located in a remote site on the South Side of the city, rather than in Lake Park at the center of the city. As we will explain, the same legal imbroglio that was then wending its way to the Supreme Court frustrated a central location. The dispute over the location of the fair also reveals, in a manner more clearly than do the legislative and judicial proceedings recounted so far, that the fate of the lakefront was caught up in a bitter dispute between rival factions of the city elite.

The federal legislation designating Chicago as the site created a dual authority overseeing the fair. A commission of representatives from every state would provide broad oversight; a directory, composed of individuals (directors) primarily from Chicago, would sell stock to raise funds for the fair and provide ongoing supervision of activities. The directory created a Committee on Grounds and Buildings and charged it with picking a site for the fair in the city, subject to the approval of the directory and the commission.[53]

The committee was quickly besieged with siting proposals from all corners of the city. Each potential site was supported by individuals who had purchased stock in the fair, as well as by real estate speculators who hoped to cash in if their neighborhood hosted the fair. Yet nearly everyone recognized the considerable logic of putting the fair in Lake Park. The park represented a point of convergence at an equal distance from the South, North, and West Sides of the city. Because the park was close to the central business district, downtown merchants would benefit from fairgoers passing by their stores. The site was also close to the city's main transportation terminals, was convenient to existing hotels and entertainment venues, and offered fine views of the lake.[54]

Lake Park nevertheless presented serious challenges. The strip of land between Michigan Avenue and the Illinois Central right of way was not wide enough for a fairground. Either the fair would have to be located on new landfill east of the railroad's tracks, or the tracks would have to disappear, presumably by being moved farther to the east. Then there was the large Interstate Industrial Exposition Building on Michigan Avenue in the center of the park (considered more fully in chapter 3), which would have to be demolished or substantially renovated. Finally, property owners on Michigan Avenue were opposed to any construction in the park, as this would bring new congestion and impair their views. Warren F. Leland, who owned a hotel on Michigan Avenue and had a suit pending seeking to demolish the Exposition Building, was especially vehement in opposing any use of the park for the fair.

The widespread support for locating the fair in Lake Park presented a golden opportunity to achieve a comprehensive settlement of the issues then pending in the *Lake Front Case*. The Illinois Central was quick to grasp the point. In a remarkable letter written in 1887—three years before Congress selected Chicago as the site—the railroad's lawyer, B. F. Ayer, informed President Fish of talk in Chicago about hosting a world's fair. He observed, "It is possible that this enterprise may furnish an advantageous opportunity for settling the Lake-Front question, and I think therefore it would not be amiss for our Company to take an active interest in shaping the policy and plans of those having the matter in charge." It was no accident, therefore, that Fish and an Illinois Central vice president would be named directors of the fair (although Fish would eventually resign, perhaps when the conflict of interest became apparent)—or that William K. Ackerman, a former president of the railroad, was named auditor, and Edward T. Jeffery, a former general manager, was named to the critical Committee on Grounds and Buildings, serving for a period as its chair. The railroad made sure that it was in a position to learn about, and to influence, the thinking of fair officials in determining the site of the fair within the city.[55]

Strenuous efforts, involving local politicians, fair officials, the Illinois Central, and Michigan Avenue residents, were made to reach a deal. During an eight-month period from the summer of 1890 to February 1891, multiple proposals were advanced to make Lake Park available for the fair.

On June 28, 1890, the fair directory adopted a resolution that Lake Park be the site of the fair, provided that the area could be increased to three hundred acres. The initial proposal called for the Illinois Central to abandon its existing right of way from Monroe Street to 22nd Street (with a slight exception between Park Row and 16th), relocate its tracks farther east on new landfill of its own making, surrender all its riparian rights in this area (with the same exception), pay $1.5 million to the City of Chicago, and allow the World's Fair to occupy the land filled in by the railroad, for a nominal rent for four years. Although the railroad would have received a three-hundred-foot right of way, the plan held little if any advantage for the Illinois Central, which promptly rejected it.[56]

Perhaps because of questions raised by some commissioners about the ongoing litigation over property rights in Lake Park, the directory quickly followed up, on July 1, with a different resolution, calling for a dual site. Lake Park was still the preferred location, with "as large a use as may be possible," but Jackson Park on the South Side was designated as a supplemental site, to be "use[d] . . . as far as may be necessary." The national commission doubted the wisdom of a dual site but, after a "long debate," accepted the resolution.[57]

Both the Chicago City Council (as it had been renamed) and the state legislature soon enacted legislation designed to make Lake Park available for the fair. But their actions introduced complications that would make a settlement more difficult. The city's ordinance transferred all of the city's rights over Lake

FIGURE 2.7. Stuyvesant Fish, ca. 1900. Library of Congress, Prints and Photographs Division, LC-DIG-ggbain-02597.

Park, from Monroe Street to Park Row, to the World's Fair for more than four years. However, reflecting mistrust of the Illinois Central (or of its influence with fair directors), the ordinance also prohibited fair officials from making any deal with the railroad without the city's first signing off. Some interpreted this to mean that the fair had to rely on city officials or the Michigan Avenue owners to negotiate with the railroad.[58]

The state legislature, in a special session, approved legislation transferring additional submerged land to be filled for the site of the fair. At the last minute, however, a clause was added providing that, after the fair, the city had to use the new land had for a public park, or else title would revert to the state. This clause made it impossible to include, as part of any negotiations, a further grant of submerged land to the Illinois Central, at least absent new legislation.[59]

In August 1890, Frederick Law Olmsted, the celebrated landscape architect retained by the directors to prepare the site for the fair, made a tour of the ground on the South Side. He had drawn up plans for the area, to become known as Jackson Park, some years before. Olmsted's report characterized the unimproved portions of the park as a swamp but found that, by dredging canals and elevating adjoining grounds, approximately 112 acres of suitable land could be made available for the fair. The local press characterized Olmsted's report as a negative verdict on the Jackson Park site.[60]

Dickering continued over possible terms that would allow the fair to be located in Lake Park. The Committee on Grounds and Buildings had proposed that the Illinois Central fill the area east of its right of way, between Randolph Street and Monroe Street, out to a line continuous with the railroad's three existing piers north of Randolph (the piers are shown above in figure 2.5). This would be rented to the fair for four years but afterward would revert to the railroad, presumably for expansion of its rail and harbor complex. This much should have been appealing to the railroad. But the committee also added a new demand, "to make it more satisfactory to the public": that the railroad abandon all of its land and facilities (other than right of way) between Park Row and 16th Street. After consulting with Fish and the board of directors, the railroad's attorney stated that this "would be impossible for the Company." Upon learning of the ongoing discussion, a state senator quickly pointed out that giving the railroad the right to fill additional land would be inconsistent with the state law, just enacted, stipulating that, after the fair, any new land had to be used as a park. Reflecting the fair's growing frustration, one unnamed director was reported to have remarked, "Instead of 'Columbus Discovering America,' it ought to be 'Directors Discovering a Site.'"[61]

Faced with an impasse in Lake Park, the fair directors increased their attention to the South Park Commission (SPC). The commission controlled not only Jackson Park but also Washington Park and the Midway Plaisance connecting the two parks. The directors now urged the SPC to make these additional parklands available for the fair. In response, in what would prove to be critical to the final outcome, the SPC agreed to add "to the original tender of the unimproved portion of Jackson Park the improved portion thereof and the Midway

Plaisance"—a total of some 650 acres, more than enough to host the fair. At a September 1890 meeting, the directory again voted to support a dual site. The national commission remained unenthusiastic about the remote location and a divided venue. Nevertheless, it accepted the decision.[62]

From this point forward, the exigencies of the situation favored the Jackson Park/Midway Plaisance solution. The South Side site now had sufficient land for the fair. The Lake Park site did not, and was embroiled in a seemingly intractable set of disputes that stood in the way of creating more land. The consulting architects, including Olmsted and Daniel H. Burnham, who would be named the fair's chief of construction and director of works, proceeded to develop plans presupposing Jackson Park as the principal site of the fair. Any role for the Lake Park venue would be far more modest.[63]

Still, the directory was reluctant to give up on the Lake Park site. One reason was intense opposition to Jackson Park on the part of investors in the fair living on the North and West Sides of the city. The directors were worried that, if they abandoned the lakefront altogether, disgruntled stockholders would sue "to enjoin collection of further assessments on their stock." Thus, efforts to achieve a settlement allowing Lake Park to be used as at least a partial site for the fair persisted throughout the fall of 1890 and the early winter of 1891.[64]

Because of the city ordinance prohibiting any direct deal between the fair authority and the Illinois Central, the settlement efforts proceeded on two tracks. One involved negotiations between the fair directors and the Michigan Avenue owners. The other involved negotiations between the Michigan Avenue owners or the city and the railroad.[65]

The courting of the Michigan Avenue owners unfolded in the fall of 1890. The property owners insisted, in largely categorical rhetoric, that no buildings be constructed in Lake Park south of Jackson Street. For example, Warren F. Leland, whose hotel sat just south of Jackson, reaffirmed his unflinching objection "to any use of the lake front except for the purposes of a park." Yet he offered a qualification: "[I]f through the necessities of this great exposition these unsightly railroad tracks can be removed further eastward . . . where they would be practically out of sight, and the lake front improved and beautified forever, why I think it a public duty, the duty of every man who has the interest of central Chicago at heart, to bring it about."[66]

In early January 1891, a proposal was advanced to move the tracks farther east, temporarily, for the duration of the fair. The Michigan Avenue owners refused to acquiesce: only a permanent relocation of the tracks would do. Lyman J. Gage, president of the directory, commented that the property owners "have acted like a man who possessed the only chair in the world and refuses to get up for a moment to let any one else sit down."[67]

With time now running out, Alderman Arthur Dixon, on behalf of the Michigan Avenue owners, proposed an ordinance designed to bring the parties together in a way that would permit construction of a handful of fair structures in Lake Park: the railroad would give up its current right of way, construct a new right of way farther east, and sink the tracks underground; in return, the railroad would be allowed to fill submerged land, east of its current right of way, from Randolph Street south to Adams Street, "to be used by them for such corporate purposes as they may see fit during the life of said corporation." There was one new twist: namely, the Illinois Central must "construct an arcade not more than 500 feet in width" above the new right of way, which could not be "higher than the established grade of Michigan Avenue." Warren Leland stated his support for the Dixon ordinance, subject to the fair authority's giving a bond to assure that any fair buildings in the park south of Jackson Street would be torn down after the fair.[68]

Fish was inalterably opposed to placing a ground-level arcade over the main line of the railroad. The tracks would have to be depressed so deeply in the arcaded area that it would create an excessively steep grade for trains leaving and entering the terminal area north of Randolph. And it was doubtful that the project could be carried out in time to permit buildings to be constructed before the start of the fair. In an effort to show some accommodation, Fish nevertheless said that the railroad was willing to sink the tracks in their current location, at its own expense, provided that it was given a three-hundred-foot right of way.[69]

With the Michigan Avenue property owners willing to consent to temporary buildings, and the Illinois Central willing to discuss modifying its line in Lake Park, the fair authority made a final push to secure a settlement. At the instruction of the directors, the Committee on Grounds and Buildings arranged for architects to prepare sketches of the buildings proposed to be erected in Lake Park. These showed five buildings between Monroe Street and Park Row: an art palace, a decorative art building, a music hall, a water palace, and an electrical palace. In a matter of days, the sketches began appearing in local newspapers, as in figure 2.8.[70]

The visual images of what the portion of the fair in Lake Park might look like achieved their intended purpose of building public support for a settlement. Meeting, as usual, at the Leland Hotel, the Michigan Avenue owners acquiesced in the idea of five temporary buildings, provided that all but the art palace would be demolished after the fair and that the fair directors would continue to pressure the Illinois Central in order "to secure the sinking or removal" of its tracks. There was "general jubilation" among the proponents of the lakefront site. The papers proclaimed, "Lake Front Question Settled at Last." The directory adopted a resolution instructing the Committee on Grounds and Buildings to take possession

FIGURE 2.8. Illustrations of the five buildings envisioned for Lake Park as part of the 1893 Columbian Exposition, reflecting street-level view from Michigan Avenue and ground plan. Left to right (going south from Monroe Street to Park Row): Fine Arts, Decorative Arts, Water Palace, Electric Display, Music Hall. *Chicago Tribune*, January 20, 1891.

of Lake Park, in accordance with a Chicago ordinance adopted in 1890, and to commence operations leading to the construction of the five buildings. Within a week, in January 1891, Lake Park had been staked off and trenches were being dug at the foot of Harrison Street for a construction headquarters.[71]

It soon appeared, however, that the agreement with the Michigan Avenue owners had papered over a difference with the Illinois Central. With their demand that the railroad either sink or remove its tracks, the property owners may have understood that if the railroad did not want an arcade, it would agree to move its tracks. But the thing to which railroad had agreed—besides a comprehensive settlement that had gained no traction—included the possibility of its merely depressing its tracks in their present location. In response to the acceptance of the proposal by the Michigan Avenue owners, Fish was said to have maintained a "golden silence."[72]

On January 27, 1891, Alderman Dixon, under the auspices of a city council committee, convened a large meeting of all affected interests. The meeting turned into a heated debate between Stuyvesant Fish, appearing for the railroad and no longer silent, and Warren Leland, for the property owners. The exchange, reported by the *Chicago Herald*, is highly revealing of the conflicting perspectives of the main antagonists and why they defied compromise.[73]

Leland insisted that Dixon's plan had the support of the public and was the best solution. Fish suggested that filling the lake to create a new right of way might cost $3 or $4 million. Leland said that the cost would be worth it, since the railroad would get "a magnificent right of way." Fish responded that the city ordinance of 1852 already gave the railroad a right of way. He noted that "[t]his land is all in litigation and we expect to own it," adding sarcastically, "You ask us to give you land above water for land under water. I might as well ask you to exchange your dwelling for your hotel." Leland retorted that the comparison was nonsense, and added, "You have to remove the nuisance of your locomotives and smoke on the lake front. . . . [I]f you don't the time will come when the people of Chicago will rise up and throw your tracks into the lake. . . . You must stop your hooting and whistling all night long on the lake front."

Fish then tried to strike a more accommodating tone, but said there were limits to the costs that he could ask his stockholders to bear. The debate moved on to other matters, including where a new passenger terminal would be located and the land south of 12th Street. When the topic returned once again to moving the right of way farther east of Lake Park, the exchange grew vehement again. Fish complained anew about being asked to move "400 or 500 feet on our own land." Leland responded that "[i]f you insist on keeping your cars there the property owners have the money raised already to fight you." Fish suggested that the property owners "have been fighting the road for years." Leland parried, "No, we haven't, but we will if you don't accept some plan within reason." Fish's response was to note that the matter was before the Supreme Court—and that the company expected to win.

This debate between the primary antagonists tells us a great deal about why they could not reach an agreement. The Illinois Central's judgment about the costs and benefits of settlement was significantly affected by its belief that the Supreme Court would uphold its position in the pending *Lake Front Case.* As Fish saw things, asking the railroad to abandon its existing right of way and build a new one on landfill in the lake was like asking it to pay for something it already owned. The Michigan Avenue owners, for their part, were uniquely affected by the smoke and especially the noise generated by the busy rail line several hundred feet from their property. Warren Leland must have heard endless complaints from hotel guests about "hooting and whistling all night long." This explains why the property owners' central demand—the one feature on which they insisted in any settlement—was to move the tracks farther away from the street. Moreover, these owners could not deliver on what the Illinois Central really wanted: secure rights to expand its harbor operations in the lake.

By mid-February, the internal correspondence of the railroad indicates, negotiations had come to a halt. The railroad's bottom line remained that, without a significant quid pro quo, it would not take on the cost and operational difficulties of relocating its line farther east. The quo it wanted was an agreement from the city and the state that would allow it to expand its existing outer harbor from Randolph Street farther south, to Monroe or Adams Street. Neither the fair authority nor the Michigan Avenue owners could bring this about. So the railroad preferred the status quo—together with its chances of winning the pending case in the Supreme Court.[74]

If the tracks were not going to be moved, then putting any fair buildings on the narrow strip of land between Michigan Avenue and the tracks was problematic. William Steinway, the New York piano manufacturer and the largest shareholder of the exposition corporation outside Chicago, voiced his displeasure at the prospect of a music hall with the tracks so nearby. Nor was the area suitable for an electrical display or the water palace, both because of the limited space and because pedestrians on Michigan Avenue would be able to see these spectacles without having paid admission to the fair. And even if the tracks were depressed in their present location, the Michigan Avenue owners noted, this would not remedy the nuisance from the smoke.[75]

So, not long after the newspapers rejoiced in proclaiming a settlement, the plan to put part of the fair on the downtown lakefront collapsed. There had been some foreshadowing. At a meeting of the directory in early January, a longtime proponent of the lakefront site had offered a "startling resolution" to abandon the lakefront in favor of Jackson Park. The resolution was tabled, but was said to echo the views of "a large number of the directors who despair of being able to secure enough ground to place more than one building in a desirable location." Then, on February 11, 1891, the directory's newly established Budget Committee reported that the lowest-cost option for construction of the fair required everything to be located in Jackson Park. The dual site would cost at least $1 million more. Given that the fair's finances were already stretched to the limit, and with no settlement of the property-rights issues on the lakefront in sight, the decision to make Jackson Park the exclusive venue was sealed.[76]

On February 20, the directory formally voted, twenty-five to seven, to abandon Lake Park as a location for the fair, and then confirmed this nearly unanimously, against a single holdout. Lake Park would be beautified and serve as the "gateway" to the fair. "Jackson Park alone simplifies the thing beyond measure," said President Lyman Gage. Warren Leland gloated that it was a "great victory" for Michigan Avenue property owners, even though nothing had been done about the railroad nuisance.[77]

That was scarcely the end of the saga of the lakefront, the railroad, and the fair. The decision to make Jackson Park the fair site presented a major logistical issue. Jackson Park was approximately seven miles south of the city center, and there were no improved streets running directly from the city center to the park. It was clear that the Illinois Central, whose tracks ran from Randolph Street south past Jackson Park, would bear a large part of the burden of transporting visitors from downtown. This would require a significant enhancement of the railroad's passenger facilities, especially the construction of a suitable depot. Fair officials also wanted steamer service, which would allow visitors to travel to the fair from Lake Park. Ideally, this would include the construction of one or more piers in the lake east of Lake Park, which in turn would require some safe means of access over the lines of the Illinois Central. Fair engineers estimated that adequate transportation facilities would cost more than $6.3 million.[78]

The transportation problem provided yet another impetus for a comprehensive settlement of the issues pending in the *Lake Front Case*. The main adversaries—the Illinois Central and the Michigan Avenue owners—had been in intense settlement discussions for months and had come relatively close to reaching an agreement in late January. And the directory's decision to abandon the Lake Park site meant that one impediment to reaching a general agreement—the prospect of erecting buildings in the park that would bring crowds and impair the property owners' view—was now out of the way.

The general outlines of a new proposal for a settlement appeared in the newspapers in March 1891. The Illinois Central made no public comment, although its attorneys were actively working behind the scenes to promote a deal. The basic terms offered major concessions to both the property owners and the railroad. The railroad agreed to move its tracks farther to the east, from Randolph Street down to Park Row, and to depress the tracks below grade so that the trains would not be visible from residential properties. The railroad would be allowed to use the area between Randolph and Adams for landfill and to construct piers and wharves. The area west of its right of way from Adams to 22nd Streets would be filled in for new parkland. The railroad would also relinquish its rights under the 1869 Lake Front Act, and Justice Harlan's decree would be set aside, ending the litigation in the Supreme Court. The final form of the settlement was to be embodied in legislation enacted by the city council and the state legislature, which was in session. The council duly enacted the proposed ordinance, albeit with certain amendments.[79]

The focus then turned to the state legislature. A deputation of interested parties traveled together to Springfield to lobby for legislation confirming the deal. Lawyers were especially well represented, including Ayer and Jewett for the Illinois Central and former US attorney William G. Ewing, now representing the property owners. Observers noted the "remarkable unanimity."[80]

The unanimity did not last long. The *Tribune* and the *Herald* editorialized against the compromise. Both suggested that the agreement reflected the interests of the Illinois Central and the property owners but not those of the broader public. A particular focus was "the four blocks," as it was here called: the area from Randolph to Adams Streets, between Michigan Avenue and the existing Illinois Central right of way. If the railroad was going to move its tracks east, where it would have plenty of land to build a new depot connecting to the new right of way, why did the railroad need the four blocks? Would it not be better for the city to retain them?[81]

Soon a representative of the Prairie Avenue owners proposed a modified deal. Then a group backed by the Michigan Avenue owners offered yet a third proposal. The newspapers became increasingly aggressive in their condemnation of the settlement as being overly generous to the Illinois Central. The scandal of the 1869 legislative session was invoked once again, along with headlines including cries of "steal." The *Herald*, in an article titled "The All Gall Lake Front Deal," claimed that the exchange of rights would yield the Illinois Central property worth $90 million, while the city got the equivalent of a paltry $1 million. As consensus collapsed and public hostility mounted, the Illinois Central quietly withdrew its support for the settlement. The state legislature adjourned without acting.[82]

The clock was ticking, with no transportation plan in place for the fair. The Illinois Central concluded that it would have to rely on its existing property rights to transport passengers to the fair. For neither the first nor the last time, the exigencies of the moment led to a land-use decision that would have a lasting effect on the lakefront.

To solve the need for better depot facilities, the railroad made a consequential decision: it decided to build a grand new passenger terminal on land east of Michigan Avenue between Park Row and 12th Street—just to the *south* of Lake Park. Construction proceeded rapidly, and the new terminal was finished in spring 1893, only weeks before the fair opened. Known simply as Central Station, the facility with its Romanesque clock tower remained a Chicago landmark for decades.[83]

More complicated was the matter of constructing piers in the lake, east of Lake Park, to transport fair visitors by steamer. The city, believing that Harlan's decision gave it the right to construct such piers, initially proposed constructing multiple piers to be reached by extensions of existing streets, with viaducts over the railroad's tracks. The Illinois Central was understandably cool to this idea. The matter of water transportation was discussed intermittently throughout 1891 and into the next year. The Illinois Central was not opposed to new piers in the lake, especially if they were paid for by the city or the fair authority. After all, if the railroad won in the Supreme Court, it would get the new piers for free. Paying for the viaducts was another matter. In public meetings with city officials

FIGURE 2.9. Central Station, 1893. Chicago History Museum, ICHi-005286.

in December 1891, the railroad emphasized the question of costs. As transcribed by a reporter, Fish said he had no objection to the viaducts, "but if they are built on our ground we must have an adequate return." Fish "casually" maintained that the Illinois Central "owned all the land between Randolph Street and Park row" and further had no need of additional passenger traffic from the fair. "'We are ready to trade something for something,' Mr. Fish added, with a wise smile, 'but we are not looking for a trade in which we will give something for nothing.'" This summed up the railroad's attitude to the fair.[84]

The city corporation counsel, John S. Miller, proposed to break the impasse by asking the Supreme Court to expedite hearing the *Lake Front Case*. The Illinois Central agreed to expedition, except as to the United States' case concerning the federal government's title to or interest in north Lake Park, which the railroad said had no bearing on the immediate controversy over the construction of piers east of the park. Miller duly filed the motion to expedite in mid-December 1891, without similar support from the United States. One week later the court granted the motion and set the case for argument in October 1892. One newspaper characterized the advancement as a "great victory," but admitted that "the hearing is still so far off that nothing can be done toward building docks on the Lake Front, except by agreement." This was correct. The court would decide the case in December 1892—too late to have any effect on the transportation arrangements for the fair.[85]

So, by the spring of 1892, it was clear that the matter of steamer piers and connecting viaducts would have to be negotiated. When the fair authority reduced its plans to one official pier with a connecting viaduct on Van Buren Street, the Illinois Central relented (see figure 2.10). Fish even offered to pay for the superstructure of the viaduct. This suited the general interests of the Illinois Central, in that its passenger depot in Lake Park at Van Buren Street was projected to serve as an especially important point of embarkation for visitors to the fair.[86]

The remaining issues involved public safety and cost sharing. The city and fair officials wanted the Illinois Central to elevate its tracks near Jackson Park, so that pedestrians might move freely in and out of the fairgrounds without having to cross busy train tracks at grade. The railroad grumbled, but eventually agreed to a cost-sharing formula and completed the work before the opening of the fair. The tracks in Hyde Park remain elevated to this day.[87]

The World's Fair turned out to be successful beyond anyone's prediction. During the fair's six months, the Illinois Central transported a staggering 8,780,616 passengers to and from Jackson Park. A ticket cost ten cents, which generated substantial revenues to help pay for the improvements, including Central Station, the viaduct, and the elevated tracks, and to make the experience, for most visitors, reasonably safe and convenient.[88]

FIGURE 2.10. Van Buren Street viaduct over the Illinois Central tracks in Lake Park, with crowds headed to the steamers on Lake Michigan for transport to the 1893 World's Fair. R. A. Beck Photo Book, courtesy of the Newberry Library, Chicago, IC Photos-3-Box 3-Folder 64.

The Supreme Court Rules

The Supreme Court heard oral argument in the *Lake Front Case* over three days in mid-October 1892, and rendered its decision with some dispatch that December. The opening of the World's Fair—the reason for expediting the case—was by then only five months away. Given the need to be ready for opening day, all relevant controversies concerning transportation facilities had by then been settled through negotiation. The Supreme Court's wisdom about the Lake Front Act of 1869 and its repeal in 1873 would provide, at best, guidance for the future.

Only seven of the nine justices participated in the decision. The reporter noted that "[t]he Chief Justice, having been of counsel in the court below, and Mr. Justice Blatchford, being a stockholder in the Illinois Central Railroad Company, did not take any part in the consideration or decision of these cases." No mention was made of Chief Justice Fuller's participation, a quarter century earlier, in a scheme to secure a grant of the submerged land for himself and other private investors. One wonders whether any actors in the case, other than Fuller himself, were even aware of this fact. Justice Harlan's right to sit in judgment of his own decision rendered on circuit passed without question.[89]

Justice Stephen J. Field, writing for the majority, followed Harlan's lead in the lower court in seeking to untangle the knot of legal issues. He began with the background understanding about ownership of the submerged land of Lake Michigan. The court in previous decisions had acknowledged that the choice between the English and American views about the ownership of nontidal submerged land was a matter of state law, and had specifically recognized that Illinois had chosen to follow the English rule of private ownership. Yet without adverting to whether the question was governed by federal or state law, Field proceeded to declaim on title to all lands under "the Great Lakes," implicitly treating this as a unique category. Relying especially on the court's decision holding that federal admiralty jurisdiction extends to the Great Lakes, he concluded that the land under the Great Lakes was indistinguishable in all relevant respects from that under tidal waters, which the court had long held to belong to the states. Consequently, the State of Illinois also exercised sovereignty over, and ownership of, submerged lands of Lake Michigan. It had done so since Illinois was admitted to the union in 1818, whether or not anyone knew it at the time.[90]

After then describing the lakefront and the midcentury legislation laying the groundwork for the Illinois Central, Field turned to address whether the Illinois Central's existing two-hundred-foot right of way and the various depots, docks, wharves, piers, elevators, and engine houses it had built on landfill in the lake encroached on the state's property rights. He concluded that mostly they did not. He relied in part on the broad powers that the state had given the railroad in its 1851 charter and in particular on the provision conditioning the location of the railroad within a city upon the city's consent. Chicago's consent in 1852 to the location of the Illinois Central's right of way in the lake therefore constituted constructive permission from the state. With respect to the facilities constructed both north of Randolph and south of 12th Street, Field, echoing Harlan, concluded that these were encompassed within the common-law right of a riparian owner to "make a landing, wharf, or pier" to reach navigable waters. The only doubt was whether the railroad had extended its facilities beyond the point of "practical navigability." The case was remanded for further proceedings to resolve this question.[91]

This disposition of the railroad's improvements failed to account for two parcels discussed in chapter 1: the triangles created by the curvature of tracks west and east approaching Randolph Street from the south, as authorized by city ordinances in 1855 and 1856. Field ratified these by ipse dixit: "[W]e do not perceive any valid objection to [the railroad's] continued holding of the same for

FIGURE 2.11. Justice Stephen J. Field, 1890. Library of Congress, Prints and Photographs Division, LC-USZ62-83944.

the purposes declared—that is, as additional means of approaching and using its station grounds."[92]

This brought the court to the outer harbor—an area "as large as that embraced by all the merchandise docks along the Thames at London," as Field described it, with "arrivals and clearings of vessels at the port . . . equal to those of New York and Boston combined." The railroad's vested-rights contention posed a real challenge, and Field departed from Harlan's approach. Focusing on the provision of the Lake Front Act purporting to grant to the Illinois Central one thousand acres along the lakefront, Field held that this portion of the 1869 act was inherently revocable. His theory was that the state's title to the submerged lands was held in trust for the public. It is, he wrote, "a title different in character from that which the State holds in lands intended for sale. . . . It is a title held in trust for the people of the State that they may enjoy the navigation of the waters, carry on commerce over them, and have liberty of fishing therein freed from the obstruction or interference of private parties."[93]

The idea that the land under navigable waters is subject to a public trust was not entirely new, even with respect to these specific waters. It had appeared fleetingly in the press in 1869, before Governor Palmer's veto of the Lake Front Act, as noted in chapter 1. Much closer to trial, the city's corporation counsel, in an analysis of the legal issues prepared for Mayor Harrison in 1886, had briefly alluded to the proposition. The state's lawyer had repeated the concept before Justice Harlan in the circuit court. And in the Supreme Court, the City of Chicago set forth the basic substance of the argument and the supporting authorities, both federal and state.[94]

In adopting the argument, however, Justice Field gave it his own spin, reflecting his general judicial philosophy. Field, a Jacksonian Democrat, throughout his career was deeply suspicious of legislatively conferred special privileges and monopolies. This is the lens through which he appeared to view the Lake Front Act of 1869. Thus, in characterizing the legislation, Field drew a picture of a powerful and privileged corporation endowed by a shortsighted legislature with unprecedented powers over a traditionally public resource. He emphasized the status of the railroad as the recipient of extensive government land grants and charter privileges even before the Lake Front Act. With respect to the act itself, he concentrated on the provisions that had the least obvious public-interest rationale, and hence made the act seem like a giveaway, concluding that "[a] corporation created for one purpose, the construction and operation of a railroad between designated points, is, by the act, converted into a corporation to manage and practically control the harbor of Chicago, not simply for its own purpose as a railroad corporation, but for its own profit generally." And although Field did not explicitly accuse the railroad of corrupting the legislature, he noted at one point that "[t]he circumstances attending the passage of the act through the legislature" had been "the subject of much criticism." In context, he could be read to refer only to certain alleged violations of state constitutional procedures, but his language hinted at darker allegations about the motivations of the legislature.[95]

There was irony in this characterization of the events of 1869. As we have seen in chapter 1, the primary motivation of the Illinois Central in 1869 was defensive—to prevent some other group from obtaining a grant of the lakefront for itself and thereby cutting off the railroad's access to it. But this was ancient history by 1892. In fact, the railroad's lawyers made no effort to describe the anxieties that drove the carrier to go to the legislature in 1869—perhaps because they did not know about them. By contrast, it is likely that the justices were familiar with the Illinois Central's recent behavior, which conformed more closely to the caricature of the bullying monopolist that Field intimated in explaining the need for a public trust doctrine.

Although he was unequivocal that the submerged land was impressed with a public trust, Field did not suggest that all dispositions of such lands were impermissible. He acknowledged that "[t]he interest of the people in the navigation of the waters and in commerce over them may be improved in many instances by the erection of wharves, docks and piers therein, for which purpose the State may grant parcels of the submerged lands; and, so long as their disposition is made for such purpose, no valid objections can be made to the grants." What was not permitted was "the abdication of the general control of the State over lands under the navigable waters of an entire harbor or bay, or of a sea or lake." In effect, Field drew a distinction between small, commerce-promoting grants of submerged land, needed for wharves, docks, and piers, and large, monopolistic grants of submerged land, which could be used arbitrarily to restrict the public's access to navigable waters for navigation and fishing. "A grant of all the lands under the navigable waters of a State has never been adjudged to be within the legislative power," he wrote, "and any attempted grant of the kind would be held, if not absolutely void on its face, as subject to revocation. The State can no more abdicate its trust over property in which the whole people are interested, like navigable waters and soils under them, so as to leave them entirely under the use and control of private parties . . . than it can abdicate its police powers in the administration of government and the preservation of the peace." Field admitted that he could not "cite any authority where a grant of this kind has been held invalid." But he thought that this was because such an extreme grant had never previously been considered by the courts.[96]

Given this framework, it was inevitable that Field would find the grant to the Illinois Central of one thousand acres of land under Lake Michigan to fall into the impermissible category—to be a breach of the trust in which this land was held. Such a grant, he wrote, was "necessarily revocable, and the exercise of the trust by which the property was held by the State can be resumed at any time." The 1873 repeal of the Lake Front Act was thus held to be constitutional.[97]

Appended as a kind of coda to the discussion of the trust obligation was an especially long paragraph addressing Justice Harlan's theory in the court below that the Lake Front Act had conveyed a mere revocable license to the railroad to build an outer harbor. This cannot be characterized as an alternative holding: the theory was described but not expressly endorsed. Perhaps the passage was added in order to secure Harlan's agreement to join in making a bare majority for the Field opinion, although this is speculation.[98]

Turning finally to the claims of Chicago, Field concluded that, under Illinois law, all land marked on plats as reserved for public uses is owned by the city where the land is located. Thus, Chicago had title to the original Lake Park. And as riparian owner of this land, the city had a common-law right to wharf out and develop the harbor outside the park, including the right to expand Lake Park by filling in the area to the original breakwater, as had happened in 1871. In these ways, the city had good title to Lake Park, as against the state and the Illinois Central.[99]

There were, perhaps inevitably, some loose ends. Field did not address Harlan's holding below that the section of the 1869 statute confirming the Illinois Central's existing rights could not be repealed consistently with the Constitution. Perhaps Field concluded that it was unnecessary to address the confirmation of rights, given that the court sustained all improvements made by the railroad up through the 1880s (assuming that they were found on remand not to interfere with "practical navigability"). But the Illinois Supreme Court would soon repudiate the common-law right to wharf out, and it would also subsequently hold that the railroad's charter did not authorize landfilling in the lake. We will see in subsequent chapters that, many decades later, when litigation was launched challenging the Illinois Central's right to dispose of the air rights above its improvements, the validity of the 1869 confirmation of rights would become an issue of potentially dispositive significance.

The outcome of the *Lake Front Case* was close, especially as to the central issue whether the state had acted unconstitutionally in repealing the grant of submerged land to the railroad. Three (of the seven) justices joined in a dissenting opinion by Justice George Shiras Jr., arguing that the Lake Front Act was a valid conveyance of property to the Illinois Central and the repeal was an unconstitutional interference with vested rights. Shiras purported not to disagree with the "able and interesting statement" by Field "of the rights of the public in the navigable waters, and of the limitation of the powers of the State to part with its control over them." Rather, he doubted the "pertinency" of that discussion, given that the Lake Front Act had prohibited the railroad from interfering with the public right of navigation and had preserved the power of the state to regulate the railroad's construction of improvements in the harbor. "It will be time enough," the dissent maintained, "to invoke the doctrine of the inviolability of public rights when and if the railroad company shall attempt to disregard them."[100]

Oddly, neither the majority nor the dissent cited the court's famous decision in *Fletcher v. Peck*. That 1810 decision also involved a state land grant followed by a repeal when the original grant was discredited by allegations of corruption, but it held that the repeal violated the Constitution's contracts clause. Harlan's opinion for the circuit court had acknowledged that *Fletcher* was the principal precedent relied on by the railroad and took pains to distinguish it, developing the revocable-license theory. This omission by both Field and Shiras may have obscured for later generations of commentators the key legal issue in the *Lake Front Case* as presented to the court.[101]

Stuyvesant Fish, president of the Illinois Central, took the defeat hard. The railroad's lawyers, seeking to explain the outcome, complained to Fish that the court had adopted a novel and unsound theory to defeat the claim of vested rights. A more accurate characterization would be that in the railroad's two lengthy briefs in the Supreme Court, one filed by Ayer and the other by Jewett, the lawyers had made a strategic decision to ignore the public trust contention advanced in Miller's brief for the city. Fish directed the lawyers to file a petition for rehearing. When this was denied without comment, Fish took the extraordinary step of hiring a prominent New York lawyer who specialized in constitutional law, William D. Guthrie, to lead an effort to file a second petition for rehearing. The court, no doubt disinclined to encourage multiple petitions for rehearing, simply ignored the second petition.[102]

The Supreme Court in the *Lake Front Case* did not address the United States' appeal, no motion having been filed to expedite it along with the others. In 1894, the court got around to hearing it. Writing again for the majority in a divided decision, and again following Harlan's lead, Field rejected the Drummond theory of retained federal rights in Lake Park. The dedication of public ground on the lakefront by the United States, Field reasoned, sufficed under Illinois law to transfer the fee to the City of Chicago. Because the United States had conveyed away its entire interest in the property, the federal government did not have standing to enforce limitations on the use of that land. With this ruling, the last cloud on the city's title to Lake Park was lifted.[103]

Although the United States did not have standing to enforce the dedication, the court stated in dictum that the Michigan Avenue owners did: "The owners of abutting lots may be presumed to have purchased in part consideration of the enhanced value of the property from the dedication, and it may be conceded they have a right to invoke, through the proper public authorities, the protection of the property in the use for which it was dedicated." As we will see in the next chapter, this dictum, along with Drummond's 1869 injunction decision, would fuel the chain of rulings by the Illinois Supreme Court, in actions brought by Montgomery Ward, enjoining the construction of any buildings in the area that became Grant Park.[104]

The Practical-Navigability Controversy

In 1896, the federal circuit court took up the task of the remand in the *Lake Front Case*: determining whether the railroad's landfills extended so far into the lake as to interfere with practical navigability. Judge John W. Showalter considered extensive evidence about how far out into the lake a pier would have to be constructed in order to accommodate the deep-draft commercial vessels then plying Lake Michigan. Showalter concluded that the Illinois Central's extensive piers and wharves north of Randolph Street and its piers south of 12th Street did not extend "into the lake beyond the point of practical navigability, having reference to the manner in which commerce in vessels is conducted on the lake." The newly created US Court of Appeals for the Seventh Circuit affirmed this judgment, in a two-to-one decision, in 1899.[105]

The final chapter of the litigation epic was written in 1902, when the Supreme Court affirmed this decision, turning aside the state's appeal. In a fitting bookend, the court spoke through Justice Harlan, who had written the original decision of the circuit court back in 1888. Since the question about the depth needed for practical navigability was "largely, if not entirely," one of fact, Harlan wrote, the judgment would not be disturbed unless it was clearly in conflict with the evidence. No such conflict being found, the order upholding the railroad's existing improvements was upheld.[106]

Harlan cautioned that the railroad could not go any farther into the lake: his original decree of 1888 had enjoined it from erecting new structures or filling with earth or other materials any portion of the bed of Lake Michigan. In short, everything the railroad had done in the past was grandfathered. As to the future, the untouched areas of the lakebed were to be under the exclusive control of public authorities.[107]

With this judgment, the vexing legal issues that had given rise to the lakefront controversy were settled, at least for the time being. Thirty-three years had elapsed since the Lake Front Act had been adopted; it took an astonishing nineteen years since litigation had commenced to confirm the validity of the act's repeal and sort out the consequences.

The *Lake Front Case* remains one of the most important decisions about property rights in American law. While the dominant mode of organizing resources is private property, the decision stands for the proposition that certain critical resources, most notably those associated with navigable waterways, must remain under the control of public authorities. Our investigation into the circumstances giving rise to the decision highlights a number of points that are not generally appreciated.

As we have seen, the central device of the *Lake Front Case*—the public trust doctrine as announced and applied—was primarily a product of the exigencies of litigation. Justice Field needed some doctrinal basis to defeat the Illinois Central's powerful vested-rights argument, reaffirmed by three of the seven participating justices. Absent the peculiar circumstances of the enactment and repeal of the Lake Front Act, there would have been no cause to invest the state's ownership of the lakebed with a trust that made large transfers to private entities inherently revocable.

We can also see how the public trust doctrine was not deployed in the litigation to freeze the submerged land in its original condition. Field was all in favor of small grants of lands for wharves and docks. He opposed what he imagined to be the conferral of a monopoly over the proposed outer harbor on a private corporation. His public trust doctrine was designed to preserve access to the lake for commercial vessels at competitive prices, not to preserve Lake Park or the shoreline from further economic development. Moreover, Field was not alone in these preferences. When the dust finally settled, all of the Illinois Central's massive landfills and improvements had been ratified by the federal courts as consistent with the nebulous trust identified in the *Lake Front Case*.

What is less clear is why Field felt compelled to reach for the blunderbuss of the public trust doctrine to defeat the Illinois Central's vested-rights claim, rather than a more fact-specific argument, such as Harlan's characterization of the grant of the outer harbor as a mere license. We can only speculate that Field was incensed by what he imagined to be a power grab by a privileged corporation, shutting out all competition from potential rivals. None of the railroad's briefs or arguments explained the railroad's motivations for seeking the Lake Front Act in 1869, or why a reasonable legislator in 1869 would likely have supported the act. Another reason may be that Field and the other justices in the majority were familiar with the more aggressive behavior of the Illinois Central starting in the 1880s, to the point where the railroad had become an effective monopolist controlling navigation in the rump "outer harbor" it had constructed in Chicago. While the decision took no account of the activity in 1867 or the events that impelled the Illinois Central to go to the legislature in 1869, it may have been influenced by the railroad's high-handed tactics in the 1880s.

The longstanding controversy generated by the Illinois Central's presence on the lakefront was by no means the only source of conflict about how to use the open space called Lake Park. As we will see in the next chapter, the Michigan Avenue property owners had their hands full fending off proposals to fill the park with structures of all kinds of description.

3

THE WATCHDOG OF THE LAKEFRONT

The published opinions resolving the *Lake Front Case* contain no hint about the role of the Michigan Avenue property owners (or the Prairie Avenue owners) in opposing the ambitions of the Illinois Central Railroad on the lakefront. As we have seen in chapter 2, however, the property owners were very much a driving force behind the scenes. Not only were they instrumental in blocking plans to locate the World's Columbian Exposition in Lake Park, but they also helped scuttle any number of settlement possibilities that would have allowed an expansion of the railroad's harbor facilities in the lake. Indeed, the property owners substantially funded the local litigation efforts in the *Lake Front Case.*

The Illinois Central was not the only antagonist with which the Michigan Avenue owners had to contend in their efforts to preserve the value of their property. The strip of land called Lake Park was also coveted for a variety of other uses inconsistent with an open view of the lake. As Lake Park began to grow through additional landfilling and became Grant Park, proposals proliferated to fill the lakefront with exhibition halls, armories, libraries, and museums. Other segments of the Chicago elite typically championed these projects, although both the proponents of openness and the advocates of buildings claimed to represent the interests of the masses. In these fights, the Michigan Avenue owners were much more visible—indeed, often as plaintiffs against local government—and, remarkably, they most often prevailed. Their immediate objective was to secure the value of their real estate by preserving their views of the lake;

the indirect effect was to save, in the center of the city, a huge open space that eventually became a cherished public park.

The legal tool employed by the Michigan Avenue owners in their battles against proposed buildings in the park was something called the public dedication doctrine. The public trust doctrine played no role in preserving what is now called Grant Park from development. Instead, various landowners, including most prominently Aaron Montgomery Ward, the famous catalog merchant, invoked the public dedication doctrine to obtain a series of state court decisions blocking construction of buildings in the park. These precedents kept Grant Park free of significant encroachments for more than a century.[1]

"Public dedication" sounds something like "public trust," and the two doctrines are easily confused. Indeed, one can find decisions enforcing the public dedication doctrine that refer to dedicated land being held "in trust" for the public. But the legal theories underlying the two doctrines are quite different.

The exact contours of the public trust doctrine have always been a matter of dispute, and, as we will see in chapter 8, the doctrine underwent a significant transformation in the later decades of the twentieth century. As developed in the *Lake Front Case*, however, the public trust doctrine referred to the right of the general public to use navigable waters for commerce and fishing. This in turn meant that the state could not transfer large tracts of submerged land to a private entity, which might deprive the public of access to those waters.

The public dedication doctrine has its share of uncertainties, many explored in this chapter. But at its core, it refers to the right of a private landowner to enforce statements on publicly recorded plats and maps that certain lands will be devoted to public uses, such as streets, public squares, or parks. Prospective purchasers rely on these representations in deciding whether to purchase nearby lots—and how much to pay for them. The public dedication doctrine allows purchasers of lots favored by such dedications to sue for an injunction against subsequent actions by developers or government officials inconsistent with the dedication.

There were no Illinois precedents endorsing the public dedication doctrine when the land along the lakeshore in Chicago was first developed in the 1830s. Yet there were a growing number of precedents from other jurisdictions—including several prominent decisions of the Supreme Court of the United States. The Illinois Supreme Court embraced the doctrine in 1850. Soon Illinois courts were enforcing it outside Chicago with vigor. These precedents would have encouraged a legally sophisticated purchaser of lots on the west side of Michigan Avenue in the 1850s and afterward to expect that he or she could go to court to enforce a public dedication restricting development of Lake Park.[2]

The Public Dedication of Lake Park

To understand the role of the public dedication doctrine on the lakefront, it is necessary to take a closer look at the original titles to land along the shore of Lake Michigan in the center of Chicago.

The Chicago lakefront was part of the Northwest Territory ceded by Virginia and other states to the general government around the time of the Revolutionary War. All land in Illinois was surveyed in accordance with the grid system established by the Land Ordinance of 1785, which divided land into square townships of thirty-six numbered sections, each containing 640 acres or one square mile. Even before Congress made the massive grant of federal land to Illinois to promote the construction of the Illinois Central Railroad, it made a similar grant to promote the construction of the Illinois and Michigan Canal, linking the Chicago River with the Mississippi River (via rivers in between). Under this grant, Illinois was given the odd-numbered sections of land for two and a half miles on each side of the proposed canal route. The state in turn granted these sections to a board of canal commissioners, created in 1829, so that it could sell land to the public to finance construction of the canal. One of these sections was fractional section 15 of township 39, located in what now includes part of the southeast portion of Chicago's Loop, or central downtown area. It was called "fractional" because of Lake Michigan: everyone assumed that the canal commissioners would not sell submerged land. Figure 3.1, taken from the *Lake Front Case*, is a map of fractional section 15.[3]

Notice that the easternmost portion of the solid land—from Madison Street south to 12th Street, save only a small block abutting 12th—was not platted. The map designates the area between the platted blocks and Lake Michigan as "Michigan Avenue." A commercial map from the same period labeled this area "PUBLIC GROUND[—]A Common to remain forever Open, Clear & free of any buildings, or other Obstructions Whatever." It is likely that the canal commissioners used this commercial map (or a similar visual aid) to convince prospective purchasers that the land east of Michigan Avenue would have an open view of the lake. The platted lots fronting on the west side of Michigan Avenue sold for higher prices than other land in fractional section 15.[4]

Soon afterward, the US Army decided to abandon Fort Dearborn, which was located in fractional section 10, immediately north of fractional section 15. The federal government opened this area for sale as the "Fort Dearborn addition to Chicago." Figure 3.2, a version of a map recorded in 1839, depicts the area. It includes the notation, in the area near the lake, "public ground for ever to remain vacant of buildings." A note in the margin of the original map, signed

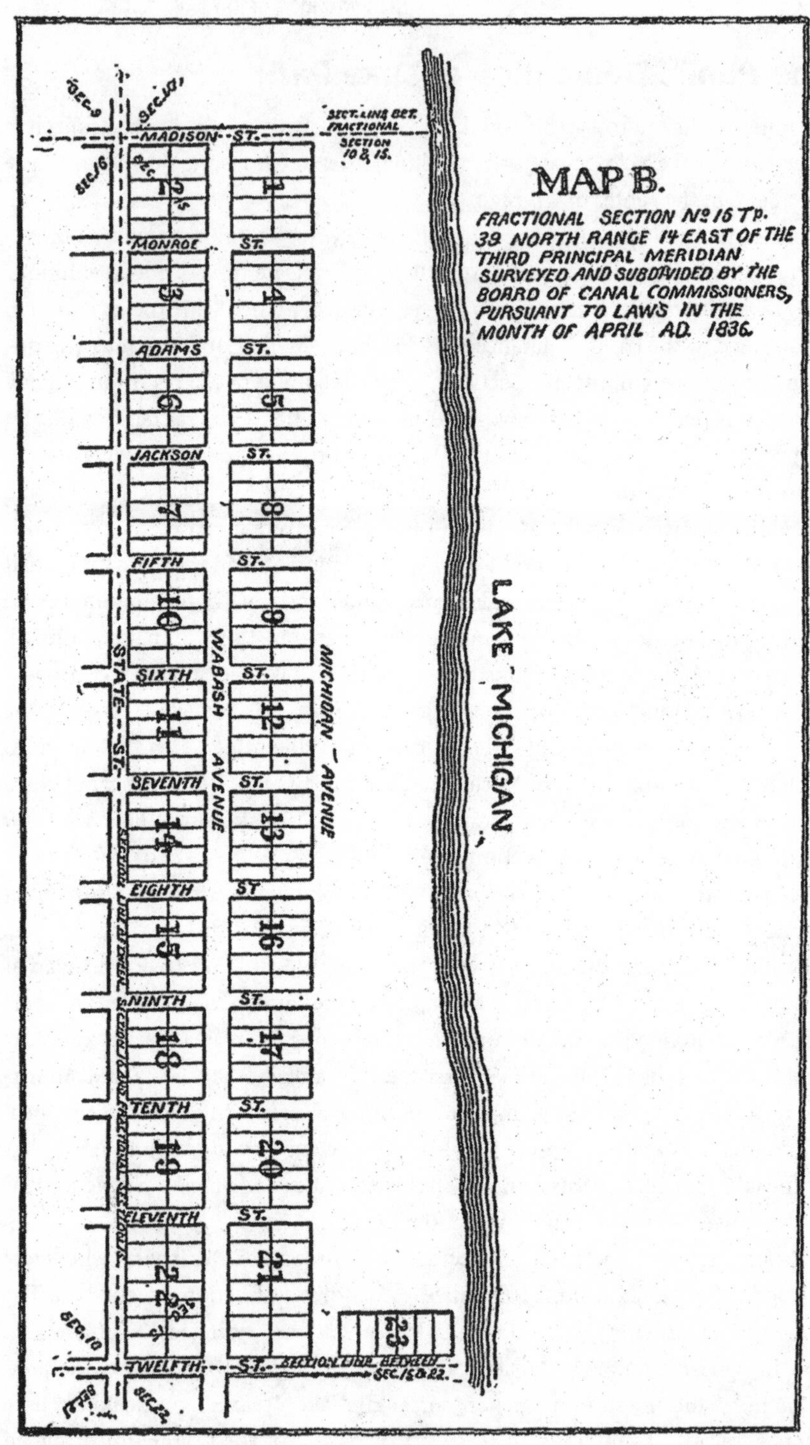

FIGURE 3.1. Fractional section 15. *Lake Front Case*, 146 U.S. 387, 397 (1892) (statement of the case).

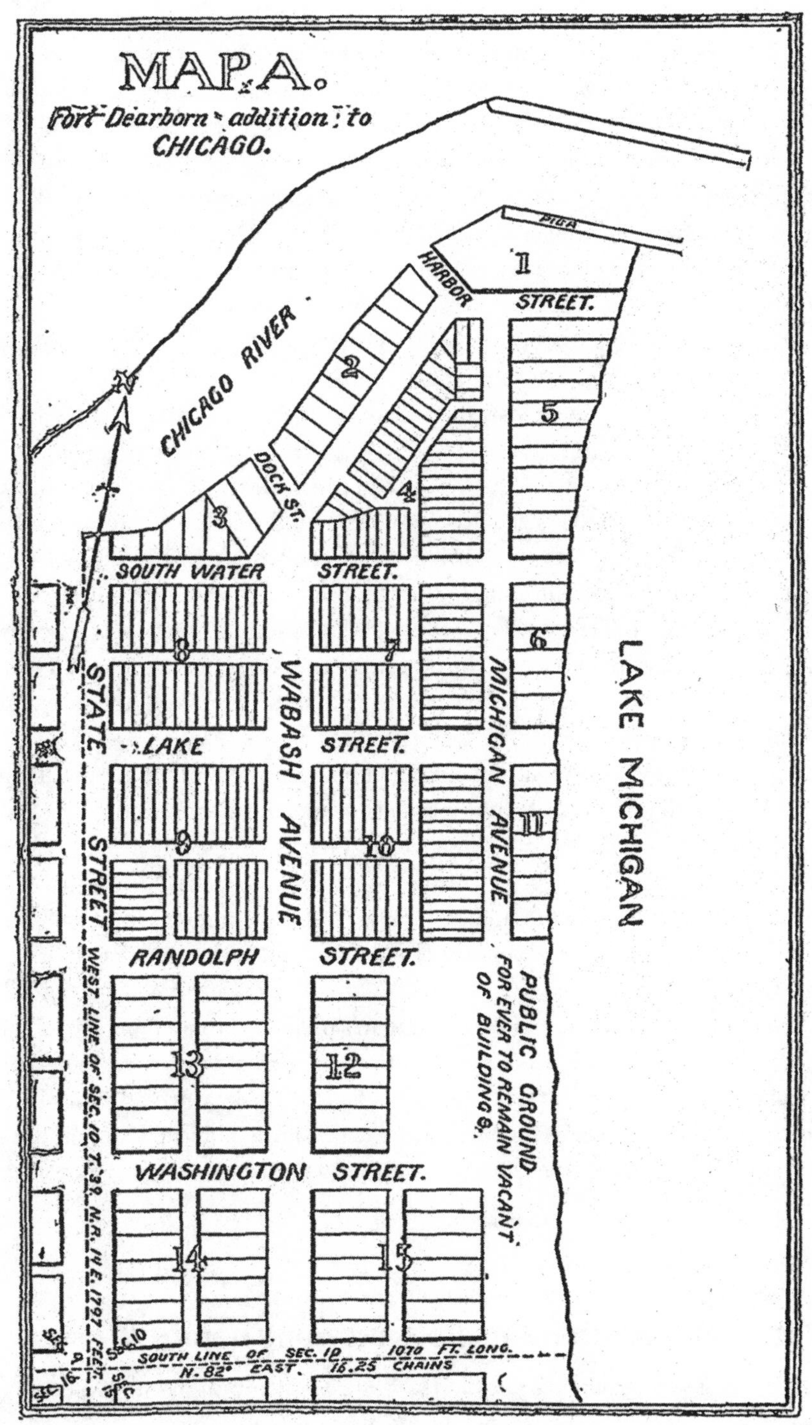

FIGURE 3.2. Fractional section 10. *Lake Front Case*, 146 U.S. 387, 392 (1892) (statement of the case).

by Matthew Birchard, the federal agent who negotiated the sales and recorded the map, read as follows: "The public ground between Randolph and Madison streets, and fronting upon Lake Michigan, is not to be occupied with buildings of any description." Madison Street, not named in figure 3.2, was at the bottom of the map, parallel to and one block south of Washington Street; it formed the boundary between fractional sections 10 and 15. As in section 15, lots abutting the protected area were sold at a premium based on the understanding that they would enjoy direct exposure to Lake Michigan.[5]

These map and plat notations would provide the legal foundation for the invocation of the public dedication doctrine by owners of land on the west side of Michigan Avenue. Otherwise, there were no legal restrictions on how land along the lakefront might be used.[6]

The use of the property on the west side of Michigan Avenue, at least initially, was largely for residential structures populated by the Chicago elite. The land to the east, in keeping with the restrictions appearing on the various maps just described, remained vacant of permanent structures. This vacant land, stretching from Randolph Street on the north to Park Row on the south, was officially given the designation "Lake Park" by city ordinances enacted in the 1840s. There was at this time, however, no formal governmental structure for preserving and maintaining a park.[7]

Once the common council allowed the Illinois Central to enter the city along the lakefront, the Michigan Avenue residents secured further protections against encroachments on Lake Park. The revised city charter adopted by the state legislature in 1861 and 1863 included a section providing in part that "[n]o encroachment shall be made upon the land or water west of [the Illinois Central Railroad right of way] by any railroad company" and permitted any owner of a lot fronting Michigan Avenue to sue to enjoin "any such encroachments or violation." For good measure, the charter provided that "[n]either the common council of the city of Chicago, nor any other authority, shall ever have the power to permit encroachments thereon, without the assent of all the persons owning lots or land on said street or avenue." Thus, critical elements of the public dedication doctrine were effectively codified, in 1861 and 1863, in state legislation applicable to the lakefront.[8]

Public Dedication on the Lakefront before Ward

The early history of public dedication lawsuits by Michigan Avenue owners can be divided between the periods before and after the Great Chicago Fire of 1871. Before the fire, public dedication actions achieved some success. The occasion for the first known lawsuit was the Democratic Party's national convention scheduled for the summer of 1864. The convention obtained the city's permission to construct a "wigwam"—a circular wooden amphitheater with a canvas roof—at the southern end of Lake Park at 11th Street. Michigan Avenue property owners argued in state court that this violated the requirement to keep the park free of buildings.[9]

The suit was perceived as politically motivated and generated some hostile reaction. In early summer, the parties filed a stipulation allowing the wigwam to go up, subject to a number of conditions, including that the building would be torn down within six days of the end of the convention. Construction resumed, and the convention proceeded to select General George B. McClellan as the party's nominee. The structure was thereupon removed.[10]

A more consequential judicial precedent arose from the litigation in 1869 challenging the Lake Front Act's provision granting north Lake Park to the Illinois Central Railroad for a new passenger depot. Judge Drummond concluded that the notation on the Fort Dearborn Addition plat was a binding dedication and that the United States, which he ruled still had title to the dedicated land, could seek its enforcement. The Drummond injunction, as discussed in chapter 1, had the effect of halting plans to construct a new depot on the north Lake Park site.[11]

After the fire, public dedication suits disappeared for more than a decade. The city, in desperate straits, leased out a portion of Lake Park for the construction of temporary commercial buildings, even before the rubble was cleared from the

FIGURE 3.3. Wigwam in Lake Park for the 1864 Democratic Party's national convention. Chicago History Museum, ICHi-001981.

west side of Michigan Avenue or used to fill and expand Lake Park between the original shoreline and the Illinois Central right of way to the east (as described in chapter 2).

Such efforts resulted, on the east side of Michigan Avenue, in a mile-long stretch of hastily built structures, generally one story in height—although some ambitious owners stretched their buildings to the permit limit of twenty feet, obtaining two low stories (see figure 3.4). Property owners tolerated these low-lying and often unsightly structures as part of the emergency atmosphere in the immediate aftermath of the fire. Once the rebuilding effort downtown was underway, these structures were torn down.[12]

In their place, the city in 1873 authorized the erection of a huge Interstate Industrial Exposition Building, south of Monroe Street in Lake Park. This

FIGURE 3.4. Temporary buildings, along the east side of Michigan Avenue in Lake Park, erected ca. 1872, after the Great Fire. Chicago History Museum, ICHi-038984.

structure was to hold an exposition of Chicago goods and wares in an effort to convince the world that the city had recovered from the devastation. The exhibition's successful first year led to the city's approving a two-year extension, and then other uses were found for the massive building. Eventually, the Exposition Building evolved into a kind of all-purpose convention center, hosting a horticultural conservatory, art exhibitions, musical concerts, and even the 1884 Republican and Democratic national presidential conventions. It remained a looming presence on the lakefront until 1892, as discussed later.[13]

Michigan Avenue landowners did not object to any of the construction activity in Lake Park in the years immediately after the fire. No doubt the shock of the fire and the sense of collective crisis had much to do with this. Moreover, the Michigan Avenue owners could hardly say that these structures were blocking their view, when their houses lay in ruins. The Exposition Building was understood to be a temporary structure when it was first proposed, and some of the Michigan Avenue elite either were sponsors of this undertaking or were actively involved in its later cultural activities.[14]

FIGURE 3.5. Interstate Industrial Exposition Building (with three cupolas), viewed to the north on Michigan Avenue from Jackson Street, ca. 1890. Chicago History Museum, ICHi-062407; J. W. Taylor, photographer.

Partly because of the passivity of the Michigan Avenue owners during this period, the city in the ensuing years permitted a variety of structures to be built in Lake Park. These included a grandstand for the Chicago White Stockings Base Ball Club, initially erected in 1878; structures to accommodate armory buildings for two companies of state militia, opened in 1882 and demolished in 1898; a passenger depot for the Baltimore & Ohio (B&O) Railroad, which had obtained trackage rights from the Illinois Central, erected in 1883 and taken down circa 1891; and a massive temporary post office building, first constructed in 1896 and demolished in 1905. Eventually, as we shall see, these structures evoked multiple objections from Michigan Avenue landowners and produced significant litigation.[15]

Michigan Avenue property owners began to rediscover their distaste for encumbrances in the park once Chicago was back on its feet again by the early 1880s. Litigation over the restriction against buildings erupted. The principal properties that would be involved in the lawsuits during the next decade are shown in figure 3.6 (and, to a lesser extent, in figure 3.11).

In 1882, two Michigan Avenue owners, John F. Stafford and Thomas Hoyne, brought the first suit, seeking to block construction of one of the buildings just mentioned: a new depot for the B&O Railroad, north of the Exposition Building. Judge Drummond, who had prohibited the construction of a depot in Lake Park in 1869, rejected the request for an injunction. He agreed with the property owners that the Exposition Building and all the other structures in Lake Park violated the dedication. Nevertheless, he concluded, the adjoining landowners, with each new building, gradually had lost their right to enforce the dedication. In essence, having not objected to these buildings, the plaintiffs were estopped or barred from now challenging the B&O terminal.[16]

The next year, Stafford filed a similar suit in state court, and achieved a measure of success, even if not quite as sweeping as he sought. He secured a temporary injunction against the erection of a building by the Trade and Labor Assembly, projected to be "two stories in height and of large dimensions and [to] contain one main hall and gallery and two ticket offices and a place for the sale of spirituous liquors, and all the other accessories of a play house or public hall and saloon." The judge said that, pending a final decree, the buildings already constructed, including the Exposition Building, could stay. "But," he stated, "there must be no further encroachments."[17]

The US attorney launched the next move in 1884 and directed it specifically at Albert G. Spalding and the Union Base-Ball Grounds in north Lake Park (see figure 3.6 for the location and figure 3.7 for an image). Relying on Drummond's 1869 holding that the United States had retained title to the land in fractional section 10, the complaint alleged that the city had violated the public dedication by

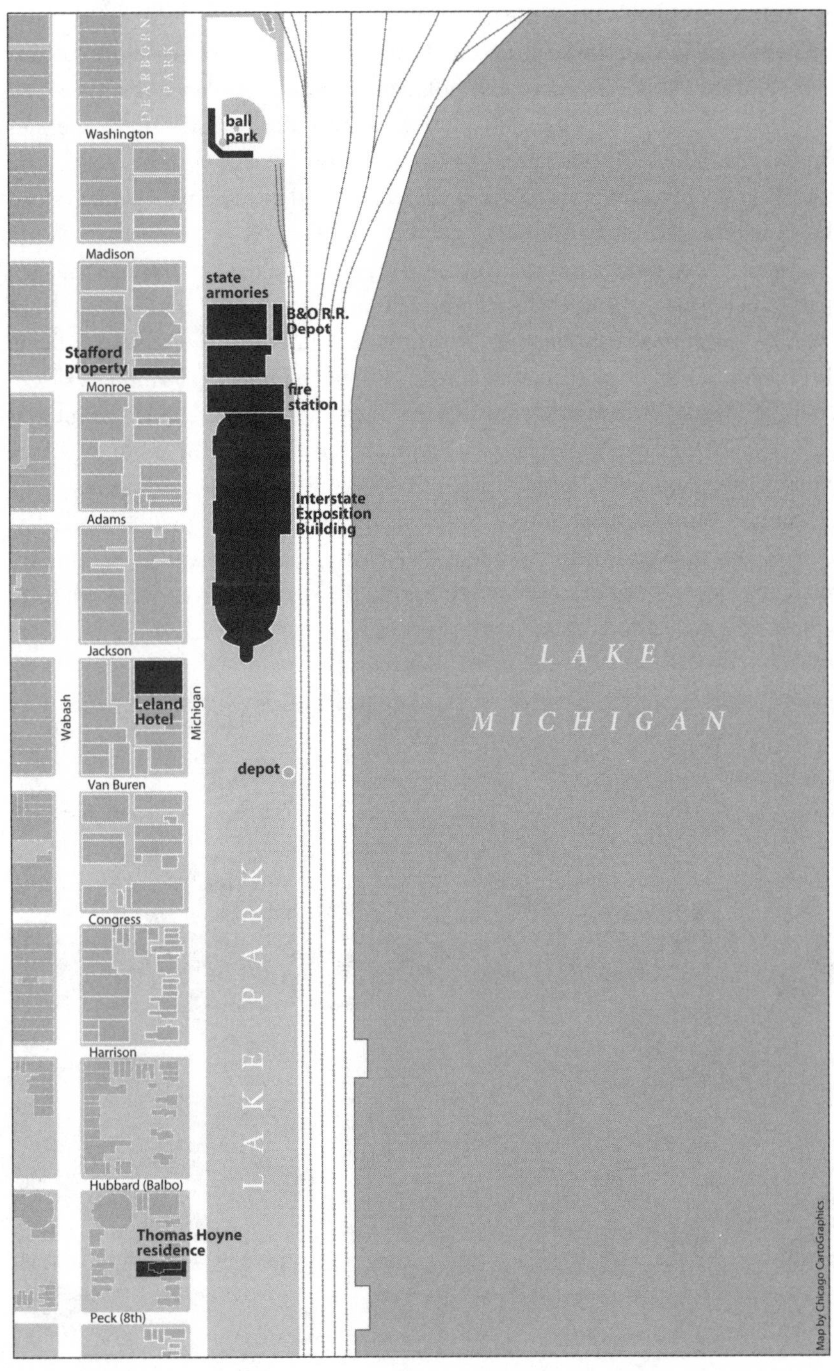

FIGURE 3.6. Location of relevant buildings and properties in and across from Lake Park, ca. 1882.

permitting Spalding's team, the Chicago White Stockings, to construct "a board fence at least ten feet in height, in such manner as to completely shut out said ground from public view or access," not to mention a grandstand with a roof and seats. The complaint noted that the public was excluded from the stadium unless it paid admission. The government stated that "this bill is filed at the request and partly on the behalf of" neighboring owners. Indeed, the complaint was verified by none other than John Stafford.[18]

Judge Henry Blodgett of the federal court enjoined the city from leasing any part of Lake Park for a baseball stadium. The ball club could finish the season, but then had to remove its structures. For the first (and only) time, a court ordered the demolition of an existing structure based on the public dedication.[19]

With Justice Harlan's ruling in 1888 that the United States retained no interest in section 10, the federal government lost its legal authority to object to construction in Lake Park. The decision meant that Michigan Avenue landowners could no longer count on accommodating US attorneys to serve as their enforcement agents, and that actions to enforce the dedication could no longer be brought in federal court. But Harlan did not question the right of private landowners to enforce the dedication themselves.

FIGURE 3.7. Union Base-Ball Grounds. *Harper's Weekly*, May 12, 1883. Chicago History Museum, ICHi-032436.

Indeed, a new plaintiff soon appeared on the scene: Warren F. Leland. The owner of the Leland Hotel on the west side of Michigan Avenue (and the brother of the proprietor of Springfield's Leland Hotel, figuring in chapter 1), he would become the leader of the property owners opposed to constructing the World's Fair in Lake Park (see chapter 2). Even earlier, in late 1886, Leland filed suit in state court, seeking an injunction against a toboggan slide that the city had permitted one J.M. Martin to erect in Lake Park, south of the Exposition Building. Martin's plea that the slide was intended to raise funds to support an impoverished widow did not move Leland. A state court issued a temporary injunction in late December and a permanent injunction early the next year. In 1889, Leland was back in court again, this time challenging the Exposition Building itself, both its very existence and a proposal to modernize and expand it by adding a powerhouse. Again, a temporary injunction against the new construction was promptly issued. It appears, however, that Leland made no effort to make the injunction broader or permanent.[20]

Ward Enters the Lists

We now turn to Aaron Montgomery Ward. He has always been something of a mystery. He has no full-length biography. He disliked publicity, rarely spoke to the press, and consistently refused permission to be written up in sketches of Chicago leaders. Ward reportedly gave generously to philanthropic causes during his lifetime, but nearly always anonymously. If he left any papers or letters, they disappeared long ago.[21]

The bare outline of what is known suggests that Ward was the quintessential self-made man. Born in New Jersey in 1843 and raised in poverty in Michigan, he left school at the age of fourteen to work as a manual laborer to help support his family. Later he became a shop clerk in St. Joseph, Michigan.[22]

After the Civil War, Ward moved to Chicago, where he worked as a clerk at Field, Palmer & Leiter, which would later become Marshall Field & Company. Ward then signed on as a traveling salesman for a St. Louis wholesaler. During his travels, he observed the often-shoddy goods sold at high prices to farm families in small-town stores. He later switched jobs again, becoming a buyer for a Chicago dry-goods company.[23]

Armed with close familiarity with rural tastes and values and a background in both purchasing and sales, Ward conceived a revolutionary scheme to buy goods in bulk and sell them directly to farmers through the US mail. After a setback from the Chicago fire, by August 1872 he had built a small inventory. His first catalog was a single page long. Business was initially slow, exacerbated by the Panic of 1873, and Ward kept his day job while he filled orders at night.[24]

FIGURE 3.8. Aaron Montgomery Ward. Chicago History Museum, ICHi-062410.

The missing ingredient was credibility with rural customers, who needed to be convinced that they would not be cheated if they sent cash to a firm in Chicago. Ward solved the problem by forging an alliance with the populist Granger Movement and by offering a money-back guarantee on all goods sold, no questions asked.[25]

The result was phenomenal. Ward's company quickly became the largest retailer in the United States. It is no exaggeration to say that Montgomery Ward was to the late nineteenth century what Sam Walton and Walmart were to the late twentieth. Starting with a focus on rural and small-town America, Ward, like Walton, revolutionized merchandizing.[26]

FIGURE 3.9. Montgomery Ward & Co. facility on Michigan Avenue, Chicago, ca. 1900. Library of Congress, Prints & Photographs Division, Detroit Publishing Company Collection, LC-D4-14730.

Within a few years, Ward and his partner, George R. Thorne, were scrambling to acquire ever-bigger office and warehouse space in Chicago. In 1887, they purchased two adjacent lots on the west side of Michigan Avenue, between Madison and Washington Streets, for $235,000. Two years later, they acquired the lot to the south for $72,000. By 1890, they had constructed a multistory "skyscraper," to which a tower was subsequently added (see figure 3.9).[27]

Ward later said that he and Thorne paid $40,000 more than they would have but for the right "to compel the property in front [of theirs] to be kept open as a public park and free and clear from all buildings." He also stated that they selected the site on Michigan Avenue in part to give their employees sunlight, fresh air, and a reasonably quiet location in which to work. Although these claims were made in litigation, they were plausible. Ward was by all accounts relatively solicitous of his employees' well-being. The lakefront site was not chosen to appeal to customers, since the catalog facility was not, at least initially, open to the public. When the Michigan Avenue facility was established, Ward, Thorne, and their employees were the only people who would be affected by the light, air, and views that the lake afforded.[28]

Ward's Lower-Court Litigation, 1890–95

Once Ward and Thorne completed their new Michigan Avenue building, they quickly joined forces with other owners who were already active in threatening and sometimes actually suing to stave off construction in Lake Park. Yet as Stafford entered into a ninety-nine-year lease of his property in 1888, Leland sold his hotel in 1892, and Sarah Daggett (to be considered soon) died in 1895, Ward gradually assumed the role of leader.[29]

The first recorded salvo from Ward & Co. came on October 16, 1890. The partners filed a complaint in state court to enjoin the City of Chicago and the Illinois Central from erecting any buildings in Lake Park. The triggering event for the suit—according to a later recounting—was when Ward looked out the window from his new office and, across Michigan Avenue, saw workers building scaffolding to load garbage into railroad cars. He summoned his lawyer, George P. Merrick, and demanded that something be done.[30]

We have uncovered no contemporaneous evidence to support this account. It may be significant that the suit was filed in the fall of 1890, when substantial efforts were underway to allow the World's Fair to be located in Lake Park (see chapter 2). A prominent feature of many of the settlement proposals was to transfer north Lake Park—opposite Ward and Thorne's property—to the Illinois Central for a new passenger depot. It is possible that the suit reflected the partners' alarm at the prospect of a large depot and throngs of passengers on the land between their property and the lake.

In any event, the court promptly issued a temporary injunction prohibiting the defendants from erecting "any structure" in north Lake Park. The action then lay dormant for several years, perhaps because the directors of the World's Fair decided to locate the fair in Jackson Park and the Illinois Central built its new depot outside Lake Park, many blocks to the south.[31]

Nevertheless, the fair had a significant impact on the future of the park. One activity affiliated with the fair was the World's Congress Auxiliary, an ambitious program of public lectures, to be delivered by scholarly, literary, and religious figures. The organizers decided that Lake Park should be the venue for the lectures. After much jockeying, it was also decided that the Exposition Building would be torn down and that, to host the auxiliary program, a new building in the neoclassical style associated with the fair would be erected in its place. After the Columbian Exposition ended, the building would become the new home of the Art Institute of Chicago.[32]

The directors of the Art Institute were well aware of the risk of litigation by the Michigan Avenue owners. Accordingly, Caryl Young, a Michigan Avenue property owner sympathetic to the project, set about to obtain consents from other property owners. Consents were sought from those owning property directly across from the proposed structure and those diagonally across (i.e., on the adjoining corners). Ward and Thorne's property was a block north of this zone, so their consents were not sought.[33]

One owner, Sarah Daggett, did not consent (see figure 3.11 for the locations of her property and the Art Institute). Young approached her husband, Isaac Daggett. Although Isaac had no ownership interest in the property and declined to sign the consent form, Young evidently got the impression that Sarah Daggett did not oppose the Art Institute construction, or at least so he reported to the directors.[34]

Armed with what it apparently regarded as a complete set of owner consents, the Art Institute entered into construction contracts on February 4, 1892. Two days later, Sarah Daggett wrote to one of the directors stating that, in fact, she did not consent to the construction. The work went ahead anyway. Shortly thereafter, on April 3, the city was served with an order in state court to show cause why it should not be held in contempt under the 1889 injunction obtained by Warren Leland. Leland had been replaced in that suit by none other than Sarah Daggett.[35]

Judge Richard S. Tuthill, who had been the US attorney in some of the early days of the *Lake Front Case*, found that the 1889 Leland injunction applied to the Art Institute building, and he ordered construction to halt. In an unusual move, with the opening of the fair rapidly approaching, the matter was reheard three weeks later by a panel of circuit court judges. Over his dissent, the court reversed Tuthill's ruling.[36]

The judges reaffirmed that the plat restrictions created an enforceable public dedication and that Daggett, as an abutting owner, had authority to enforce the restrictions. They nevertheless held that Daggett was not entitled to an injunction, primarily on the grounds that she had slept on her rights even while the Art Institute was acting. Given that Daggett had voiced her opposition shortly after she learned about the project, this was a weak rejoinder.[37]

The court modified the Leland injunction to the extent necessary to permit construction of the Art Institute to go forward. Daggett did not appeal, whether for want of time or because of the requirement of posting a large appeal bond. The building was still under construction when the World's Congress Auxiliary took possession in late spring 1893.[38]

It is doubtful that Ward harbored any reservations about the project. He served as a governing member of the Art Institute from 1888 to 1913, and as the museum commented after his death, "During all his years as the 'watch-dog of the Lake Front' he was always friendly to the Art Institute and considerate of its interests."[39]

Another significant institution that emerged at this time was the Chicago Public Library (today the Chicago Cultural Center), built in the space previously known as Dearborn Park, on the west side of Michigan Avenue between Randolph Street and Washington Street. As reflected in figure 3.2 above, this space had been included as part of the "public ground" on the Fort Dearborn Addition map that was "for ever to remain vacant of buildings." It had served for years as a rare empty space west of Michigan Avenue. Nevertheless, consents to use Dearborn Park as the library site were readily obtained from abutting landowners—specifically, from the owners of property that abutted Dearborn Park in the horseshoe fronting Washington Street on the south, Garland Place (previously Dearborn Place and now Garland Court) on the west, and Randolph Street on the north. At that time, Ward's property, in the block to the south, did not extend all the way north to Washington Street, and thus Ward was not approached to sign the consent. The library would be built in the same neoclassical style as the Art Institute.[40]

Ward soon found himself back in court in several disputes arising under the temporary injunction that he had obtained in 1890. In May 1891, a petition was filed, with the city's support, to modify the injunction to permit the Adam Forepaugh Shows to erect a circus tent in Lake Park. Ward objected, arguing that such a tent was a building. Judge Kirk Hawes said that the park had been neglected by the city for twenty years, and he asked the parties to submit authorities on whether abutting property owners had standing to prevent temporary use of a "mud hole." The judge eventually allowed the traveling circus to erect the tent.[41]

In 1892, a deal was struck to allow another wigwam to be built, this time for the Democratic Party's national convention during the coming summer. Ward initially opposed the wigwam but eventually yielded, having been assured that it would be torn down after the convention. He later regretted the decision, telling the *Tribune* that "it took five years of litigation to undo the precedent thus established."[42]

In April 1893, the City of Chicago petitioned for a modification of the injunction to permit another circus in the park. Ward and Thorne again objected, and this time they found a measure of success. The court entered an order enjoining all defendants "from erecting any buildings, sheds, plat-forms, tents, or other structures upon [Lake Park]."[43]

Ward's attitude toward use of the lakefront nevertheless remained selective. In 1895, Chicago's corporation counsel concluded that the city could not allow a proposed temporary post office to be built in north Lake Park without first obtaining permission from Ward and the other abutting property owners. After some equivocating, Ward gave his oral consent, which the federal authorities regarded as sufficient. Once the building was completed, however, he again drew the line. Ward obtained an injunction to stop the construction of a bicycle track next to the temporary post office building. And when the post office decided to expand the temporary building in 1899, Merrick was back in court for Ward. He secured an injunction in state court, but when the case was removed to federal court (because the construction company was essentially acting on behalf of the federal government), the injunction was dissolved. The Seventh Circuit reasoned that the "original plan" called for a larger post office than had been initially constructed, and thus Ward's previous consent should be construed to include the enlarged structure.[44]

Grant Park and *Ward I*

Unquestionably the most important effect of the Columbian Exposition was its powerful impression on the public imagination. Under the guiding hand of Daniel Burnham, Chicago had built a magical "White City" in Jackson Park, featuring large neoclassical buildings, public plazas, monumental statuary, and, perhaps most enchantingly, electrical lighting. The year before the fair, the *Lake Front Case* had quashed any claim by the Illinois Central that it could build an outer harbor east of Lake Park, and had further determined that the city had clear title to all the filled land in the park (other than the railroad's right of way). With these matters settled and the fair concluded, the White City served as a model for how Lake Park might be reconstructed. Chicago's business and cultural elite proceeded to draw up numerous plans for the lakefront. The most influential of these plans, not coincidentally, was authored by Burnham himself.[45]

The process culminated in the *Plan of Chicago*, which would eventually be published by Burnham and his junior colleague and successor, Edward H. Bennett, in 1909. Burnham and Bennett's plan was a dazzling utopian vision, featuring a greatly enlarged lakefront park. The park would be flanked by huge piers reaching out into the lake, with a large oval harbor for yachts in the middle. Marshall Field promised to fund a magnificent natural history museum, which Burnham and others envisioned as the centerpiece of the park. A new Crerar Library, funded by a bequest, was also slated to be added to the park.[46]

With most of the Chicago elite behind this developing vision, the Chicago City Council enacted ordinances in 1895 and 1896 designed to make ideas such as these a reality, and the Illinois General Assembly adopted authorizing legislation.

FIGURE 3.10. View of neoclassical structures at the 1893 World's Columbian Exposition in Jackson Park. Courtesy of the Newberry Library, Chicago, case oversize T500.C1 J3.

The emerging plan called for a massive landfilling project, covering the area from the Illinois Central tracks east to the harbor line established by the army engineers. The ordinances provided that the newly filled area north of Monroe Street would be used for purposes of constructing an armory and parade or training ground for the Illinois National Guard. The southern portion of the park would be transferred to the South Park Commission (SPC) for development of a formal park and sites for museums, libraries, and other civic and cultural buildings. Finally, in 1899, the entire area was renamed "Grant Park" in honor of President (and onetime Illinois resident) Ulysses S. Grant.[47]

Armed with this authority, the SPC quickly set about filling in the lake east of the Illinois Central tracks. Between 1896 and 1907, the SPC engaged in steady landfill activity, starting with about 6 acres per year and accelerating to more than double and triple that rate in the second half of the decade. By 1906, more than 128 acres of new land had been created.[48]

For more than thirty years, from 1864 to 1896, litigation over the construction of buildings in Lake Park had been confined to local courts in Chicago. Then, rather abruptly, the action shifted to the Illinois Supreme Court. The explanation is simple: the stakes were suddenly higher. The resolution of the title question in favor of the city, combined with the burst of civic energy associated with the Columbian Exposition and (for a rather different matter) rising anxiety about social unrest associated with the Pullman strike of 1894, unleashed a flurry of plans to fill the park with permanent structures. Yet in order to proceed with these plans, the city and its allies had to obtain a definitive resolution of the public dedication issue.

The inexorable movement to the state supreme court began when the city reasserted its request to dismiss Ward's lawsuit. Ward vigorously fought back, and the case proceeded to evidence and a judgment in 1896. Judge Theodore Brentano ruled in Ward's favor and ordered that the temporary injunction be made permanent. His order prohibited the city and the Illinois Central from building any new railroad tracks, sheds, or other structures in the park. A temporary exception was made for the existing armory buildings in north Lake Park. The injunction also specifically exempted the Art Institute and the post office, both of which enjoyed owner consent and the latter of which was temporary. The next day an article appeared in the *Chicago Tribune* naming Ward the "watch dog of the lake-front." The paper would continue to use the tagline up to its publication of Ward's obituary.[49]

In 1897, on appeal, the Illinois Supreme Court upheld Ward's victory. Most of the unanimous decision authored by Justice Joseph N. Carter was devoted to recapitulating the complex history of the park, from the initial marketing efforts of the canal commissioners and the United States through the balance of the nineteenth century. Carter concluded that the restrictions on buildings included on maps of the original plats were legally binding public dedications, enforceable by adjoining property owners. All of this was, as we have seen, relatively uncontroversial, given the existing precedents on public dedication, both in Illinois generally and as to the lakefront specifically.[50]

The court likewise had little trouble concluding that it made no difference that the two parts of Lake Park had been dedicated by two different owners—the canal commissioners and the United States—at different times. Both had represented to prospective purchasers that the land east of Michigan Avenue would be clear of buildings. "Besides," the court emphasized, "this open space has always been treated by the city and the public as *one* park."[51]

Turning to the most seriously contested question, the court rejected the city's argument that the adjoining property owners were barred from enforcing the public dedication because they had acquiesced in other violations of the restriction in the park. This, of course, had been Judge Drummond's rationale in 1882 for denying an injunction against the B&O depot. Since then, however, the owners had roused themselves, and the Illinois Supreme Court recounted the extensive record of litigation surrounding the park for more than a decade. The only seemingly permanent exception, the court noted, was the Art Institute, and property owners had consented to it. The owners had not "waived all of their rights in the premises because they may have chosen to waive some of them."[52]

In affirming the injunction, no mention was made of the new armory projected for the ongoing landfill activity to the east of north Lake Park. This set the stage for the next case. That case and Ward's other future battles would be more difficult because they concerned proposed buildings that enjoyed widespread support among the civic elite, the local newspapers, and presumably a majority of the populace.

The National Guard Armory and *Ward II*

A severe recession beginning in 1893 created widespread social unrest, nowhere more so than in Chicago. George M. Pullman, who manufactured and leased railroad sleeping cars on the far South Side of Chicago, responded to financial reverses by cutting his employees' wages 25 percent or more, but refused to reduce the rents in their company-owned housing. In 1894, angry Pullman workers went on strike, which in turn elicited a supportive boycott by Eugene V. Debs's American Railway Union against switching Pullman cars. The result was largely to paralyze rail traffic on major railroads. When John Peter

Altgeld, the first Democrat elected governor of Illinois since before the Civil War, hesitated to call out the state militia, President Grover Cleveland ordered federal troops to Chicago. This triggered mob violence in support of the strikers. Before order was restored, much of the White City in Jackson Park had burned to the ground (a fire of uncertain origin but blamed on the strikers), hundreds of rail cars had been destroyed, and more than a few individuals were dead or wounded.[53]

These events were deeply traumatic to Chicago, especially its elite, which helps explain why the first concrete proposal for the newly enlarged land on the lakefront was to construct a permanent home for the Illinois National Guard. Even before the Pullman strike, the *Tribune* had reported one business leader's opinion that "it would be of great benefit in case of riots to have the headquarters of an entire brigade of militia within a few minutes' march of the center of the city."[54]

When construction of the new armory finally began in June of 1900, Ward sought an injunction. He prevailed in the trial court, and the defendant in the suit, the board of commissioners for the armory, appealed to the Illinois Supreme Court. The appeal did not maintain that the state's power to preserve social order—its police power—overrode whatever rights private property owners had under the public dedication doctrine. Perhaps with the economy on the mend and labor unrest subdued, the need for troops on the lakefront had lost its urgency.[55]

Instead, the primary issue on appeal in *Ward II* was whether the public dedication recognized in *Ward I* applied only to the land *west* of the Illinois Central tracks, closer to the original shore, or extended to the newly made land east of the tracks as well. Ruling for Ward, the court concluded that the dedication applied equally to the newly filled land. Justice James H. Cartwright's opinion was less than clear in its rationale. One argument was based on an analogy to natural accretion. Cartwright was unable to perceive any difference between augmentation of riparian land by natural accretion and by artificial filling. This ignored the obvious fact that landfilling is not a natural event—nor is it gradual and imperceptible like an accretion (see chapter 4 for further discussion of accretion and artificial landfilling).[56]

The court's decision also suggested that extending the dedication to the newly created parkland was necessary to fulfill the purposes of the original dedication. "[T]he property owners on Michigan avenue," the state supreme court said, "bought their lots with the distinct understanding that there should never be any building between their lots and the lake." In these circumstances, "when the limits of the park were extended into the lake, no right was acquired to erect buildings between the lots and the lake although at a greater distance from the lots." This did not address the obvious fact that structures erected farther from Michigan Avenue would have less impact on light, air, and view for owners of land abutting Michigan Avenue. Yet whatever its deficiencies, the decision was another major victory for Ward.[57]

Ward versus the Philanthropists

At this point, the disputes between Ward and the SPC turned to two monumental civic projects supported by private philanthropy. The principal properties and proposed construction sites are shown in figure 3.11.

When John Crerar, a railroad mogul, died in 1889, he left a bequest estimated at $2.5 million for the building and operation of a public library, as well as a separate $100,000 bequest to support construction of a statue of Abraham Lincoln. In 1901, the city council settled on Grant Park as the location for these projects. The state legislature promptly passed an act authorizing both the library and the statue to be erected in the park. The act provided that consent had to be obtained from all abutting owners.[58]

George Merrick, Ward's attorney, initially responded that Ward would not consent to any buildings in the park. A few weeks later, in April 1901, Merrick issued another statement, saying that Ward would consent to the library, but only if the authorities built it south of Jackson Boulevard—that is, south of the Art Institute, rather than to the north where Ward's property lay. The SPC was adamant that the library be placed to the north of the Art Institute.[59]

The trustees of the library quickly obtained consents from most of the other property owners on Michigan Avenue, and indicated that they would go to court to overturn the requirement of unanimous consent. But it appears that they did not do this. Instead, in 1903, the legislature enacted statutes permitting the SPC to legally condemn the public dedication rights of abutting owners, in order to strip Ward and others of their ability to block libraries and museums. In early 1905, the SPC gave final approval to build the Crerar Library on the lakefront. Finally, in 1906, the contractors set up their equipment and prepared to break ground.[60]

Merrick immediately initiated contempt proceedings on Ward's behalf. The library board and the SPC argued that they were not bound by the 1896 injunction against the city upheld in *Ward I*. Judge Brentano, who had issued that injunction, did not buy the argument. He ordered all building materials removed from the lakefront. There was no appeal.[61]

The battle soon flared with new intensity on another front: the Field Museum. After the Columbian Exposition closed in 1893, Marshall Field helped launch

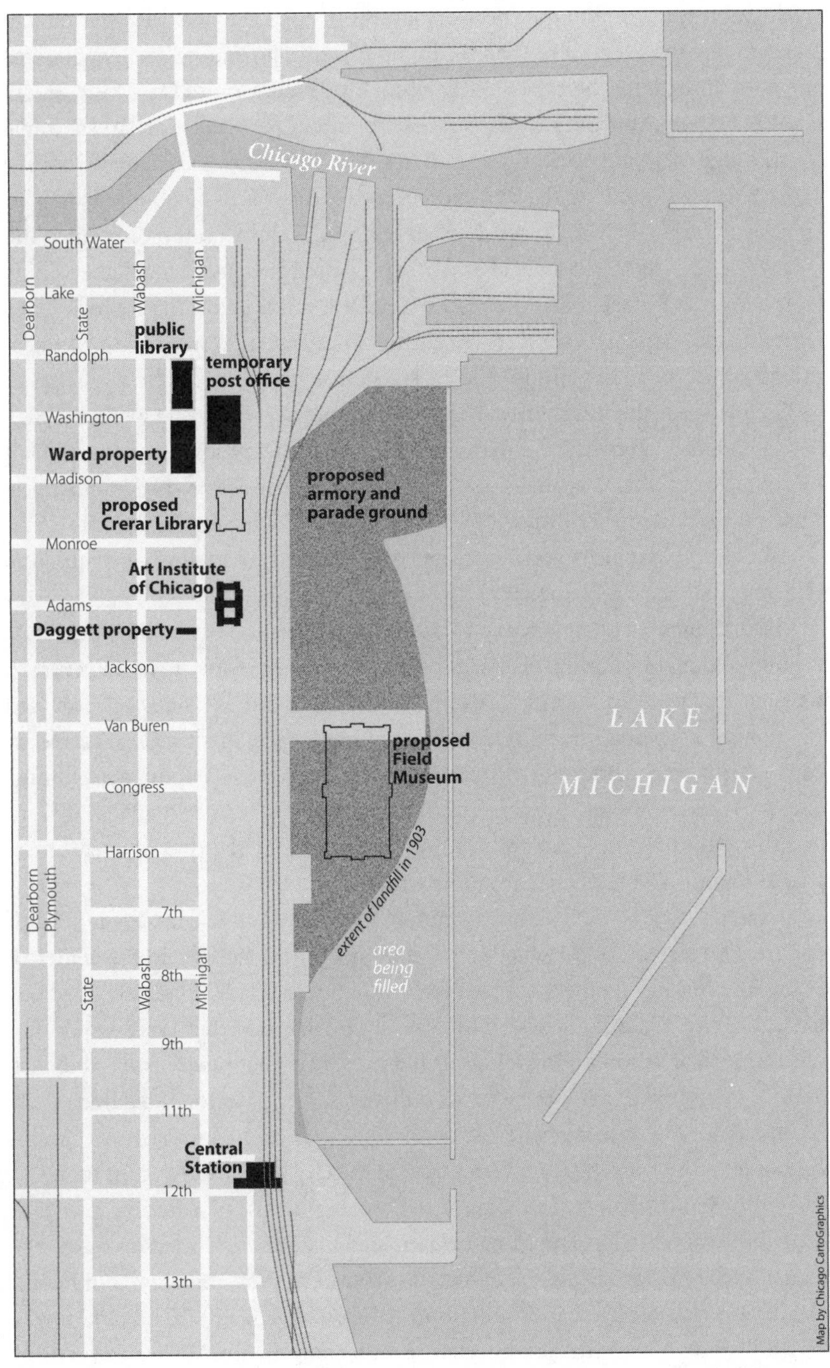

FIGURE 3.11. Location of proposed buildings and relevant properties in and across from Grant Park, ca. 1903.

a campaign to house a collection of natural history artifacts in a permanent museum. He donated more than $1 million in initial funding and encouraged others to contribute their World's Fair stock to such a museum. Montgomery Ward & Company, ironically (as matters would happen), was the largest initial contributor, donating one thousand shares. The museum was originally housed in the Fine Arts Building, the sole surviving structure originally built for the fair in Jackson Park (today the reconstructed building is the Museum of Science and Industry). As early as 1896, Field and others wanted to construct a new building for the museum in what was then Lake Park, and the 1896 ordinance included a provision authorizing this. However, the SPC was reluctant to commit to a specific site until the final plans for the park system were complete.[62]

The plans for the museum were put on hold for several years while the SPC cleaned up and expanded the park and planned its next move. In early 1903, it was announced that Marshall Field would donate funds for the "handsomest museum building in the world," to be built on the lakefront. In 1904, the SPC submitted a proposal to voters for approval of a tax to support the museum, which passed overwhelmingly.[63]

Marshall Field died on January 16, 1906, leaving $8 million for the purpose of building the Field Museum. His will provided that the bequest would revert to his estate if within six years of his death "lands and premises" were not "provided for" the museum and "given to it or devoted to its permanent use . . . as a location and site for the building or buildings to be erected as its permanent home." Harlow N. Higinbotham, president of the museum trustees, declared that if Ward kept the museum off the lakefront, it would amount to "the ruin of what otherwise ultimately will be the greatest museum in the world."[64]

In early 1907, the SPC ceded a tract of land for the museum at the foot of Congress Street on the east side of the Illinois Central tracks—in the center of Grant Park but half a mile south of Ward's building at Madison Street. Ward was not in the city when the news was released. Merrick said that Ward would not take immediate action and would wait for some overt act before going to court. Higinbotham stated that Ward was the only remaining objector and dared others in opposition to come forward. He declared that Ward had no right to contest the museum building, because the people of the city had already voted on it.[65]

The museum trustees were concerned about the cost of entering into construction contracts that would be delayed by litigation, and Merrick agreed to a symbolic act of driving a stake into the ground so that litigation could commence. Merrick filed for an injunction on February 23, 1907. The SPC filed a cross-bill to enjoin Ward from interfering with construction.[66]

The matter was assigned to Judge George A. Dupuy, who had been involved in the *Ward I* litigation in the 1890s, as assistant corporation counsel to the city, before entering private practice and then joining the bench; he was clearly unsympathetic to Ward's position. Dupuy promptly ruled that buildings consistent with "park purposes" would be allowed in the park, setting a trial to decide whether the museum so qualified. With this ruling, Dupuy implicitly adopted the understanding that the dedication was an affirmative command to use the space for park purposes, even though the language on the original maps expressed a negative restriction on "buildings."[67]

As the lawyers prepared for trial, Ward offered to settle the matter and allow the Field Museum in Grant Park, so long as the SPC would agree not to sponsor any more buildings. The SPC immediately rejected Ward's offer, saying that it did not want to go "hat in hand" to Ward every time it wanted to build in the park. The patience of the parties and their lawyers had grown thin by this time, and courtroom exchanges were often heated.[68]

At the close of evidence, Dupuy ruled that the museum was a proper park building, and that it could be built, as planned, east of the Illinois Central's right of way, a distance from Michigan Avenue, and thus rejected Ward's request for an injunction. Both Ward and the SPC were unhappy with the decision—the SPC was still hoping to build the Crerar Library and a new city hall on the west side of the Illinois Central tracks, closer to Michigan Avenue—and both immediately appealed to the Illinois Supreme Court. This would be *Ward III*.[69]

The high court reversed Dupuy's decision, ruling for Ward once again. Speaking again unanimously through Justice Cartwright, it held that there was no basis for dividing the park in two, for the court in *Ward II* had already determined that the filled land was of the same character as the rest of the park, just as if the additional land had naturally accreted. Relying on its decisions in *Ward I* and *Ward II*, the court summarily dispensed with Dupuy's idea that "proper park buildings" could be erected in the park.[70]

This was a seemingly decisive blow in favor of the no-buildings conception of the dedication. Nevertheless, the court went on to address the contention that certain buildings—such as rain shelters, band shells, and lavatories—are absolutely necessary in a park. Those types of facilities, the court stated, "can be provided without the erection of what would properly be characterized as a building." This was as close as the Illinois Supreme Court would come to offering a definition of "building" in the *Ward* cases. It was not clear whether the court regarded certain kinds of structures as being too important to be excluded from the park, whether it thought the listed structures would be so innocuous that they would not jeopardize the interests of the abutting landowners, or some combination of both.[71]

A triumphant Ward finally gave the *Tribune* an interview following the decision. He said that his fight was "for the poor people of Chicago—not for the millionaires." He had come to understand that the SPC had "nineteen" building projects lined up for Grant Park, and he feared that the park would become littered with buildings if he did not object. He also said that if he had known how long the fight was going to last, he might not have started it. He alluded to the money that he had spent in the fight and added, with more than a touch of self-pity, that he was not even getting gratitude in return.[72]

Perhaps as an implicit quid pro quo for the interview, the *Tribune*, a noted booster of the museum, printed an editorial the next day commending Ward for his perseverance in protecting the park, even while it expressed hope that a compromise permitting this one structure might still be possible.[73]

The SPC Moves to Condemn Ward's Interest

The SPC remained confident. It immediately announced that, as authorized by the legislature in 1903, it would begin proceedings to condemn Ward's public dedication rights. Throughout the *Ward III* proceedings, the SPC had threatened this. Now both the directors of the Crerar Library and the trustees of the Field Museum requested that the SPC file a condemnation case, and the former agreed to pay the SPC's legal fees.[74]

The SPC filed the condemnation action on January 27, 1910. In addition to Ward and his company, the suit named as condemnees Levy Mayer, who owned the Stratford Hotel, and various other objectors. The SPC indicated that more condemnation actions would follow.[75]

Judge William H. McSurely dismissed the condemnation action. He was satisfied that the previous suits had determined the rights of all the parties, including the right of the SPC to condemn any "easements" that Ward or others might have. The SPC appealed.[76]

On December 21, 1910, Ward won in the Illinois Supreme Court for the fourth time, although now the court was closely divided, ruling by a vote of four to three. Speaking once again through Justice Cartwright, who had authored *Ward II* and *Ward III*, the court acknowledged that the power of eminent domain (or condemnation) extends to every kind of property or interest. Nevertheless, the legislature could not authorize a taking for an illegal use, and the court reasoned that the previous *Ward* cases had established that it was unlawful to erect buildings in the park. The city could not use the device of eminent domain to escape the consequences of its earlier decision to accept the dedication of the parkland with the restriction that it would be kept free from buildings. The three dissenters noted that eminent domain is an inherent attribute of sovereignty and maintained that the state could not divest itself of its condemnation powers.[77]

By today's lights, *Ward IV* seems hard to defend. If one assumes that the acquisition of land for a museum open to the public is a public use, then the state should be allowed to condemn all interests in land necessary to secure such a use, whether those interests are characterized as property rights, contract rights, or public dedication rights.[78]

In retrospect, the commissioners and their allies overreached by failing to proceed toward condemnation immediately after the decisions in *Ward I* and *Ward II*. Their litigation strategy made it appear as if they were trying to obtain a valuable right without paying for it, and that they were willing to pay (through the condemnation or eminent-domain process) only after they failed. It is not surprising that a majority of the Illinois Supreme Court took a dim view of this strategy. The SPC and Higinbotham apparently had been so exercised by Ward's opposition that it impaired their judgment.

In any event, *Ward IV* had a decisive impact on the future of Grant Park. Whether there were as many projects in the SPC's sights as the nineteen that Ward maintained, it is a virtual certainty that a variety of buildings would have followed the Field Museum into the park if the decision had gone the other way.

Following the December 1910 decision in *Ward IV*, the Field Museum trustees had to scramble to find a site outside the protected area. The bequest would expire and revert to the estate in mid-January 1912, six years after Field died. After multisided negotiations, described more fully in chapter 7, the SPC acquired a new site between 12th and 16th Streets, in a complex land swap with the Illinois Central. The museum was finally completed in 1921.[79]

Ward's Other Actions

While the high-stakes fight between Ward and the civic elite was playing itself out in the Illinois Supreme Court, Ward continued to perform his accustomed role of park watchdog. The results were mixed.

Ward succeeded, without litigation, in blocking the erection of a tent to be used for a major speech by William Jennings Bryan, who was touring the country in 1900 as the Democratic Party candidate for president. The Democrats held the event in the open air. Ward's action was viewed as politically motivated, and James K. Jones, senator from Arkansas and chairman of the Democratic National Committee, urged Democrats to boycott Montgomery Ward & Company in protest. Ward engaged in damage control by issuing a statement in which he claimed that he had not known the purpose of the tent and had supposed from a sign on a wagon, "Great American Show," that "a circus was about to start business on this forbidden ground." He said that he was merely "guilty of trying to give the people of Chicago a free park."[80]

The next year, the federal government began to build a fence outside the temporary post office to block dust from mail wagons taking shortcuts through the park. Ward immediately objected, and the fencing project stopped.[81]

These actions suggest strongly that Ward was not motivated by any particular animus toward Marshall Field, with whom he occasionally socialized, or his museum, as has sometimes been suggested. Indeed, Ward's early financial support for Field's museum initiative, and his offers to settle with the Crerar Library and then with the Field Museum on terms that would permit those structures to be built in the park, indicate that he was relatively sympathetic to the construction of monumental buildings in the park. At the same time, Ward's actions after 1900 suggest a growing imperiousness as he came to assume that he had unilateral authority to approve or disapprove practically any construction activity between Michigan Avenue and the centerline of the lake. His willingness to pay the legal bills necessary to enforce his judgments helped ensure that reality closely corresponded with this assumption.[82]

By 1912, Montgomery Ward & Company had outgrown the facility on Michigan Avenue and moved its operations to Chicago Avenue, north of the city center. Ward, who had sold the controlling interest in his company almost twenty years earlier but was then the sole owner of the Michigan Avenue property, quickly sold the property in three different transactions. The next year, Ward broke his hip while at his winter home in Pasadena, California. He returned to Chicago but died of pneumonia on December 7, 1913. Although it was thought that Ward would make a provision in his will for the ongoing fight against buildings in Grant Park, he left nearly all of his money to his wife and daughter.[83]

Ward's Legacy

The cumulative effect of the four *Ward* decisions was to leave a huge vacant space in the center of the much-enlarged Grant Park. Under some circumstances, this would have caused a complete rethinking of the lakefront's future. But the tremendous momentum built up behind the Burnham Plan, with its animating vision grounded in what would be called the "City Beautiful" movement, could not be turned back. Implementation of the Burnham Plan moved ahead under the guiding hand of Edward Bennett, but the multiple cultural institutions contemplated for the center of the park were relegated to the periphery. After a site for the Field Museum was found to the south, a site for the Crerar Library was found on the northwest corner of Michigan Avenue and Randolph Street, again just outside the protected area. Other cultural buildings, such as the Shedd Aquarium and the Adler Planetarium, were also erected at 12th Street or to its south, just as in the late nineteenth or very early twentieth century the Public Library, the Auditorium Building, and Orchestra Hall had been built on the west side of Michigan Avenue—all outside the perimeter of the park. One of the piers contemplated by the Burnham Plan was eventually constructed—the enormous Navy Pier stretching into the lake north of the park area. One of the offshore islands contemplated by the plan—the so-called Northerly Island—was created and eventually became an airport and now is something of a nature preserve. In a direct echo of the original plan, two yacht clubs were allowed to locate at the foot of the park.[84]

The otherwise vacant park itself was landscaped in accordance with the neo-classical dictates favored by Bennett, who had studied at the École des Beaux Arts. Like the gardens at Versailles, the park was divided into large rectangles joined by long walkways. Eventually the rectangles were filled in with trees, shrubs, neo-classical concrete balustrades, and statuary, as well as the splendid Buckingham Fountain. The park had a solitary band shell but, other than the Art Institute, no buildings to grace it. In the summer, the park served as a gathering place for collective celebrations, such as Fourth of July pageantry and free concerts. But for most of the year, it stood relatively empty.[85]

Nature is said to abhor a vacuum. If the 319-acre space that was Grant Park could not be occupied with buildings, it could be filled with automobiles. Over the course of the twentieth century, Grant Park was crisscrossed by multilane roadways. The landfill area east of the railroad tracks and north of Monroe Street, which had been slated in the 1896 ordinance to become a National Guard armory and training ground, became a vast outdoor parking lot. After World War II, the parking gradually moved underground; eventually much of Grant Park would be perched on top of four huge underground parking structures. Like much of the rest of the United States, Grant Park was created by the railroad, but came to be dominated by the automobile.[86]

Ward's Motives

What are we to make of Ward's motives for his remarkable crusade? For starters, Ward's record as "watchdog" was largely consistent with his interests as an investor in commercial real estate. Ward's lakefront actions began when he acquired significant Michigan Avenue property, and they ended when he sold that property, admittedly after a final victory and shortly before his death. Yet it may be notable that his effort to protect the park intensified in the mid-1890s, when he had acquired Thorne's interest in the property and become its sole owner. In any event, from that time until he sold it, the Michigan Avenue property was Ward's largest asset, apparently forming the bulk of his estate's value.[87]

Ward's enforcement activity was also selective in a way that reflected his interests as a property owner. He did not challenge the Art Institute or the Public Library, he consented to the Democratic Party's wigwam and the temporary post office, and he was prepared to consent to both the Crerar Library, if it would be located in the south park, and the Field Museum, if the SPC would agree that there would be no more buildings. He opposed loading platforms, storage sheds, garbage, circuses, bicycle tracks, tents for political rallies, armories, and railroad structures. His guiding principle was not big versus little—he sometimes opposed small structures (storage sheds, bicycle tracks, fences) and other times did not oppose large ones (the Art Institute, the Public Library, the post office). Nor was it permanent versus temporary—sometimes he opposed temporary structures (circuses, tents for political rallies) and other times he maintained no objections to permanent ones (the Public Library, the Art Institute).

Overall, Ward appears to have been guided by a sure sense of how different projects would affect the market value of his real estate. Nuisances, clutter, unsightly temporary platforms, fences, and—especially—noisy crowds would likely impair real estate values on Michigan Avenue. Stately and decorous structures such as the Public Library and the Art Institute would not. Ward's opposition to the Crerar Library and the Field Museum is arguably inconsistent with this generalization. But recall Ward's apparent willingness to settle with the proponents of these two structures if he could put the buildings where he wanted them to go and could preserve his control over everything else.

Ward's consent to the temporary post office is particularly revealing. This ungainly building would impair somewhat the view of the lake and the flow of air and light enjoyed by Ward's facility on the other side of Michigan Avenue. But by 1895, Montgomery Ward & Company had become the single largest customer of the US Postal Service. A well-functioning postal system was an imperative for the company, and it was clearly in Ward's financial interest to consent to the temporary post office.[88]

Still, although Ward's financial interests undoubtedly motivated and shaped his behavior, they do not fully account for his remarkable zeal in enforcing the public dedication. For one thing, he spent an estimated $50,000 on litigation during his period of ownership—well more than $1 million in today's value. Ward himself suggested that the expenditure was not economically justified. His litigation activity also took on a fanatical quality, especially as the years went on. Preventing the Bryan campaign from putting up a tent for a one-day rally was

FIGURE 3.12. Temporary post office in Grant Park, as viewed to the north from just outside Ward's property on Michigan Avenue, ca. 1900. Chicago History Museum, ICHi-032436.

hardly in the interests of Montgomery Ward & Company, as evidenced by its quickly eliciting a national call for a boycott. And it is hard to see how Ward's property values would be affected by the construction of a yacht club in the lake (as discussed below).[89]

Ward himself suggested that populist sympathies drove his litigation. He claimed that he did it for the "poor people" as opposed to the "millionaires." Ward started life as a manual laborer, strongly empathized with struggling farm families, and was affiliated commercially with the Granger Movement.[90]

But the pattern of Ward's actions does not support the thesis that he was seeking to protect the interests of the masses. The Chicago City Council and the Illinois General Assembly had expressly approved a number of the projects he blocked. One, the Field Museum, not only was supported by representative bodies but also had received an overwhelming affirmative vote in a public tax referendum. Further, Ward showed striking hostility toward popular entertainment in the park, bringing multiple actions to block circuses. It is highly doubtful that the "poor people" approved of these actions. It is worth noting that Ward's catalog business did not depend on what people in Chicago thought about him.

His market was rural and small-town America. Thus, in contrast to Marshall Field, for example, he could incur the displeasure of Chicagoans without any significant personal hardship to his firm or its profits.

Another hypothesis is that Ward was a naturalist or environmentalist ahead of his time—in effect, that he wanted to preserve the park in an unspoiled condition free of artificial encumbrances. Ward made some statements consistent with this hypothesis, and he supported the removal of the armories and other clutter in Lake Park. A reporter characterized him as telling a meeting of fellow Michigan Avenue owners at his company's office in 1893 that city authorities should not be "always trying to convert one of the most beautiful locations for a people's park into a dumping ground for garbage or a speculative site for builders and railroads." Rather, they should follow the model of other great cities, especially those in Europe, which were "tearing down marble blocks and widening thoroughfares to create breathing spaces and pleasure grounds for the people."[91]

The evidence for this hypothesis is somewhat stronger than for the populist claim. Ward often expressed distaste for garbage, refuse, and litter in the park. And his opposition to gatherings in the park for circuses and political rallies might reflect an austere naturalist vision of the proper uses of a park, akin to what many proponents of national parks and wilderness areas often express today. Again, however, the data do not fully conform to the thesis. Ward was clearly more sympathetic to the erection of monumental public buildings such as the Public Library and the Art Institute than he was to lesser intrusions such as tents. The temporary post office building was about the most unnatural addition to the park imaginable, but it had Ward's consent.

Yet another interpretation is that Ward had a strong antipathy to disorder. His retailing empire was characterized by its precise organization and attention to detail. Ward was said to be drawn to intervene in the lakefront by his disgust at seeing garbage piled in the park for loading onto trains. Once he assumed the role of watchdog, he consistently opposed any activity or structure that would generate nuisances or involved the gathering of large and boisterous crowds, such as circuses and political rallies. In contrast, large, well-ordered institutions such as public libraries and the post office were less likely to incur Ward's displeasure.[92]

To use the modern vernacular, Ward may have been something of a control freak. He had the financial resources and, thanks to the public dedication doctrine, the legal power to attempt to impose his vision of a more orderly world on the lakefront park. He did not fully succeed, of course, for large public spaces in major urban centers are inherently disorderly—they are subject to the vagaries and whims of the random clusters of people who venture into them.

Whatever his motives, Ward's persistence and willingness to spend large sums of money on litigation left a body of law—in particular, four Illinois Supreme Court precedents—that would protect Grant Park from major intrusions for more than a century. The Chicago lakefront would look very different today had it not been for Aaron Montgomery Ward.

The Limits of the Public Dedication Doctrine

The *Ward* precedents were strong stuff—no buildings in Grant Park, period. So it is not surprising that courts were soon asked to prescribe limits to this proscription in terms of the territory covered by the public dedication and the type of intrusions proscribed. The process began while Ward was still fully engaged in the role of watchdog. It continues to this day.

Ward was responsible for defining the territorial boundary of the Grant Park public dedication—north, south, east, and west. *Ward I* established that the doctrine applied to the original fractional section 10, from Randolph Street on the north to Madison Street on the south. *Ward II* extended the doctrine to landfill east of the original area encompassed by Lake Park. *Ward III* established that the doctrine applied in the original fractional section 15, from Madison Street on the north to the edge of Grant Park (today Roosevelt Road) on the south, and to landfill east of this original area. Ward also launched two other battles that further delineated the eastern and western boundaries of the dedication.

In 1898, the Chicago City Railway Company started construction of an electric trolley on Michigan Avenue. The company planned to put poles along Michigan Avenue from which to hang trolley wires. Ward secured a temporary injunction from Judge Brentano, based on *Ward I*. The Illinois Appellate Court dissolved the injunction, holding that Ward had not established that the width of Michigan Avenue itself was subject to a public dedication. And even if the dedication did cover Michigan Avenue, the court ruled, the dedication was to establish a "public ground," which could be a street as well as a park. The practical effect seems to have been to fix the western boundary of the dedication at the eastern—rather than western—edge of Michigan Avenue.[93]

Another battle launched by Ward would even more clearly delineate the *eastern* boundary of the dedication. In 1899, the Columbia Yacht Club began to fashion a clubhouse on pilings in the lake at the foot of Randolph Street, just beyond the docks. Pursuant to the 1895 ordinance, the SPC was in the midst of its multiyear project of filling the park to the harbor line, so the yacht club would eventually be situated just off the shore. Ward sued. A state judge ruled against him on a rationale not altogether clear from the reportage: it seemed to involve Ward's not having riparian rights, given that there were other landowners (the city and the railroad) between his property and the lake. In fact, Ward was seeking to enforce a different sort of right: the public dedication. In any event, despite an early statement of intent, it appears that Ward did not appeal.[94]

This was only the beginning of the controversy over the yacht clubs. In 1901, a second club, the Chicago Yacht Club, undertook to build a permanent clubhouse on landfill at the foot of Monroe Street, also just outside the harbor line. Clarence W. Marks, who owned property on the same Michigan Avenue block as Ward, sought to enjoin both the Chicago and Columbia Yacht Clubs. Marks was represented by Merrick, Ward's lawyer throughout the litigation over the lakefront. It is conceivable that Marks agreed to undertake the litigation at the urging of Ward, who was presumably precluded by the prior judgment from challenging the Columbia Yacht Club. There is no direct evidence of such an arrangement, although it may be telling that after an initial victory for his client, Marks, in the trial court, Merrick stated to the press, "Mr. Ward is in Europe and I have no instructions to begin any new suits."[95]

Marks acknowledged in his complaint that the yacht clubs were being located on submerged land technically outside the boundary of the lakefront park. But he insisted that this location was deliberately chosen to frustrate the rights of Michigan Avenue owners and reflected a conspiracy on the part of the clubs to evade the law.[96]

Marks initially had better luck than Ward, securing an ex parte injunction against the Chicago Yacht Club from Judge Elbridge Hanecy, Merrick's former law partner—and Ward's former (and future) lakefront lawyer with Merrick. On appeal, however, the Illinois Appellate Court concluded that the public dedication doctrine stopped at the eastern border of Lake Park, wherever that might be located. One can detect in the opinion significant skepticism about the bona fides of Marks's contentions, given the modest size of the clubhouse and its distance from Michigan Avenue. The court observed that "the view from appellee's premises at the corner of Washington street and Michigan boulevard can scarcely be said, from the allegation of facts in the bill, to be obstructed by a building in the lake opposite the foot of Monroe street," two blocks to the south.[97]

Conflict over the Chicago Yacht Club would resume decades later in 1925, after the park and the harbor line were extended farther east into Lake Michigan in order to construct Lake Shore Drive. The clubhouse had to be relocated and reconstructed; like the original, it would be built in the area just outside the eastern boundary of the park. Two Michigan Avenue property owners, fortified now by four *Ward* decisions rather than just one, sought to enjoin its reconstruction.

In two separate decisions, the Illinois Supreme Court rejected the renewed challenge. One action was brought by the Stevens Hotel, which was owned by the family of future Supreme Court justice John Paul Stevens and would become the Conrad Hilton Hotel (and more recently the Hilton Chicago). Although it did not cite *Marks*, the reasoning of the Illinois Supreme Court was equally formalistic: the proposed yacht club building was outside the legal boundary of the park and thus beyond the public dedication.[98]

It is puzzling why the yacht clubs triggered such persistent litigation activity from Michigan Avenue landowners. One can understand why these owners would be upset by baseball stadiums, armories, depots, and even circus tents blocking their view of the lake and bringing congestion, noise, and litter to the park across the street. These structures and their associated activity would depress the market value of property on the west side of Michigan Avenue. Yet it is difficult, at least at this distance in time, to understand any threat from the existence of the yacht clubs. The clubhouses were relatively small and not visible from street level on Michigan Avenue. Indeed, from the perspective of modern sensibilities, the clubs' neat rows of boats bobbing in the harbor during warm weather would add to, rather than detract from, the aesthetics of the vista. It is also hard to imagine that yacht clubs would inject significant traffic or uncouth crowds into the park, at least to a degree that might affect property values.

We can only speculate that the owners feared that the yacht clubs would become a precedent that would allow more extensive construction in the water just beyond the park. The principal fear may have been construction of an outer harbor. That would bring, inevitably, more railroad tracks and, very likely, warehouses and other structures associated with an active harbor, all of which would jeopardize the ambience of the park and the views enjoyed by the Michigan Avenue owners. Agitation for an outer harbor continued well into the twentieth century. Of course, whether or not their apprehensions were warranted, the owners, by suing and losing, enhanced the very risk they feared.[99]

Defining "Building"

Other controversies helped define what sorts of structures would be regarded as "buildings" prohibited by the public dedication. In contrast to questions about territorial limits, where bright-line boundaries have prevailed, the definition of "building" frequently has been influenced by the purposes of the dedication. To be sure, the ordinary meaning of "building"—a structure enclosed by walls and a roof large enough to accommodate some form of human activity—has established the core of the definition. But, at least on occasion, the courts have turned to the purposes of the dedication.[100]

The many decisions and controversies up to 1910 established the outer limits of the term "building." At one end of the spectrum, the Illinois Supreme Court had made clear that libraries, museums, armories, post offices, and depots were buildings, and the court in dictum in *Ward III* added that powerhouses and stables would be buildings as well. The decree in *Ward I* also established that loading platforms and storage sheds were regarded as buildings. Local precedent had held that a baseball stadium was a building. At the other end of the spectrum, it appears that no one has ever argued that the viaducts spanning the Illinois Central tracks are buildings, or that statues and fountains in the park are buildings. And the court had opined (in dictum in *Ward III*) that storm shelters, bandstands, and lavatories would not be buildings.

As for temporary as opposed to permanent structures, the local precedents were mixed. Ward believed that tents and wigwams counted as buildings, and his aggressive litigation achieved some success in this regard. But a number of local decisions went the other way, both before and after Ward's reign. The practice today is to allow tents to be erected during various park festivals.

The most extensive consideration of the definitional issue occurred in a decision of the Illinois Supreme Court in 1952, involving the construction of the first parking garage under the park. The court noted that once construction was finished, nearly all of the parking garage would be underground, except for entrances and exits and several five-foot-high vents and air intakes, the latter being concealed by shrubbery.[101]

As to whether these minor intrusions above the surface were buildings, the court emphasized the purposes of the dedication. That purpose, the court said, "was to keep the public tracts free of buildings so that there would be unobstructed view of Lake Michigan" and thus make "lots abutting on such tracts more desirable." The vents and intakes did not violate the dedication because they occupied only an "infinitesimal portion" of the whole park, would be concealed with shrubbery, and would "not obstruct the view of any tenant of the plaintiff or any tenant of other abutting property."[102]

The decision strongly implied that, in borderline cases, whether a particular structure violates the dedication should be determined by asking whether the "right to view, light and air will be interfered with." The decision eventually led to the construction of three more underground garages, making Grant Park—below the surface—one of the largest underground parking garages in the world.[103]

Another controversy directly implicating the definition of "building" was the longstanding saga involving the Grant Park band shell. Free summer band concerts appeared in the park as early as 1915, when a small wooden bandstand was built. In the early 1930s, a much larger "temporary" band shell was constructed in south Grant Park. It proved to be immensely popular. Yet the band shell fell into disrepair. "By the 1970s," as Timothy Gilfoyle has recounted, "an assortment of stagehands, performers, and even grand pianos had fallen through the stage floor."[104]

The park district was eager to build a more permanent structure. A long progression of proposals, many by famous architects, followed. The most ironic was a 1961 plan, jointly sponsored by the park district and the A. Montgomery Ward Foundation, for a $3 million band shell dedicated to the memory of Montgomery Ward. Over about a thirty-year period, all proposals foundered, largely because one or more property owners on Michigan Avenue either refused to consent or threatened to bring litigation invoking the *Ward* precedents.[105]

The impasse was broken in 1977–78, when officials announced that a new "demountable" band shell would be erected, just east of Columbus Drive and the Art Institute. No one sued. When the summer concert season ended, Edmund L. Kelly, superintendent of the Chicago Park District, said that the district would not waste funds—stated to be $389,352—on dismantling the structure. The park district in effect called the bluff of the Michigan Avenue owners. The Petrillo Music Shell remains a fixture of the park to this day.[106]

The three-decade struggle to replace the decrepit Grant Park band shell tells us a great deal about the power and the pitfalls of the public dedication doctrine. It is not surprising that one or more Michigan Avenue landowners might object to the building of a structure that would attract masses of humanity to the park. What is more surprising is that owner opposition prevailed for so long. In *Ward III*, the Illinois Supreme Court had said that "certain structures are absolutely necessary for the comfort of the public and the proper use of the park, but most of them, such as shelters in case of storms, *band stands*, lavatories, toilets and the like, can be provided without the erection of what would properly be characterized as a building." This was dictum but would be taken seriously by any later court.[107]

The puzzle is why the Chicago Park District did not move ahead directly with a new band shell project, daring one or more landowners to initiate litigation. The answer is unclear, although increasing political conflict between the park district and newly formed advocacy groups such as Friends of the Parks may provide part of the answer. Park advocates came to view the *Ward* precedents as an important tool in fighting for parks, and the courts began to show increasing sympathy with environmental and preservationist views (as discussed in chapter 8). As a result, the park district may have been gun-shy about risking a showdown with park advocates over the band shell.[108]

The Consent Mechanism

The public dedication doctrine is a unanimous-consent mechanism. Any abutting landowner can block a forbidden use, provided that he or she is willing to incur the expense of a lawsuit. But if all abutting owners consent to a use, the project can go forward, even if it would otherwise violate the dedication. The consent mechanism has been successfully invoked on four occasions with respect to the area protected by the Grant Park dedication: the public library, the Art Institute, the temporary post office, and Millennium Park (considered in chapter 9). Three of those invocations—all except the temporary post office—have had a lasting effect on the visage of the park.

The Art Institute is by far the largest permanent building in the park. We have previously described the circumstances of its original construction. The *Daggett* case held that all necessary Michigan Avenue owners except Sarah Daggett had consented to the building, and it ruled that her objections were untimely. The idea that the Art Institute had obtained unanimous consent from Michigan Avenue owners received the imprimatur of the Illinois Supreme Court in *Ward I*, and from that time forward the consent mechanism has been understood to be the legal foundation for the Art Institute complex.

The original legislation authorizing construction of the Art Institute limited it to four hundred feet of frontage on Michigan Avenue. In ensuing years, both before and after World War I, the Art Institute would continually expand its facilities, though always to the east, and always in such a way as to neither increase its frontage along Michigan Avenue nor raise the height of the original structure. Never during this relentless expansion did any Michigan Avenue landowner object.[109]

The Art Institute received permission from the SPC in 1928 to embark on still-further additions east of the Illinois Central tracks, and this finally elicited a legal challenge. The next year, which also saw its lawsuit against the Chicago Yacht Club, the Stevens Hotel retained George Merrick to seek an injunction against the Art Institute. Merrick was more than successful in the circuit court, obtaining a broadly worded injunction that barred construction of any building or structure "of any kind, size, nature or description whatever, or for any purpose whatsoever, anywhere within the limits of Grant Park." An alarmed Art Institute went to the Illinois Supreme Court, which transferred the case to the Illinois Appellate Court.[110]

The appellate court rendered a remarkable decision in 1931 that has effectively served as the legal charter for the Art Institute to the present day. The court was significantly handicapped because the original consents were not introduced into the record. It accordingly proceeded by indirection, looking to language in the statutes and ordinances authorizing the original construction, as well as to the language of the *Daggett* and *Ward I* decrees validating the consents. The court concluded that the consents must have contemplated that the building would be permanent, that it would accommodate the reasonable needs of the Art Institute, and that it would provide for "necessary enlargement of the building" over time as the museum's needs grew with Chicago's population.[111]

The court reinforced these conclusions with a discussion of the conduct of the Michigan Avenue owners in the almost forty years since the building was initially authorized. The court noted that the many additions and enlargements had all been discussed in the press and had been well known to the abutting property owners; that the construction had taken place "in plain view"; that no owner at any time had commenced a legal proceeding against the Art Institute; and that, notwithstanding all this, during the same time "abutting property owners ha[d] vigorously and successfully opposed the construction of any other buildings in Grant Park." This analysis supported a construction of the consents based on the course of conduct by the owners. It could equally have been used to establish a finding of waiver or estoppel on their part; conceivably, it might even have established that the Art Institute had extinguished by prescription (that is, by adverse possession) the dedication as to the portion of the park covered by its frontage.[112]

The court concluded by observing that the Art Institute had offered at trial to enter into a number of stipulations: it did not claim the right to exceed a boundary marked by Monroe Street on the north, Jackson Street on the south, Michigan Avenue on the west, and what we know as Columbus Drive on the east; to occupy more than four hundred feet of frontage on Michigan Avenue; or to build a structure higher than the then-existing building on Michigan Avenue. The court observed that "these stipulations might well be incorporated in the final decree," which in fact occurred on remand. The result was in effect a regulatory injunction granting the Art Institute the right to construct an enormous complex, subject to height and frontage restrictions. As long as the Art Institute adhered to the terms of the final decree, it would have no further worries based on the public dedication doctrine. With its most recent additions, the Art Institute has filled virtually the entire area described by the stipulations.[113]

Assessing the Public Dedication Doctrine

What more general lessons can be drawn about the public dedication doctrine from its role in preserving Chicago's premier public park?

One advantage of the doctrine, it would seem, is that it incorporates a rule-like protection of public spaces, which encourages judicial enforcement. Armed with a specific dedication, such as the "vacant of buildings" restriction on the Chicago lakefront, the doctrine empowers abutting property owners to insist on strict compliance. "Vacant of buildings" means vacant of buildings. Even in the case of a general dedication, such as an open space on a map, the doctrine often enshrines the status quo as reflected in longstanding public uses.

The public dedication doctrine also incorporates a unique rule about who has standing to enforce it. In addition to public authorities, a finite group—abutting landowners—can enforce or waive the dedication. Abutting landowners will be motivated to prevent deviation from uses that enhance the value of their property. Thus, if momentary enthusiasm for development of public spaces overcomes civic leaders, abutting landowners can step forward to resist the idea, and in so doing protect longer-run interests.[114]

The doctrine also has features that permit its modification over time. Minor deviations having a small impact on values of abutting land are unlikely to be challenged, and once such projects have been completed, challenges will be barred as untimely. Major deviations are more difficult to achieve, but if it is sufficiently clear that they will enhance the value of abutting property, they may also take place, pursuant to the consent mechanism.

No legal doctrine functions perfectly, of course, and the history of the Chicago lakefront reveals some disadvantages of the public dedication doctrine. One clear limitation is that the private interests of abutting landowners will often fail to generate a level of enforcement activity commensurate with the total value to the community of preserving public spaces. Almost by definition, the value to abutting landowners will be a fraction of the total community value. Thus, although the public dedication doctrine may generate significant enforcement activity, it is unlikely to generate optimal levels of enforcement.

In the context of Chicago's lakefront park, the public dedication doctrine generated a fairly consistent level of enforcement activity by abutting landowners from 1864 until the end of the twentieth century, with the exception of the decade immediately after the 1871 fire that destroyed most of the structures along Michigan Avenue. Nevertheless, Montgomery Ward unquestionably engaged in enforcement activity at a higher and more sustained level than any owner before or since. Other owners sought and obtained temporary injunctions, but usually they dropped out of the picture after a few years. Rarely did they persist in litigating to the point of securing a permanent injunction. And only Ward was willing to fund repeated rounds of appellate litigation.

This suggests that perhaps one or more abutting owners must have unusually large stakes if they are to serve as a persistent enforcement agent for the public dedication doctrine. If every abutting owner has an equal and relatively small stake, then it will be difficult to form a coalition to share the costs of litigation, because of familiar problems in forging agreements for collective action. The Ward history also suggests that effective enforcement may depend on one or more owners being rather fanatical, either because they have unusually intense preferences for preservation or for some other reason. Obviously, the conditions that call forth a champion who fights to defend a public dedication will be somewhat rare.[115]

History suggests another limitation: the preferences of abutting owners and of the general public may diverge, sometimes significantly. On the largest question—whether to maintain a public space—there is likely to be a convergence of interests. But on subsidiary issues, abutting landowners may harbor very different preferences. To simplify the history of the Chicago lakefront, abutting owners are likely to prefer peace and quiet, whereas the general public may want fun and games. As we have seen, Michigan Avenue owners tended to oppose baseball stadiums, toboggan slides, circuses, political conventions held in wigwams, and pavilions for outdoor concerts. It is likely that a public referendum would yield different views on these activities. Ward, who became the park's most important enforcement agent, may have harbored even more negative views about public gatherings than most abutting owners.

However one assesses the advantages and disadvantages, why did the public dedication doctrine enjoy such powerful support from state court judges? It is tempting to say that judges enforced the doctrine because it was clearly established in law—that we see here an example of judges following the law even in the face of demands from public officials and the civic elite to do something else. There is something to this. As the precedents enforcing the public dedication doctrine piled up, this clearly reinforced the confidence of the judges in enforcing it. But if we consider the adjudicated controversies individually, we can see that there was almost always a plausible basis for ruling *against* enforcement of the dedication. *Ward I* could have been decided on the grounds that storage sheds and scaffolding are not "buildings"; *Ward II* on the grounds that the dedication did not extend beyond the original boundary of Lake Park; *Ward III* on the grounds that the dedication was not violated by buildings compatible with park purposes; and *Ward IV* on the grounds that a sovereign state can never give up the power of eminent domain. Like the common law more generally, the public dedication doctrine presented ample grounds for the exercise of judicial discretion one way or the other. The question is why the judges so consistently exercised their discretion to enforce the doctrine.

Was it because the judges were sympathetic to the interests of the diffuse general public in preserving space for a park that all could enjoy? This, too, may have played a role. But for most of the nineteenth century, the area now known as Grant Park was not really a park; it was, to use Judge Hawes's words in 1891, a "mud hole." It was traversed by a busy and dangerous railroad line spreading out, as it reached Randolph Street, in a massive rail complex, and the waters of the lake on its eastern edge were polluted with raw sewage discharged by the Chicago River (see chapter 5), which discouraged swimming and water sports. Moreover, as we have seen, the public dedication doctrine was often invoked to bar circuses, baseball games, and toboggan slides—not to mention public museums and libraries—all of which suggests a significant degree of hostility to mass public tastes and interests.

The hypothesis most consistent with the facts is that the local judges sympathized with the private property owners who had purchased lots on Michigan Avenue. They understood that these owners had paid premium prices for their property on the assumption that they would enjoy light, air, and unobstructed views of the lake. And the owners could point to the public dedication of Lake Park, and the mounting number of precedents enforcing such public dedications more generally, as establishing that their reliance was justified. The judges of the era came from substantially the same social class as the Michigan Avenue landowners, and identified with their aspirations to protect these reliance interests. And so it happened that a doctrine designed to protect private property rights was enlisted by judges solicitous of those rights into the service of protecting public rights.

In this sense, the behavior of the judges in the *Ward* cases is broadly consistent with what we have seen in the *Lake Front Case.* The watchword was to protect established reliance interests—the status quo on the ground. The Illinois Supreme Court justices in the *Ward* cases protected the established interest of the Michigan Avenue property owners in being able to see the lake.

As we will see in chapter 8, the public dedication doctrine has largely disappeared in Illinois. The history of Grant Park suggests that this is regrettable. The park would not exist today were it not for the understanding that public dedications create rights in abutting owners, allowing them to insist on strict adherence to public uses. Generations of property owners on Michigan Avenue, most prominently but not exclusively Montgomery Ward, called on the public dedication doctrine to fight off a seemingly endless series of proposals for erecting structures in the park. The result of their efforts was to create a spectacular public space in the center of Chicago—one of the most dramatic urban spaces in the world today. Various fortuities entered into the story of how this happened, including large events such as the Great Chicago Fire and the Columbian Exposition and quirks such as the personality of the mysterious Mr. Ward. But the law was also a major contributing force, and the demise of the public dedication doctrine will make it more difficult to preserve such public spaces in the future.

No other segment of the lakefront was favored with a public dedication like the one used to keep Grant Park free of (most) buildings. Indeed, the area immediately north of the Chicago River had no official plat or survey at all. As we shall see in the next chapter, its fate would be very different from that of Grant Park.

4

THE STRUGGLE FOR STREETERVILLE

The struggles chronicled thus far took place within the bounds of the law. When Henry Shepard and Melville Fuller wanted to build an outer harbor, they sought a grant from the legislature. The Illinois Central did the same. Even after repeal of its grant in 1873, the railroad could cite legal justifications for its aggressive landfilling in the 1880s. And the many conflicts between the Michigan Avenue property owners and the civic elite over whether structures could be built in Grant Park all unfolded in court under the public dedication doctrine.

Here we look north of the Chicago River, to the neighborhood known today as Streeterville.* The land in question was created by a combination of natural accretion, unauthorized landfilling, and a legally sanctioned public works project. The result was great uncertainty about who had title to the newly formed land—greater uncertainty even than that which produced the *Lake Front Case* south of the river. The competition over resources unleashed by the uncertainty afflicting Streeterville often took place outside the bounds of the law—and included at times massive fraud and outright violence.

* "Streeterville" is an informal name for an area whose boundaries are somewhat imprecise. For general purposes, we regard Streeterville as the land north of the Chicago River and south of Oak Street that lay beneath Lake Michigan when Chicago was originally founded as a city. This makes St. Clair Street roughly the western border of the area.

Streeterville is also unique in that it is the only area of the lakefront in which the "haves" entered into direct competition with the "have nots" for control of a portion of the resource. The haves ultimately prevailed, but the means they used were sufficiently controversial that they stimulated support for public control of remaining portions of the lakefront. This was an important factor in creating the greenspace that dominates the lakefront today—though not in Streeterville itself.

The struggle for control of the land of Streeterville can be divided into three periods. The first, which lasted from roughly 1850 to 1885, was relatively decorous, consisting largely of litigation over rights to land formed by natural accretion. The second, from roughly 1885 to 1915, was intense and largely extralegal. This period included everything from a gun battle involving the followers of George Wellington Streeter, a notorious squatter, to a conspiracy to secure the land by using scrip given by Congress to the survivors of a Mexican-American War hero, to an attempt to claim the land for a branch of the Potawatomi Indians. The third period, from roughly 1915 to 1930, was when the wealthy landowners who claimed the land by riparian rights consolidated their control over the area, abetted by construction undertaken by institutions of impeccable social standing, such as Northwestern University.

A central puzzle is why it took so long for the struggle over Streeterville to be resolved. The answer would seem to be the following cycle: as long as the new land stood vacant, it remained, in the minds of many, a resource that was up for grabs; as long as it was perceived as being up for grabs, competition to establish property rights in the land continued; as long as the competition continued, it discouraged development, with the result that the land remained vacant; and because it remained vacant, to end where we began, it was perceived as being up for grabs. Resolution came only when the claimants with the most resources started to build substantial structures on the land. This eliminated the perception that the land was up for grabs and instead fostered the impression that it was no different from other solid land that is actively possessed.

A second puzzle is why the filled land in this area of the lakefront is overwhelmingly held in private hands, whereas the land south of the Chicago River, in what is now Grant Park, is public. The public trust doctrine, as developed in the *Lake Front Case*, is not the answer. The doctrine was invoked in challenging the artificial filling of submerged land in Streeterville, but the Illinois Supreme Court found no violation, as we shall explain.

A primary reason for the difference is that Grant Park to the south of Streeterville—as well as Burnham Park to the farther south and Lincoln Park to the north—came to be actively controlled by public park districts. Such public control was partially triggered by what happened in Streeterville, but came too late to be much of a factor in the area itself. Of equal importance, Grant Park, as we have seen, was protected by a public dedication promising that the land in that area was "for ever to remain vacant of buildings." No such public dedication applied to Streeterville. Indeed, the new land had no official plat or survey at all.

Accretion, Avulsion, and Unauthorized Landfilling

To understand the story of Streeterville, it is necessary to consider some additional legal doctrines that apply to new soil attaching to riparian land—that is, to land that borders on some kind of ocean, lake, or river.

From Roman times to the present, a distinction has been recognized between gradual and imperceptible changes to a shoreline and sudden and perceptible changes. The former, when they involve the deposit of new soil, are called accretions; such new land is deemed to belong to the owner of the preexisting *riparian* land. In contrast, sudden and perceptible changes to the shore are called avulsions. These do not modify preexisting property boundaries. If a large chunk of land washes away in a storm, the boundary remains as before, although some of the riparian owner's land is now underwater. Likewise, if a storm fixes new land to the shore, the new land belongs to whoever owned the submerged land before the augmentation.[1]

What about additions to solid land from *artificial* landfilling (often euphemistically referred to as "reclaimed" land)? Awarding artificially filled land to the riparian owner would provide an incentive for unauthorized landfilling. Consequently, many courts have assumed that riparian owners who engage in deliberate filling of submerged land, or who erect structures in the water that cause their riparian land to be augmented by accretion, cannot claim title to the new land.[2]

The logic of the accretion/avulsion distinction likewise suggests that artificially created land should belong to whoever owned the submerged land on which the landfilling occurred. If someone dumps enough dirt on submerged land to cause it to turn into solid land, the change will usually be perceptible, and thus is in the nature of an avulsion. If such artificial avulsions are treated like other avulsions, title should remain as it was before the change took place—that is, with the owner of the submerged land.

Yet the relatively few existing cases that explicitly treat deliberate filling as an avulsion admit of unease about this result. The Supreme Court has described the result as "arguably odd" and "counter-intuitive." Perhaps this is because, in addition to providing an incentive for unauthorized landfilling, allowing the owner of submerged land to engage in such filling could interfere with public rights of navigation and fishing or with the rights of riparian owners by blocking their access to or view of the water.[3]

When we turn from formal law to historical practice, the matter is clouded even more. Many states in the nineteenth century and earlier permitted or even encouraged artificial filling, with the newly formed landfill awarded to abutting riparian owners. It is also probable that surreptitious filling has been tolerated as a way of augmenting riparian land, if only because it is difficult to detect and prevent.[4]

In short, although much of the logic of the common-law distinction between accretion and avulsion would seem to support awarding title over land created by artificial filling to the owner of the submerged land on which the fill is placed, the competing principles and the actual treatment of such conduct have created significant uncertainty about the legal status of artificially filled land.

There was yet a further complication in Illinois. Up to about 1860, the general consensus was that riparian owners on Lake Michigan owned the land under the lake (see chapter 1). By this understanding, riparian landowners were free to dump fill in the lake—provided that in doing so they did not interfere with public navigation—because they would be filling their own property. After about 1860, legal opinion increasingly took the view that the State of Illinois owned the bed of Lake Michigan. This was explicitly confirmed by the circuit court and the Supreme Court in the *Lake Front Case*. Thus, after 1888 or 1892 (or 1896, when the Illinois Supreme Court officially endorsed this view), any landfilling of Lake Michigan by a riparian owner would create land that belonged to the state. Yet one can easily see that, during the transition period from 1860 to the 1890s, the legal significance of artificial filling of Lake Michigan would present an especially vexing question.[5]

A final factor contributing to uncertainty about rights to filled land was the weakness of the state as a political institution. Weak state governments, such as Illinois in the nineteenth century, could easily be prevailed on to convey rights to submerged lands. And even when they retained title, they were unable to assert effective control over such lands. Illinois, like other states of the era, had no department of parks or natural resources to monitor encroachment on submerged lands.[6]

In short, the absence of clear authority about the law governing artificial landfilling, changing understandings about ownership of submerged land, and weak state institutions all converged in nineteenth-century Illinois to create conditions ripe for conflict between rival groups—including some marginal groups prepared to use extralegal means—seeking to capture new land. This, in capsule form, explains the struggle for Streeterville.

Kinzie's Addition

Chicago began as a military outpost. In 1803, Fort Dearborn was built on the south bank of the Chicago River, where Michigan Avenue is located today. On the north bank was the small farm of one John Kinzie, who arrived in 1804 and returned several years after the War of 1812. In 1821, a certain John Wall surveyed the area for the federal government. Wall's hand-drawn map demarcated the area occupied by Kinzie's farm as north fractional section 10, township 39 North, range 14 East of the third principal meridian. He calculated that it contained 102.29 acres of land.[7]

In 1831, Robert A. Kinzie, John's son, applied to the federal government to obtain title to north fractional section 10 under the preemption acts. Two years later, the younger Kinzie subdivided this so-called "Kinzie's Addition" to the city of Chicago into blocks and lots, with the plat being recorded in 1834. The subdivision was bounded on the south by the Chicago River, on the east by Lake Michigan, on the north by what we now know as Chicago Avenue, and on the west by State Street (at that point known as Wolcott Street). The street running north and south nearest the lake was called Sand Street (later renamed St. Clair Street); approximately between Huron Street and Chicago Avenue (heading north), as the shore of the lake bent to the west, Sand Street was cut off by the water (as reflected in the upper right-hand corner of figure 4.1). In 1837, the United States issued Robert Kinzie a patent conferring fee-simple title to the tract and noting the acreage as stated on the 1821 survey. Chicago had begun its phenomenal growth, with real estate values, including those in Kinzie's Addition, rising dramatically around this time.[8]

As noted in chapter 1, the current in the southern part of Lake Michigan generally moves in a counterclockwise direction. Once the mouth of the Chicago River was straightened by piers jutting into the lake, the current's movement produced erosion south of the piers. North of the piers, by contrast, this produced accretion—and lots of it. As early as 1837, a chart labeled "Cap Allen's Map," prepared by an officer stationed at Fort Dearborn, indicated that the shoreline north of the piers had moved outward into the lake from where it had stood when the straightening of the river occurred (see figure 4.2). The chart showed additional sandbars forming farther offshore, on a diagonal line running from the northwest to the southeast. The 1840s saw further accretion, so that soon an estimated 1,200 feet of new land had augmented the original land platted as Kinzie's Addition. It was a gift of nature—new solid land. Legal maneuvering soon broke out over who owned nature's gift.[9]

Although accretion in the area was well underway by 1850, it was some time before the first reported judicial controversy over rights to the new land appeared. The explanation for the lag may be that the accreted lands—nicknamed "the Sands"—had become Chicago's premier vice district, "the vilest and most dangerous place in Chicago," as the *Chicago Tribune* characterized it in 1857. After many failed attempts, that same year a posse and some thirty policemen led personally by Chicago's new mayor, "Long John" Wentworth, delivered writs of ejectment and tore down "five disreputable houses, and four shanties."[10]

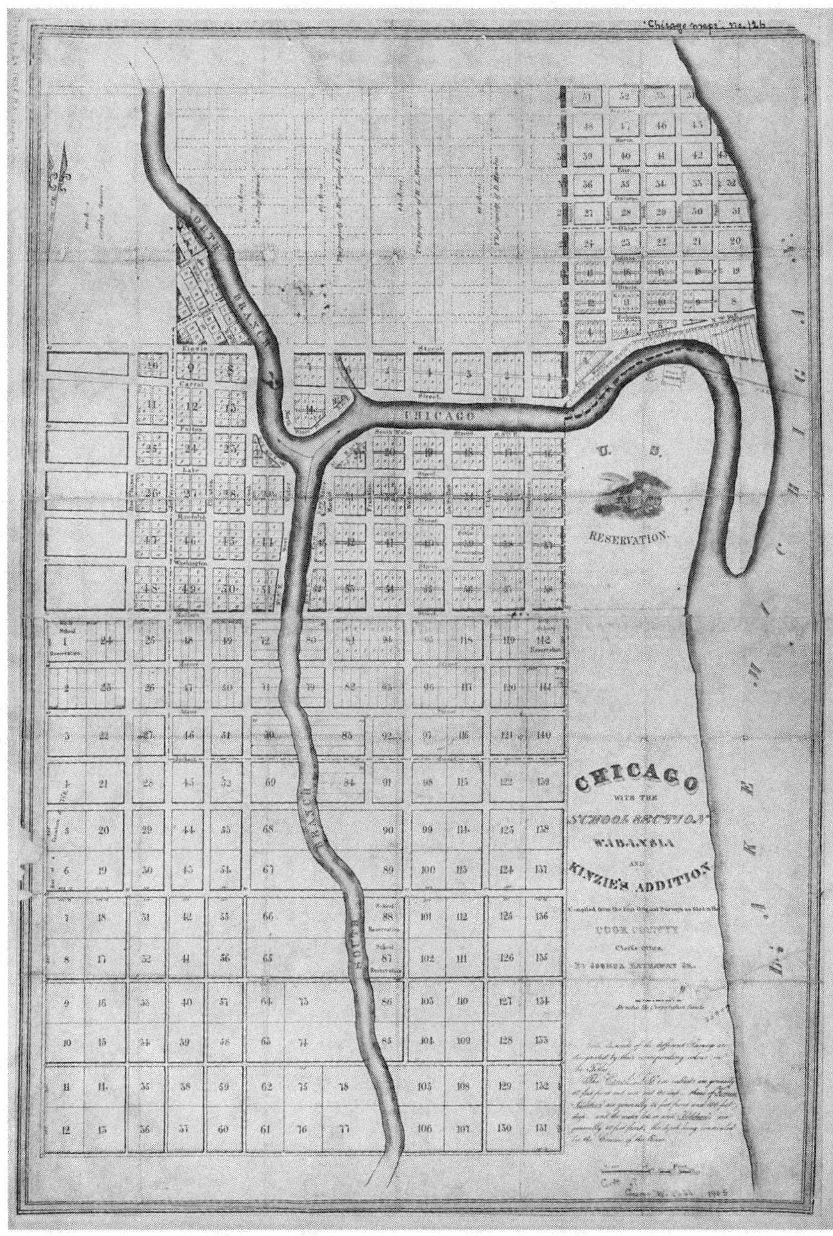

FIGURE 4.1. Chicago, including Kinzie's Addition, 1834. Kinzie's Addition is the platted land in the upper right-hand corner of the map. Chicago History Museum, ICHi-037308.

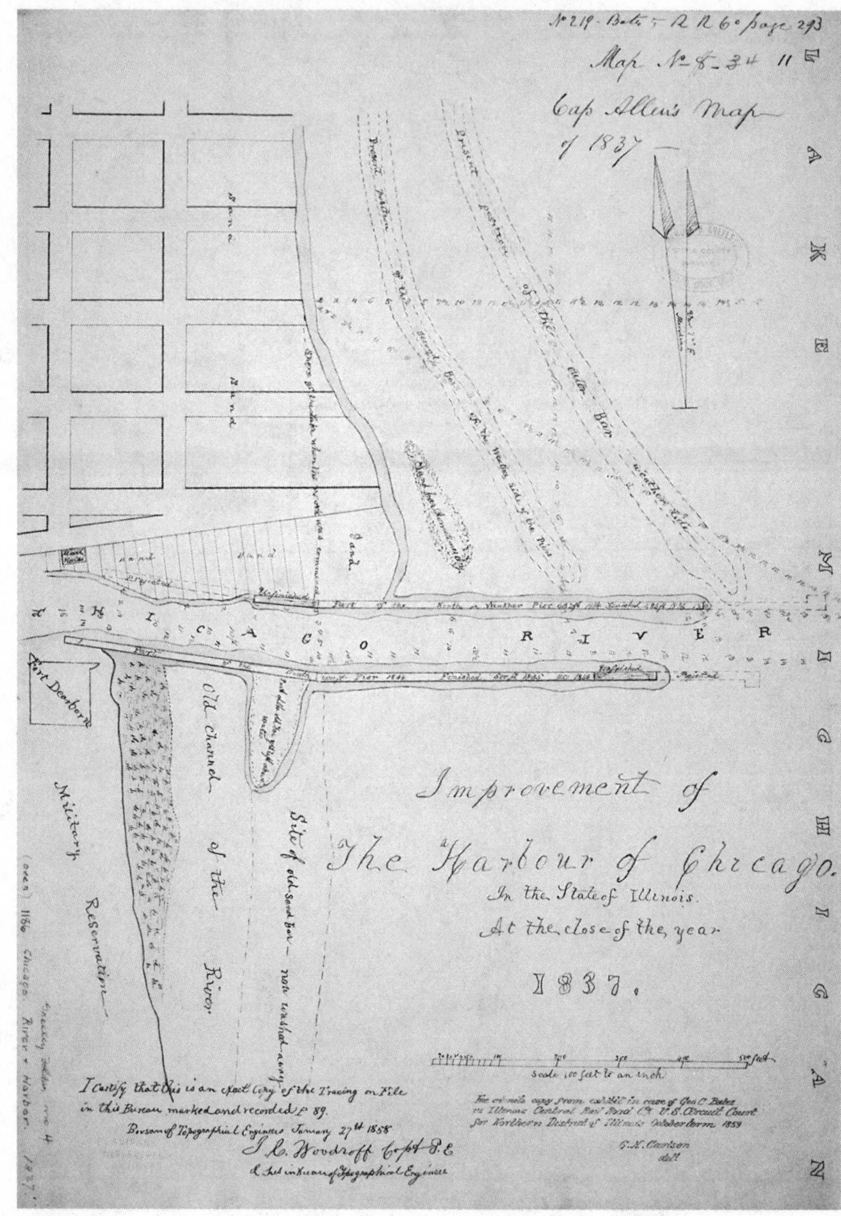

FIGURE 4.2. Cap. Allen's Map of 1837. Chicago History Museum, ICHi-067019.

Whether or not the Wentworth raid put an end to the vice, enough respectability was established to convince owners with titles in Kinzie's Addition to attend to the land's development potential. The Ogden family, owners of land in Kinzie's Addition just north of the Chicago River, formed an entity called the Chicago Dock and Canal Company, which obtained a charter from the state legislature in 1857. The charter broadly authorized the company to construct on its own lands, "and on the shore and in the navigable waters of Lake Michigan," various wharves and docks, as well as to appropriate parts of the streets in this area, which accretion had augmented. The firm eventually filled in the area north of the river's north pier, with the result that land extended a half mile into the lake east of the 1830s shoreline. Here it constructed a long slip, parallel to the river, which still exists, being known today as the "Ogden Slip." Like the extensive landfills of the Illinois Central across the river, this massive landfill could arguably be justified under the wharfing-out privilege. Yet the new construction unquestionably accelerated the accretion to the north.[11]

Soon, various owners began investing in litigation to secure title to the new land. At least seven controversies involving claims of accretion in the Sands reached the appellate level starting in the 1850s, yielding four opinions of the Illinois Supreme Court and, remarkably, four of the United States Supreme Court.[12]

The most consequential dispute concerned the legal significance of Sand Street, standing between the original subdivision and much of the newly formed land to the east (and depicted in figure 4.3, at its original northern extent, near Superior Street, which is to say between Huron and Chicago). If Kinzie had made a *statutory* dedication of the street, then under Illinois law the City of Chicago held fee-simple title to the street, making the city the riparian owner entitled to all the newly formed land to the east. But in 1865, in *Banks v. Ogden*, the Supreme Court of the United States ruled that Kinzie's recordation of the subdivision did not occur pursuant to the Illinois statutes. Consequently, Sand Street was a *common-law* dedication, which meant the public had only an easement in the street. The fee remained with the dedicator, Kinzie, and passed to his assignees. Kinzie's assignees thus could claim, as riparian owners, title to accretions that formed to the east.[13]

Litigation over accretions in Kinzie's Addition persisted until 1879. The initial cases assume that the accretion was not the intended consequence of any human intervention. The last reported opinion, however, notes in passing that the accretions had created a half mile of new land, "partly by natural causes and partly by artificial means." This was an oblique acknowledgment that the efforts of Mother Nature had been augmented by the shovel. As the secretary

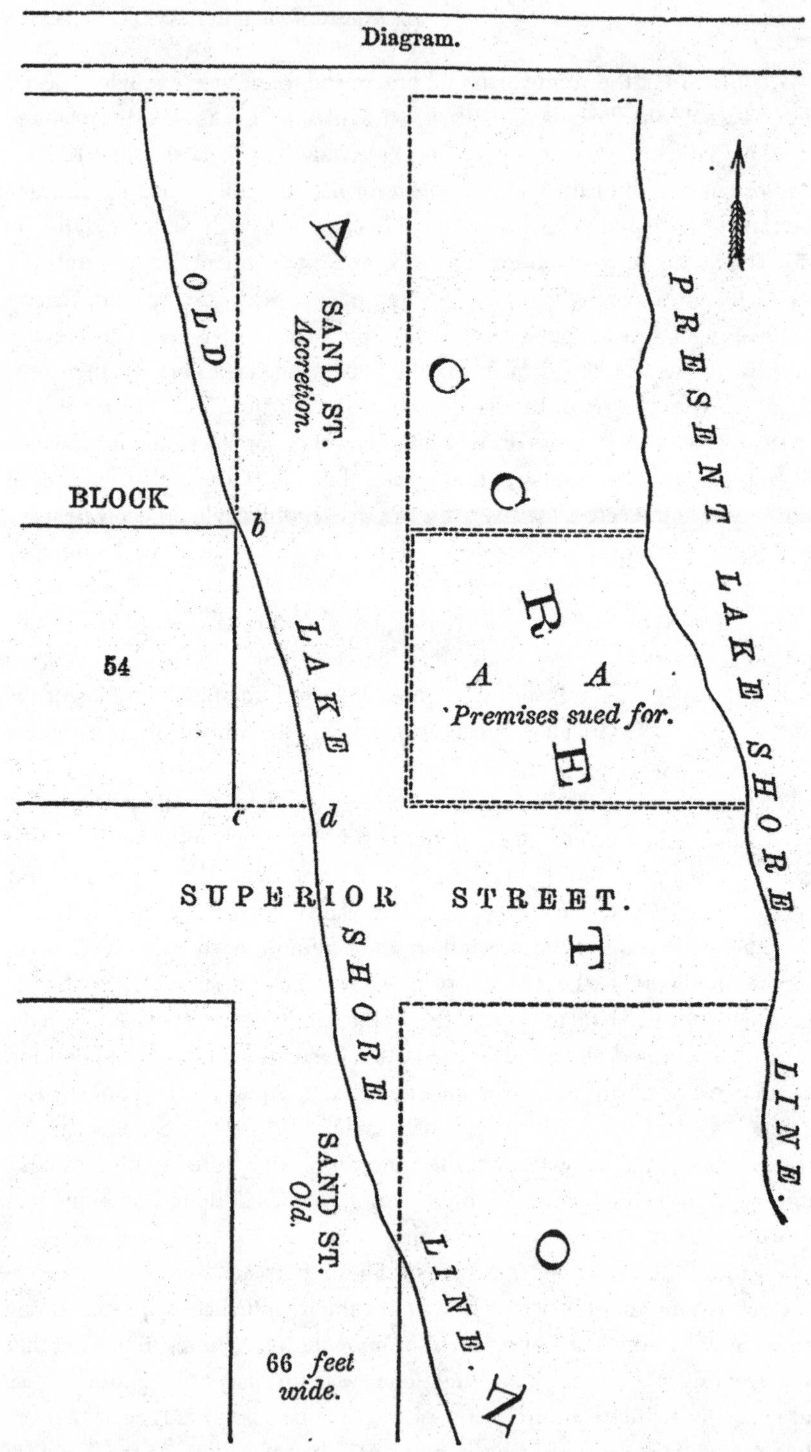

FIGURE 4.3. Illustration from *Banks v. Ogden*, 69 U.S. (2 Wall.) 57, 59 (1864) (statement of the case).

of the interior observed later, the initial "natural accretion . . . was afterwards accelerated by the building of piers into the lake and by the dumpage of refuse from the city."[14]

160 Acres of Vacant Land

In the 1880s, litigation over accretion was replaced by largely extrajudicial schemes to obtain rights to the new land east of the original Kinzie's Addition. The root cause of this shift in the mode of conflict, we believe, was mounting uncertainty over the legal status of the new land.

One reason for increased uncertainty was that artificial filling had largely supplanted natural accretion. All structures in Kinzie's Addition burned to the ground in the Chicago fire of 1871. It is probable that, as with the area south of the river (where this is a certainty), some rubble from the fire was dumped into the lake. Even apart from the fire, while details are elusive, some additional fill was undoubtedly used to augment the extent of the solid land.[15]

The state of development in the accretion area east of Kinzie's Addition is revealed by Robinson's *Atlas of the City of Chicago*, published in 1886 (see figure 4.4). The atlas shows that the shoreline had moved dramatically to the

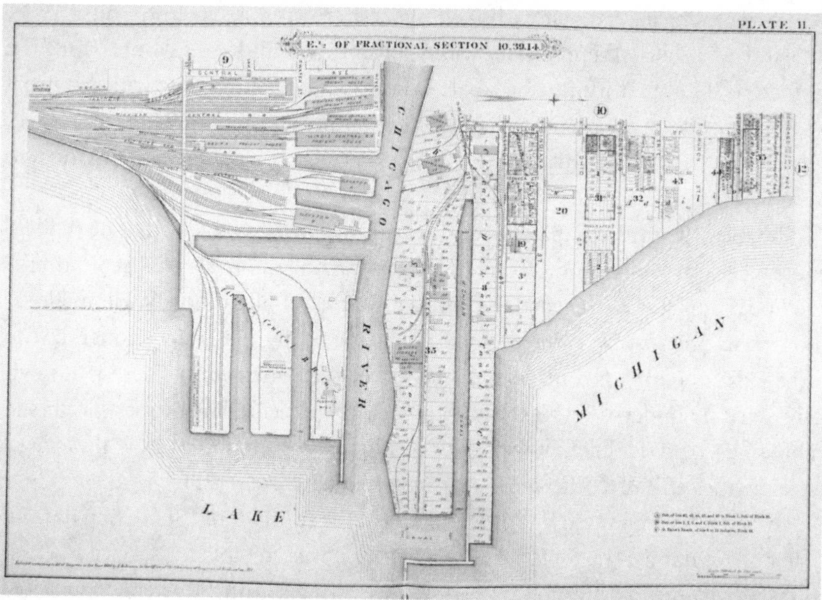

FIGURE 4.4. Map of where Lake Michigan and the Chicago River meet (west is at the top, north to the right). From E. Robinson, *Robinson's Atlas of the City of Chicago* (New York: E. Robinson, 1886), vol. 3, plate 11. Chicago History Museum, ICHi-065925.

east, relative to the original Wall survey of 1821 or even when the accretion cases of the 1860s and 1870s had been brought. An extensive landmass, later calculated to be 160 acres, had been formed in Streeterville, north of the river and east of the original boundary of Kinzie's Addition.[16]

Also striking is the dearth of buildings in Streeterville. Most of the blocks had been subdivided into lots, but not all. Even the subdivided areas showed few or no structures. For example, the area south of Chicago Avenue, now occupied by Northwestern University, is shown as "Lills Chicago Brewing Co[']s. Sub" (the northernmost area of the map). But only one small structure is shown in the subdivision. In contrast, the land on Pine Street and on both sides of St. Clair, as Sand Street had been renamed, was relatively full of structures. The difference? That area was part of the original Kinzie's Addition (most of the area, including Pine Street, is just outside the atlas excerpt that is figure 4.4, which has St. Clair Street at the top). Title there was secure.

The Deestric of Lake Michigan

In the late 1880s, rather suddenly and simultaneously, four separate efforts were launched to gain title to the largely vacant land east of St. Clair Street. As Edward O. Brown, a Chicago attorney who left the best eyewitness account, would write, the land "dazzle[d] the eyes of various adventurers and speculators," for "[i]t seemed to them that it must be a sort of no-man's land, teeming with potential wealth beyond the dreams of avarice." The story lies substantially in three unsuccessful efforts, which we discuss here and in the next two parts, before we turn to the effort that succeeded.[17]

The most famous campaign—and the most persistent—was that of the legendary George Wellington Streeter. Streeter was the quintessential scoundrel—profane, pugilistic, a braggart, and contemptuous of all authority. He made, as more than one observer noted, good newspaper copy. He knew enough law to forge legal documents and defend himself in the courtroom. There is no evidence that he understood all the legal intricacies presented by property rights in submerged land. He had, however, an intuitive appreciation of how these legal uncertainties afflicted others. This he exploited with great skill.[18]

The story, as recounted by Streeter, starts in the summer of 1886, when he built a steamboat named the *Reutan* to see whether it was suitable for service in Honduras. Returning to Chicago from Milwaukee on a trial run, Streeter encountered a sudden gale that caused the *Reutan* to ground offshore, near Superior Street. He decided to stay put, and an island soon formed around the boat, augmented by fill. For years, Streeter and his then wife, Maria, continued to live on the *Reutan* and to fill in the submerged land around it. Streeter boasted that by 1893 he had filled in an area amounting to 186 acres and connecting to the previous shore. Streeter proclaimed the new land "The Deestric of Lake Michigan" (the spelling varied), asserted that it was independent of the city, county, or state (the claim varied), and had himself acclaimed leader of this new "district" by an entourage of scruffy followers (who no doubt themselves over time varied).[19]

This tale was mostly false. A more plausible version, emerging in a later fraud trial, is that Streeter's boat was intentionally grounded at the foot of Superior Street, and he was allowed to leave it there by Nathaniel K. Fairbank, arguably the riparian owner, whereupon Streeter overstayed his welcome and became a squatter.[20]

In any event, as the tale reflects, Streeter initially claimed the land east of Kinzie's Addition by right of original discovery. He claimed to have discovered the land, which had emerged from the lakebed, and to have labored to extend the land into a large tract. Streeter undoubtedly contributed to, or at least invited, further artificial filling of the submerged land. But there is no way that he was responsible for all of it. Most of the land was created by natural accretion, augmented, before his arrival, by artificial filling (as discussed above) and, in the 1890s, by the filling performed by the Lincoln Park Commission in building the Lake Shore Drive extension (as discussed below).

Streeter also tried a second device for claiming the land: he secured a copy of the original Kinzie patent, used acid to remove certain portions of the writing, and forged various signatures and information to make it appear that he had a valid federal patent to the land. Before the forgery was exposed, Streeter managed to record his claim with the county, whereupon the Rascher Insurance Map Publishing Company issued an early 1890s map showing a portion of the area as "Streeter's Land."[21]

Later, perhaps in emulation of rival claimants, some of whom we shall discuss in the next section, Streeter developed a theory of title separate from his discovery claim. It was based on the Wall survey of 1821, reflecting the original Kinzie's Addition. Streeter claimed that the line on the map demarcating the shore of Lake Michigan was a boundary line. Boundary lines were understood to be fixed delimitations of property rights established by survey. In contrast, meander lines were mapped by surveyors along the edge of a body of water for purposes of ascertaining the quantity of land available for sale. They were understood to be subject to revision later, when the exact boundary would be established. If the shoreline was a meander line, then the patent issued to Kinzie included the right to claim subsequent accretions. But if it was a boundary line, as Streeter maintained, then the accretions were arguably part of the public domain, open for claiming.[22]

Relying on the theory that the Wall survey had established a boundary line, Streeter applied in 1895 for a patent on the "unclaimed" land outside Kinzie's Addition, invoking Maria's status as the purported widow of a Civil War soldier. As administratively affirmed, the General Land Office rejected his application on the grounds that the formerly submerged lands, east of St. Clair Street, "do not belong to the government, and, therefore, this Department [of Interior] has no jurisdiction to direct their survey or disposal."[23]

As he shifted back and forth from one theory to another, Streeter intuitively perceived that it would strengthen any claim of title, certainly in a psychological if not a legal sense, if he were in actual possession of some part of the land. Like the seafaring explorers of the sixteenth century, Streeter felt that it was imperative to plant a flag in the soil marking his "discovery" of the contested land. This explains his dogged efforts from 1886 to 1915 to maintain a foothold on some portion of the contested terrain. Whether it was the grounded *Reutan*, a makeshift fortress, a tent, a shack, a boat club house, a broken-down motor truck, or a small brick building, Streeter nearly always sought to maintain some physical presence on the land. The principal exceptions were when he was in jail or when others in league with him maintained a presence on the land.[24]

FIGURE 4.5. Streeter's house on an old scow, 1892. Chicago History Museum, ICHi-019835.

Streeter's efforts were greatly assisted by the halfhearted attempts of the original riparian owners to evict him. Nathaniel K. Fairbank, who owned land between Huron and Superior Streets, went further than most. In 1890, Fairbank sued Streeter for forcible entry and detainer and secured an order of recovery, but he failed to enforce it before Streeter tied the matter up in further litigation. Periodically over the years, one or more owners would persuade the police to intervene or would hire private "detectives" to evict Streeter and his cohorts.

FIGURE 4.6. Streeter with his wife, "Ma," ca. 1915. Chicago History Museum, ICHi-012593.

Most of these attempts were rebuffed by a show of force by Streeter and Maria and later by Streeter and his last wife, "Ma" Streeter. On several occasions, Streeter was forced to retreat, but he always came back.[25]

The most serious episode occurred in 1902, when a guard in the service of an attorney for riparian owners was shot and killed in a battle with Streeter's gang. Streeter was indicted for murder. His first trial, in which he defended himself, ended with a hung jury; the second resulted in a manslaughter conviction. After spending less than a year in the Joliet penitentiary, Streeter was released by a sympathetic judge.[26]

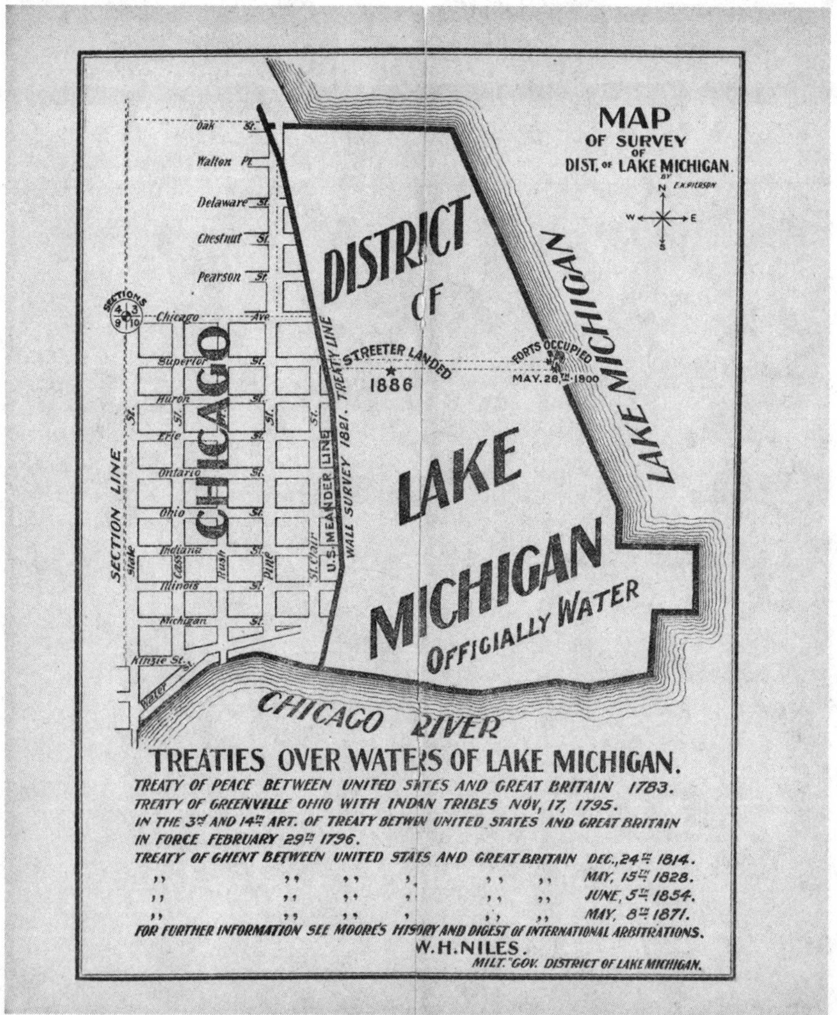

FIGURE 4.7. Advertising map for District of Lake Michigan, ca. 1903. Chicago Public Library, Special Collections and Preservation Division, STR box 1, folder 43.

What was Streeter's objective in all this? There are occasional suggestions that he wanted to make a pest of himself in an attempt to get the riparian owners to buy him off. He was certainly a pest, but there is no indication that he ever extracted an offer of payment in return for forfeiting his "claim." More obviously, Streeter made a living by duping unsophisticated real estate investors into buying deeds to lots in his District of Lake Michigan. One newspaper estimated that he had received $100,000 in his nearly thirty-year career of engaging in sham land transactions.[27]

There are two striking facts about Streeter's marathon career as a squatter. First, there is no publicly reported judicial decision establishing that he was trespassing on land owned by the riparian owners. We know of at least two forcible-entry-and-detainer actions—a statutory cause of action that presupposes the defendant to be in wrongful possession—brought by riparian owners against Streeter. But neither resulted in a judgment that resolved the title question. The numerous other legal actions against, and sometimes by, Streeter involved ancillary issues such as fraud, assault, murder, or selling liquor on Sundays.[28]

It is probably no coincidence that the riparian owners avoided a definitive judicial determination of their title in litigation with Streeter. Fear of popular sympathy for the wily scoundrel may have been one reason. But a more likely explanation is that their title—at least to much of the land in question—was doubtful.

The second striking fact about Streeter's long career is that the State of Illinois showed no interest in his agitation. This was so even though it became increasingly likely that the state held title to the artificially filled land. Streeter had his run-ins with the Chicago police, and he fought pitched battles with private security guards hired by the riparian owners. But the State of Illinois was entirely absent from these conflicts. This underscores the weakness of the state as an institution at the time. The emerging legal consensus that the state owned the artificially filled land was nice in theory, but in practice it was little different from saying that no one owned it at all.

The McKee Scrip Claim

Captain Streeter was not the only one maneuvering to obtain property rights in the vacant land east of Kinzie's Addition. William R. McKee, a colonel from Kentucky, was killed in action during the Mexican-American War. In 1853, Congress awarded each of his orphaned children "one quarter section of land, to be located upon any vacant land of the United States." As frequently happened in such instances, the McKee children sold their rights for cash. In 1889, Congress was prevailed on to remove the restriction that such land must be "located where and in such manner as the President of the United States shall direct." The McKee scrip, as it was called, eventually came into the hands of a group of adventurers led by Harvey M. La Follette, a real estate speculator, and Matthias Benner, former chief of Chicago's fire department; they set their sights on acquiring the land east of the original Kinzie's Addition. In 1896, the General Land Office rejected their initial application seeking a patent to the area as "vacant land of the United States."[29]

The La Follette group refiled its application, and the commissioner of the Land Office, Silas W. Lamoreaux, quickly responded by sending a number of clerks to conduct a survey of "unsurveyed public land" in the tract in question. Fairbank, one of the riparian owners, got wind of this and filed a protest. This was evidently rejected, for within a month the La Follette group filed an amended application, this time seeking to patent the land as shown "on the plat of the official survey of such lands approved October 15th, 1896." This was all the land east of St. Clair, which the survey calculated as comprising roughly 160 acres. Being depicted on an official survey, these lands were deemed to be part of the federal public domain open for claiming.[30]

After further proceedings with the applicants and the riparian objectors, Lamoreaux signed a written opinion on February 20, 1897, awarding a patent to the entire 160 acres to the McKee scrip claimants led by Benner and La Follette. Lamoreaux put the decision in a sealed envelope and left it with his deputy, with instructions that it was to be opened and officially "promulgated" the following Tuesday, February 23, after the holiday for Washington's birthday. Lamoreaux immediately left the capital.[31]

Once promulgated, decisions by the commissioner of the Land Office awarding patents to federal lands were very difficult to reverse. In an administrative appeal, the secretary of the interior would not take additional evidence and would reverse a decision only based on clear error appearing on the record made by the commissioner. Courts were even more reluctant to intervene.[32]

Lamoreaux's decision came in the waning days of President Grover Cleveland's second term. Part of the scheme, evidently, was to release the decision during the general exodus in the turnover of administrations so that it would not be noticed before it was promulgated. The riparian owners nevertheless got word that something was up. Being well connected, they interceded with Cleveland, who directed that no action be taken to promulgate any decision on the McKee scrip without his approval.[33]

The nervous owners sent an emissary to Washington, attorney Edward O. Brown, who also served as a key adviser to the Lincoln Park Commission (see chapter 6). His trip was brief but seemingly efficient. Arriving the morning following William McKinley's inauguration and after meeting that day with the outgoing secretary of the interior and the next day with his successor, and receiving assurances, Brown left to return to Chicago. On the morning of Monday, March 8, he stepped off the train in Harrisburg, Pennsylvania, to purchase a Chicago paper. There he read a sensational article proclaiming that the La Follette application had been granted, complete with the full text of the Lamoreaux opinion. A flurry of panicked telegrams ensued.[34]

It turned out that Lamoreaux had secretly given a copy of the decision to the La Follette applicants, and they had leaked it to the press. Fortunately for the riparian owners, the official copy still sat in Washington, unpromulgated.[35]

Lamoreaux, now convalescing in Wisconsin, lamely confessed to the new secretary of the interior, Cornelius N. Bliss, that he had given a copy of the decision "to a party," but with instructions that it not be released until promulgated. Bliss directed that Lamoreaux grant an immediate rehearing on the application. Lamoreaux issued the order and was allowed to resign before the rehearing took place, without any further action against him.[36]

On rehearing, Lamoreaux's successor rejected the application. La Follette appealed the decision to Bliss, who affirmed in a published opinion cleared with the Justice Department (in particular, Willis Van Devanter, assistant attorney general and future Supreme Court justice). Bliss rejected La Follette's contention that the order for the survey in 1896 was a final determination that the land in question was public land and binding on the Department of the Interior. Bliss reasoned that the approval of a survey should not bar the department from reexamining the question of public title "at any time before the legal title has passed from the United States." The decisions cited by La Follette and Benner, to the extent contrary, were overruled.[37]

On the merits, Bliss concluded that the line east of the north half of fractional section 10, as shown on the Wall survey of 1821, was a meander line, not a boundary line. Thus, there were no federal public lands available to claim in the area. The survey ordered by Lamoreaux in 1896 was annulled. The opinion said nothing about who in fact was the owner of the 160 acres east of Kinzie's Addition. Bliss noted only that the United States had "ceased to be a riparian proprietor and is therefore not entitled to subsequent accretions."[38]

The scheme did not immediately die away. Several years later, one still read of deeds based on the "McKee scrip" being recorded by out-of-state investors. The riparian owners laughed at these claims. Yet the land, despite its prime location, remained largely undeveloped.[39]

The Potawatomi Claim

A third effort sought to claim the newly formed land for a band of the Potawatomi Indians. Before European settlers arrived, the Potawatomi inhabited the area where Chicago is located. In 1833 and 1846, the Potawatomi agreed to relinquish their claim to five million acres of land, including Chicago, and to move west of the Mississippi. These treaties were understood to extinguish the Potawatomi's right of occupancy, which was a precondition to opening the lands to sale by the federal government. No mention was made in these treaties of the submerged land beneath Lake Michigan.[40]

One band of the tribe, known as the Catholic Potawatomi, received permission to remain in the St. Joseph River Valley in southwest Michigan. In the second half of the nineteenth century, the Catholic Potawatomi, led by an elected business committee, pursued multiple claims for breaches of treaty obligations before Congress and in litigation, with some success. In the mid-1890s, the business committee stripped of any authority its onetime leader, Simon Pokagon, a colorful but self-interested figure who was frequently away on the lecture tour. Pokagon previously had turned to two Chicago lawyers in an effort to pursue the idea of asserting rights for the Potawatomi to the reclaimed land along the Chicago waterfront, including Streeterville. The lawyers eventually lost interest in the scheme, and in 1897, Pokagon, in desperation, purported to sell by quitclaim deed the band's interest in the Chicago lakefront to William H. Cox, a schemer who had previously joined forces with Streeter.[41]

Armed with this deed, Cox filed a claim on behalf of the tribe with the Department of the Interior. The gist of the argument was that the Potawatomi had never relinquished their right of occupancy to the land submerged under Lake Michigan and, therefore, that the United States would have to acquire the land by a new treaty if it wished to permit settlement by non-Indians. The commissioner of the Indian Bureau rejected the claim, on the grounds that the Potawatomi had ceded by treaty all land east of the Mississippi River. In 1900, a congressional committee reached the same conclusion.[42]

Simon Pokagon died in 1899, and his son, Charles Pokagon, took up the "Sandbar Claim" as his own cause. Charles was, if possible, more melodramatic than his father. In the spring of 1901, as the *Tribune* presented the matter to its readers, he held a press conference announcing a planned "invasion" of the reclaimed land by a chartered steamer filled with "Pottawatomie braves," embarking from St. Joseph, Michigan. The announced invasion generated some bemused press coverage. According to the newspaper, some wags declared that "inasmuch as the mooted property lies along the lake front Montgomery Ward would see that no one got near it." The invasion never materialized.[43]

Stimulated by Charles Pokagon's fervor, the Potawatomi reasserted their claim before the Indian Bureau commissioner in 1902, but he reaffirmed the earlier determination. With respect to the argument that the land ceded in the treaties did not include "the lands under the water," the commissioner held that this was contrary to settled principles of international law. Such land was transferred to the new sovereign—which by the terms of the treaties had been the United States. The Potawatomi claim fell quiet for a number of years.[44]

The Lake Shore Drive Extension

The fourth effort to gain title to the newly created lands east of Kinzie's Addition was that of the riparian owners—those who traced their title to Kinzie's original patent plus natural accretions. They ultimately succeeded, although the statute the owners used to secure their claims contained a substantial gap that left a portion of the reclaimed land unaddressed.

Who exactly were the riparian owners? It is difficult to say with complete certainty because the titles were held in trust. But various investigations, contemporaneous and subsequent, extracted the information that the owners included the Chicago Dock and Canal Company (controlled by the Ogden heirs), the Cyrus McCormick estate, W. C. Newberry, the Potter Palmer estate, Nathaniel K. Fairbank, John V. Farwell, and Ogden, Sheldon & Company. This was a virtual who's who of wealthy Chicago families, most of whom had augmented their wealth through real estate dealings. Collectively and individually, they would have had an acute appreciation of the potential commercial value of the reclaimed land, and they possessed the resources needed to advance their interests in securing the rights to it.[45]

The riparian owners used the Lincoln Park Commission as the vehicle to advance their cause. The park district had been established by state legislation in 1869, the same year as the South Park Commission, which we saw contending with Ward in chapter 3, and one for the West Side. The inaugural statutes provided that the Lincoln Park district would be controlled by a board of commissioners who, after the first group, would be appointed by a state court judge and hence would be independent of the mayor and city council. Under the law, however, while the commissioners could make an annual recommendation, elected officials had to set all taxes to be levied in support of the park district.[46]

The main activity of the Lincoln Park Commission during its early years was to secure land a mile or more north of the heart of Streeterville (specifically, between North Avenue and Diversey Avenue) along the lakefront and to fill and landscape this area for what would become Lincoln Park. The resulting park would include a pleasure drive along the lake, called Lake Shore Drive, partly in order to protect the lakeshore from erosion. The original legislation also gave the commissioners authority to lay out an approaching drive from the end of Pine Street (now Michigan Avenue), near Oak Street, northward to the south end of the park (at North Avenue), a project to be paid for by special assessments. With squabbles over assessments, construction of this segment of the drive was not completed until 1875. A breakwater was constructed but was inadequate to keep out the lake waters after storms.[47]

In the early 1880s, Potter Palmer astonished the Chicago establishment by turning away from the fashionable Prairie Avenue area on the South Side and building an enormous residence—"by all odds the most imposing in [the] city"—on Lake Shore Drive, several blocks north of Streeterville. Other wealthy families soon followed suit. Tax revenues and voluntary supplemental assessments of the property owners allowed the park commissioners to improve Lake Shore Drive between Oak Street and North Avenue by enhancing the breakwater, rebuilding the drive, and making some sidewalk and landscaping improvements. Property values on the drive, which enjoyed unobstructed views of the lake, skyrocketed.[48]

Palmer, and perhaps other wealthy individuals and families who migrated to this "Gold Coast," also held lakefront interests just to the south, in Streeterville. The Lake Shore Drive owners and the commissioners of Lincoln Park became well acquainted when they were making common cause to fund the enhancements to the drive north of Streeterville. And it cannot have hurt that one of the commissioners was a lakeshore owner in Streeterville.[49]

In any event, the Streeterville riparian owners enlisted the aid of the commissioners in helping to secure their interests. According to an early history of Lincoln Park, the riparian owners' scheme was initially devised in 1886 by Henry Sheldon. A member of Ogden, Sheldon & Company, a large Streeterville owner, he would proceed to act on behalf of the Ogden, Fairbank, Farwell, and Newberry interests. As refined over several years (and shown in figure 4.10), the plan called for the commissioners to construct a southward extension of Lake Shore Drive: it would swing to the east of Pine Street, near Oak Street, proceed several blocks and then turn south, outside the existing accreted and landfilled area of Streeterville, and terminate at Ohio Street. Special assessments imposed on the Streeterville riparian owners would pay for the extension. The commissioners, in turn, would transfer to the owners title to the submerged land between the new drive and the existing shoreline (to the west), as compensation for their assistance in funding the construction.[50]

The only plausible rationale for the project was to secure title to the contested land for the riparian owners. As soon characterized, the proposed extension of Lake Shore Drive was a road that "leads nowhere." It would dead end at Ohio Street, its progress blocked by the Ogden Slip and beyond that by the Chicago River. There were no structures of any consequence along the route. There were no existing cross streets. There would be views of the lake to the east but, to the west, nothing save mud, garbage, and a few squatter shacks. Anyone out for a Sunday carriage ride would find the segment of Lake Shore Drive in the original

FIGURE 4.8. Streeterville, 1909. DN-0007184, Chicago Daily News negatives collection, Chicago History Museum.

FIGURE 4.9. Lincoln Park on a Sunday, undated. Library of Congress, Prints & Photographs Division, Detroit Publishing Company Collection, LC-D4 18849.

Lincoln Park infinitely more pleasant. Photographs of the respective areas from about this time confirm this (contrast figure 4.8 with figure 4.9).[51]

The scheme was temporarily abandoned when the Illinois attorney general sued to stop construction. The interested parties then sought legislation authorizing the plan of the commissioners and riparian owners. The Illinois General Assembly promptly obliged in 1889. One section of its 1889 act, critical for our purposes, provided as follows:

> [T]he submerged lands lying between the shore of such public waters and the inner line of the extension of such boulevard or driveway shall be appropriated by the board of park commissioners to the purpose of defraying the cost of such extension and to that end such board of park commissioners are authorized to sell and convey such submerged lands in fee simpl[e] by deeds duly executed on its behalf by its president and under its corporate seal, and every deed executed in pursuance hereof shall vest a good title in the grantee to the premises intended to be conveyed thereby.

In other words, the drive would be funded by selling off submerged land between the existing shore and the right of way for the new drive. Under the act, the extension of the drive itself would become part of the Lincoln Park Commission and subject to its control.[52]

Although the statute called for selling the lands between the shoreline and the new drive to the east, Edward O. Brown recalled in a memoir that "it was not the intention of the persons instrumental in securing the passage of the act that this course should be adopted." Rather, "[f]rom the first it was plainly the intention to come by negotiation between the Commissioners and the shore owners to some agreement" in which the landowners would fund the construction and, in return, gain title to the submerged land from the shore to the drive, which they would then fill "and thus largely increase their land holdings."[53]

Brown acknowledged its being "foreseen that some opposition would undoubtedly develop to this scheme." To mute the anticipated outcry, a carefully orchestrated series of consultations was planned. First, a "selected committee" of three eminent citizens was asked to opine whether the scheme was in the public interest. The committee duly rendered such a judgment. Second, the Army Corps of Engineers was asked to determine whether the plan presented any interference with the rights of navigation. The chief engineer in Chicago reported to the War Department that he saw no objection, and proponents heralded the department's reaction as approval.[54]

Under contracts executed in 1891, deeds conveying title and the right to fill submerged land between the shoreline and the roadway to the east were made out to the riparian landowners and placed in escrow with the Northern Trust Company. They were to be delivered when the owners complied with their contractual obligations to underwrite the cost of the fill and construction. The work was scheduled to be completed by 1893, but two investigations were launched that quickly brought construction to a halt.[55]

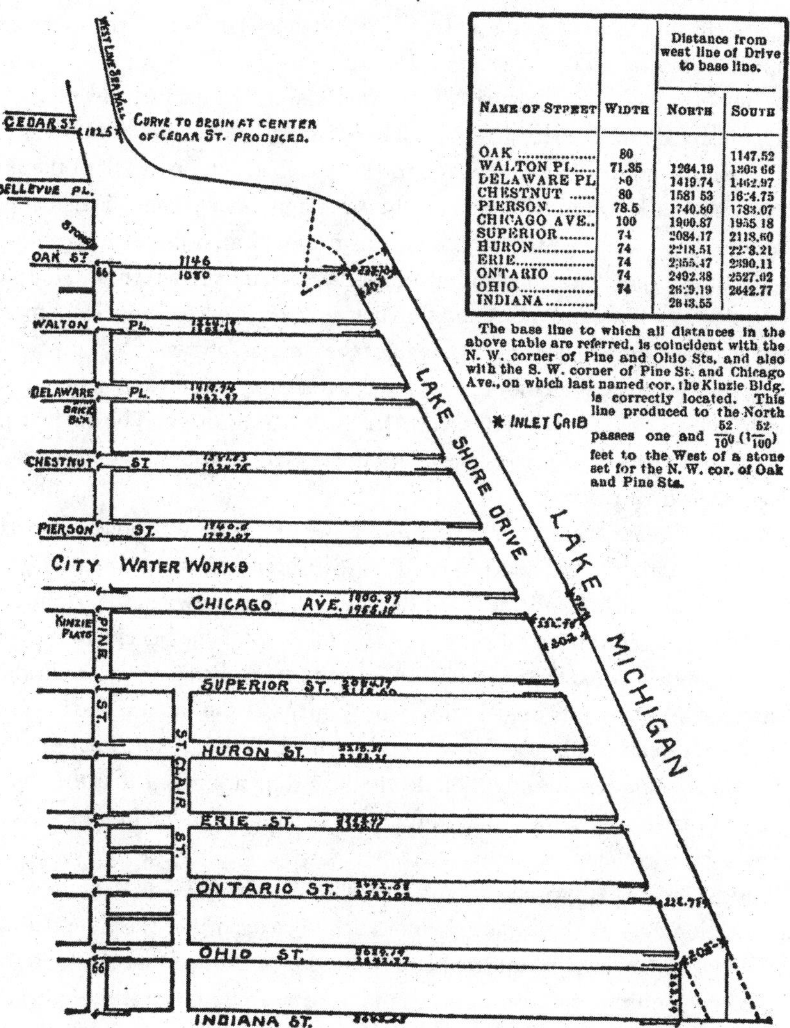
EXHIBIT C.

MAP OF THE OHIO STREET EXTENSION OF THE LAKE SHORE DRIVE.

ISHAM RANDOLPH, Consulting Engineer.

NAME OF STREET	WIDTH	Distance from west line of Drive to base line. NORTH	SOUTH
OAK	80		1147.52
WALTON PL	71.35	1264.19	1303 66
DELAWARE PL	80	1419.74	1462.97
CHESTNUT	80	1581 53	1624.75
PIERSON	78.5	1740.80	1783.07
CHICAGO AVE.	100	1900.87	1935 18
SUPERIOR	74	2084.17	2118.60
HURON	74	2218.51	2253.21
ERIE	74	2355.47	2390.11
ONTARIO	74	2492.38	2527.02
OHIO	74	2629.19	2642.77
INDIANA		2843.55	

The base line to which all distances in the above table are referred, is coincident with the N. W. corner of Pine and Ohio Sts, and also with the S. W. corner of Pine St. and Chicago Ave., on which last named cor. the Kinzie Bldg. is correctly located. This line produced to the North passes one and $\frac{52}{100}$ ($1\frac{52}{100}$) feet to the West of a stone set for the N. W. cor. of Oak and Pine Sts.

FIGURE 4.10. Plat of Lake Shore Drive extension, *People ex rel. Moloney v. Kirk*, 45 N.E. 830, 832 (Ill. 1896).

A special committee of the Illinois Senate, named after its chairman, Henry C. Bartling, undertook the first investigation. The committee's report excoriated the project, describing it as a "theft from the navigable waters of Lake Michigan," a drive that "is valuable only to the abutting and contiguous property owners as an exit from the made land." The committee surmised that "the property owners by undue influence of some sort used the Lincoln Park Commissioners." It gave a "conservative estimate" of the value of the newly made land "at from 8 to 12 Millions." The Bartling Committee recommended that the state attorney general "take all necessary steps to obtain possession of the lands created in the waters of Lake Michigan and do all in his power to prevent greedy owners of riparian rights from encroaching upon the waters of the Lake."[56]

The attorney general, Maurice T. Moloney, launched his own investigation, and concurred that an excessive amount of submerged land would be taken from the public, primarily for private gain. In 1894, he filed suit on behalf of the state against the park commissioners and the riparian owners. The suit demanded that the 1889 statute be pronounced unconstitutional, all construction contracts declared void and canceled, all filling of submerged lands removed, and the submerged lands restored to their condition before any encroachments. The Chicago Title & Trust Company, acting on behalf of the riparian owners, filed suit against the commissioners, demanding that the contracts be enforced as written. The commissioners filed a cross bill asking that their title to the land be quieted and their right to levy special assessments on the owners to complete and maintain the drive be declared.[57]

Moloney's case against the Lake Shore Drive extension was powerfully reinforced by the then-recent decision of the US Supreme Court in the *Lake Front Case*. The court had confirmed that the State of Illinois owned the submerged land but qualified this by saying it was held in trust for the benefit of the public. Moreover, it ruled that "[t]he trust . . . cannot be alienated, except in those instances . . . of parcels used in the improvement of the interest thus held, or when parcels can be disposed of without detriment to the public interest in the lands and waters remaining." Moloney had a strong argument that the legislature's conveyance of some ninety-three acres of submerged land to the adjacent shore owners violated this public trust.[58]

Judge Thomas G. Windes, of the circuit court, dismissed the attorney general's action against the project. Windes acknowledged that the state held the submerged land "in trust for the people," but he concluded that the legislature had plenary authority to convey such land "for the accomplishment of purposes beneficial to the people of the State." Moloney appealed.[59]

In 1896, in a decision styled as *People ex rel. Moloney v. Kirk*, the Illinois Supreme Court unanimously affirmed. Reflecting popular hostility toward the scheme, the court voiced its displeasure with the legislation. But the propriety or impropriety of such a grant, it held, was a matter for the legislature to determine, not for the courts: "The legislature represents not only the State, which holds the title which at common law was vested in the crown, but the legislature also represents the public, for whose benefit the title is held, and in that capacity it possesses the sovereign power of parliament over the waters of the lake and the submerged lands covered by the waters." The court found no compelling evidence that the extensive landfill would interfere with navigation or with fishing. And because the new drive would remain "in the hands of the park commissioners for park purposes," the legislature had made "no attempt . . . to relinquish its governmental powers or place them beyond the power of future legislation."[60]

The *Kirk* court also upheld the critical provision of the act that allowed the submerged lands between the existing shore and the new drive to be transferred to private parties in return for their funding the construction of the drive. There could be no objection to this provision, the court concluded, so long as the commissioners received full value for the submerged land. The court failed to address the obvious objection that the government *did* relinquish control with respect to these more extensive submerged lands, between the shore and the drive, as they would fall into private hands. Yet the court concluded with a cryptic sentence, which no doubt caught the eyes of the lawyers at Chicago Title & Trust: "The right of a shore owner on Lake Michigan to fill up portions of the lake and thus extend his lands does not arise in this case and that question will not be considered."[61]

The Slow Birth of Streeterville

The riparian owners had won. Or had they? One of the puzzles of the history of Streeterville is that development of the area failed to take off after *Kirk* blessed the Lake Shore Drive extension in 1896, including the transfer of ninety-three acres of submerged land to the riparian owners, or even after 1903 when the extension was finally completed.[62]

To be sure, new buildings eventually followed. But the pace of development was exceedingly slow, especially given the prime location of the land. In 1912, a ten-story apartment building went up where the new drive turned at Oak Street (as extended) near the lake. In 1916, an office building was constructed along Ohio Street—in such a way as to be easily converted into a factory, if the unusual location did not support the initial venture. Starting in 1920, the Drake Hotel graced Michigan Avenue, although this was at least partially on original solid land. Other buildings came along only slowly, such as the east side of the

FIGURE 4.11. Streeterville, ca. 1923. Courtesy of the Newberry Library, Chicago, Midwest MS Sloan No. 3090.

American Furniture Mart, now 680 North Lake Shore Drive, which arrived in 1923. Strikingly, however, an aerial photograph (figure 4.11) taken around this time—nearly three decades after the *Kirk* decision—reveals that much of the land in the area remained vacant.[63]

One reason is that agitation and litigation over ownership rights to the reclaimed land did not end with the decision in *Kirk*. Streeter lay low for several years after his release from prison in 1904. But by 1909 he was back on the vacant land, living in a motor truck and selling lots as of old. In 1912, a sympathetic Chicago alderman arranged for Streeter to occupy a small brick store-cum-living-quarters on Chestnut Street, where he and Ma Streeter sold sandwiches, soda pop, liquor, and, eventually, copies of his "autobiography."[64]

Streeter remained enough of a nuisance that in 1915 the Chicago police bloodied him in a massive attack, which apparently was provoked by Streeter's having insulted Mayor William Hale "Big Bill" Thompson. Although Streeter got the worst of the encounter, he was charged with assaulting a police officer with intent to kill. He presented his own closing argument at trial, whereupon the jury acquitted him. When an effort coordinated by Chicago Title & Trust finally obtained an order to demolish the Streeters' makeshift store in 1918, the couple retired to a boathouse in Indiana Harbor.[65]

Streeter died in 1921. His funeral was attended by Mayor Thompson, who led a forty-car motorcade to Graceland Cemetery, final resting place of the Chicago elite. The president of Chicago Title & Trust, who no doubt had mixed feelings about the event, wrote a short eulogy for a newspaper: "The Cap'n's ideas of law were somewhat at variance with that of the preponderant legal opinion but he was a gallant and able protagonist nevertheless. We shall miss him more than might be imagined. He kept two lawyers and one vice president busy for twenty-one years. . . . [M]ay he rest in peace and find his lost 'deestrict' in some fairer land where the courts cease from troubling and title companies are at rest."[66]

Streeter may have found lasting peace, but the title company did not. Ma Streeter continued the quest for vindication, filing a lawsuit in 1924 seeking $100 million in damages from Chicago Title & Trust and various riparian property owners, purportedly some 1,500 defendants in all. The next year, a federal judge ruled that she had not been properly married to Streeter—he had failed to terminate at least one previous marriage—and so she did not inherit any of his "right."[67]

Meanwhile, the Potawatomi claim sprang back to life in 1909. The stimulus was a proposal for state legislation permitting the Illinois Steel Company to engage in extensive landfilling to enlarge its plant site on Lake Michigan near the Calumet River, on the far South Side (chapter 8 takes up this proposal in detail), and another plan to construct a massive new public pier into the lake at Grand Avenue (what became Navy Pier). The Indians' claim was raised as a potential complicating factor in both instances, but public officials were unmoved.[68]

In a final effort, the Potawatomi tribe decided to test the claim in litigation. The US District Court for the Northern District of Illinois dismissed the complaint in 1914. The Supreme Court affirmed in a terse decision. Justice James C. McReynolds saw no need to construe the treaties or determine the original rights of the Potawatomi to the submerged lands: "If in any view [the Potawatomi Nation] ever held possession of the property here in question we know historically that this was abandoned long ago and that for more than a half century it has not even pretended to occupy either the shores or waters of Lake Michigan within the confines of Illinois." After decades of agitation in multiple forums, the claim advanced on behalf of the Potawatomi was rejected on a simple theory of abandonment.[69]

In short, the period from 1909 to 1924 witnessed continued contestation over ownership of the vacant lands between St. Clair Street and the new Lake Shore Drive extension. Although in hindsight none of the protests or lawsuits posed a particularly serious threat to the interests of the riparian owners, this may not have been so clear at the time. Moreover, it is striking that, once again, the claims of the rival contestants were not resolved on the merits, with an affirmation that the riparian owners had title to the land. Instead, the rival private claims were disposed of on collateral grounds—such as Ma Streeter's invalid marriage and the Potawatomi's abandonment of any claim to the land.

The emergence of new assertions of *public* rights in the reclaimed land magnified the uncertainty. Legally speaking, the most notable call for public ownership and control came from a joint committee appointed by the state legislature to ascertain the extent of the state's rights in submerged and shore lands—and to determine how far those rights had been "usurped by private individuals, corporations, and companies." Called the Submerged and Shore Lands Legislative Investigating Committee, it was known informally as the Chiperfield Committee or Commission, after its chairman, Burnett M. Chiperfield, then a member of the Illinois House. The committee produced a three-volume report in 1911 calling for a robust assertion of public rights in order to end "piratical encroachments for private gain." In the best spirit of the Progressive Era, the committee argued that government ownership of submerged and reclaimed shore lands should be vigorously maintained, a new commission created to monitor public rights in submerged lands, and the attorney general charged to roll back existing private encroachments. The objective was not to preserve submerged lands in their natural state, as would become the animating focus of the public trust doctrine later in the century (see chapter 8). Rather, it was to ensure the use of land for "commercial uses," such as the construction of an outer harbor for Chicago and the development of "waste lands" adjacent to the shore.[70]

Turning to the Lake Shore Drive extension, the Chiperfield Committee condemned the project as having no evident purpose other than "to acquire title in behalf of special interests." It urged that the attorney general commence new litigation to determine anew "whether or not [this] property worth millions of dollars should be given to private property owners to further augment and swell their holdings." The committee thought it self-evident "that such lands are irrevocably dedicated for public purposes." These official sentiments were undoubtedly noted by the riparian owners and their legal advisers, and could only instill further caution in them about proceeding with development.[71]

More specific plans were also afoot to use the reclaimed land for public purposes. With the publication of the influential *Plan of Chicago* in 1909, the notion of building a new outer harbor east of Grant Park and downtown lost its allure. Instead it now seemed to many that the logical place to put the outer harbor was on the other side of the river's mouth: that is, in Streeterville. Indeed, Burnham and Bennett's plan featured two gigantic piers jutting into the lake, one on each side of the downtown lakefront. The northern pier was depicted at

Chicago Avenue—squarely in the middle of Streeterville. Other sketches in the plan showed multiple docks jutting off the northern pier to accommodate freight steamers. At least implicitly, the plan contemplated that the area around the Lake Shore Drive extension would develop as a giant maritime port.[72]

This was scarcely the only plan to convert the area into a new outer harbor. The Pugh Terminal Company proposed a plan in 1908 to build three piers north of the Chicago River. The Chicago sanitary district released a plan in 1910 for six piers to be built in essentially the same area, each with a warehouse designed to accommodate four million tons of freight annually. The next year, perhaps thinking those somehow to be little plans, Mayor Carter H. Harrison Jr. proposed a plan calling for twenty-five miles of docks and recreation piers in the area from Chicago Avenue south to 29th Street. Eventually, in 1912, the city council approved a plan to begin by building two piers, one three thousand feet long for passengers and package freights and the other somewhat shorter. This evolved into the plan for Municipal Pier No. 2 (now Navy Pier), construction of which started in 1914 at the foot of Grand Avenue. The other pier never came to fruition.[73]

The 1896 *Kirk* decision, far from suppressing dreams about grand public plans for the lakefront in this area, could be read as encouraging them. The opinion reaffirmed the overriding importance of navigation on the lake and stated that the 1889 legislation did not relinquish the legislature's governmental powers over the lake "or place them beyond the power of future legislation." A public claim on the development of the lakefront in this area as a new harbor thus remained a distinct possibility well into the first decades of the twentieth century. This, too, magnified the uncertainty associated with the land, and undoubtedly caused those who might otherwise have initiated commercial development to hesitate.[74]

In hindsight, the *Plan of Chicago*, the investigations such as the Chiperfield Committee report condemning the Lake Shore Drive extension, and the construction of Navy Pier marked an important turning point in public deliberation about the lakefront. The lakefront was increasingly regarded as a resource belonging to all the people, not something to be exploited for private gain. Although it was too late to reverse the privatization of Streeterville, this changed perspective added momentum to the efforts of the park districts, already underway in Grant Park, to preserve the lakefront as parkland open to the public.

Overcoming a Flawed Title

A deeper reason for the slow and uneven development of Streeterville is that the title claims of the riparian owners were seriously flawed—and they were flawed in a way that the 1889 legislation and the *Kirk* decision did not cure.

Oversimplifying slightly, one can picture the question of title to the Streeterville land as involving three layers (or increments) of new solid land formed on submerged land to the east of Kinzie's Addition, as shown in figure 4.12, which reflects our reconstruction. The first layer consisted of ordinary accretion, immediately east of the 1821 shoreline, formed by the action of the counterclockwise current in Lake Michigan over a period of three decades or so, especially after the straightening of the river in the mid-1830s. This land rightly belonged to the riparian owners under settled rules of title by accretion. The second layer, east of the 1853 shoreline, consisted primarily of artificial fill added outside the original area of accretion in any number of ways: the depositing of refuse in the lake after the fire of 1871, the use of the area as a general dump for refuse, or the efforts of Streeter and his followers. These fills were not authorized, and in any event could not be claimed as accretions. Once it became clear that the state owned the submerged land, this layer of fill presumably belonged to the state.

The third layer (including most of the area east of the 1883 shoreline in figure 4.12) consisted of the ninety-three acres of new submerged land transferred to the original riparian owners and (with respect to the drive itself) to the Lincoln Park Commission. The Illinois Supreme Court had blessed this transfer of submerged land in the *Kirk* decision. Yet there remained the nettlesome final sentence, saying that the right of the riparian owners to "fill up portions of the lake" was not being adjudicated in the case. Did this refer to artificial filling that occurred before the Lake Shore Drive extension—that is, to filling primarily in layer two? Or did it refer to the filling authorized in layer three—in other words, was the court upholding the transfer of submerged land to the riparian owners but not their filling it? Or was the sentence a reference to neither layer but rather a more general point about the limits of the court's decision? In short, the third layer, like the first, most likely belonged to the riparian owners, but even this was not entirely clear.

We can be sure that more than one lawyer for the Chicago Title & Trust Company puzzled over the state of title created by this three-layered cake. What did it mean if title to layers one and three was probably good but to layer two likely bad? Would the soundness of the surrounding layers rescue the middle? Or did the lack of good title to the middle infect and invalidate the outer? In retrospect, the riparian owners had erred in not securing language in the 1889 legislation ratifying their title to *all* landfills between the original shoreline of 1821 and the new Lake Shore Drive extension. In 1889, it might have been possible to insert language in the legislation doing just that. But even as early as just a few years later, the public outcry over the Lake Shore Drive "steal" meant that a legislative fix was out of the question.

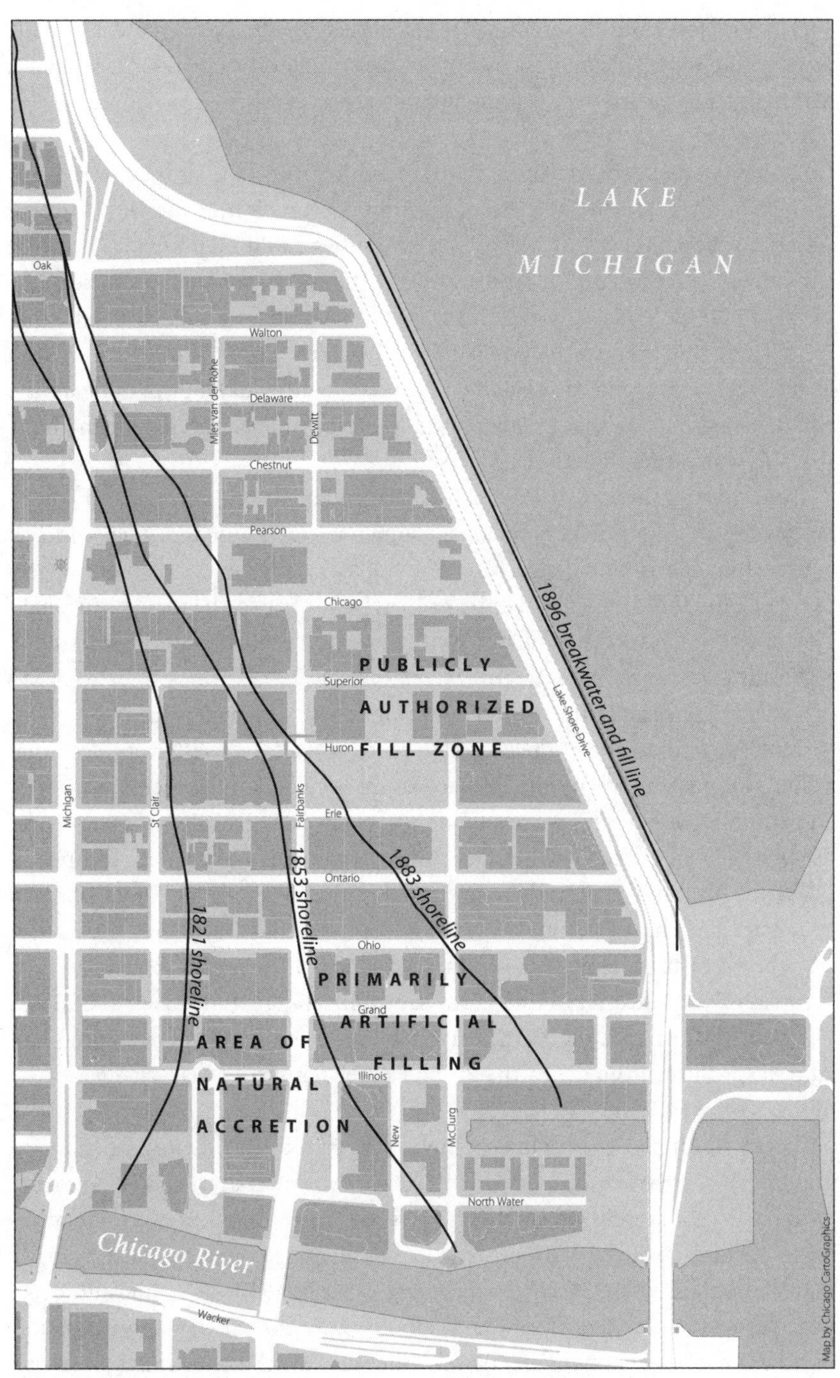

FIGURE 4.12. Depiction of Streeterville's "Three Layers."

The straightforward solution would have been for the riparian owners to file an action to quiet title and ask a court to declare that they owned Streeterville. Surely this was considered. But the judgment was evidently reached that it was too risky.[75]

So how were the riparian owners to secure the fruits of their legal maneuvering? The only answer was to establish visible occupation of the land through significant development. If individuals or entities could be persuaded to build substantial structures on the land, especially structures occupied by institutions engaged in respectable activities, this would soon establish a collective sense that the riparian owners held title to the filled land. After a time, if someone tried to challenge the occupants' title based on the unextinguished claims of the state, the riparian owners could claim estoppel, undue delay, or abandonment—and hope that this would prevail with the courts.[76]

This strategy presented a difficult collective-action problem, as each riparian owner would rationally prefer that someone else be the first mover to risk constructing a substantial structure. The full story of how the riparian owners overcame the problem will never be known. Nevertheless, the manner in which Northwestern University came to acquire a significant portion of the land in the 1920s provides a window into how Streeterville eventually came to be regarded as solid land of secure title, no different from other land in Chicago.

In the second decade of the twentieth century, the Northwestern professional schools located in the city of Chicago—in particular, law, medicine, dentistry, and commerce—all were interested in new quarters. Each of the schools preferred to stay in Chicago rather than move to the university's main campus in Evanston. Although they initially sought a location west of Pine Street (soon to be renamed Michigan Avenue), Nathan William MacChesney joined the university's board of trustees in 1913 and soon persuaded the various players to turn their attention to Streeterville. Options to acquire land in the area were obtained, but expired during World War I. After the war, new options were secured and land was acquired from the Fairbank and Farwell families and later from the heir of the Newberry family.[77]

The deeds of conveyance hint at the uncertain state of title to this land. The grantors of the Farwell property in 1920 gave the university a special-warranty deed—that is, a deed in which the grantors warranted that they had done nothing to impair title during their ownership but did not guarantee against preexisting defects in title. The Newberry property came in 1927 via a quitclaim deed, which provided no warranty of title at all. Typically, special-warranty deeds and quitclaim deeds signal potential flaws in the title. As for the Fairbank property, whose title Northwestern took via a "trustees' deed" in 1920, Northwestern was aware of "certain objections to the title to a small portion of the property" and regarded it as "unwise" to obtain that portion "at the present time." Citing "litigation pertaining to the titles in this neighborhood," the university also decided to seek title insurance for the Farwell and Fairbank properties—policies whose expense the grantors helped underwrite and that Chicago Title & Trust provided at a special discount.[78]

There is also an interesting clue as to how at least some of the money to pay for the 1920 purchases was raised. MacChesney served on the board of directors of an organization called the North Central Business District Association, consisting mostly of real estate investors and businesses having interests in the area north of the Chicago River. The association's board included, in addition to MacChesney, representatives of the Palmer, Ogden, McCormick, Farwell, Fairbank, McClurg, and Pelouze estates and families. The North Central Association, as it was also known, actively solicited its members to contribute to Northwestern to provide funds for the purchase of the Streeterville property. A "bulletin" issued to "members" and "friends" stated bluntly that the proposed project "is of particularly great commercial value to the surrounding neighborhood." Specifically, "[i]t will encourage to the South of Chicago Avenue, a high type of business development which will be of tremendous value to the surrounding real estate; it will also protect the wonderful residential section to the North from business encroachment."[79]

MacChesney was, to put the best face on it, working to advance the interests of both sides of the deal. His friends and clients among the riparian owners wanted a development with prestige to enhance the reputation of Streeterville and legitimize it as a location for future projects. Meanwhile, Northwestern needed a site for a new campus and was short of cash to pay for it. There is no evidence that university trustees had any explicit understanding that the owners would donate part of the funds that the university required to acquire the land. But it seems likely that this is what happened.

Once the Farwell land was acquired in 1920, further efforts commenced to raise the money for construction. At the encouragement of its dean, John Henry Wigmore, who had been a longtime leader in the Chicago campus effort, Levy Mayer's widow and Judge Elbert H. Gary (of judiciary fame, the song attests, but of US Steel wealth) provided support for a new law school, on which the university broke ground in 1925. Elizabeth Ward, widow of Montgomery Ward (of chapter 3 fame), made a major gift that made possible the construction of the medical school building at the same time. The collection of buildings included Wieboldt Hall, bearing the name of another Chicago retailer, for the business school.[80]

FIGURE 4.13. Northwestern University's Chicago campus in Streeterville, sometime after 1926, with view south/southwest toward buildings on Chicago Avenue and the American Furniture Mart (with tower) in the background on the left. Courtesy of McCormick Library of Special Collections and Northwestern University Archives.

Development of Streeterville began to accelerate after Northwestern's Gothic-revival Chicago campus went up. Northwestern's commitment was not the only cause. The opening of the Michigan Avenue bridge over the Chicago River in 1920 and the widening of the formerly named Pine Street made the area more accessible. And the opening of the posh Drake Hotel the same year lent considerable cachet to the northern end of the neighborhood. Still, the central area of Streeterville remained largely vacant of buildings until Northwestern made its move. After 1926, commercial construction activity proceeded at a more rapid pace. Further development would be disrupted by the Great Depression and World War II—but never again by doubts about the validity of the legal title to the land.[81]

Whether by chance or design, Streeterville was eventually transformed from submerged land into a neighborhood of Chicago regarded as conventional (if especially valuable) real estate. The transformation, which started in the 1830s and was fully completed only a century later, was marked by extraordinary competition over who would garner the prize of new solid land.

The competition was made possible in significant part by legal uncertainty over the status of the new land formed where water once stood. The only solution was for one of the contesting groups to seize control of the asset, engage in substantial development, and hang on. Filled land, at least when it has been occupied in a visible way, is a resource susceptible of stable control and use. Vacant land reclaimed from water without clear legislative authority is not.

It is also noteworthy that Streeterville, which consists predominantly of artificial landfill, is overwhelmingly private property. The public trust doctrine, as interpreted in the *Kirk* case, posed no barrier to legislatively authorized transfers of submerged land to private owners in this area. The court deferred to the legislature as trustee with respect to the proper disposition of this resource. Grant Park, to the south, was saved for public use by the public dedication doctrine, not the public trust doctrine. But given the repudiation of the 1896 Land Office survey, Streeterville has no official survey or plat. Thus, there is no formal designation of public space to which the public dedication doctrine might attach. By the time property rights in Streeterville were sufficiently settled to permit development, institutions of local government such as the park district were robust enough

FIGURE 4.14. Streeterville, as viewed to the southwest, in the foreground, with Lake Shore Drive to the east and north and Oak Street Beach to the right, ca. 2014. Iwan Baan, photographer.

to protect public rights along the lakeshore, without the aid of private rights such as dedication. But by then, the path toward private rights in the interior of the area was far too entrenched to turn back. Streeterville was destined to be an area of glittering high-rises along the lakefront, not a public park.

The history of Streeterville was nevertheless instrumental in changing public attitudes about what to do with remaining areas of the lakefront north and south of the city center. The outcry over the role of the Lincoln Park Commission in enriching the St. Clair Street property owners meant that future landfilling by the park districts would be legislatively restricted to creating parks and pleasure drives (see chapters 6 and 7). Meanwhile, major engineering projects designed to protect the city water supply, considered in the next chapter, had the effect of making the lakefront a much more attractive venue for family outings and recreation. This, too, would have a powerful effect on public attitudes about the proper use of the lakefront.

5

REVERSING THE CHICAGO RIVER

It is time to take a closer look at the Chicago River and its effect on the lakefront. We have seen that the efforts of the army engineers in the 1830s to straighten the mouth of the river produced erosion of the lakefront to the south and accretion to the north, with major consequences in both areas. Our story also has considered how, as the nineteenth century unfolded, congestion in the river stimulated plans, by the Illinois Central Railroad and others, to construct a new outer harbor on the lakefront. In this chapter, we will see how efforts to combat pollution in the river had the effect of cleaning up the water along the lakefront. The long-term effect was profound. The lakefront ceased to be seen as a conduit for commerce—or as a repository for garbage and waste—and came to be regarded as an environmental and recreational amenity.

The Chicago River as a Commons

Chicago owes its location to the Chicago River, whose virtues included being perceived as a logical place to forge a link between Lake Michigan and the Mississippi River. The watershed divide between the Great Lakes and the Mississippi River basins lies very close to the Chicago lakefront, and the elevation marking the divide is scarcely above the level of the lake. The Native Americans who lived in the area developed a portage from the south branch of the river around a marsh, sometimes called Mud Lake, to reach the Des Plaines River, which flows into the Illinois River, which in turn flows into the Mississippi. The French explorers Louis Jolliet and Jacques Marquette wrote enthusiastically about the potential of the site for a canal connecting the Great Lakes to the Gulf of Mexico. Many of the fur traders who followed in their wake offered similar assessments.[1]

When Illinois became a state in 1818, Chicago was little more than Fort Dearborn and a trading post. The promoters of Illinois's statehood nevertheless successfully persuaded Congress to move the state's northern boundary from its originally envisioned location—directly west of Indiana and too far south to touch Lake Michigan—to a point some sixty miles farther north. The objective was to assure that the new state could capitalize on a potential canal linking the lake and the Mississippi basin. It would take nearly two decades of political wrangling in the federal and state legislatures before the necessary rights were obtained for what was eventually called the Illinois and Michigan (I&M) Canal. In fact, it was unclear until the 1835–36 state legislative session that the Chicago River, as opposed to the Calumet River, would be the jumping-off point for the canal. The winning argument for the Chicago River was that the Calumet was too close to Indiana, and thus while Illinois would have to bear the costs of constructing the canal, Indiana would capture much of the benefit. On this narrow point of interstate rivalry, the location of the future city of Chicago was determined.[2]

Chronic funding problems meant that progress in completing the I&M Canal was interminably slow. It also meant that the canal commissioners were forced to abandon the desired "deep-cut" plan in favor of a cheaper, "shallow-cut" plan. Consequently, the finished canal could accommodate only flat-bottom barges. The official opening took place in 1848. By that time the railroad boom had begun, and Chicago was on the verge of becoming the critical rail hub for the central United States. The canal would never be much of a financial success. It was responsible for the location of Chicago, but it played only a secondary role in the city's growth and development.[3]

Much more important to the future of Chicago was the Erie Canal, completed in 1825. This created a continuous water highway all the way from New York City, up the Hudson River to Albany, then across the canal to reach Buffalo on the eastern edge of Lake Erie, and through the Great Lakes. Chicago became the western terminus of this water route. Grains and livestock were transported to Chicago, mostly by rail, from Illinois and nearby areas north and west; grains, flour, and processed meats were then shipped by water from Chicago to the East Coast. In the other direction, clothing, manufactured goods, and immigrants came to

Chicago by water from the East Coast, along with timber from the upper Great Lakes, all then transported by rail throughout the Great Plains.[4]

The harbor in which this water-and-rail interchange took place was the Chicago River. From the late 1840s through the beginning of the twentieth century, Chicago experienced phenomenal growth, more than tripling and then doubling each decade for almost the entire period. Traffic in the city's river grew apace. Inevitably, given its short length and narrow width, the Chicago River became incredibly congested. Property law abetted the development and the congestion. As detailed in chapter 6, anyone with land abutting the river could "wharf out" into the river so long as this did not interfere with public navigation. Soon it seemed that nearly everyone had built a wharf, dock, or pier. There were many disputes over whether such structures interfered with the ability of boats to maneuver around existing docks, but the law's primary answer was a common-law nuisance action. This was costly to pursue and uncertain in result.[5]

The congestion on the water was only the beginning of the frustration associated with the Chicago River. The river and its branches formed a *T*, with the central business district located south of the main stem and east of the south branch. As business grew in this area, later largely to be called "the Loop," the number of persons who worked in this downtown district and lived or had business on the other side of the river also multiplied. They had to cross the river. Soon, bridges were built over many of the major arterial streets leading north and west from the city center (see figure 5.1). Most of these were "swing" or "pivot" bridges, which could be rotated on their centers, thus opening ninety degrees to allow vessels to pass. The bridge tenders were often perceived as being more solicitous of river vessels than of wagons and pedestrians waiting to cross. By 1858, an early historian wrote, "all the pugnacity of the city was divided in the fierce warfare which raged between river navigators and those persons who were obliged to use the thoroughfares."[6]

The underlying condition that gave rise to the overcrowding of the river was its status as a resource open to all. No one had the right to exclude anyone else from using the river. The principle of openness was enshrined in the Constitution: the Supreme Court had held that the commerce clause prohibited impediments to navigation unless authorized by Congress. The principle was also reflected in the public trust doctrine, as developed in Justice Stephen Field's opinion in the *Lake Front Case* (see chapter 2). Both the understanding of the commerce clause and the public trust doctrine were grounded in the perception that the general public has an inalienable right to use navigable waters for travel, commerce, and fishing. This gave rise to what a later generation of commentators would call the tragedy

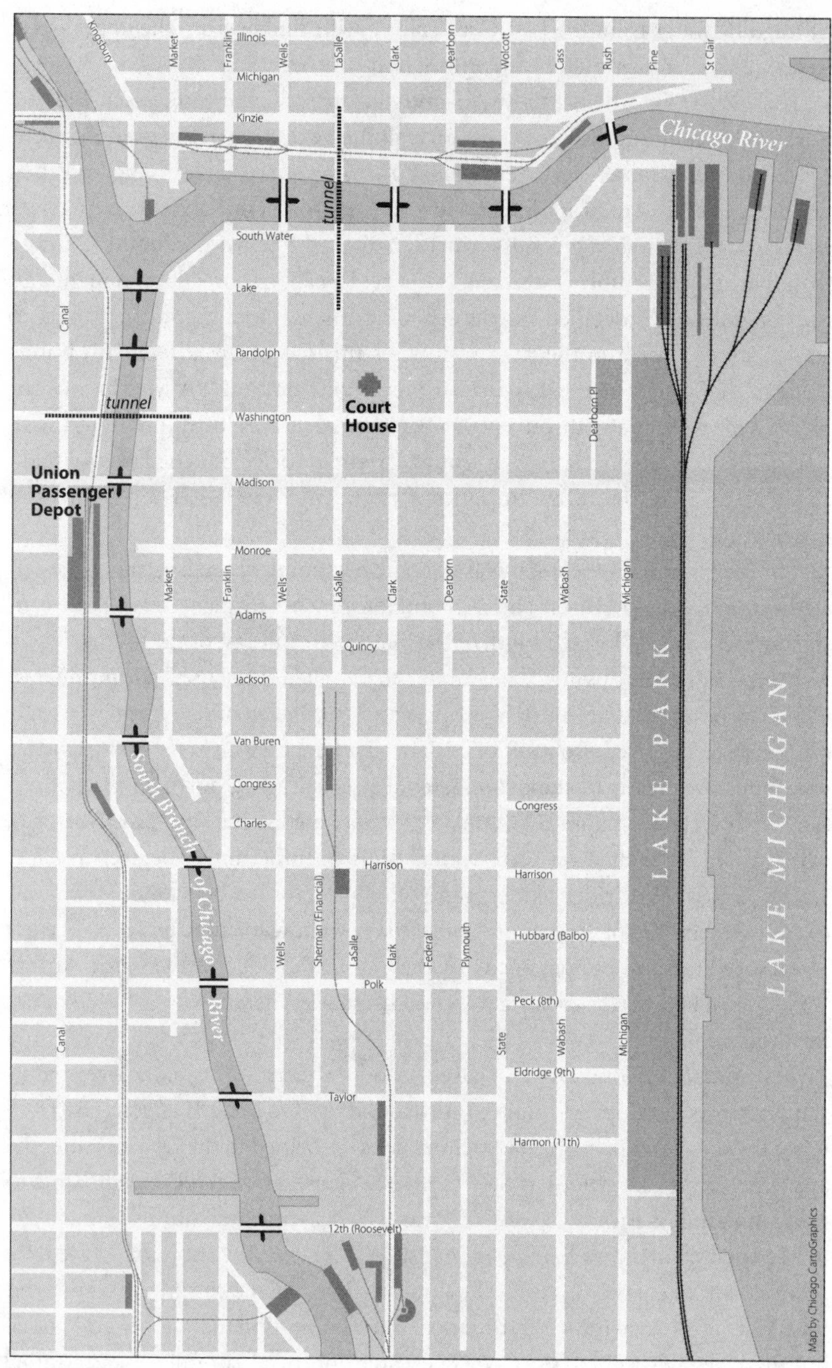

FIGURE 5.1. Chicago River bridges and tunnels, ca. 1872.

of the commons. Anyone extracting resources from the commons—whether in the form of navigation or wharfage services—realized the full benefit of that consumption. By contrast, the *cost* imposed by each person's use was distributed among all who wished to make similar use of the water. The result was a classic prisoner's dilemma: each person selfishly pursued an individual interest, with the result that everyone was worse off than would have been the case if some collective means of mutual restraint could have been devised.[7]

The city was not entirely inert in the face of rising frustration over the congestion of the Chicago River. In 1848, the city and the canal commissioners commenced to construct a turning basin at the confluence of the main stem with the north and south branches. Tunnels were opened under the south branch in 1869 (at Washington Street) and the main stem in 1871 (at LaSalle Street), allowing carriages and pedestrians to pass under the river without encountering bridge delays. The city also attempted to regulate the construction of piers and docks, most notably by action in the late 1840s related to leases of public land.[8]

The most persistently voiced solution to the river congestion was to construct an outer harbor in Lake Michigan. Although Lake Michigan also is an open-access commons, it is so enormous that congestion (at least away from the shore) is unthinkable. But political and legal squabbling consistently foiled attempts to build a harbor in the lake, as we have seen.

The ultimate solution to the congested state of the Chicago River came from evolution in the commercial shipping industry. When the modern iron and steel industry began to emerge in the 1880s, a new generation of lake freighters was built to haul raw materials to the large blast furnaces and rolling mills south of Chicago's downtown and in northern Indiana. The new vessels had drafts too deep for the Chicago River, especially with passenger tunnels located a mere sixteen feet below the surface. Consequently, the Calumet River, which could be dredged to the required depth, became the harbor of choice for transportation of bulk materials to Chicago. Freighters carrying grain, salt, and other bulk commodities soon joined those hauling iron ore and coal in docking in the Calumet Harbor or in northern Indiana. The Chicago River continued to function as a harbor for lighter commodities that could be transported by smaller vessels. But the railroads (and later interstate trucking) would gradually capture most of this business.[9]

Although no one was aware of it at the time, the end of the nineteenth century marked the peak of landings of commercial ships in the Chicago River. Whereas the Chicago River was the port for eleven million tons of cargo in 1889, part of an era in which it was reportedly the fourth-busiest harbor in the world (after New York, London, and Hamburg), by 1907 the number had fallen by more than half. The Chicago River had entered a long decline as a commercial port relative to the Calumet River. Today, the Chicago River is used almost exclusively by recreational and excursion vessels.[10]

The River as Sewer

The open-access status of the Chicago River had an even more irksome consequence: the river became the repository of all sorts of refuse, industrial byproducts, and human and animal waste. No one argued that there was an inalienable public right to dump garbage and sewage in the river, along the lines of the public right of navigation. The commerce clause and the public trust doctrine did not protect the right to pollute navigable waters. It was simply that everyone dumped waste in the river, or dumped it in such a way that it would end up in the river, and it was taken for granted that this was one of the functions of a navigable body of water. This was not crazy. Over time, garbage and sewage deposited in a body of water will largely decompose and turn into sediment due to the action of bacteria and dissolved oxygen in the water. The problem is that if too many people dump too much waste into a waterway such as the turbid Chicago River, the capacity of the river to absorb the waste becomes exhausted, and the river effectively becomes a rancid sewer. This is another illustration of the tragedy of the commons: each individual captures the benefits of the river as a depository of waste, while the costs are spread to everyone else in the community, with the result that everyone suffers.[11]

By the 1840s, there was ample evidence that the Chicago River was well on its way to becoming seriously polluted. The city relied on a primitive system of roadside ditches and open sewers running beneath plank streets. These receptacles often became clogged, "leaving standing pools of an indescribable liquid . . . to salute the noses of passers-by," according to one 1850 account. When it rained, the waste eventually washed into the river. Foul odors were one thing; rampant disease was another, and in the early 1850s, Chicago was hit by a series of severe cholera epidemics, with one year said to have seen more than 5 percent of the city's population killed. The germ theory of communicable disease had not yet been developed; instead, disease was commonly attributed to miasma or "death fogs" that emanated from wastewater, river pollution, or sewage.[12]

Fear of disease and death can be powerfully motivating—enough to overcome the commons tragedy that characterizes a pollution problem such as the one then afflicting Chicago. In 1855, the state legislature required the creation of a Board of Sewerage Commissioners, which promptly hired Ellis S. Chesbrough, of Boston, to serve as its chief engineer. Chesbrough developed a plan for what became the first comprehensive sewerage system in a US city.[13]

To improve the flow of sewage, Chesbrough's plan required raising the grade of Chicago's streets. A system of enclosed brick sewers would run down the center of the streets, covered by fill from the river. The new sewer system would be elevated at a "sufficient angle" to "drain by gravity into the river." And the dredging of the river would enhance its capacity to receive sewage. The plan was implemented at what was then regarded as a great cost. In 1864, the project was responsible for $2 million of Chicago's $3.5 million public debt. But it significantly reduced the stench in the streets.[14]

Chesbrough's public sewer system led to one of the more remarkable engineering events in Chicago history. With the raising of the street level, existing structures had to be raised as much as a full story, unless a new entryway was cut into what had previously been the second story. A young George Pullman, the future manufacturer of rail passenger cars, helped develop a jackscrew system that allowed brick buildings to be gradually raised without damaging the structure. The Tremont House hotel was raised in this fashion, reportedly while patrons continued to go about their business as if nothing were happening.[15]

The Chicago Waterworks

In the city's early days, some Chicagoans got their water from private wells, others from horse-drawn carts with barrels containing water scooped from the lake. Attention soon focused on the lake as a more systematic source of drinking water. In 1842, a private water company began operating on a limited scale, pumping water from an intake in the lake and distributing it through wooden pipes to customers. A public water company was later established and began supplying water in 1854. The public company built an intake into the lake at Chicago Avenue, although the rough waters prevented construction as far out as initially planned. This intake fed into three reservoirs, one for each division of the city, where the water was distributed by pipe to individual businesses and homes.[16]

Chesbrough's sewer system did not eliminate waste and filth but simply directed them more effectively into the river. And the river continued to flow, however sluggishly, into the lake—the source of the city's drinking water. So it soon became clear that Chesbrough's sewer system posed a threat to the waterworks system. Especially during the spring snowmelt and after heavy rainstorms, the volume of water in the river would surge, and untreated waste and sewage would flow out into the lake, contaminating the water supply.[17]

After considering a number of options, Chesbrough proposed that a new water intake be constructed two miles east into the lake, to be connected by a tunnel to a new city pumping station. The city agreed, and Chesbrough proceeded to supervise another project that was considered one of the engineering marvels of the time. It included towing an enormous pentagonal structure, called a "crib," into the lake, weighing it down with stone, and setting it on the bottom of the lake, as the site of the intake. Tunnels connecting the shore and the crib, dug in arduous conditions, met on November 30, 1866.[18]

To receive and distribute the water, the project also entailed the construction of a new pumping station and water tower on opposite sides of Pine Street (now Michigan Avenue) near Chicago Avenue. Encased in cream-colored stone and designed in a "castellated Gothic" style, these structures survived the Chicago fire and stand today as iconic landmarks for the city.[19]

Upon opening in 1867, Chesbrough's waterworks was considered a great success. The city's phenomenal growth continued to outpace all predictions, however, and Chicago officials soon realized that a second tunnel was needed. Eventually, nine water-intake cribs would be built in the lake, two of which are still in use. Today, when it is too cold for recreational boating, the cribs are often the only manmade features visible on the vast and empty expanse of water lying east of the lakefront.[20]

The location of water intakes two or more miles offshore was at best only a temporary solution to the threat posed by the tainted Chicago River. As population and industry grew, the quantity of raw sewage discharged through the sewer system grew apace. Perhaps most notoriously, the creation of the Union Stockyards south of 39th Street in 1865 meant that a highly concentrated stream of offal and animal blood was discharged into a stem of the south branch of the river; it came to be known as "Bubbly Creek" because the mass of decomposing organic matter caused bubbles to rise to the surface. Like every Chicago sewer, Bubbly Creek flowed into the river. And because the river flowed into the lake, the more concentrated the pollution in the river became, the more the lake became contaminated.[21]

Chesbrough had long been aware of the contamination problem and proposed a solution. This was to expand the I&M Canal to its original "deep-cut" plan. Chesbrough calculated that if the carrying capacity of the canal were greatly expanded, the water in the Chicago River would flow into the canal instead of Lake Michigan. In effect, the current would be reversed, flowing away from, rather than into, the lake. The plan was adopted, and a $3 million bond issue was approved to pay for it. By 1871, the expansion of the canal was completed. Large pumps were installed on the South Side, at Bridgeport, to further encourage the movement of the water into the canal. Chesbrough was hailed as a genius.[22]

The plan worked—for one year. Then, as Donald Miller has summarized, the river's current "slowed down and eventually stopped, and it became its old stagnant, pestilential self." The causes included an increased volume of water in

FIGURE 5.2. First water crib in Lake Michigan, ca. 1870. Chicago History Museum, ICHi-020501.

FIGURE 5.3. Construction under Lake Michigan. *The Great Chicago Lake Tunnel* (Chicago: Jack Wing, 1867), frontispiece. Chicago Public Library, Special Collections.

the Des Plaines River, coming from farmers draining their wetlands. They also included the Ogden-Wentworth Ditch, an excavation about twelve miles west of the city. Because its effects included carrying overflow from the Des Plaines River into the Chicago River, the ditch counteracted the Bridgeport diversion. It is indicative of the times that no regulatory body had authority to prevent the construction of such a private "canal" working at cross-purposes with the public canal. In any event, the named promoters of the ditch were William B. Ogden and "Long John" Wentworth, two former mayors and among the most powerful figures in Chicago. Clout mattered.[23]

It was only a matter of time before the contamination of the river became an unacceptable threat to the water supply in the lake. Another cholera epidemic struck the city in 1873, followed by recurring outbreaks of smallpox and dysentery. In 1879, heavy rains caused the river to discharge filthy water into the lake for thirty consecutive days. In 1881, the state legislature directed the city, if other solutions did not work, to pump water out of Lake Michigan, through the south branch of the river, into the I&M Canal. By 1883, pumps had been installed to add one thousand cubic feet of water per second to the canal. This, along with a number of dry seasons, reduced the frequency of pollutant discharges into the lake and the water intakes.[24]

Then, in August 1885, the city was struck by a storm that dumped more than five and a half inches of rain in one day. Fear that the resulting flood would send polluted river water into the lake and then into the cribs set off widespread alarm. Fortunately, a change in the weather—in the form of a strong wind from the northeast that drove the contaminated water away from the cribs—saved the day. For some time, Chicago residents and newspapers had been clamoring for something to be done about the condition of the river. The close call associated with the summer storm caused collective anxiety about a significant epidemic of waterborne diseases such as cholera and typhoid fever to rise to a new and higher level.[25]

The Sanitary and Ship Canal

The flood of 1885 finally spurred the city to take action. A citizens' committee recommended consideration of a multijurisdictional sanitary district to remedy the lake contamination problem. Its report suggested that digging a new trench deep enough and wide enough to draw the entire volume of the Chicago River away from the lake and into the Mississippi River basin might be the best solution. The report acknowledged that "the sewage must be diluted to that point which will speedily produce complete oxidation, or the growing populations along the [Illinois] river will not permanently tolerate so insufferable a nuisance," but it offered no advice on how this might occur. Both the city and state undertook formally to study the problem. In the interim, Chicago sought to broaden support for the project by clarifying that the new trench, unlike the I&M Canal, would be large enough to accommodate Mississippi River–style riverboats. This revived dreams of a "Great-Lakes-to-the-Gulf Waterway" and drew support from the business community throughout the state, as well as from farmers eager for alternatives to rail transportation. It also explains why the new government entity would be called the "Sanitary and Ship Canal."[26]

In 1889, the Illinois General Assembly authorized the creation of a new governmental entity, a "sanitary district," today known as the Metropolitan Water Reclamation District of Greater Chicago. This new body would be notable in two respects. First, its jurisdiction extended beyond the city of Chicago to include a number of suburban communities affected by contamination of the river and the water supply. Indeed, as amended in later years, it came to encompass virtually all of Cook County. Thus, the legislation recognized that the problem was regional and required an authority that could act outside the limits of existing political boundaries.[27]

Second, any sanitary district created pursuant to the statute would have independent authority to tax and to borrow funds for a massive project. At that time, the state constitution limited municipalities to borrowing 5 percent of the total assessed taxable property within their corporate limits, and Chicago and other cities in the region had exhausted their borrowing capacity. The sanitary district would be subject to the same 5 percent limit but of course had no preexisting debt. The district also had a very large base of assessed property, given its multijurisdictional reach. In view of the magnitude of the proposed canal project, such new tax revenues were imperative.[28]

As required by the enabling act, the proposal to create the sanitary district was put to a referendum of voters in affected areas, where property would be subject to the new taxes. In November 1889, it passed by a staggering margin of 70,958 to 242. Almost no one wanted to die of cholera or typhoid fever.[29]

The sanitary district was governed by nine directly elected trustees. It took two years to get started on construction. Problems included finding the right supervising engineer (it could not be Ellis Chesbrough, who had died in 1886) and determining the route of the new channel and its capacity. The final design specified a channel starting just below the confluence of Bubbly Creek and the south branch of the Chicago River, proceeding parallel to and on the northerly side of the Illinois and Michigan Canal, and running about twenty-eight miles southwest to Lockport. It would be large enough to convey ten thousand cubic feet of water per second—the maximum measured flood flow of the Chicago River—at a velocity less than two miles per hour. Overall, the channel bottom would have a slight downward slope, dropping some 5.7 feet from beginning to end.[30]

An official groundbreaking—"shovel day"—occurred, with great fanfare, on September 3, 1892, in the town of Lemont, southwest of Chicago. The herculean project would take more than seven years to finish. Fifty steam shovels were used, some weighing as much as seventy-two tons, as well as a massive grading machine, pulled by a team of twelve to sixteen horses. Other custom-designed machinery included a conveyor with a hopper able to separate dredged material such as clay and rock, special dredges for excavating wet areas, and machines to chisel the sides of the channel in rock sections. Much of the technology developed in digging the Chicago Sanitary and Ship Canal was later adapted to construct the Panama Canal.[31]

More than $21 million was spent on excavation, $3 million on acquiring the right of way, and $4 million on building railroad and highway bridges over the canal. With interest on the bonds issued to acquire the funds, the total price tag came to roughly $34 million.[32]

The district's trustees saw no need to obtain the federal government's permission before beginning. This was apparently predicated on the belief that the new channel was simply an updated and bigger version of the I&M Canal. The trustees knew from the start, however, that it would also be necessary to enlarge the Chicago River if the high volume of water passing from the lake to the new

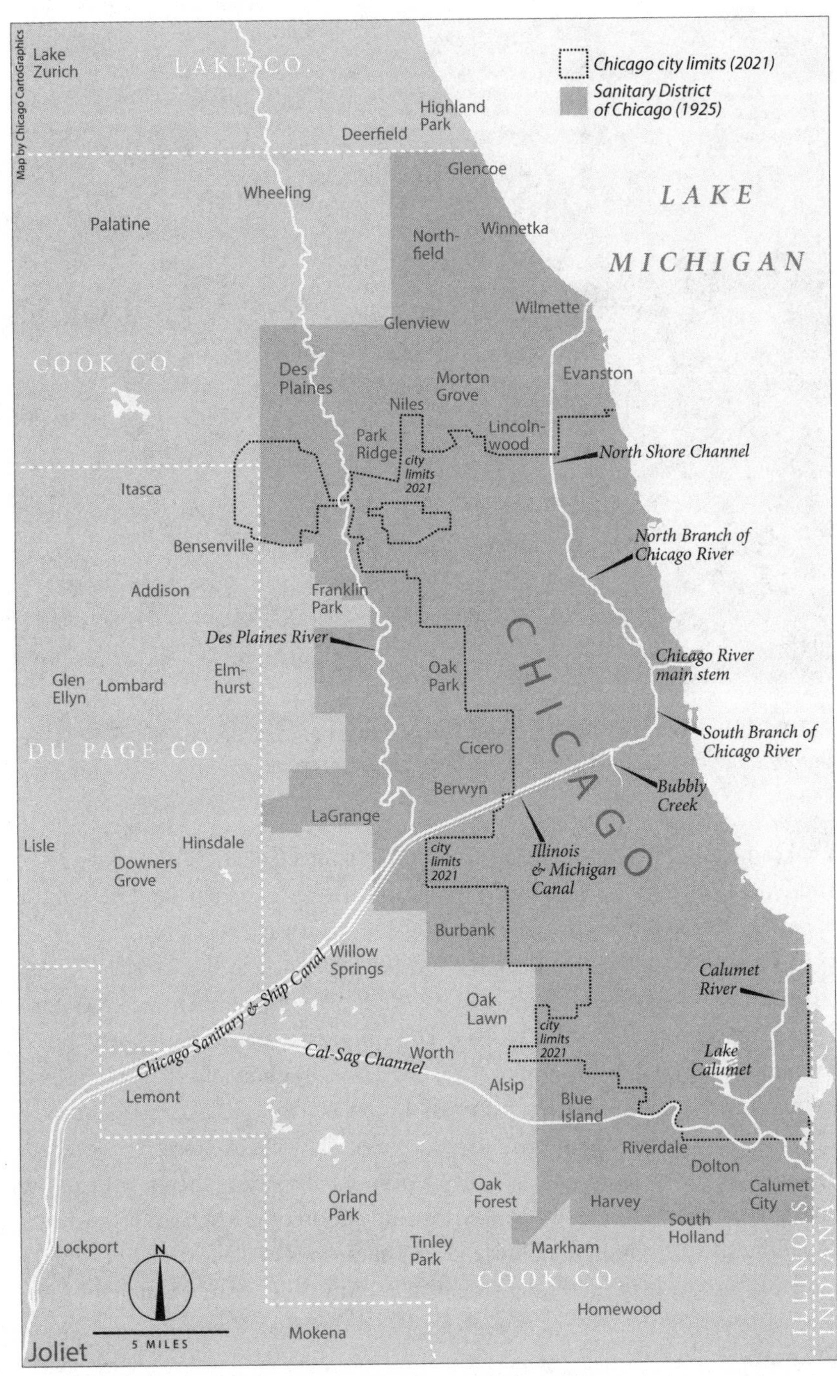

FIGURE 5.4. Map showing the Chicago River, Chicago Sanitary and Ship Canal, and Des Plaines River.

FIGURE 5.5. Chicago Sanitary and Ship Canal construction, ca. 1895. Chicago History Museum, ICHi-040068; J. W. Taylor, photographer.

canal came to create such a strong current that it affected navigation in the river. And federal legislation, starting in 1890, explicitly required a federal permit for any modification of the channel of a navigable waterway.[33]

In the middle of the decade, attention finally turned to the Chicago River's expansion. A commission appointed by the federal government in 1895 confirmed the need to improve the river. The commission also predicted that the diversion would lower the level of the Great Lakes by about six inches. This was the first official mention of such a possible consequence, and it raised an issue that would loom over the project to the present day. The expansion proceeded, and in 1899, the secretary of war issued a permit authorizing the opening of the new canal, subject to only two things: the imposition of restrictions if the diversion induced a current in the Chicago River hazardous to navigation or property and an assumption of liability by the district. Any other matters, including the issue of lowering the level of the lakes, were referred to Congress, which took no action.[34]

The plan to reverse the river, sending sewage through the new canal into the Des Plaines River (whence to the Illinois River), had obvious implications for Illinois communities downstream from Chicago, such as Joliet and Peoria. Representatives of both cities sought unsuccessfully to obtain legislation repealing the state law enabling the sanitary district, but apparently did not threaten any judicial action.[35]

There is no indication that St. Louis or other cities in Missouri paid much attention to the canal project during the early years of its construction. Yet St. Louis drew its water from the Mississippi River, and the Illinois River empties into the Mississippi, less than forty miles north of St. Louis. The sewer water that the sanitary district was planning to add to the Illinois River would eventually admix with the water drawn by St. Louis. So, given the emerging acceptance of the germ theory, it is no surprise that St. Louis residents would become alarmed. Economic competition no doubt played a supporting role in engendering opposition to the project. Chicago and St. Louis were fierce competitors during these years, and it was increasingly apparent that Chicago was winning. Political leaders in St. Louis may have worried that the Chicago Sanitary and Ship Canal would divert freight traffic away from the Mississippi.[36]

In any event, St. Louis became agitated about the project beginning in 1898, six years after construction began. Its first response was to attempt, without success, to rouse political opposition to the project in southern Illinois. Then a study committee was appointed. After its report was issued in 1899, focusing on the threat of disease, St. Louis was determined to take action. It took time to decide how or what, but from the beginning of this period it was a known possibility that the State of Missouri might file an original action in the Supreme Court, asking the nation's high court to enjoin the canal project.[37]

The sanitary district trustees concluded that it was imperative to finish the canal as quickly as possible, before any suit was filed. This had some legal basis. Courts of equity frequently decline to enjoin action if the objecting party is guilty of "laches," or undue delay in seeking relief. But there is no indication that the trustees hastened to open the canal on the basis of legal advice. Rather, they seemed to respond to a basic intuition that once the canal became fully operational, it would become part of the reality on the ground and would be harder to shut down.[38]

The upshot was a race to see whether the canal could be finished before lawyers got to the courthouse with Missouri's papers. Each side sought to conceal its actions, as much as possible, from the other. Most of the work on the canal had been finished. About a mile west of the starting point of the canal, a temporary earthen dam held back the waters of the Chicago River. In the morning hours of January 2, 1900, in a freezing wind, trustees gathered at the site of the dam with a crew of workers, determined to breach the dam. There was no general advance notice of the event, but a few individuals were invited to witness or memorialize the proceedings. When two reporters belatedly hurried up, the *Chicago Tribune* would report the next day, it "caused a small panic until it was seen they carried no injunctions with them." Shovels and a dredge were inadequate to move the frozen soil. Dynamite, too, proved unsuccessful. Finally, a fire composed of burning timbers lighted to keep the participants warm was set on top of the dam, which softened the soil sufficiently for the dredge to finish the job. The water cascaded into the main channel. "Like schoolboys on a vacation," as the newspaper painted the picture, "the drainage officials waved their arms and shouted." They retired for a celebratory lunch.[39]

The race was not yet won. Under the sanitary district enabling act, a three-person independent commission had to report to the governor that all work had been completed satisfactorily, and the governor had to personally give his permission to lower the Bear Trap Dam at Lockport, sending the canal's waters into the Des Plaines River. The commissioners and the trustees had engaged in substantial back and forth toward the end of 1899, and late on January 16, 1900, the groups convened in Joliet. The next day, January 17, in an early-morning

FIGURE 5.6. Crowd of people aboard the *Juliet*, the Sanitary District of Chicago inspection boat, 1900. Chicago History Museum, ICHi-014876.

phone call placed by the commissioners, the governor authorized the opening of the dam. The group boarded a special waiting train to Lockport, and late that morning, a weary crowd watched as the water spilled into the Des Plaines. By midafternoon, when the trustees were back in Chicago celebrating over lunch, news arrived that, also that morning, the Missouri side had filed for an injunction in the Supreme Court.[40]

The race between the sanitary district and the Missouri lawyers reveals another feature of resources in a commons: they generate competitions to see who will be the first to gain the use of the resource. Such competitions are thought to be wasteful, because the losers expend effort that generates no payoff, and even the winners may overinvest to claim the prize. We have previously seen evidence of such racing behavior in the competition between various private cabals, the city, and the Illinois Central Railroad to be the first to obtain a grant of the bed of Lake Michigan to construct an outer harbor (see chapter 1), and in the many-sided competition between Captain Streeter and others to secure title to the accreted lands north of the Chicago River (see chapter 4). Streeter's claim to have been the first to "discover" the accreted lands is a particularly obvious manifestation of the instinct that being first confers a kind of moral entitlement to control an open-access resource.[41]

Missouri v. Illinois

Chicago had won the race, if just barely. But did it matter? Missouri charged that the State of Illinois and the sanitary district, characterized as an "agency" of the state, were engaged in a "direct and continuing nuisance" to the citizens of Missouri who relied on the Mississippi River for their water. The complaint alleged that the opening of the canal would inject 1,500 tons of "undefecated filth and sewage" per day into the Des Plaines River, which would eventually flow into the Mississippi, and that this would "poison and pollute said water with the germs of disease of various and many kinds." Missouri asked for a temporary and permanent injunction against Illinois and the sanitary district. In form, the complaint asked only that the discharge of sewage be stopped. In reality, of course, it would be impossible to do this without undoing the entire project. The "filth and sewage" were going into the Chicago River, where they had to flow either, as before, toward Lake Michigan or, as now, into the new channel and to the southwest.[42]

In March 1900, Illinois and the sanitary district formally responded that the Supreme Court did not have jurisdiction and requested dismissal. Illinois asserted that the controversy was not properly brought by a state, as the federal Constitution and implementing statutes required for this sort of case to begin in the Supreme Court itself. Rather, Illinois maintained, the suit was between public corporations established by the respective states—the sanitary district on the Illinois side and the municipalities of Missouri using the Mississippi as a source of drinking water on the other. In any event, the defendants argued, no sovereign right of Missouri was involved, nor was any property right of Missouri directly affected.[43]

Acting with considerable dispatch, the Supreme Court heard oral argument on the jurisdictional question in mid-November 1900, and released its decision eleven weeks later, on January 28, 1901. Writing for a majority of six, Justice George Shiras Jr. allowed the case to proceed. The bulk of his opinion was designed to show, by reference to constitutional history and the precedents, that it was appropriate for the court to hear a dispute such as the one brought by Missouri. When he finally got around to addressing the particular issues presented, Shiras made three important rulings.[44]

First, the State of Missouri could properly act on behalf of its residents in complaining of pollution emanating from another state. In the most memorable passage in the opinion, Shiras had this to say: "If Missouri were an independent and sovereign state all must admit that she could seek a remedy by negotiation, and, that failing, by force. Diplomatic powers and the right to make war having been surrendered to the general government, it was to be expected that upon the latter would be devolved the duty of providing a remedy and that remedy, we think, is found in the constitutional provisions [for original jurisdiction in the Supreme Court] we are considering." The passage is startling in suggesting that the actions of Illinois and the sanitary district, in opening the canal to send pollution in the direction of Missouri, would amount to a *casus belli* in an international context. The court implicitly adopted Missouri's perspective. The Illinois engineering project was seen as a deliberate attempt by one political jurisdiction to thrust deadly filth on a neighboring jurisdiction—an act so outrageous that it would justify taking up arms.[45]

Second, the court concluded that Illinois was a proper defendant. The sanitary district had been established by state law "to do the very things which, according to the theory of the complainant's case, will result in the mischief to be apprehended." The district was "a public corporation, whose existence and operations are wholly within the control of the State." This established for interstate pollution disputes what in the international law context would be called the principle of attribution. If subordinate actors within a political jurisdiction are causing injury to another political jurisdiction, the source state is legally responsible for their conduct.[46]

Third, the court rejected Illinois's claim that the complaint should be dismissed because Missouri was guilty of laches. The claim had considerable force, given that Missouri, as we have seen, had remained silent for more than seven years, while Illinois spent tens of millions of dollars on constructing a mammoth ditch for the sole purpose of reversing the flow of the Chicago River. This was a legal version of the intuition universally shared by the politicians in Illinois that once the canal were opened, it would be impossible to stop it. The majority dodged the argument, however, observing that Missouri was not asking that the ditch be filled up; it only sought "relief against the pouring of sewage and filth through it." Of course, this misstated the reality of the canal project. The sanitary district could stop pouring sewage and filth through the canal only by damming up the canal and rendering it useless. Wastewater treatment plants would not come into widespread use for several decades.[47]

Chief Justice Melville W. Fuller, the former Chicago lawyer, dissented, joined by two other justices. The chief justice developed a more subtle argument that made the completion of the canal not only relevant, but dispositive. He noted that when the governor of Illinois signed off on the decision to open the dam at Lockport, the state performed its last relevant act under the enabling legislation. Thus, there was no longer any basis for regarding the state as a proper defendant, and no basis for the court's retaining the case under its mandatory original jurisdiction, which required that the suit be one properly brought against a state.[48]

Although the court held that it had jurisdiction over the controversy, it also denied Missouri's request for a temporary injunction. The matter would have to go to trial. The Supreme Court is a tribunal composed of nine justices, with almost all of its work being appellate review, and it is not well suited, nor does it have the time, to conduct trials. Consistently with its emerging practice in original-jurisdiction cases, the court in November 1902 appointed Frank S. Bright to serve as "commissioner" to take evidence (such appointees would later be called "special masters").[49]

As the contest thus moved to proof, animosity ran high between the cities. In 1903, when Chicago's National League baseball team traveled to St. Louis for opening day, it was greeted by a crowd of "newsboys and street urchins" who derided the Chicago team as "de Chicago microbes." The nickname stuck, and continued to be used in the St. Louis papers for several years. It was even adopted by the Hearst newspapers in Chicago, perhaps because of their rivalry with the *Chicago Tribune*, an enthusiastic proponent of the river-reversal project.[50]

More than fifteen months were consumed in the presentation of evidence to Bright, including the testimony of more than 350 witnesses and more than one hundred exhibits; the final record consisted of some 13,160 pages. Bright thereupon took a year and a day to prepare and submit his report to the court. The court then heard oral argument over a three-day period, on January 2–4, 1906.[51]

Missouri's principal argument was based on what today would be called epidemiological evidence. St. Louis had experienced a 77.7 percent annual increase in typhoid deaths in the years immediately following the opening of the Chicago Sanitary and Ship Canal. Each life lost was valued at $5,000, with $10 per day assigned as the value "for loss of labor, medical treatment and nursing." Given these losses, Missouri maintained, the appropriate remedy against the nuisance was simply that Illinois and the sanitary district be enjoined from dumping untreated sewage into the tributaries of the Mississippi.[52]

Illinois's principal argument in rebuttal was that, if anything, the construction of the canal had improved the quality of water in the Mississippi. The Illinois River had always flowed to the Mississippi, and its now-higher volume of water, on account of the addition from Lake Michigan, diluted the pollutants. The state pointed to evidence that the Illinois River was less polluted than the Missouri River, which also flowed into the Mississippi north of St. Louis and made a greater contribution to the volume of the Mississippi than did the Illinois River. Illinois maintained as well that the bulk of the pollution at St. Louis came from Missouri's own cities.[53]

A mere month and a half after argument, the court released its decision. In an opinion written by Justice Oliver Wendell Holmes Jr., the injunction requested by Missouri was denied. The Holmes opinion, as was characteristic of much of his judicial work product, was succinct, eloquent, richly suggestive, but rather oblique. He gave two principal reasons for rejecting Missouri's complaint.

First, building on a closing comment by Justice Shiras in the previous opinion about the need for Missouri to demonstrate a "real and immediate" danger, Holmes suggested that Missouri had to meet a high burden of proof in demonstrating a causal link between the opening of the Chicago Sanitary and Ship Canal and the incidence of typhoid fever in St. Louis. Without exhaustively reviewing the evidence, he cited a number of reasons to doubt that Missouri had sustained its burden. He noted that no one maintained there to be "a nuisance of the simple kind that was known to the older common law." The sanitary district had done "nothing which can be detected by the unassisted senses—no visible increase of filth, no new smell." He took it as "proved that the great volume of pure water from Lake Michigan which is mixed with the sewage at the start has improved the Illinois River. . . . Formerly it was sluggish and ill smelling. Now it is a comparatively clear stream to which edible fish have returned." As for the epidemiological evidence, Holmes was skeptical. He noted that if one went back to the 1890s, the incidence of typhoid deaths in St. Louis often had been as high as or higher than it was in the years immediately after the completion of the canal.[54]

The studies submitted by the warring expert witnesses on both sides clearly fascinated Holmes, who characterized them as "the most ingenious experiments."

FIGURE 5.7. Justice Oliver Wendell Holmes Jr., ca. 1902. Library of Congress, Prints & Photographs Division, LC-USZ62-58677; Frances Benjamin Johnston, photographer.

In one trial, presented by a Missouri expert, barrels containing a type of unusual bacteria were released in the Mississippi River near the mouth of the Illinois River, and some of the bacteria were found at St. Louis four weeks later. Against this, Illinois set what Holmes regarded as "a no less striking experiment with typhoid germs suspended in the Illinois River in permeable sacs." These were shown to have survived for only three or four days. All this was a clear forerunner of the types of disputed scientific evidence that would roil environmental law—and vex reviewing courts—in later decades. The bottom line for Holmes was that inconclusive proof of causation of disease was not sufficient to carry the day.[55]

The second reason given by Holmes for denying relief was that Missouri was also responsible for the pollution it decried. He put it this way:

> It is a question of the first magnitude whether the destiny of the great rivers is to be the sewers of the cities along their banks or to be protected against everything which threatens their purity. . . . If we are to judge by what the plaintiff itself permits, the discharge of sewage into the Mississippi by cities and towns is to be expected. . . . Where, as here, the plaintiff has sovereign powers and deliberately permits discharges similar to those of which it complains, it not only offers a standard to which the defendant has the right to appeal, but, as some of those discharges are above the intake of St. Louis, it warrants the defendant in demanding the strictest proof that the plaintiff's own conduct does not produce the result, or at least so conduce to it that courts should not be curious to apportion the blame.

Holmes concluded that "[t]he presence of causes of infection from the plaintiff's action makes the case weaker in principle as well as harder to prove than one in which all came from a single source."[56]

This was an invocation of equitable principles, reflected in the traditional maxims "He who comes into equity must come with clean hands" and "He who seeks equity must do equity." They can be seen as a kind of reverse golden rule: Do not ask of others what you do not do yourself. The principle would recur in later transboundary pollution cases decided by the court, most prominently between New Jersey and New York over water pollution.[57]

The question of who had been first to capture the use of the water—the question that so animated the players in the January 1900 race by Illinois to open the canal before Missouri could get to the courthouse—did not make a legal appearance in the Holmes opinion. Conceivably, however, it exercised an unstated influence on the justices, who were now unanimous in rejecting Missouri's plea. By the time the court ruled, the canal had been in operation for six years. It was the new status quo, which Missouri was seeking to upset. The relevant question, in the minds of the justices, may have been which party had to construct a water filtration plant—St. Louis or Chicago. The fact that diversion of the Chicago River had become part of the reality on the ground, and that St. Louis might have to build a filtration plant in any event, given the pollution of the Mississippi River from Missouri sources, may have made it seem that the least disruptive solution was to require Missouri to filter. In fact, that is what Missouri did.[58]

The creation of the sanitary district is a dramatic illustration of growth in the energy and efficacy of local governments at the close of the nineteenth century. As Jon Teaford has written, the United States' major cities during this era were dominated by political machines notorious for their graft and corruption. But somehow these cities also managed to undertake major infrastructural improvements, such as the construction of water systems, sewerage systems, and parks, often because the state legislature was convinced to create boards and commissions that operated independently of the local city councils. Chicago's sanitary district and, before it, the city's Board of Sewerage Commissioners under the leadership of Ellis Chesbrough are primary examples of this phenomenon. Chicago's park districts, which we will see in action in the next two chapters, are another. Armed with independent funding authority, and possessed of their own administrative structure, these entities were able to undertake immense projects designed to provide public goods desired by their constituents. As Teaford has written about Chicago, "In the 1850s the city council had ordained that the level of the swampy city be raised ten feet, and it had been done. In later decades the municipal authorities had ordered that the flow of the Chicago river be reversed, and so it was reversed. The achievements of government in Chicago at times rivaled the feats of the Old Testament God."[59]

By all accounts, the opening of the Chicago Sanitary and Ship Canal produced a dramatic improvement in the quality of the water in the Chicago River. An early report in the *New York Times* exclaimed, "The impossible has happened!" The Chicago River, it said, "now resembles liquid." More importantly, the city's mortality rate from typhoid fever dropped dramatically once the canal was opened.[60]

Of particular significance for our story, the opening of the canal and the river's reversal produced an equally dramatic improvement in the quality of the water in the lake bordering Chicago. The open sewer of the river now flowed away from Lake Michigan. The lakefront suddenly became a much more attractive place for swimming, fishing, recreational boating, or simply strolling along the edge of the shore. This all helped build support for plans to beautify the lakefront. It is no coincidence that the South Park Commission's plans for expanding Grant Park by landfilling along the lakeshore (see chapter 3) commenced during the years when the sanitary canal was under construction and accelerated after it opened. The park district could be confident of public support for a huge lakefront park if the waters of the lake were relatively free of sewage and pollutants. Nor is it a coincidence that during the years immediately around and after the reversal of the river, plans were hatched to extend Lincoln Park up and down the north shore of the lake (see chapter 6), and to build what became Burnham Park along the south shore (see chapter 7). No matter how offensive the project may have been to communities such as Joliet, Peoria, and St. Louis, it greatly enhanced the appeal of the Chicago lakefront as a venue for public respite and recreation.[61]

The Water Diversion Controversy

With the Supreme Court's definitive judgment in *Missouri v. Illinois* in 1906, the most significant threat to the project to reverse the river had passed. But Chicago and the sanitary district were not in the clear. The better part of the next century would be taken up with repeated challenges to what came to be called the "Chicago diversion" of the waters of Lake Michigan. The Army Corps of Engineers, states such as Wisconsin and Michigan, and even the Canadian government were all involved in these disputes. The primary umpire with final authority to resolve the disputes was the Supreme Court of the United States, acting in a new series of original-jurisdiction actions.

Recall that, as early as 1895, a federal commission had noted that the diversion would lower the level of waters throughout the Great Lakes. This issue was not resolved but continued to fester. The initial estimate was that the diversion of waters contemplated by the original plan for the Chicago Sanitary and Ship Canal would lower the level of water in the Great Lakes by about six inches. This may not seem much, given that the level of water in the lakes can vary by two feet or more from one year to another. But a reduction of six inches during years of low water would limit the size or, at least, the carrying capacity of lake freighters that could use many of the ports and harbors throughout the region, without extensive dredging.[62]

Here was another example of the tragedy of the commons on a very large scale. Illinois had a legitimate reason for diverting water—to protect Chicagoans from disease. But the costs of the diversion would be borne by all the other states bordering on the lakes, from Wisconsin and Minnesota all the way to New York, plus Canada, not to mention the consumers who would have to pay higher costs for goods because of the increased costs of water transportation. Who had authority to police this commons, to decide whether the benefits to Chicagoans were more or less important than the higher costs to other states and consumers?

The ensuing years witnessed an endless stream of attempts to resolve the water diversion controversy. At first it seemed that the army would be given authority to arbitrate the conflicting claims. But when the army set a permissible level of withdrawals that seemed to favor Chicago, other states bordering the Great Lakes were incensed. With Wisconsin the lead plaintiff, the states brought a new original action in the Supreme Court, demanding that Illinois and the sanitary district be directed to cease any diversion that would pose harm to navigation on the lakes. The court referred the matter to a special master: Charles Evans Hughes, who had been a justice of the Supreme Court before stepping down as the Republican Party's candidate for president in 1916, would take evidence and recommend a decree. The court accepted Hughes's factual findings, but insisted that it, and not the army, would prescribe the appropriate limit on diversions. Eventually the court entered a decree in 1930 requiring that the sanitary district reduce withdrawals to no more than 1,500 cubic feet per second (CFS) by the end of 1938.[63]

The court would come to regret its decision to become the umpire of the multisided dispute over Great Lakes water levels. The sanitary district could not keep up with the schedule of construction of wastewater treatment plants contemplated by the court's schedule. Partly this was due to its lack of diligence, but a major factor was the collapse in tax receipts during the Depression. The sanitary district's struggles required further hearings before the court to modify the decree. And this was only the beginning; the court modified its decree multiple times in ensuing years. The most significant revision occurred in 1967, when the court issued a new decree, effective in 1970, increasing the volume of water permitted to flow out of Lake Michigan into the Mississippi basin from 1,500 CFS to 3,200 CFS.[64]

Frustrated by their continual litigation against the Chicago water diversion, and alarmed by other ideas for diversions of Great Lakes waters in the 1980s, the states and Canadian provinces bordering the Great Lakes began moving toward a more implacable antidiversion posture. In 1985, the governors of the affected states and provinces signed a document called the "Great Lakes Charter." Though not legally binding, the charter committed the signatories to securing the unanimous consent of the Great Lakes states and provinces before any new large-scale diversion or consumptive use of water would be permitted. The next year, the affected US states obtained an amendment to a federal statute, the Water Resources Development Act, that made it a requirement of federal law that all eight governors consent to any new diversion of water outside the Great Lakes basin.[65]

The efforts of the Great Lakes governors to block future diversions were driven by what a generally sympathetic account describes as "anti-diversion paranoia."

None of the diversion proposals floated in the 1980s had any chance of success. Yet the idea festered among many that permitting any new diversion would set a precedent that would lead to more. It was a classic slippery-slope argument: if we permit even one more diversion, there will be no way to stop other, more massive diversions, and eventually there will not be enough water left for surrounding communities.[66]

Significant questions were raised about the constitutionality of state-level legislation barring diversions, as well as about the provision in the 1986 federal legislation allowing governors to block diversions without any hearing or judicial review—or, more substantively, in each governor's complete discretion, without any requirement to consider the size, purpose, or conditions of a proposed diversion. These concerns led to prolonged negotiations between the affected states to develop an interstate compact that would effectively stifle future diversions. In 2005, agreement on a text was finally reached, with approval following from the legislatures of the eight Great Lakes states. Congress enacted the Great Lakes–St. Lawrence River Basin Water Resources Compact, with President George W. Bush's signature, in 2008.[67]

The interstate compact, which is federal law, with all its force and effect, continues the policy of requiring unanimous consent of the states surrounding the Great Lakes to authorize any new diversions. Of particular relevance to our story, however, Article 4 specifically grandfathers diversions consistent with the Supreme Court's decree in *Wisconsin v. Illinois*. Illinois insisted on this exception as a condition of its joining the compact. Thus, the Chicago River diversion now enjoys the imprimatur of not only the Supreme Court but also a binding interstate compact.[68]

The antidiversion movement in the Great Lakes region reveals yet another feature of an open-access commons. As Elinor Ostrom has emphasized, a commons can be governed by norms or rules that restrict the access of outsiders to its resources. This is an apt characterization of the commons known as the Great Lakes, at least on the dimension of consumptive uses of the water. The political jurisdictions bordering the lakes have banded together to make it very difficult for anyone outside these jurisdictions to make use of the waters of the lakes. Meanwhile, they have adopted rules that permit significant (but regulated) consumptive uses by themselves.[69]

Both the original rationale for the reversal of the Chicago River and the source of hostility to the diversion that animated surrounding states for most of the twentieth century are now of greatly diminished importance. To begin, the reversal's purpose was to keep sewage and industrial pollutants out of the Chicago River, and hence out of Lake Michigan. This purpose is now largely irrelevant, given both the construction of plants that treat domestic waste before it enters the Chicago River and the imposition of strict limits on discharges from industrial point sources under the Clean Water Act of 1972.[70]

Further, the primary objection to the river reversal voiced over time—and the animating concern behind the Supreme Court's original-jurisdiction decisions—was that the reversal jeopardizes navigation on the Great Lakes by lowering the level of the waters. This is also of significantly diminished importance. The volume of commercial shipping on the Great Lakes is now but a shadow of what it once was. The Chicago River is no longer used as a commercial harbor. Some freighters still ply the waters of the Great Lakes and dock in the Calumet River and northern Indiana, and there would be some increased costs to the firms that use such services if they had to turn to railroads or interstate trucking instead. But the basic objection concerning navigation on the Great Lakes, made during most of the twentieth century, can no longer be advanced as a substantial reason for limiting the diversion.

The primary source of antipathy to diversion today is grounded instead in environmental values. One significant concern is the ecological threat posed by the invasion of alien species, such as Asian carp, into the Great Lakes. The Chicago Sanitary and Ship Canal creates a link between the Great Lakes and the Mississippi River basin that otherwise would not exist; closing that link (which would mean re-reversing the river) would reduce the risk. Of course, there are other points of entry into the Great Lakes, such as the St. Lawrence Seaway, which have introduced other invasive species. And it may be that the electronic protective barrier installed by the Army Corps of Engineers to block the Asian carp from entering the Great Lakes via the Chicago River will succeed in deterring this particular threat.[71]

Another manifestation of the environmental perspective is the emergence of a significant segment of opinion within the environmental community that decries—even if selectively—any deviation from what is understood to be the "natural" condition of the physical environment. For persons of this view, as Peter Annin has captured them (and it), the reversal of the Chicago River is an "abomination that should never be repeated." This perspective is the same as the one animating the extreme version of the public trust doctrine that gained currency after the 1970s and views any landfilling of Lake Michigan as abhorrent (see chapter 8).[72]

Whatever policy is adopted regarding diversions elsewhere in the Great Lakes, the Chicago River is not going to be re-reversed anytime soon. The interstate compact that now governs the Great Lakes gives Illinois a veto over any such demand. However unfair to the other jurisdictions that share the Great Lakes, the river reversal was a key factor in transforming the Chicago River and the

Chicago lakefront from a commons devoted to commerce and a repository of waste into a venue for respite and recreation. The construction of the Chicago Sanitary and Ship Canal was but one of a series of engineering feats that have secured a water quality for Lake Michigan along the shore of Chicago that is second to none. These feats are vital elements in the making of the specular lakefront that exists today.[73]

6

NORTH LAKE SHORE DRIVE

The growing conception of the lakefront as an environmental amenity was very much in evidence in the completion—in fits and starts from 1870 to 1954—of Lake Shore Drive and associated parks. This chapter traces the construction north from the original Lincoln Park to Hollywood Avenue. The story, as contained in sources such as legislation, court decisions, and park plans, is remarkable and never has been told before.

As we have seen, it became increasingly likely after 1860 that the State of Illinois would be found to have title to the bed of Lake Michigan, an understanding confirmed by the Illinois Supreme Court in the *Kirk* decision in 1896. This emerging clarification of ownership set off a series of seismic disturbances along the lakeshore, such as the competition among rival interests to build an outer harbor (see chapter 1) and the struggle to capture the reclaimed land in Streeterville (see chapter 4). It also laid the groundwork, legally speaking, for the construction of north Lake Shore Drive. The drive was built by the Lincoln Park Commission on landfill atop what originally had been the bed of the lake. Transfer of title to the lakebed for this purpose from the state was unproblematic after *Kirk*, which upheld the construction of the drive in Streeterville. The problem going forward was how to acquire the riparian rights of the private landowners farther north along Lake Michigan's shore.

Riparian rights are rights that attach as a matter of law to land abutting a body of water; they include the right to access the water, to use the water, and to enjoy accretions that form by the water's natural action. Riparian rights are regarded as especially valuable rights, and courts often say that the government can extinguish them only on the payment of just compensation. Thus, even with title to the lakebed in the state, everyone agreed that if such land were to be reclaimed from the lake for creating parks or even just boulevards, it would be necessary first to acquire the existing riparian rights of abutting private landowners.[1]

The Lincoln Park Commission and the First Plan for North Lake Shore Drive

The original Lincoln Park, located on the lakefront between North and Diversey Avenues, came to include a pleasure drive along the lakeshore, called Lake Shore Drive. As we have discussed, the drive was extended south of the original park, the first extension being finished in 1875, in the area that soon welcomed Potter Palmer's mansion and came to be known as the Gold Coast, and the second coming from 1889 legislation, which authorized the drive to be extended farther south, out and around the area that would be called Streeterville. The legislature in 1889 also authorized extension of the drive to the *north* of the original park and conveyed the state's interest in submerged land for purposes of landfilling to accommodate the new construction in either direction.[2]

The story of the southerly extension around Streeterville was recounted at length in chapter 4. The Illinois Supreme Court in the *Kirk* case upheld its controversial financing scheme, in which the Lincoln Park Commission (LPC) transferred title to submerged land to the existing riparian owners in return for their agreeing to underwrite the cost of the project. Yet given strong criticism of that scheme, excoriating the transfer of submerged land for private gain, it was clear that public sentiment would not tolerate an overt transfer of submerged land as a means of funding the northerly extension.

New legislation in 1895 clarified how the northerly extension of the park and drive was to proceed. As before, the state agreed to transfer its title over the submerged land to the park district and authorized landfilling to create a new drive to be protected by a breakwater. The act further provided that the riparian rights of the owners of land along the shore were to be acquired by purchase, or if necessary by condemnation. Significantly, however, the new legislation also specified that the land reclaimed by the park district had to be used and improved "for the purposes of a public park under its control and management." The legislative mandate seemingly assured that any landfilling along the lakeshore north of the original Lincoln Park would generate a new breakwater, a new boulevard, and a public park—but no residential or commercial development.[3]

FIGURE 6.1. Map showing Lincoln Park and Lake Shore Drive ca. 1902, and also the shoreline today.

FIGURE 6.2. Edward O. Brown, 1904. Chicago History Museum, ICHi-092977.

The mandate to devote future reclamation for use as a "public park" created a major dilemma for the LPC: it was unclear how the commission was going to pay for the northerly extension of the park and drive. The 1895 act provided that funds for any extension were to be raised by special assessments imposed "upon property benefited by the proposed improvement." Resistance to such special assessments was always intense. Later legislation authorized the park district to seek voter approval for issuing bonds to raise revenue for the project, but these, too, would have to be funded by special assessments or increased property taxes. In order to tamp down opposition to special assessments or higher property taxes, it would be critical to keep the costs of the project as low as possible.[4]

The park district struggled continually to secure funds for the northern extension of the park and drive, which largely explains why the project proceeded in fits and starts. But one important dimension of the cost problem—the expense of acquiring the riparian rights of those who owned land on the lakeshore—was tackled with great ingenuity by the park district's counsel during these years, Edward O. Brown. This is the same Brown whom we encountered in chapter 4 doing work for the riparian owners in Streeterville, including his dramatic trip to (and from) Washington, DC, in 1897. For the northern extension, Brown devised a two-part strategy for reducing the cost of acquiring riparian rights, effectively to zero. One part consisted of a carrot, the other a stick.

The carrot, which was probably of greater importance, was a surreptitious variation on the method used to pay for the extension of Lake Shore Drive in Streeterville: the LPC transferred submerged land to riparian owners in return for a release of their riparian rights. How was this possible, given the explicit command in the 1895 act (prompted by the adverse reaction to the 1889 legislation) that all new land between the shoreline and the drive was to be a public park? The answer is that the 1895 act said nothing about where the *precise boundary* between the riparian land and the newly created public park was to be located. Brown's practice was to enter into negotiations with riparian owners whereby the LPC would agree to locate the boundary an average of one hundred feet to the *east* of the original shoreline. In other words, the riparian owners would get one hundred feet of submerged land, which they no doubt would fill to create new solid land; in return, they would convey a deed to the LPC releasing their riparian rights. As the Chiperfield Committee observed in 1911, "[T]he Park Board accomplished by indirection the results that the original act of 1889 permitted them to do directly."[5]

Brown's practice was abetted by a 1903 statutory amendment that specifically authorized such boundary-line settlements. The amendment allowed boundary-line agreements to be presented to a local circuit court judge, who would enter a "final decree" establishing the "dividing or boundary line between the lands of the [riparian owner] and the lands of the said board of park commissioners adjacent thereto." It further provided that the boundary line so established "shall be the permanent boundary line of said shore lands . . . and the owners of said shore lands shall have the right to improve, protect, sell and convey the shore lands up to the boundary line so established, *free from any adverse claim in any way arising out of any question as to where the shore line was at any time in the past* or as to the title to existing accretions, if any, to said shore land." In other words, once the decree was entered, the riparian owners would get clear title to a portion of the submerged land, and presumably could fill it, for development or sale—a sub rosa version of the Streeterville scheme. Evidently, most owners valued the additional land more than retention of their riparian rights. The court proceedings establishing the new boundaries were invariably uncontested, generated no published decisions, and allowed the transfer of submerged land to the riparian owner to be validated and recorded.[6]

The program of swapping submerged land for riparian rights explains how the commissioners were able to obtain large numbers of voluntary contracts to convey riparian rights to the LPC without any stated monetary consideration and without resorting to condemnation proceedings. Some of these conveyances pertained to riparian land as far north as Devon Avenue, the projected northern terminus of the extended Lincoln Park and Lake Shore Drive. The practice was described in detail and condemned by the Chiperfield Committee in 1911. The committee further documented that once the boundary line was established, riparian owners frequently began landfilling and constructing breakwaters to secure their new rights, well before the park district commenced its improvements. Notwithstanding the committee's denunciation of the practice, no steps were taken to curtail it.[7]

Wharfing Out in the Nineteenth Century

The stick side of the strategy was even more audacious. To understand it, we must delve somewhat more deeply into one of the most important riparian rights—the right to "wharf out" to reach water deep enough to support navigation.

Throughout most of human history, the preferred way to transport people and goods over any distance has been by water. This was especially true before the advent of the railroads and is the reason that nearly all major cities are located on some navigable body of water.

Transporting people and goods by water requires moving them between the land and the vessels on the water. Usually this involves the construction of some kind of wharf that connects the dry land with water deep enough to allow vessels to approach the shore without grounding.* The advantages of transport by water—and the necessity of allowing people to gain access to navigable water—made it clearly in the public interest not only to permit but to encourage the construction of wharves. So the common law did this. As stated in one nineteenth-century decision by the US Supreme Court, "The navigable streams of the country would be of little value for that purpose if they had no places where the vessels which they floated could land, with conveniences for receiving and discharging cargo.... Wharves and piers are as necessary almost to the successful use of the stream in navigation as the vessels themselves.... But to be of any value in this respect they must reach so far into deep water as to enable the vessels used in ordinary navigation to float while they touch them and are lashed to their sides."[8]

Moreover, in the context of the weak governments that characterized nineteenth-century America—governments with small budgets and small or nonexistent bureaucracies—it was universally understood that wharves would have to be built by private riparian owners. Riparian owners would have the necessary access rights over the land to reach the body of navigable water. They would also have a strong incentive to build a wharf in order to maximize the value of their land. Some would do so for their own comings and goings. Others would see the advantage of building a wharf and allowing the general public to use it—in return for some fee.[9]

Not surprisingly, the nineteenth-century judiciary developed a jurisprudence of wharf rights to promote private construction of wharves while also allowing for public regulation to prevent abuses, which might take the form of monopolies, overbuilding of wharves, or the construction of structures intruding too far into the navigable water. A large body of decisions created what amounted to a general right of private riparian owners to wharf out to navigable waters. The details varied from one state to another. Nevertheless, a trio of US Supreme Court cases decided shortly after the middle of the century—*Dutton v. Strong*, *Railroad Co. v. Schurmeir*, and *Yates v. Milwaukee*—illustrated the prevailing judicial attitude. In each case, the court spoke approvingly about the need for private wharves on navigable waters in order to promote commerce and assure public access to navigable waterways. The third of these decisions said explicitly that the right applied without regard to whether the riparian owner also owned the bed of the body of water on which the wharf was built. As was common during this era, the court's decisions about wharfing

* There are a variety of terms for structures used to connect dry land with vessels floating on navigable waters, including wharf, pier, dock, slip, quay, and landing. Our discussion should be understood to cover all of these types of structures under the general heading "wharf."

out were framed in terms of the general common law, with no real distinction being drawn between federal and state law on these matters.[10]

The decisions of the Illinois courts up to the end of the nineteenth century were fully consistent with this jurisprudence. In 1868, the Illinois Supreme Court decided two cases recognizing the right to wharf out. One involved wharves constructed in the Ohio River, the other a wharf in the Chicago River. In both decisions, the court upheld the right of landowners along the shore to construct wharves in navigable waters, provided that they did not interfere with the public's general right of navigation. As the court commented in the first case, "The right of dockage and wharfage is, perhaps, coeval with commerce, connected with marine and inland navigation." Appellate decisions later in the century reaffirmed this understanding.[11]

No Illinois state court decision involved the right to wharf out into Lake Michigan, which is no surprise given that the local commerce and the congestion were on the Chicago River. Yet the federal courts in the *Lake Front Case* made the logical extension. Recall that the Illinois Central Railroad had acquired riparian land on the lakefront between Randolph Street and the Chicago River in order to construct a depot and related facilities. The carrier also had acquired riparian land between roughly 12th Street and 16th Street, which it used for a roundhouse and repair yard. Justice Harlan, in the trial court decision in the *Lake Front Case*, held that the railroad's landfilling and its many improvements in these areas were justified in part by its rights as a riparian owner to wharf out. The exercise of such a right, Harlan noted, was supported by numerous cases, including the three Supreme Court decisions noted above.[12]

The Supreme Court affirmed this aspect of the judgment. Writing for the court, Justice Field observed that "[t]he riparian proprietor is entitled, among other rights, as held in *Yates v. Milwaukee*, to access to the navigable part of the water on the front of which lies his land, and for that purpose to make a landing, wharf or pier for his own use or for the use of the public, subject to such general rules and regulations as the legislature may prescribe for the protection of the rights of the public." The court concluded that the railroad's claim to control and use various slips, wharves, and piers "is well founded so far as the piers do not extend beyond the point of navigability in the waters of the lake."[13]

Although the right to wharf out into navigable waters may have seemed secure when the *Lake Front Case* was decided, a deeper probing would have revealed some latent ambiguities. In jurisdictions where the riparian owner was deemed to own the bed of navigable water to the center of the stream (such as Illinois for navigable rivers), the right to wharf out presented no significant difficulty. A riparian owner who built a wharf into the water would be building on submerged land that he or she already owned. If, however, the state was deemed to be the owner of the submerged land where the wharf was located, the foundation of the right was much less clear. Was wharfing out in these circumstances based on an implied license from the state? If so, then it would seem that the state could revoke the privilege at any time, since licenses are generally regarded as revocable at will. Or was the right to wharf out part of the package of rights that attach to riparian ownership as a matter of law, such as the right to future accretions or the right of access to the water? If so, then it would seem to be more logical to regard wharfing out as a kind of appurtenant property right or easement that could not be abrogated by a state, at least not without the payment of compensation. Once it was clear that the State of Illinois owned the bed of Lake Michigan, these latent ambiguities would be brilliantly exploited by attorney Brown to eliminate any right under Illinois law to wharf out on Lake Michigan.[14]

The *Revell* Cases

In contemplating the costs of purchasing or condemning the riparian rights of owners north of the original Lincoln Park, the commissioners were concerned about the costs of acquiring the rights of owners who had constructed piers or wharves into the lake, especially if those piers had augmented the size of their holdings by accretion. Brown soon devised a litigation strategy designed to reduce these costs—to zero: he would simply persuade the Illinois Supreme Court to repudiate the right to wharf out.[15]

The key to the strategy was that in 1894, just two years after its decision in the *Lake Front Case*, the Supreme Court had decided to look to the states on all issues about the nature and scope of riparian rights within each state. The scholarly opinion by Justice Horace Gray in *Shively v. Bowlby* reaffirmed that, under federal law (the equal-footing doctrine), the state governments presumptively owned the land beneath navigable waters. But as to the details—such as whether states could convey submerged land to private parties or allow riparian owners to wharf out on state-owned submerged land—the court said that these were questions of state law. The court went out of its way to minimize the significance of its statements endorsing the right to wharf out in *Dutton v. Strong*, *Railroad Co. v. Schurmeir*, and *Yates v. Milwaukee*, stating that "none of the three cases called for the laying down or defining of any general rule, independent of local law or usage, or of the particular facts before the court."[16]

Nothing in the lengthy opinion in *Shively* suggests that the Supreme Court was hostile to wharfing out. The motivation for the decision appears, rather, to have been a growing recognition by the court that it was impossible to articulate a general common law on the subject. It is also possible that the expanding role of

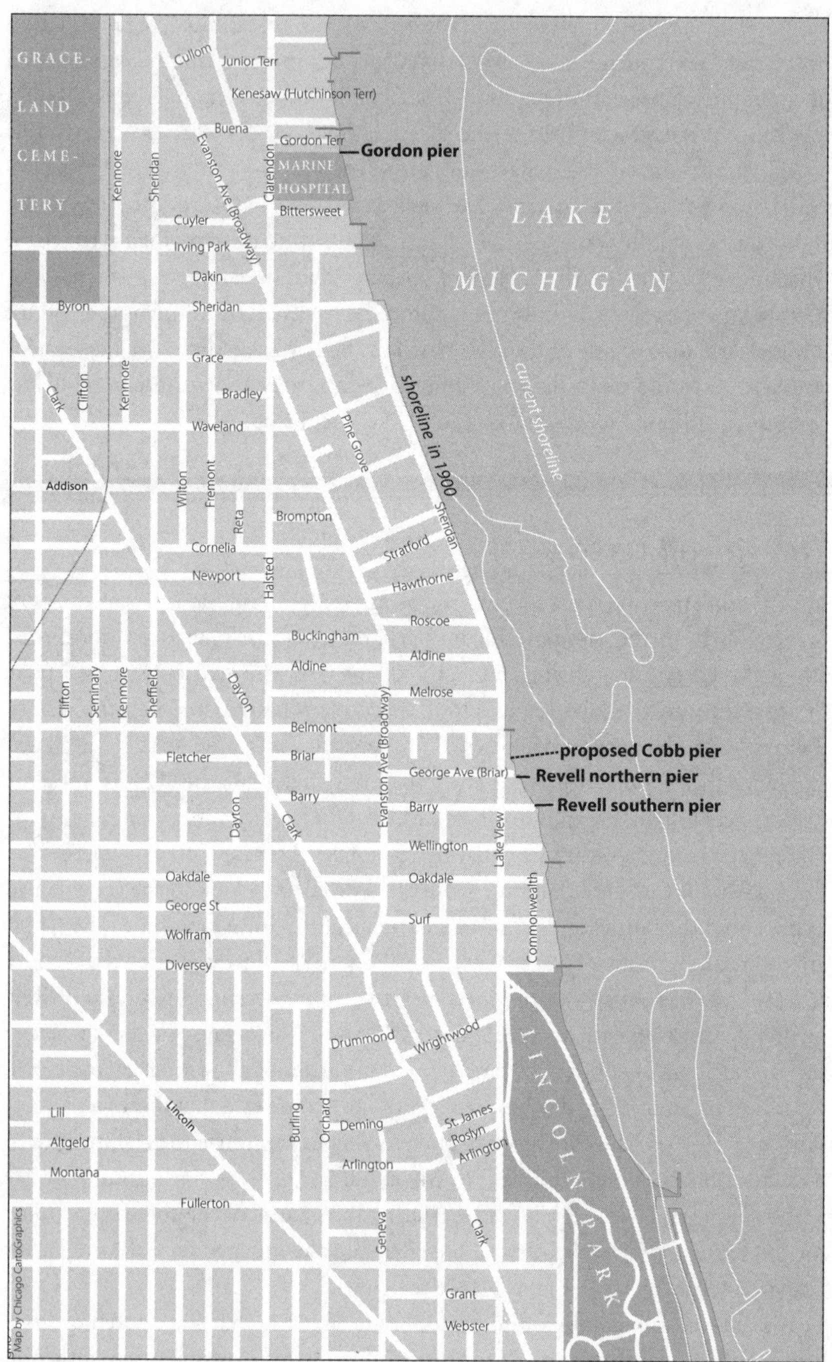

FIGURE 6.3. Locations of the Revell and other properties involved in wharfing-out cases, north of the original Lincoln Park.

the War Department in protecting navigable waters from local encroachments, under authority conferred by Congress starting in 1890, gave the court confidence that the interest in preserving navigation would be adequately protected by federal administrative action.[17]

In any event, shortly after *Shively* was decided, Brown, as counsel to the Lincoln Park Commission, launched a legal assault on the right to wharf out in Lake Michigan. The original targets were landowners north of the original Lincoln Park who had built piers that Brown regarded as designed to induce accretion. For the first suit, in 1895, Brown elected to proceed against Alexander Revell, who owned lakefront property a short distance north of Diversey Avenue, the northern end of the original park. Revell had constructed a pier running perpendicularly into the lake at each end of his property, the longer one extending about two hundred feet. Brown cleverly harnessed the "well-known zeal at that time of the attorney general to prevent the submerged shallows belonging to the state from becoming private property." Specifically, as he later recounted it, he persuaded Maurice Moloney "to allow his name and the authority of his office to be used" in this "test" case. The second suit, against Charles Gordon, who owned riparian land approximately two miles farther north, was filed shortly afterward, in 1896. These locations are shown in figure 6.3.[18]

Brown had two advantages over Revell and Gordon. First, neither defendant could claim that the piers had been constructed for purposes of navigation—the traditional rationale for the right to wharf out. Instead, Brown could credibly allege that they had been constructed to induce artificial accretion. Second, Brown out-lawyered Revell and Gordon. While the briefs in *Revell* have been lost, it is evident from the briefs in *Gordon*, where the same law firm appeared in support of the riparian owner as had represented Revell, that the defendants' lawyers were no match for Brown.[19]

Revell was decided first and became the decisive precedent on the right to wharf out in Illinois. It took the form of a simple syllogism. The first premise was that Illinois held legal title to the bed of Lake Michigan, having succeeded to the rights originally held by the king of England with respect to submerged lands under navigable waters. The second was that Illinois had adopted the common law of England as it stood in 1606, which "must control" in "the absence of any statute of the state changing the common law in regard to the rights of riparian or littoral owners." The third was that the common law as of 1606 had held that any encroachment on submerged land owned by the king was a "purpresture," which "may be enjoined or abated in a court of equity although it is not injurious or not a public nuisance." Ergo, the state could order that a wharf encroaching on submerged land in the lake be abated—torn down at the wharf owner's expense—without regard to whether it caused any injury or inconvenience to the public.[20]

The validity of this syllogism is questionable for several reasons. That the king in fact had title to submerged land under tidal waters was a proposition invented by lawyers for the Stuarts seeking enhanced royal revenues, and was in fact sharply contested in 1606. Only later was the theory accepted. Even then, it is hard if not impossible to find a case in which a pier or wharf was actually torn down as a "purpresture" unless it was a public nuisance. At most, such a wharf would be "arrented," meaning that the king would demand a rental payment from the wharf operator. All this can be gathered from a careful reading of the treatises of the time, including those cited by the court in *Revell*. Moreover, the English courts developed a procedure allowing a riparian owner to obtain an advance judicial determination that a wharf would not be a public nuisance, and a judgment to this effect would immunize the owner from any demand that the wharf be "abated." This also was documented in the treatises. The proposition that the common law allowed the English Crown to destroy any wharf constructed on royal tidal lands for any reason was a caricature at best.[21]

A deeper irony was the inconsistency between the court's first and second premises about the nature of the common law. The first premise of the court's syllogism understood or assumed that the common law tolerates or encompasses pragmatic adjustments in light of changed circumstances. Recall that, at English common law, it had been understood that the king's title to submerged land extended only to waters subject to the ebb and flow of the tide. This particular common-law rule, however, had been significantly modified by American courts, including the Illinois Supreme Court in the *Kirk* case, which extended sovereign title to important nontidal lands, including the Great Lakes. The change was not prompted by any statutory revision, but by the judicial perception that the Great Lakes are vital in the same way as the water subject to the tides is vital to navigation in England. The second premise, by contrast, was based on the proposition that the common law had been frozen as of 1606 and could be changed only by legislation. The court never explained why judicial pragmatism was appropriate in defining one premise while rigid positivism was required for the other, even when both premises concerned the nature and scope of riparian rights on navigable watercourses.[22]

And what about the precedent of the *Lake Front Case*, which had recognized a right to wharf out on Lake Michigan? This was shunted aside on the authority of *Shively v. Bowlby*. The *Lake Front Case* had relied on *Dutton*, *Schurmeir*, and *Yates*, the *Revell* court said. But the doctrine laid down in those three cases had been "substantially repudiated" by *Shively*, which held that "each State has the right to determine for itself the title and rights of riparian owners within its border." The Illinois Supreme Court determined that it was "a better policy for all concerned to adhere to the common law rule [i.e., the rule in 1606] rather than follow the doctrine laid down in the *Illinois Central* case."[23]

The bottom line, the court ruled, was that Revell had no "right to construct piers upon the submerged lands without the consent of the State." This made *Gordon* a foregone conclusion. The injunction at the behest of the LPC ordering Gordon to tear down his pier was affirmed by the Illinois Supreme Court one year later, in a terse opinion citing only *Revell*.[24]

There was one possible reservation. Although the court in *Revell* said that it chose to follow "the common law" of 1606 rather than the *Lake Front Case* of 1892, it also acknowledged that the right recognized in the *Lake Front Case* was "the right to wharf out in aid of navigation." This had no application to *Revell*, "as the piers erected by the appellant in this case were not constructed in aid of navigation." Thus, the court arguably reserved for the future the question whether the right to wharf out might be recognized if its purpose was navigation rather than erosion control or an attempt to induce accretion.[25]

A few years later, the Illinois Supreme Court was given the opportunity to resolve that question. Henry Ives Cobb owned riparian land just north of Revell's property. Cobb developed a plan to build a wharf that would extend five or six hundred feet into the lake, reaching waters deep enough to permit lake steamers to load and unload. The LPC, which held title to the submerged land based on its plan to extend Lake Shore Drive north of Diversey, refused to consent. In 1900, Cobb unsuccessfully sought an injunction against the park district.[26]

On appeal to the Illinois Supreme Court, Cobb's lawyers advanced the key argument that had been missing in *Revell*: Cobb as a riparian owner had an undisputed *right of access* to the water, and "as incidental to that right he is entitled to use the submerged land in shoal water, which is the property of the state, in order to make that right available, otherwise the right is no right at all." Cobb submitted a massive brief supporting the right of access and the incidental right to wharf out as critical to the maintenance of commercial navigation. The court, guided by a brief from the LPC nearly as formidable, distinguished as many of these authorities as it could. The only thing the court did not do was to explain why Cobb's argument was wrong. In the end, once again, the Illinois Supreme Court simply relied on *Revell*.[27]

Although *Revell* laid the intellectual foundations, *Cobb*'s repudiation of the right to wharf out for purposes of navigation was the bigger departure from legal tradition. The *Cobb* decision is a plausible candidate for the now-much-mooted controversy about "judicial takings." In the face of dozens of decisions assuming or upholding a right, independent of title, to wharf out to engage in commercial navigation—including a high-profile US Supreme Court decision involving the same body of water—the state court embraced a contrived syllogism based on the supposed prerogatives of the king of England in 1606 in order to deny the existence of the right. Moreover, it did so at the behest of an entity that was eager to reduce the amount of compensation it would have had to pay for condemning such rights.[28]

The practical implications were profound. After *Cobb*, it was difficult to imagine how any private owner would agree to construct a harbor facility in Lake Michigan. The *Lake Front Case* closed off the possibility of a reliable grant of the state-owned lakebed to a private entity to build a harbor. And if, as *Cobb* establishes, the government can order any private pier or wharf "abated"—torn down—for any or no reason at all, and without any obligation to pay compensation, no riparian owner will build a pier or wharf on such submerged land.[29]

In short, the decision in *Cobb* meant that the government would have to undertake any future construction of harbor facilities in the lake. Progressives such as Brown and Moloney may have assumed that the government was prepared to step into this breach. And, in fact, discussion of various plans for constructing a public outer harbor on the lakefront continued at this time. But given the absence of funding for such a project, coupled with endless disagreement about where such an outer harbor should be located, the aspiration gradually faded away. With the single exception of Navy Pier, no wharves for the purpose of commercial navigation would ever again extend from Chicago into Lake Michigan itself.[30]

The repudiation of the right to wharf out in *Revell* created a new argument for the courts to wrestle with on remand in the *Lake Front Case*. The federal trial court found that the railroad's extensive landfills did not extend beyond the point needed to reach navigable waters. By the time this judgment was on appeal to the Seventh Circuit in 1899, both *Shively* (1894) and *Revell* (1898) had been decided. In light of these developments, the state argued vigorously that under Illinois law the Illinois Central's wharves, piers, and other improvements were unauthorized purprestures, which the state could order abated.[31]

The Seventh Circuit dodged what it described as "this most interesting question," concluding that it was outside the scope of the remand and upholding the decision in favor of the railroad. In affirming, the Supreme Court also framed the issue in such a way as to avoid any consideration of the implications of *Shively* and *Revell*. Speaking for the court, Justice Harlan observed that his original circuit court decision in 1888 had rejected all challenges to the railroad's improvements. This decision had been fully affirmed in the 1892 *Lake Front Case*—save only the question whether the improvements exceeded the scope needed to reach navigable waters. This was the only issue that had been open for consideration on remand. On this technical ground, the Illinois Central was able to retain its extensive improvements in the lake. In 1902, as ten years earlier, the Supreme Court was not eager to dismantle one of the major rail complexes in the United States.[32]

Yet given *Revell* and *Cobb*, any *additional* landfilling by the railroad based on the right to wharf out was now impossible. In 1898, the Illinois Supreme Court had also rejected the claim that the Illinois Central's 1851 charter authorized landfilling in the lake. Thus, further expansion by the railroad in the lake was seemingly foreclosed. More subtly, the legitimacy of the railroad's existing improvements was undermined. The Chiperfield Committee soon called for the Illinois attorney general to launch a new assault on the railroad's right to occupy what had once been lakebed. The railroad would remain on the defensive about its rights to these lands for years—until a boundary-line agreement and another court decision came to its rescue (see chapter 7).[33]

Building North Lake Shore Drive

But first we must finish Lake Shore Drive on the North Side. With the decisions in *Revell* and *Cobb*, and the 1903 statute allowing the negotiation of fixed boundaries with riparian owners, the LPC's lawyers were able to reach no-cost settlements with many landowners. The park district's policy in the next several years, according to its report in 1908, was "to establish shore lines [if] at least a half-mile of frontage could be included in one proceeding." In this fashion, by the end of that year, through four separate court proceedings, boundary lines had been established as far north as Bryn Mawr Avenue, with boundaries for a few smaller areas in between remaining unfixed. There was a hint of problems to come: according to the report, it might be necessary to resort to individualized boundary proceedings, "inasmuch as in several instances [property owners] have been unable to get the consent of their neighbors to such action."[34]

The original plan for Lincoln Park's north extension, as promulgated in 1895, was unimaginative. As seen especially toward the top of figure 6.4, it called for a more or less rectangular band of reclaimed land approximately one thousand feet in width, running parallel to the original shore, consisting of a new breakwater at the eastern edge, a narrow pleasure drive just inside the breakwater, and a new park between the drive and the western boundary of the landfill. The plan divided the extension into two rectangular segments: a short span from Diversey to Belmont, followed by a gap of approximately a mile, and then a resumption in a long span running all the way north to Devon.[35]

Construction of the park extension proceeded at a glacial pace. Evidently, the LPC was able to do some work in the more southern of the two segments during

EXPLANATION.

The shaded portions, indicate parks already established. The dotted portions are extensions, plans for which have been adopted by the Board of Commissioners of Lincoln Park. That portion east of the Park, and between Diversey and Fullerton Boulevards, require a plan, none having been adopted. The dotted lines on the map show a proposed plan which may, or may not, be adopted. The letters indicate. ‘A” Land; “B” Bathing Beach; “C” [illegible]nd Steamer Harbor.

In order to proceed with these improvements, all of which are in the Town of Lake View, it is necessary to have the consents of the Assessor and Supervisor of the town. With these having been secured, the work of improvement can be at once proceeded with, the money necessary being obtained from long time, low interest bonds.

With these additions, Lincoln Park would have somewhere near 1200 acres, exclusive of Boulevards.

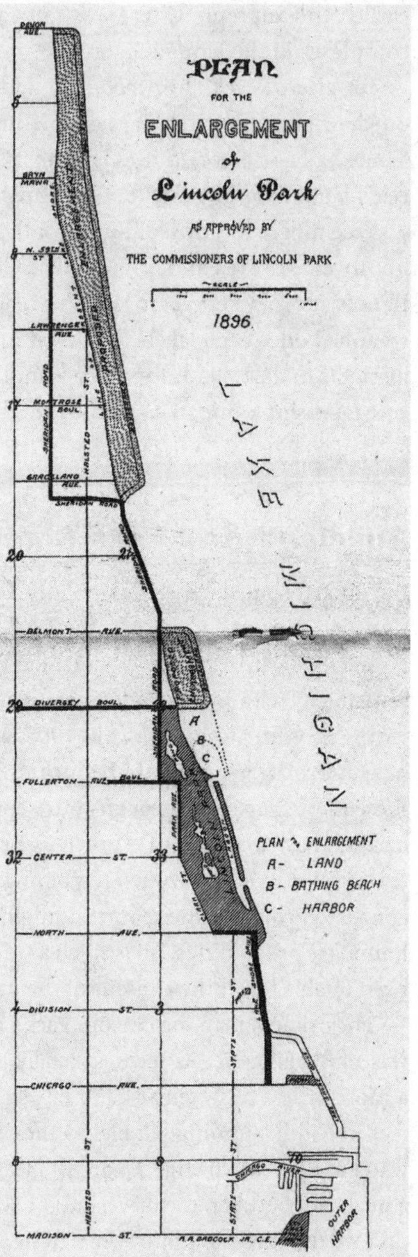

FIGURE 6.4. 1895 plan for north extension of Lincoln Park and Lake Shore Drive as approved by the Commissioners of Lincoln Park. From the *Report of the Commissioners of Lincoln Park*, April 1, 1895–March 31, 1896.

the first decade after the 1903 act. But construction on the more northern segment did not start during this time. Even by 1920, the only work that had been completed in the northern segment was the construction of a breakwater at its very beginning.[36]

Sometime around 1923, with the revenue picture improving, the LPC started to rethink its plans for the northern extension of Lincoln Park. Statements appeared in the press that focused on the increasing use of the drive by motorists commuting to downtown. The commission announced its intention to construct two drives—termed in the press an "inner park drive" on the western edge of the park and an "outer or shore drive"—in order to give "autoists" more ways to commute to and from the center of the city. Eugene R. Pike, president of the LPC, said that this "illustrates the commission's policy—to avoid grandiose announcements and litigation, and to go on with its work section by section, letting each section show to the people how nice the completed whole is going to be." Early in 1925, the *Chicago Tribune* published an article by Pike detailing a number of modifications the LPC had made to improve the flow of traffic and announcing that "[t]he commissioners of Lincoln park have under consideration further plans for relieving traffic congestion and adding to the safety of the public." He added, "These plans will be completed as fast as we have funds available for the purpose."[37]

True to Pike's word, when work began in earnest on the more northern segment of the park extension in 1926, it bore little resemblance to the narrow band of park set forth in the 1895 plan. The park district began following a radically different conception, calling for filling approximately four times as much land as the 1895 plan had contemplated. Far from creating a straight shoreline parallel to the original shore, the new work featured an undulating shoreline, with multiple harbors and lagoons, beaches, and a golf course all extending into the lake. Instead of a narrow pleasure drive, nestled against a breakwater at the eastern edge of the park, Lincoln Park would have a multilane, limited-access expressway running along the *western* edge of the landfill. This would be near the boundary line of the original riparian property, with the parkland to the east of the roadway, punctuated by a variety of interior drives and parking lots.[38]

The Robbins family owned riparian land in this construction zone, as reflected in figure 6.5. In 1906, Burr Robbins had conveyed his riparian rights to the LPC in return for an agreed boundary. Two decades later, his heirs saw park district workers constructing an embankment 15 to 20 feet high in front of their property, impairing their view of the lake, and a 100-foot-wide roadway on top of the embankment, cutting off their property from the projected park. They sued for an injunction from the circuit court. The Robbinses pointed out that the original plan called for landfill of 1,000 feet in front (east) of their property; the

FIGURE 6.5. Locations of Robbins, Schmidt, Wall, and Saddle and Cycle Club properties (the latter three discussed later in the chapter).

construction underway reflected a shoreline 3,500 feet east. The original plan put the drive nearly 1,000 feet from their property line; the construction placed the much larger roadway only 122 feet away from them.[39]

The Robbinses were obviously irritated, but did they have a claim? The 1906 contract promised submerged land in return for a release of riparian rights. Burr Robbins had gotten the new land and released his rights. The family could point to no language in the contract promising that the park extension would adhere to exact features shown in the 1895 plan. Indeed, their claim could be seen as a plea for a partial restoration of the riparian rights that their ancestor had agreed to give up. In the summer of 1927, the circuit court dismissed their claim for want of equity. The Robbinses appealed, but there is no indication that they sought a stay pending appeal. Meanwhile, the LPC proceeded aggressively with construction under the new plan, largely completing the expanded project north to Montrose Avenue late that year.[40]

When the Illinois Supreme Court rendered its decision the next spring, it gave a surprise victory to the Robbinses. The court found that the 1906 contract contemplated that the project would comport with the purposes set forth in the 1895 act. The dominant purpose was to create new land dedicated to a park. Now the contemplated use of the filled land adjacent to the Robbinses' property was not "for park purposes but for a public highway." The opinion was unclear about how far the park district would be permitted to deviate from the 1895 plan without violating the restriction to park purposes. But it ruled against the park district and directed that on remand the lower court consider whether to enter the injunction sought by the Robbinses.[41]

The *Robbins* decision and mounting resistance by property owners obviously required the LPC to rethink its course of action. It determined to press forward with the more ambitious concept for the expanded park, taking three steps in response to the decision.

First, the commission commenced at least twenty-six eminent-domain actions seeking to condemn riparian rights along the lakeshore that it had not acquired through negotiated boundary agreements, focusing on the northernmost area of the projected extension (between Bryn Mawr and Devon). It appears that only one of these actions, *Commissioners of Lincoln Park v. Schmidt*, was tried. That case disclosed why the LPC had been wise in its initial strategy of avoiding condemnation. The suit, filed in 1928, dragged on for eighteen years, generated four appeals to the Illinois Supreme Court, and, though formally abandoned in 1943, was not finally resolved for three more years (the last two appeals involved attorneys' fees the park district had to pay). The result at trial suggests that condemnation would be expensive, even aside from litigation costs. As urged by the LPC, the trial judge instructed the jury to measure compensation based on the value of the Schmidt property before and after the completion of the proposed project. The LPC assumed that the projected improvements would increase the value of the Schmidt property, substantially or completely offsetting the loss of riparian rights. Yet the jury returned a verdict that the park district owed the Schmidts $32,550. The jury evidently found that the greater distance from the lake, together with the noise and inconvenience of having a multilane, controlled-access highway inserted between the property and the park, significantly *reduced* the market value of the property. The park district asked for a new trial, but the Illinois Supreme Court concluded that it was effectively objecting to the very method of calculating compensation it had proposed at trial. The LPC dropped any further attempt to condemn the Schmidts' riparian rights—and all other pending condemnation actions as well.[42]

The second response to *Robbins* was for the park district to return to the Illinois legislature. Legislation in 1927 had authorized the construction of lagoons and harbors within the area reclaimed from the lake. This still left in place the 1895 plan, however, which under the reasoning of *Robbins* was incorporated by reference into all existing contracts with riparian owners. So, in 1931, the LPC obtained legislation that replaced the 1895 act. The new law made clear that the LPC was authorized to construct multiple boulevards and driveways on the filled land, as opposed to a single driveway as under the original act; it also removed the requirement that the driveway be located at the eastern edge of the reclaimed land next to a seawall.[43]

The third response was to create new plans for the extension of Lincoln Park and Lake Shore Drive north of Montrose. For these purposes, the LPC employed a consulting engineer, Hugh E. Young, of the Chicago Plan Commission. In 1929, Young oversaw development of an elaborate plan showing proposed features north to Devon Avenue. Young's design, as seen in figure 6.6, was even more exuberant than the one pursued in 1926. It showed a curvilinear shoreline, numerous boat harbors, bathing beaches, playing fields, and a large golf course. Lake Shore Drive was a limited-access expressway, running along the western edge of the landfill. Underpasses at major cross streets, with connecting exits from the drive, provided access to the park. Within the park itself, winding roads and parking lots served various recreation venues. Later, in 1931, the LPC formally adopted a new plan, as seen in figure 6.7, showing an even more imaginative conception for the park, especially between Foster Avenue and Devon, complete with a large harbor with an island at Thorndale Avenue. This plan would never be fully implemented.[44]

If the park district expected these actions somehow to overcome the resistance by landowners to its enlarged ambitions, it was mistaken. In 1937, Julia Wall and others, owners of riparian property on the final stretch of the proposed

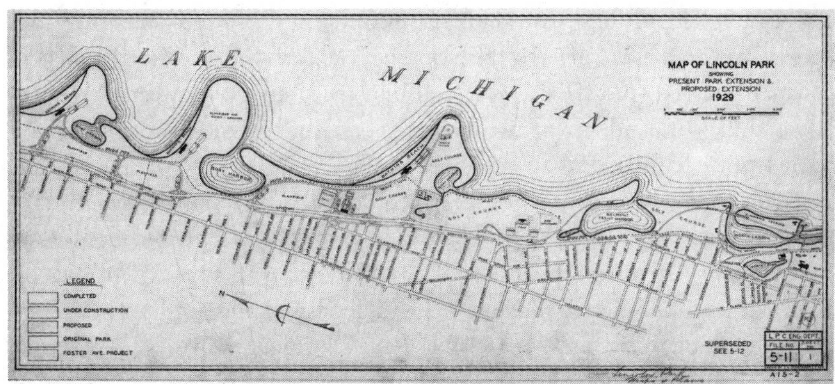

FIGURE 6.6. 1929 plan for the extension of Lincoln Park and Lake Shore Drive. Chicago Public Library, Special Collections, Chicago Park District Archives, Drawings, CPD3254.

FIGURE 6.7. 1931 plan for the extension of Lincoln Park and Lake Shore Drive. Chicago Public Library, Special Collections, Chicago Park District Archives, Drawings, 0100-0123-1931-1.

extension (see figure 6.5), just south of Devon Avenue, also filed suit. Their predecessors in title had conveyed their riparian rights to the park district in 1912 and had obtained a judicial decree establishing the boundary between their property and the parkland. The plaintiffs sought rescission of the 1912 contract and reconveyance to them of the riparian rights.[45]

Their argument had two parts. First, echoing the decision in *Robbins*, the plaintiffs argued that the contract had been executed in contemplation of the 1895 plan. A very different plan based on a different act had now replaced this plan. The plaintiffs alleged that this was a material alteration of the 1912 agreement, justifying rescission. The 1895 plan showed a "narrow park" 740 feet wide outside their property, with a 212-foot boulevard on the outer or eastern edge. The new plans called for a park 4,660 feet wide opposite the plaintiffs' property, "lying between it and Lake Michigan," with the first thing east of the property being a double highway, with a traffic separator in the center and a uniform width of 225 feet from curb to curb. East of the new drive, the plan included, among other things, a 30-foot driveway, then a bridle path, and a lagoon as much as 1,340 feet wide, west to east.[46]

Second, neither the LPC nor its successor as of 1934, the Chicago Park District, had fulfilled the promises made in the 1912 contract, at least implicitly, to construct a breakwater protecting the plaintiffs' property. The Walls and the other owners had incurred major expenditures in 1929 and 1930 (and would again in 1938), in an effort to restore their land following storm damage. The persistent failure of the LPC to build the breakwater, the plaintiffs argued, also supported rescission. The circuit court agreed and ordered the restoration of the plaintiffs' riparian rights.[47]

In 1941, the Illinois Supreme Court affirmed the judgment for the plaintiffs. The court noted that expert testimony about the effect of the changed plan on the value of the plaintiffs' property was in "hopeless conflict." But the court credited testimony that "the uncertainty resulting from the adoption of the 1931 plan, and as to when it would be consummated," had given rise to a "chaotic condition . . . which had impaired the marketability of property in the vicinity for a considerable period of time." It found that, generally speaking, "the market value of the plaintiffs' property has been diminished as a result of the condition described, although the amount of the diminution is not susceptible of precise mathematical computation." With these findings, the outcome was inevitable.[48]

The *Wall* decision was a hard blow to the park district. The park and drive had been extended to Foster Avenue, but the park district now faced severe difficulties in completing the project to the intended northern terminus, a mile and a half north, at Devon Avenue. The combination of the *Schmidt* decisions and the language in *Wall* about the damaging effects of the enlarged project on property values meant that any effort to acquire riparian rights by condemning the rights of the remaining holdouts—which potentially included anyone seeking rescission of a contract entered into before 1931—would be prohibitively expensive. This explains why all the condemnation suits were dropped.[49]

The difficulties of pressing farther north were nevertheless overcome one more time, in a manner that starkly confirmed the daunting price of completing the project. After World War II, the park district negotiated with the Saddle and Cycle Club, the owner of land north of Foster Avenue, where the drive then ended (see figure 6.5). The club had conveyed its riparian rights to the LPC previously (the date being reported variously as 1928 and 1931), in return for a generous boundary agreement giving the club new reclaimed land. In 1938, echoing the complaint filed by the *Wall* plaintiffs one year earlier, the club filed suit seeking rescission. The action was evidently held in abeyance during the war; after *Wall* and the war, the park district secured a new settlement. Specifically, in 1947, the parties agreed to relocate the boundary line of the club's property farther east, giving the club an additional four acres of submerged land. In 1950, the *Tribune* reported that the Saddle and Cycle Club was selling all of its original land that fronted on Sheridan Road, to the west. The article explained that "[t]he nearly three acres along Sheridan rd. to be sold thus are offset by the more than four acres acquired from the park board." In other words, in exchange for giving up its objections to the new plan,

FIGURE 6.8. Original Saddle and Cycle Club, ca. 1915. Chicago History Museum, ICHi-092978.

the club was able to pocket the proceeds from selling prime real estate and still end up with more land than it ever had previously.[50]

On November 27, 1954, the Lake Shore Drive extension from Foster to Hollywood was officially opened. A Cook County commissioner expressed the hope that someday the drive would extend all the way to the Wisconsin border. It was not to be. Hollywood—little more than a half mile north of Foster and less than half the distance from Foster to the proposed northern terminus of Devon—marks the farthest extension of the drive to the north. Though not apparent to most observers at the time, the ability of the park district to acquire riparian rights had reached a dead end. The original contracts negotiated under the authority of the 1895 act were no longer valid in light of *Robbins* and *Wall*. Condemnation of riparian rights would be very expensive under *Schmidt*. The only other option was to locate the boundary between the riparian owners and the new park in such a way as to give riparian owners vastly more reclaimed land. Even with such a sweetener, this was unlikely to interest the riparian owners on Sheridan Road north of Hollywood, some of whom now were planning to build high-rise apartments favored with views of the lake. Continuation of the

FIGURE 6.9. Lincoln Park and Lake Shore Drive, looking south from Foster Avenue, 1935. Landfilling and drive construction farther north to Hollywood Avenue were not yet underway. Chicago Public Library, Chicago Park District Archives, 154_004_002; Chicago Aerial Survey Co.

project had become financially infeasible. Once the high-rise towers were built, it would be politically infeasible as well.[51]

In this chapter, we have seen how the Lincoln Park Commission devised two methods for acquiring the riparian rights of landowners in order to extend Lincoln Park to the north. One was the boundary-line mechanism, the other the judicial elimination of any right to wharf out in Lake Michigan. Edward O. Brown, a creative lawyer working for the LPC in the late nineteenth and early twentieth centuries, deserves credit for conceiving and advancing both ideas. Brown's motivation was the very short-term objective of acquiring riparian rights without having to pay for them, made necessary by the LPC's having little money at the time. The long-term effects were profound.

If one thinks that having a largely unspoiled expanse of park along the shore of Lake Michigan at the front door of Chicago is a wonderful thing—as most everyone who experiences Chicago today does—then Brown's skillful manipulation of the courts to eliminate the right to wharf out turned out to be a good thing. If any private wharf can be abated by the government for any or no reason, then private wharves will disappear, as they did in Chicago. Those who cheered the elimination of the right to wharf out were not antiwharf: the dream of constructing an outer harbor in the lake continued to be a theme of public discussion well into the twentieth century. But the only public wharf built in the lake to accommodate commercial traffic was Navy Pier, which was never large enough by itself to attract significant landings of freight traffic. It has been converted into a mixed-use tourist attraction. The Calumet River, much farther south, became the commercial harbor for Chicago. Without private wharves, and only one public wharf, the lakeshore was free to be filled with parkland nearly from one end to the other. In any event, an obscure lawyer working out solutions to a mundane property-rights problem at the end of the nineteenth century had a profound impact—one that was entirely unimagined at the time—on the visage of the city.

As we will see in the next chapter, Brown's ideas would also be instrumental in the construction of south Lake Shore Drive, where they encountered a more formidable adversary: the Illinois Central Railroad.

7

SOUTH LAKE SHORE DRIVE AND BRIDGING THE RIVER

The project of constructing Lake Shore Drive on the South Side of Chicago was different from the North Side, although the legal method of acquiring riparian rights was the same. History and geography produced the differences. On the North Side, the project started as a park with a pleasure drive, which gradually extended to the south and north. It came to include a limited-access highway only after traffic volume began to surge in the 1920s. On the South Side, there was a major park at each end—Grant Park on the north and Jackson Park on the south—and the drive was conceived as a boulevard linking them together. As a result, south Lake Shore Drive was more of a highway project, and less of a park, from the beginning.

The aesthetics were also different. Lincoln Park, featuring a winding drive and a lagoon, was an arboreal refuge for quiet family outings. On the South Side, the lakefront development was heavily influenced by Daniel Burnham and the City Beautiful movement. Jackson Park (the site of the 1893 World's Fair) and Grant Park both featured neoclassical structures, and Grant Park sported formal gardens in the Beaux Arts style. Major public buildings along the route of south Lake Shore Drive were built in the neoclassical style. Thus, south Lake Shore Drive, as it eventually emerged, was relatively stark, formal, and treeless compared to the drive on the North Side.

This chapter tells the story of Lake Shore Drive on the South Side, including how it became one with its counterpart on the North Side.

The Origins of South Lake Shore Drive

The idea of south Lake Shore Drive, in a very general sense, can be traced to the World's Fair. One proposal during the transportation planning was to construct a boulevard system from Lake Park south to Washington Park, just west of the fair site, with the northernmost part (south of Park Row) being near the lake. Whether for lack of time, money, or need—or because some viewed it as a project for the vanity of the Prairie Avenue types—the idea did not move forward until after the fair.[1]

The concept began to gain traction when Daniel Burnham, who had been the director of works for the fair, was asked by the Commercial Club of Chicago to present a plan for the south lakefront. His presentation prominently included the construction of a drive connecting Lake Park—where aggressive landfilling had just started and which was soon to be renamed Grant Park—and Jackson Park. A map prepared by the city in 1896 shows a "Proposed Drive and Waterway" linking the two parks. Figure 7.1, emerging from Burnham and Bennett's *Plan of Chicago* and the events described below, is a somewhat later, widely publicized variation on the idea.[2]

Part of the spate of state legislation in 1903 was a new statute authorizing the South Park Commission (SPC) to build the proposed drive connecting the lakefront parks. The statute authorized the park district to "extend any such park" by constructing a connecting drive, but the emphasis was not on the park but on the drive. In order to extinguish the riparian rights of abutting landowners, the act provided that the park district was to acquire these rights "by contract with, or deeds from, any such owner or owners," the cost to be paid by the park district "out of its general revenue." The SPC had greater taxing power than the LPC on

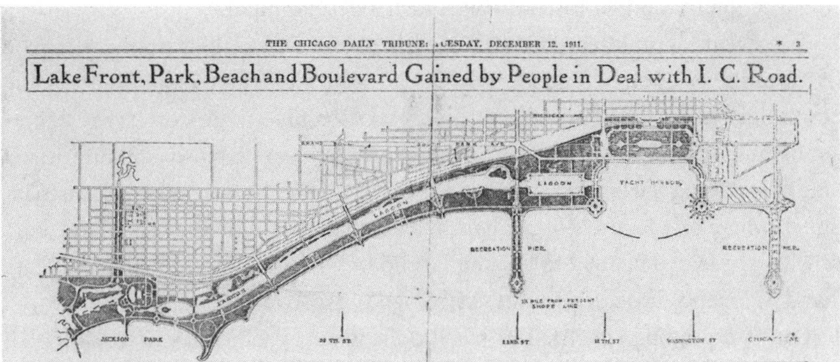

FIGURE 7.1. Plan for a boulevard and waterway linking Jackson and Grant Parks. *Chicago Tribune*, December 12, 1911.

the North Side, but competing projects and the extraordinary levy necessary to support a purchase of riparian rights discouraged it from immediately moving forward.[3]

Meanwhile, as we have seen, a solution to the funding problem had been devised by the LPC in the form of land-for-rights swaps embodied in boundary-line decrees. The Commercial Club went to Springfield in 1907 and came away with a new statute authorizing the SPC to acquire riparian rights using boundary agreements. The 1907 act included the familiar promise that land west of the boundary line would be "free from any adverse claim." At the same time, there were several significant modifications of the Lincoln Park model. In one respect, the 1907 act went beyond the earlier statutes: it authorized the riparian owner to "fill in" the "submerged lands up to the line so established" and thus expressly acknowledged that the boundary-line decree could be used to transfer submerged land to the riparian owner. But unlike the 1895 and 1903 statutes used for Lincoln Park, the 1907 act provided that condemnation could be used to acquire riparian rights on the South Side only if the owner was *non sui juris*, in the statutory phrase (e.g., a minor or an insane person), or unknown. The act also included an unusual provision allowing "[a]ny legal voter or taxpayer" in the district to intervene in a judicial proceeding to establish a boundary line, and to voice his or her objections. The court was instructed to confirm and establish the agreed boundary line only if it found, "upon a hearing, . . . that the rights and interests of the public have been duly conserved in and by such agreement."[4]

The SPC did not immediately proceed. The explanation, apparently, is that the city's new mayor was actively exploring building an outer harbor, one possible location being on the near South Side, and the SPC did not want to engage in any construction that might interfere with such a development.[5]

Two events soon intervened that moved the project to the front burner. The first was the election of Theodore K. Long to the city council in 1909 from the South Side, near Hyde Park. Long quickly focused his energies on trying to create bathing beaches on the lakefront. The problem was extensive unauthorized landfilling along the lakefront on the South Side. This included an area, near 51st Street, where one James Morgan had created nearly eight new acres of land, part of which he leased in 1892 to Warren Leland (whom we encountered in chapters 2 and 3) for the construction of the Chicago Beach Hotel.[6]

Long's crusading spirit led to his appointment by Chicago's mayor in 1910 as head of a new entity—the Lake Shore Reclamation Commission—to investigate unauthorized landfilling on the lakefront. Long helped persuade the Illinois attorney general to file suit in the spring of 1910 against all known riparian owners between 12th Street and Jackson Park, seeking to recover for the public all

FIGURE 7.2. Theodore K. Long. *History of the Long Family of Pennsylvania*, by William Gabriel Long (Huntington, WV: Long Family Organization of Pennsylvania, 1930), 64.

lands that had been unlawfully reclaimed from the lake in this area. The defendants included the Morgan and Pullman heirs, but by far the most powerful defendant was the Illinois Central Railroad, whose line ran along the lakeshore from 12th Street to 51st Street. Although its charter from the state gave it a two-hundred-foot right of way for railroad purposes, the Illinois Central claimed to have acquired, in separate transactions, nearly all the riparian rights along the lake in this roughly five-mile stretch, more land than all the other defendants combined. The railroad had relied on these riparian rights to justify the construction of breakwaters protecting its tracks as well as to establish a substantial rail yard between 12th and 16th Streets (see chapter 2). The SPC became interested in the suits, and forged an alliance with Long and the attorney general, suggesting that the suits could be used to extinguish existing riparian rights and transfer submerged land to the SPC for construction of the drive. Long was willing to settle the cases on this basis, but little progress was made at first in bringing the suits to trial or securing settlements.[7]

The other catalytic event was the Illinois Supreme Court's decision in *Ward IV*, handed down at the end of 1910. This decision dealt a fatal blow to the SPC's plan to locate the Field Museum in the center of Grant Park, as recounted in chapter 3.

FIGURE 7.3. Illinois Central Railroad right of way and yard along Lake Michigan, viewed to the southeast near 12th Street (likely from Central Station), 1907. After the boundary-line agreement of 1912, the visible area, including this portion of Lake Michigan, was filled and became the site of the Field Museum and today's Museum Campus. Chicago History Museum, ICHi-068374.

Marshall Field's will required that a site be provided for the museum by January 16, 1912, or the bequest would fail. Now in a crisis, the SPC had to find an alternative location. The most logical spot was just beyond the southern boundary of the park, on the landfill peninsula that the Illinois Central had created to support its railroad operations, as augmented by new landfill extending farther out into the lake. The peninsula was one of the two areas that the courts in the *Lake Front Case* had held to be justifiably reclaimed by the Illinois Central under the common-law right to wharf out.

The pieces were now in place for one of those grand bargains that have a transformative effect on a city. During the summer and fall of 1911, a series of meetings took place between some of the most powerful actors in Chicago, including the mayor, members of the Chicago Plan Commission and the South Park Commission, Stanley Field (nephew of the late Marshall Field), several newspaper editors, Alderman Long on behalf of the Reclamation Commission, and, scarcely least, officers of the Illinois Central. The basic outline of a deal emerged, calling for the Illinois Central to convey its land east and south of Central Station to the SPC for the purpose of building the Field Museum. In return, the park district would enter into a boundary agreement with the Illinois Central, which would receive new submerged land south of 16th Street, to be filled and occupied by the railroad for new rail lines and repair yards replacing the ones given up.[8]

On December 11, 1911, the Illinois Central and the SPC signed a comprehensive agreement providing for a complicated exchange of rights. The settlement fixed a new permanent boundary starting at the southern edge of Grant Park, at a point 761 feet east of the west line of Michigan Avenue, and proceeding in a southeasterly direction (following the lakefront) for distances ranging generally from 700 to 400 feet east of the railroad's existing right of way. This had the effect of transferring most of the peninsula built by the railroad between 12th and 16th Streets to the SPC. This area, as augmented by further landfilling, would be the location for the Field Museum. In return, the railroad would acquire an estimated 162 acres of new land from 16th Street to 51st Street. The agreement further provided that the Illinois Central would permit the SPC to construct viaducts over the railroad's expanded property at select cross streets: this would permit the public to gain access to new reclaimed lands to the east, where the park district would construct a drive connecting the two parks. The agreement implied that the railroad would electrify its line at some point in the future, whereupon the SPC would be allowed to cover over part of its tracks in Grant Park. The railroad also promised to relocate Central Station to a new location south of 12th Street within five years, and to convey to the SPC, for park purposes, the property on which the terminal was located (in fact, the station

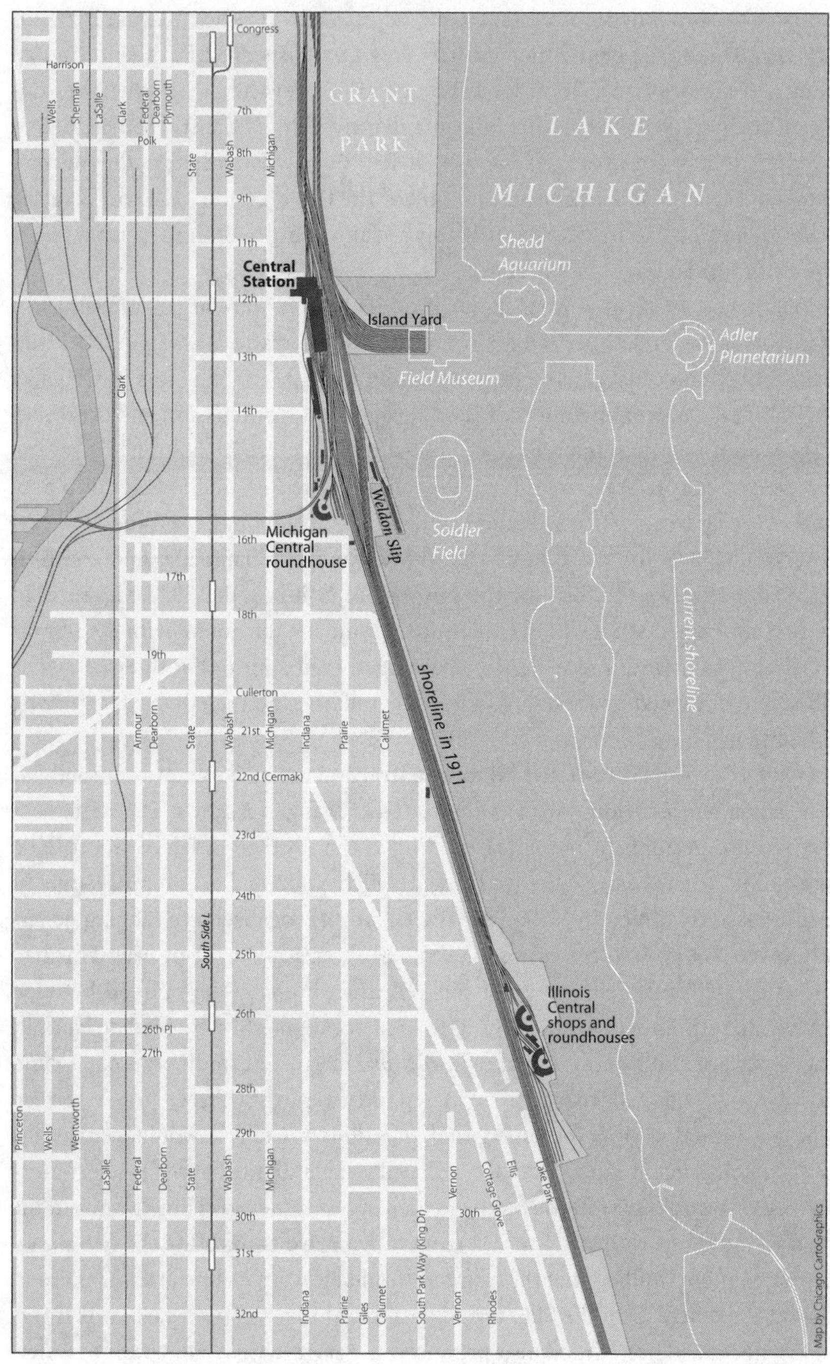

FIGURE 7.4. Map showing Illinois Central peninsula and other facilities south of 12th Street, ca. 1911, and also the shoreline today.

remained in its original location until it was demolished in 1974). The agreement was made conditional on the approval of the Chicago City Council.[9]

In the winter of 1912, an extraordinary public debate ensued over the proposed settlement. The debate reprised most of the elements of the public controversy that had raged more than forty years earlier, in 1869, over the Lake Front Act. Opponents of the settlement characterized it as a massive "steal," in which the Illinois Central obtained lands of enormous value relative to what it would give up. They accused the state legislature of being corrupted by the railroad when it adopted the 1907 act, the provision limiting the power of condemnation to persons *non sui juris* being singled out as inexplicable on any ground other than the influence of the Illinois Central—which was very much *sui juris* and thus immune from condemnation. Proponents of the measure pleaded that it was essential to secure a proper location for the Field Museum, which would be a beautiful ornament to the city. They argued that the rights vacated by the Illinois Central involved largely solid land and could be used for museum construction immediately, whereas the submerged land given to the railroad was not so valuable, given the substantial cost that the railroad would incur to fill it in.[10]

As the debate wore on, opponents began to complain about not only steals and property values but also environmental concerns. They pointed out that there was no guarantee the Illinois Central would electrify its lines. It might instead intensify the level of its operations on the South Side or provide trackage to other railroads, producing more smoke and soot for adjacent property owners. And there was no assurance against the railroad's using its expanded holdings to build new facilities, driving down property values in residential neighborhoods. Interestingly, there was little mention in the debate of the advantages of constructing a new drive connecting Grant and Jackson Parks.[11]

A committee of the city council voted eight to three to reject the agreement. Instead it recommended that the governor propose legislation conferring on the SPC the power to condemn all riparian rights. On February 19, 1912, the full city council concurred. In June of that year, the General Assembly duly adopted the requested legislation.[12]

Once the SPC acquired general condemnation authority, all riparian landowners between Grant Park and Jackson Park agreed to land-for-rights boundary decrees with the park district. The inference is unmistakable that the statute conferring condemnation authority was the critical event that induced the South Side riparians to settle. Given the Lincoln Park Commission's disastrous experience with condemnation on the North Side later in the century (see chapter 6), one might think that perhaps the South Siders capitulated too readily. But there were important differences. For one thing, the SPC project as then conceived called for little more than the construction of a modest drive along the edge of the extended shore, as opposed to (recall the subsequent case of the LPC) a sprawling expanse of land in front of the riparian's property and the placement of the drive right next to that property; this would limit any compensation received for the loss of riparian rights. For another, a jury would not have great sympathy for the South Siders—especially the Illinois Central, but also the Pullman heirs, the wealthy Shedd family, and the Chicago Beach Hotel, successor to the rights of Morgan, who had engaged in illegal filling. Certainly, it would react differently from the future jury that, in the North Side condemnation, apparently identified with the Schmidt family as residential property owners. If the South Siders could expect only a modest award in an eminent-domain action, they were clearly better off agreeing to a settlement that confirmed their title to any landfilling they had done and gave them additional submerged land to augment their holdings.[13]

With respect to the Illinois Central, the SPC decided that it could not wait for the legislature to confer eminent-domain authority, for the clock was ticking on identifying a site for the Field Museum (indeed, the time had already passed). On March 30, 1912, the railroad and the park district signed a new settlement agreement, superseding the agreement of the previous December. The site for the museum did not change—thus enabling the SPC to argue, if challenged, that the site had been timely "provided" by January 16, 1912. However, the width of the submerged land conveyed to the Illinois Central was trimmed back by 100 to 150 feet south of 31st Street. The railroad also promised that none of its property from 31st Street to 51st Street would be used to erect any structures except "switch shanties, switch towers and signal towers when necessary . . . for the actual operation of the railroad of the Company." Presumably to avoid further debate and delay, the revised settlement omitted any requirement of approval by the city council.[14]

The revised settlement agreement was filed in the circuit court for a May hearing and approval as a permanent boundary decree. Numerous opponents, many of whom had testified in the hearings conducted by the city council committee, intervened, as the 1907 act allowed them to do based on their status as voters or taxpayers. In a further effort to placate the intervenors, on June 26, 1912, the Illinois Central and the SPC entered into a "supplemental agreement" providing further concessions by the railroad. In the agreement, which was not subject to approval by the court, the Illinois Central promised, once the March 30 boundary agreement was approved, to "convey" back to the park district an additional strip of submerged land between 18th and 39th Streets, ranging in width from one hundred feet at 29th Street to fifty feet at 39th. Further restrictions on railroad operations in residential areas south of 28th Street were also added. Based on the supplemental agreement, all but three intervenors withdrew their opposition to the deal. The circuit court then ruled in favor of the agreement and approved a decree implementing the March 30 settlement and establishing a permanent boundary line from 12th Street to 51st Street. In the spring of 1913, the Illinois Supreme Court dismissed an appeal filed by the three remaining intervenors. The court reasoned that although the 1907 act gave voters and taxpayers the statutory right to intervene in the circuit court proceedings, the law gave them no right to appeal in the absence of property rights directly affected by the decree.[15]

The Illinois Central was clearly backpedaling throughout the negotiations that produced the 1911 and 1912 settlement agreements. A primary reason was the proposal to confer condemnation authority on the SPC that was working its way through the General Assembly. In fact, condemnation was uniquely threatening to the Illinois Central, although it is not clear from the internal correspondence of the railroad that its officers initially appreciated this. If the SPC could condemn the railroad's riparian rights, what would this do to all the improvements that the railroad had built on landfill on the South Side? The landfilling between 12th and 16th Streets had been vindicated in the *Lake Front Case* on the theory that it was an exercise of the railroad's riparian rights. If the riparian rights were taken, would all the improvements have to go too?[16]

More generally, the railroad desperately needed a more secure foundation for its property on the South Side. Under a mounting pile of precedent, including *Revell* and *Cobb* and the decisions on remand from the *Lake Front Case* (see chapter 6), the Illinois Central could claim no more filled land than that which had existed at the time of Justice Harlan's circuit court decision in 1888. The railroad had continued to engage in extensive filling in the ensuing years, much of it south of 16th Street, which was not covered by the Harlan decree. The attorney general's 1910 lawsuit against the Illinois Central, prompted by Long and challenging unauthorized landfilling, was still pending. If the action went to trial and exposed unauthorized filling, the augmented lands would be vulnerable to being abated as purprestures. Even if the railroad could be shown to have strictly adhered to its rights as fixed by the Harlan decree, this would leave no room for it to expand its rail operations south of 12th Street, or to reconfigure those that existed in 1888 in a more efficient layout.[17]

The only leverage that the Illinois Central could exercise, as the railroad's president, Charles H. Markham, noted to its board, was "[t]he necessity for setting an early date for beginning work on the Field Museum." So the urgency facing the SPC to ensure that it had a site for the museum became "the controlling influence in [the railroad's] negotiations with the South Park Board."[18]

There was one more large bump in the road. The War Department quickly approved the modest additional landfilling required to create a site for the Field Museum; however, the secretary of war denied the request to permit the extensive landfilling, farther south, contemplated by the boundary-line agreements. His principal concern was that the legislation invoked as authorizing the project, a 1912 congressional enactment, spoke of park extension work "desired by the municipal authorities" in Chicago. He construed this to mean "*elected* authorities," which did not include the SPC. In short, approval by the city council was needed. (The secretary was undoubtedly aware that the council had declined to approve the original settlement agreement, which thereafter had been revised so as to avoid any requirement of its approval.) He was also concerned that the Illinois Central might be able to use its enhanced property rights to claim the authority to operate any outer harbor that might be constructed outside the proposed fill area. The ghost of 1869 evidently reached into the military bureaucracy in Washington, DC.[19]

The War Department's intransigence increased the leverage of the city council. Prolonged negotiations over the terms of an ordinance authorizing the project, interrupted by World War I, ensued. The city's primary demand was that the railroad firmly commit to electrifying its lines, which would reduce the noise and pollution from coal-burning engines. The Illinois Central balked because of the large costs involved. It also hoped to build a huge terminal on its new lands south of 12th Street, accessible by trains from other lines, which would not be electrified. Agreement on the terms of an ordinance was finally achieved in 1919, calling for the Illinois Central to electrify its line north of Roosevelt Road (as 12th Street had just been renamed) by 1930 and to depress its tracks in Grant Park below grade level, among a variety of other things. The Lake Front Ordinance, as it was called, was formally approved by the city council in July 1919. Early the next year, the War Department gave its blessing, the Illinois Central followed with its formal acceptance, and the voters approved bond issues by the South Park Commission.[20]

After the Field Museum opened in 1921 in its isolated location (see figure 7.5), the SPC concentrated on Grant Park and a multilane drive along its outer edge. Construction of the drive and park south of 12th Street was slowed by the need to secure additional bonding authority to build viaducts over the Illinois Central's tracks. The drive was completed to 23rd Street by 1925, and in the ensuing years it was extended in additional segments. By the end of 1929, one could drive all the way from Grant Park to Jackson Park without stopping. The construction project, which included grade separations (or viaducts) at 23rd, 31st, 39th, and 47th Streets, extended into the 1930s. The SPC also had to expend substantial

FIGURE 7.5. Recently completed Field Museum, ca. 1921. Chicago Public Library, Special Collections, Chicago Park District Photos, box 33, folder 2, image 16.

energies to create additional landfill to accommodate the World's Fair exposition, called the Century of Progress, which began in 1933 on reclaimed land, including Northerly Island, stretching south to 39th Street.[21]

As the drive was stitched together, from both the new construction that has been our focus the past two chapters and existing roadways, different names—not all of them official or consistently used—proliferated. On the North Side, it was called Lake Shore Drive or the Outer Drive. South of the river, there were sections known as Field Boulevard, Leif Eriksen Drive (a nod to Scandinavian voters and spelled variously), and Columbus Drive (to please the Italians), with some stretches having a different name southbound from the corresponding northbound portion. Starting in the late 1930s, newspapers periodically agitated for a single name. With the different park commissions having been folded into the unified Chicago Park District in 1934, the name was officially changed to Lake Shore Drive, throughout, in 1946. So it has remained ever since.[22]

FIGURE 7.6. Landfilling and construction of the new drive on the South Side, 1926, viewed to the north from near 31st Street. Chicago Public Library, Chicago Park District Archives, 153_001_003; Chicago Aerial Survey Co.

Bridging the River

The 1912 boundary-line decree did not directly affect the Illinois Central's improvements between Randolph Street and the river. Yet once the 1919 Lake Front Ordinance committed the railroad to electrifying its trains in the city and depressing its tracks below grade in Grant Park, the glory days of the huge rail and shipping complex north of Randolph Street were numbered. Anticipating the completion of the electrification project, the railroad began a long process of winding down its freight operations on the peninsula. Between 1921 and 1924, the railroad filled in five large slips on the complex. The filling was done with the permission of the city, the War Department, and the Illinois Department of Public Works and Buildings. Evidently, it did not occur to anyone at the time that this might have serious consequences for the railroad's property rights: *once the slips were filled, they no longer could function as wharves.* Thus, a key rationale for upholding the railroad's right to occupy the area, endorsed by the *Lake Front Case*, disappeared. Moreover, the lakebed between the slips belonged to the state, and none of the agencies that approved the project had any delegated authority from the state to convey the submerged land to the Illinois Central for filling. Under the logic of *Revell*, the fill areas were purprestures, and could be taken by the state at any time without compensation. Indeed, once the slips facing the lake were filled, the state, not the railroad, was arguably the lakefront riparian owner between Randolph and the river. All of these questions, unlike the land itself, would remain submerged for another forty years.[23]

Meanwhile, with construction of the drives fully underway on both sides of town, interest grew in transforming the roads into an expressway running the length of the city from north to south. The main problem was the gap separating the north and south drives at the Chicago River. The Chicago Plan Commission, created by the city in 1909 to help implement Burnham's *Plan of Chicago*, took the lead in building support for a bridge linking the two drives together. A committee appointed in 1926 by Charles H. Wacker, longtime chairman of

FIGURE 7.7. The massive Illinois Central complex bisected by Randolph Street, viewed east of Michigan Avenue (to the northeast), 1920s, before the wind-down had begun in earnest. The trackage to the right (south) of Randolph was evidently justified by the triangular grants of submerged land in 1855 and 1856. Chicago History Museum, ICHi-005225.

the plan commission, relied on Hugh E. Young, the commission's chief engineer, for a leading role in the project.[24]

Over the next three years, the committee worked assiduously, securing the cooperation of the two park districts on either side of the river, obtaining the necessary approvals from the federal government, helping the Lincoln Park Commission obtain legislative authority to issue bonds needed to pay for its share of the costs, and preparing blueprints showing alternative plans. One barrier was a massive warehouse constructed by the Chicago Dock and Canal Company next to the Ogden Slip, which stood directly in the path of the proposed extension. The LPC brought condemnation proceedings to cut the warehouse into two parts, with the right of way for the drive running in between them. Another problem was a property owned by the federal government's lighthouse service at the mouth of the river. Its use required legislation not just from Congress releasing the property to the city but also from the state conveying substitute submerged land to the city and from the city transferring that land to the federal government. Suffice it to say, all of this took much time and effort.[25]

For the river crossing, the committee eventually produced detailed drawings showing three alternatives: a bascule drawbridge, a tunnel, and a suspension bridge. Its recommendation of the drawbridge was accepted by the full Chicago Plan Commission and then by the LPC, the SPC, and the city. In November 1929, the plan commission published a fancy booklet replete with photographs and illustrations detailing the three options and its efforts in building a consensus. The Illinois Central was largely invisible in the booklet. There were, however, tantalizing references to the need to accommodate "intensive development" of the "Illinois Central property." And in the middle of the booklet was a sketch (see figure 7.8) showing a wall of skyscrapers along the north edge of Randolph Street between Michigan Avenue and the lake, with the caption, "Study showing possibility of air right development between Randolph Street and the Chicago River east of Michigan Avenue." It is thus clear that as early as 1929 the Illinois Central was contemplating moving its remaining rail operations underground and using the so-called air rights above the area for a spectacular real estate development.[26]

As the plan commission concluded its work, the city moved toward acquiring and granting the necessary property rights to complete the bridge. The first step took the form of an ordinance, adopted on October 24, 1929, amending the 1919 Lake Front Ordinance to address the area north of Randolph Street. The ordinance authorized constructing an "Outer Drive Viaduct" over the river, as well as a network of elevated streets over the area occupied by the Illinois Central's rail complex. (Some of these streets, such as Columbus Drive, including

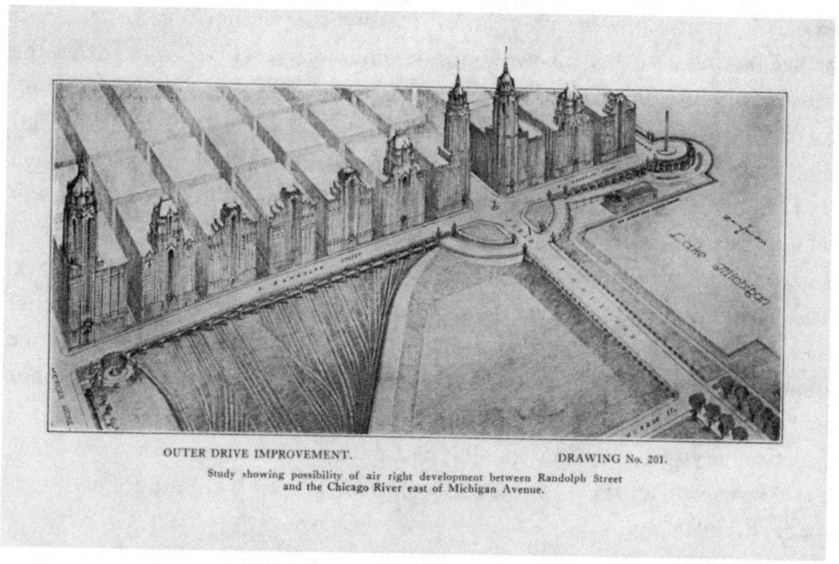

OUTER DRIVE IMPROVEMENT. DRAWING No. 201.

Study showing possibility of air right development between Randolph Street and the Chicago River east of Michigan Avenue.

FIGURE 7.8. Possible development of air rights, along Randolph Street at the northern edge of Grant Park, above the Illinois Central peninsula. 1929 Bridge Report, Drawing No. 201. Courtesy of the University Library, University of Illinois at Urbana-Champaign.

its bridge over the river, would not be completed until many decades later.) The ordinance was accepted by the SPC and the Illinois Central, among others, and was regarded as a contract binding on the city and these parties.[27]

Once everyone had signed on to the engineering and financial features of the plan, the boundary-line mechanism made another appearance. Along the lines of the various legislative enactments in 1903, 1907, and 1912, the Illinois Central and the SPC entered into an agreement in which the railroad would relinquish its assumed riparian rights and, in return, a new permanent boundary would be established east of the existing shoreline—in this case meaning the outer edge of the landfill peninsula occupied by the Illinois Central. Indeed, the agreement called for a new boundary line 280 feet east of the existing landfill. Approval of the boundary line would allow the Illinois Central to engage in further landfilling for this distance into the lake, and would presumably give the railroad unimpeachable title to all its land to the west of the new boundary line. In other words, the entire peninsula, even if no longer used as a wharf and even if composed in significant part of fill never authorized by the state, would be confirmed as belonging to the Illinois Central.[28]

Other features of the agreement would also have long-term consequences. From the south, it called for the new drive to cross Randolph Street, turn sharply east as it approached the river, and then turn sharply north across the new bridge (see figure 7.9). Thus was born the infamous "S-curve" in the drive, the cause of innumerable fender benders in future decades. The logical explanation for the S-curve was to preserve as much land as possible for future development by the Illinois Central. Interestingly, once the route of the drive crossed Randolph, it crossed filled land declared to belong to the Illinois Central, not land to be created by the SPC. Indeed, there were no plans for the SPC to fill any of the submerged land east of the new boundary line for additional park. The explanation for this is less clear. Most likely it was to spare the park district the cost of landfilling to support the new drive. But it is also possible that the Illinois Central was hedging its bets on the location of any new outer harbor that might be created in the future. By forgoing any new fill for park purposes, the boundary agreement gave the Illinois Central direct access to the lake, which could be used in an effort to create new slips or wharves if economic conditions made this attractive.[29]

FIGURE 7.9. Lake Shore Drive's S-curve approaching the Outer Drive Bridge from the south, 1960. Chicago History Museum, ICHi-000157; Don Honick, photographer.

Dusting off the old script, the SPC, on June 16, 1930, filed a complaint in the Circuit Court of Cook County seeking confirmation of the boundary-line agreement and naming the Illinois Central as a defendant (these details would become important more than a generation later). The Illinois Central answered and filed a cross-bill alleging its ownership of the shore lands and asking for a declaration that it held title to these lands. The attorney general received notice of the proceedings and filed a statement with the court disclaiming any interest in the involved lands on behalf of the people of the state of Illinois. With no one objecting to either the confirmatory proceeding or the cross-bill, the court, on August 1, 1930, entered a decree confirming the new boundary line and granting the Illinois Central's request for a declaration of ownership of the lands west of the boundary line. The railroad could now claim fee-simple title to the entire peninsula, plus 280 feet more to the east—scores of acres of prime real estate.[30]

The financial challenges of the Great Depression delayed construction of the link spanning the Chicago River. After several years, additional monies were secured from the new federal Public Works Administration. An extraordinary civic celebration, including President Franklin D. Roosevelt himself and some thirty-six thousand motorists, attended the opening on October 5, 1937.[31]

The Air Rights Controversy

The Depression and World War II also put on hold any plans that the Illinois Central had to capitalize on the air rights—the authority as a matter of property law to control space above the surface of land. After the war, with the economy finally on the mend, the Illinois Central bought out an interest in the land that had been conveyed to the Michigan Central Railroad, making itself the sole claimant to the former peninsula. In 1951, the Illinois Central sold to the Prudential Insurance Company the air rights necessary to construct a forty-one-story commercial office building on the peninsula, essentially where the railroad's original train shed had been located in the nineteenth century. This transaction, which also included the rights to place caissons and supporting columns on the land, netted the railroad $2,270,315. When completed in 1955, the Prudential Building, along Randolph Street, was the tallest building in Chicago. Later, in 1961, the Illinois Central sold the rights to construct a large apartment house, called Outer Drive East, for around $2,750,000. This was constructed on landfill *east* of Lake Shore Drive (as it then stood), over formerly submerged land that under the 1930 boundary-line agreement belonged to the railroad.[32]

FIGURE 7.10. Prudential Building shortly after its completion, 1955. Chicago History Museum, ICHi-092969.

The Illinois Central was seemingly on its way to millions of dollars in sales of air rights. In 1959, however, a cloud appeared on the horizon. An obscure Chicago law firm called Young & Hickey filed a lawsuit in federal district court, claiming that the Illinois Central had no title to the air rights in the area north of Randolph Street. The members of the small firm, who named themselves as plaintiffs, claimed standing to sue as federal taxpayers, state taxpayers, and representatives of a class of citizens of Chicago. As for relief, the complaint demanded that all monies received by the Illinois Central on account of the sale of air rights above the filled land "be deposited with the court pending determination of who is entitled thereto." The motives for the suit are unclear; perhaps it was simply an early exercise in a sort of class-action entrepreneurialism, in which lawyers seek out cases to bring in the hope of earning large fees.[33]

It was probably not a coincidence, however, that one of the lawyers involved, Burton Hugh Young, was the son of the late Hugh E. Young, who had worked as the principal engineer for the Chicago Plan Commission in bridging the river (and whom we also encountered in chapter 6 planning the north extension of the drive for the Lincoln Park Commission). Before his death in 1951, Hugh Young must have discussed with his son the history of the Illinois Central's title to the land north of Randolph Street, which the son, and his partners, later turned into a theory that the company had no claim to the air rights.[34]

The Illinois Central had little difficulty getting the lawsuit dismissed on the grounds that the plaintiffs had no authority to bring such a claim in federal court. When the law firm refiled in state court, the City of Chicago intervened in its support. The Illinois Central got this new suit dismissed as well, this time on the grounds that the state was an indispensable party. But in 1963, on appeal to the Illinois Supreme Court, the state attorney general, in a change of position, moved to intervene as well. Since this intervention supplied the party whose absence had constituted the obstacle to the suit, the Illinois Supreme Court remanded to the circuit court for proceedings on the merits.[35]

Back before the trial court, the state aligned itself with the plaintiffs and the city. It asked for "a declaration of the State's title to all lands east of the 1852 Lake Michigan shoreline (roughly Michigan Avenue) between the Chicago River and Randolph Street and between 11th Place (Park Row) and Hyde Park Boulevard (51st Street) subject to the easement of the Illinois Central to such portions of these lands as are necessary to its railroad operations." It demanded that the railroad account for the proceeds of its wrongful dispositions of such lands and air rights, that upon the railroad's payment to the state the rights of existing grantees and lessees (e.g., the Prudential Insurance Company) be confirmed, and that the railroad be permanently enjoined from "future sales, leases, or other dispositions of the lands or air rights." What started out as a long-shot suit by private plaintiffs was suddenly transformed into another major showdown between the state and the Illinois Central over manmade land in the lake.[36]

The financial stakes were enormous. Each side hired one of the city's top law firms. The railroad turned to a firm whose office was on-site (Kirkland, Ellis, Hodson, Chaffetz & Masters, in the Prudential Building); the state retained lawyers from Mayer Brown (as it is now called). The parties assembled a voluminous record, including many of the central legal documents pertaining to the railroad's development projects in the lake dating back to 1852. Finding that the boundary-line decrees controlled the matter and that the Illinois Central had fee-simple title to the grounds in question, the circuit court dismissed the suit.[37]

On appeal to the Illinois Supreme Court, the plaintiffs—the state, the city, and the private plaintiffs—joined together once again. In order to prevail, they had to establish two propositions: first, that the railroad did not have fee-simple title to the land north of Randolph Street and south of 12th Street under the decree in the *Lake Front Case*; and second, that it did not have fee-simple title based on the 1912 and 1930 boundary-line decrees.

As to the first question, the Illinois Central relied heavily on Justice Harlan's decree in the *Lake Front Case*, entered in 1888 and affirmed on the second appeal to the Supreme Court in 1902. The decree provided that the railroad was "the *owner in fee* of all the wharves, piers, and other structures erected by it" north of Randolph Street and between 12th and 16th Streets. The railroad naturally argued that "owner in fee" meant that it had full ownership rights to all of the made land in these areas.[38]

The plaintiffs responded that what Harlan must have meant was that the railroad was the "owner in fee" of the various *structures* it had built on the made land. Harlan could not have meant that its interest in the made land itself was anything more than an easement. Under the *Lake Front Case* and the *Kirk* decision, the State of Illinois owned the bed of Lake Michigan. Unless and until the state conveyed these lands to the Illinois Central, the railroad's only entitlement to fill the lake and construct structures on the landfill, according to the judgment in the *Lake Front Case*, was based either on the right to wharf out to the point of navigability or on its 1851 charter authorizing its appropriation and use of state "lands" and "streams" to construct railroad facilities. The right to wharf out authorized the construction of docks, piers, and wharves to reach navigable water, but did not transfer any rights to the submerged land itself. The charter right authorized construction of depots, roundhouses, switching yards, and other railroad facilities, but did not convey any interest in the submerged land itself. Thus, on any construction of the judgment in the *Lake Front Case*, the Illinois Central had at most an easement to use the submerged land for railroad purposes; it did not own the air rights above its landfills.[39]

The second barrier the plaintiffs had to overcome was the boundary-line decrees entered in 1912 and 1930, declaring the railroad to be the owner of the disputed lands in fee simple. Here, the plaintiffs were on weaker ground, but not without an argument. Their principal contention was that the state had not been a party to those proceedings. Although the enabling state legislation required that the attorney general participate in the proceedings with respect to any state lands involved, and the attorney general had received notice but disclaimed any interest on the part of the state, the plaintiffs claimed that this feature of the legislation violated a state constitutional provision stating that "[t]he State of Illinois shall never be made defendant in any court of law or equity." The plaintiffs further maintained that the Illinois Central was not a riparian owner in any of the contested areas governed by a boundary-line decree. In all these areas, the railroad had engaged in landfilling beyond that allowed by the decree in the *Lake Front Case*, and under *Revell* this filled land belonged to the state. If the SPC wanted to extinguish riparian rights, it should have entered into a boundary-line agreement with the state. By dealing instead with the Illinois Central, the commissioners were "in the position of the proverbial purchaser of the Brooklyn Bridge." Lastly, the plaintiffs claimed that the 1930 boundary-line decree was invalid on its face, since no park improvement was planned outside the boundary line, as the legislation required.[40]

The railroad responded that the relevant legislation authorized the attorney general to appear if he thought it proper to do so, but if he elected to make an appearance, it would be as an intervening plaintiff, not as a defendant. The Illinois Central further argued that the procedure established by the legislature had been "meticulously followed." To permit the state many years later to "collaterally attack" the resulting decrees, the argument continued, was manifestly improper. The boundary-line decrees were final and binding as to all issues decided, including that the railroad, not the state or any other party, held riparian rights that had to be extinguished before Lake Shore Drive could be constructed. The Illinois Central had proved that it owned the shore in 1912 and again in 1930. "Certainly," the railroad argued, "it cannot be compelled fifty years later to prove it all over again."[41]

At the end of the day, the Illinois Supreme Court, overwhelmed perhaps by the complexity of the history, declined to rule either on the nature of the railroad's title under the decree in the *Lake Front Case* or on the binding effect of the 1912 and 1930 boundary-line decrees. Instead it accepted an affirmative defense proffered by the railroad: that the state was legally precluded—estopped—from asserting its claim to the air rights because this was inconsistent with multiple representations that it had made in the past, on which the railroad had relied to its detriment.

Specifically, the court recited "a remarkably lengthy series of official acts, statements and declarations by various officials, bodies or representatives of the State, indicating that the now disputed title to these lands was then vested in the Illinois Central." These included, among the more recent things, the sales of air rights to the Prudential Insurance Company and to the investment company that built Outer Drive East, both of which had been approved by the Illinois Commerce Commission. None of these acts or statements was, "individually, of a conclusive nature." But they were adequate to demonstrate "why it may fairly be said that the prevailing governmental attitude, both State and city, since near the beginning of this century has regarded the Illinois Central Railroad as the owner, in fee, of the now disputed lands."[42]

The court acknowledged considerable uncertainty about whether or when a public body such as the state could be estopped. Ordinarily, principles of laches (undue delay) or estoppel do not apply against the state. But the rule was not absolute. In the context of the "extraordinary circumstances here prevailing," the court concluded that "basic concepts of right and justice preclude the State from now asserting any claim to the lands involved in these proceedings." So, because the state had waited too long to assert that the Illinois Central had only an easement, the railroad got the air rights.[43]

The *Hickey* decision was a fitting bookend to the *Lake Front Case* decided almost seventy-five years earlier. Both involved the Illinois Central and its efforts to secure the submerged land under Lake Michigan for its own advantage. Superficially, the outcomes were different: the Illinois Central lost the *Lake Front Case* but won *Hickey*. Considered more fully, the decisions have some important common themes.[44]

Both cases suggest that big, highly visible grabs of state-owned submerged land are vulnerable to reversal, whereas incremental, behind-the-scenes grabs are much more likely to succeed. The Illinois Central was poorly advised in 1869 to think that it could get away with a legislative grant of the lakefront in the city's center for a mile into the lake without stimulating a backlash. Refusing to compromise with the city and staking everything on a constitutional vested-rights argument proved further ill-advised. In contrast, the 1869 legislature's confirmation of the Illinois Central's existing landfills was upheld by the courts, as were the railroad's efforts to validate later, unauthorized encroachments with boundary-line agreements. Boundary-line agreements proved to be a nearly ideal mechanism for snitching submerged land from the state. Settlements with politically powerful actors could be quietly negotiated in advance and then ratified in court proceedings that received no publicity. Afterward, challenges to the title of the reclaimed land could be rebuffed on the grounds that the matter had been settled by prior decree.

Perhaps more fundamentally, the two cases reinforce the importance of *possession* in predicting the outcome of disputes over the use of submerged or reclaimed land. This is an implicit subtheme of chapter 3, where we considered the contrasting fates of projects that had been proposed but not yet built—such as the Field Museum, the Crerar Library, and the National Guard Armory, which were enjoined—and structures that had been erected and occupied, such as the Interstate Exposition Building and the Art Institute, which were allowed to stand (and even to expand). It is even more clearly a lesson of chapter 4, where we saw that Streeterville remained largely undeveloped until the perception gained currency that the land was actively possessed. In the case of the Illinois Central, virtually every foot of land that the railroad reclaimed from the lake and over which it exercised active management and control became an asset that remained on the corporate books. The only exception is the part of its filled land below 12th Street that was given up as a site for the Field Museum, but this was a voluntary exchange by the railroad for which it received compensation in the form of more land in return. In contrast, the area of the lake that the railroad never occupied, most notably the grant in 1869 of the one mile into the lake to build an outer harbor, was rescinded by the state in 1873, and the rescission was upheld by the courts. Here the railroad could claim ownership, in the form of a grant of fee-simple title from the state, but never acquired possession. Indeed, the Illinois Supreme Court's invocation of estoppel in *Hickey* to rebuff the state's belated effort to take away the air rights associated with the railroad's occupation of the filled land could just as easily have been written as a judgment conferring title by adverse possession. Whether or not possession is generally nine points of the law, it clearly is with respect to land reclaimed from water along the Chicago lakefront.

The physical projects recalled in this chapter were made possible by the boundary-line agreements pioneered by Edward O. Brown and the Lincoln Park Commission for acquiring riparian rights to extend Lake Shore Drive on the North Side. However, in keeping with the architectural style that prevailed in Grant Park and along south Lake Shore Drive, the boundary-line agreements on the South Side were monumental compared to those on the North. The 1912 boundary-line agreement between the Illinois Central and the South Park Commission had enormous consequences for the lakefront. It ratified the Illinois Central's property rights south of 12th Street, which had become increasingly precarious once the Illinois Supreme Court in 1898 eliminated the common-law right to wharf out (the *Revell* cases in chapter 6) and interpreted the railroad's charter as not permitting landfilling in the lake (discussed in chapter 8). Of greater long-range significance, it led to the creation of the Museum Campus, Burnham Park, and south Lake Shore Drive. The agreement also produced the 1919 Lake Front Ordinance, which required the electrification of the railroad, the lowering of its tracks in Grant Park below grade, and, indirectly, the abandonment of the massive rail complex north of Randolph Street.

The 1930 boundary-line agreement was equally consequential. The immediate effect, of course, was to facilitate the completion of Lake Shore Drive as a continuous highway spanning the greater part of the Chicago lakefront. It also solidified the shaky property rights of the Illinois Central in the peninsula that the railroad had created between Randolph Street and the river—an area eventually worth hundreds of millions of dollars. As time passed, the peninsula, including the development now known as Illinois Center, became the second area along the lakefront where glass and steel skyscrapers extend virtually to the water's edge. The 1930 agreement was a public-private trade of truly monumental proportions. There was virtually no public awareness of what was at stake when the deal was struck; certainly the press did not appreciate that the Illinois Central was being given fee-simple title to extremely valuable land where it previously had at most an easement. When the deal was eventually questioned in the *Hickey* litigation many decades later, the Illinois Supreme Court decided, unsurprisingly, that it was too late to undo what had already occurred.

Were the monumental boundary-line agreements worth the cost in forgone public rights? Certainly most people would today regard the 1912 agreement in favorable terms. It produced huge new public amenities—museums, parkland, and the south drive. The cost was barely a hundred acres of lakebed, a tiny fraction of the area of the vast lake. The 1930 agreement presents a closer case. Yes, the public got the bridge. But it got no new parkland. On the other side of the ledger, the Illinois Central received a windfall of gigantic proportions. In theory, the railroad could have been required to reconvey to the park district the peninsula it had created, allowing the district to create an extension of Grant Park running all the way to the river. Instead the railroad got fee-simple rights, which eventually allowed developers to create a neighborhood of commercial structures interrupting the stretch of parkland along the lakefront. We do not think the result a disaster, either aesthetically or in terms of public recreational opportunities. Whether a better deal could have been struck, from a public-rights perspective, if the participants in the 1930 negotiations had had a better understanding of the convoluted property rights at issue, is a matter of

FIGURE 7.11. Portion of Chicago skyline showing the Prudential Building overshadowed by skyscraper development to the east along Randolph Street, 2017. Bruce Leighty/Alamy Stock Photo.

speculation. Just as uncertainty over property rights foiled the development of an outer harbor, greater transparency about the property-rights mess might have led only to interminable litigation and no bridge over the river.

The public trust doctrine played no role in the monumental decisions associated with the 1912 and 1930 boundary-line agreements. Nor did it factor in the litigation that awarded the Illinois Central the air rights above the landfill peninsula created by the railroad for its massive terminal facilities. By the time *Hickey* was decided in 1966, the public trust doctrine had largely been forgotten. Yet, as we will see in the next chapter, it would soon experience a remarkable rebirth, becoming the primary legal rubric for resolving controversies about what is permitted and forbidden on the lakefront.

8

THE TRANSFORMATION OF THE PUBLIC TRUST DOCTRINE

It is time to return to the public trust doctrine and trace the arc of its development on the Chicago lakefront in the twentieth century. As in other states, the public trust doctrine took on new form and force in Illinois starting around 1970. Given its origins as a limitation on state title to submerged lands, however, the doctrine in Illinois retains some features not universally shared elsewhere. Most prominently, the trust inheres in the title to certain public land; hence, the state cannot eliminate the trust, even by amending its constitution. This makes the Illinois version of the doctrine uniquely impervious to change. The title theory probably also accounts for the fact that, with a single exception, Illinois courts have limited the trust—or, at any rate, its effect—to submerged or previously submerged land under navigable waters.

Starting Points

At the dawn of the twentieth century, there were three notable precedents addressing the public trust doctrine in Illinois. The first and most important, of course, was the US Supreme Court's decision in the *Lake Front Case* of 1892, described in chapter 2. Justice Field used the doctrine in order to counter the Illinois Central's far-from-trivial vested-rights argument concerning the state's grant of submerged land in 1869. Although the State of Illinois held title to the bed of Lake Michigan, he wrote, that title could not be freely alienated; rather, it was "held in trust for the people of the State that they may enjoy the navigation of the waters, carry on commerce over them, and have liberty of fishing therein freed from the obstruction or interference of private parties." Field made clear that the doctrine afforded no objection to the grant of small parcels of submerged land for the construction of wharves, docks, and piers, which are aids to navigation and commerce. But the state could not abdicate its general control "over lands under the navigable waters of an entire harbor or bay, or of a sea or lake"; in any event, it could revoke such a grant.[1]

The court did not rule or even suggest that the trust extended to other state-owned lands, such as parks. The decision also left open who was supposed to be the trustee of the protected lands and (for a different question) who had standing to bring a claim that a particular conveyance violated the public trust.

The *Lake Front Case* was likewise silent about whether the trust obligation was grounded in federal law or state law. The court soon clarified, in a case arising out of a dispute over filled land in Oregon, that state law controls. The final expositor of a state's law is, of course, the state supreme court. So the future elaboration of the public trust doctrine as relevant here was in the hands of the Illinois Supreme Court, not the US Supreme Court.[2]

The second important precedent was the Illinois Supreme Court's 1896 decision in *People ex rel. Moloney v. Kirk*, considered in chapter 4. The court upheld landfilling to extend Lake Shore Drive around Streeterville. The court professed to agree with everything said about the public trust in the *Lake Front Case*. But it also said that the legislature should make decisions about the proper disposition of submerged land and that courts should give significant deference to these decisions. So the primary remedy of those objecting to the disposition of navigable waters or submerged land lay not with the courts, but in electing different representatives to the legislature.[3]

A third significant decision involved landfilling by the Illinois Central outside its tracks between 25th and 27th Streets. The railroad wanted to fill in about four acres of land to construct an engine house, and the army engineers had signed off. When the city objected, the railroad filed suit in state court. Its principal theory was that its original charter authorized the filling because it permitted the railroad, for construction of "engine houses" (among other things), to take possession of and use "all and singular any lands, streams, and materials of every kind" belonging to the state.[4]

In 1898, in what we will call the *IC Charter Case*, the Illinois Supreme Court rejected the carrier's position. The court held that "lands" referred to solid land and did not include land beneath the lake and that the reference to "streams" also did not encompass lakes. More relevantly here, the court said that even if the charter were broad enough to include the proposed project, it would violate the trust obligation recognized in the *Lake Front Case* and reaffirmed in *Kirk*.

The court concluded that the proposed use was not for the erection of wharves, docks, or piers to aid navigation. Rather, it was "for the private use of the railroad company." Two years later, the US Supreme Court affirmed.[5]

The two state supreme court decisions—*Kirk* and the *IC Charter Case*—are in some tension with each other. *Kirk* allowed the transfer of substantial submerged acreage to private parties to provide funding for a public highway. It seemed to say that courts would defer to the legislature on matters involving the disposition of the lakebed, unless a significant impairment of public rights of navigation or fishery was shown. The *IC Charter Case* two years later prohibited the filling of a small area of lakebed to augment the facilities of a common carrier. There was no basis for arguing that the proposed landfill would impair public rights of navigation or fishery, given the approval by the army engineers. The best way to reconcile the decisions is to note that the project in *Kirk* had been authorized by the legislature recently and expressly, whereas the proposed landfilling in the second case rested on a state charter that was nearly fifty years old and ambiguous as to whether it included submerged land. Together, the decisions seem to say that landfilling is permissible if it is clearly authorized by the legislature and does not interfere with navigation and fishing, but landfilling without the clear authority of the legislature is prohibited unless, at a minimum, it can be said to enhance the public's ability to engage in navigation and fishing.

In setting the stage for the controversies to come, it is also important to recall that, at the beginning of the twentieth century, legislatively authorized landfilling under the supervision of park districts was rapidly transforming the lakefront. The South Park Commission was building out the lakefront to construct an enlarged Grant Park following the ideas of the *Plan of Chicago* (see chapter 3). The Lincoln Park Commission was extending Lake Shore Drive north from Diversey, and plans were afoot to extend it farther, toward the northern boundary of the city (see chapter 6). Soon a corresponding project on the South Side would be underway as well (see chapter 7).

Once *Kirk* upheld legislatively authorized landfilling by park districts, and the park districts embarked on filling the better part of the Chicago lakefront, the primary places where public trust issues might arise were at the far ends of the city, north and south. This is indeed what we see for the better part of the twentieth century. The most sharply contested public trust issues arose on the far North Side, beyond the north end of Lake Shore Drive, and the far South Side, beyond the drive's south end. Only with the transformation of the public trust doctrine starting in 1970 do we see the migration of the doctrine back to the center of the city, with very mixed results.

The South Works—Part I

The first major lakefront controversy to erupt in the twentieth century involved lands used for a steel plant on the far South Side of Chicago, between 79th Street and 92nd Street, just before the mouth of the Calumet River (as visible in figure 8.1). The South Works, to use the common name, would also be the site of two subsequent public trust cases during the century (its current status will be considered in chapter 9).

The South Works plant was first constructed in 1880. It would become part of the United States Steel Corporation in 1901 but nevertheless retained its separate identity as the Illinois Steel Company into the twentieth century.[6]

In 1900, the Cook County board of assessors asserted that the Illinois Steel Company was occupying a much larger tract of land than was listed on the tax rolls. The company responded that any new land was the product of natural accretion. After further investigation, Charles M. Walker, the city's corporation counsel, alleged that some two hundred acres of land had been created by the company through artificial filling. When the steel company sought to record a map showing its enhanced holdings, Walker instructed that the filing be rejected. The company retaliated by refusing to allow city officials to enter the property. But no action was taken at the time to recover the land for the state.[7]

One night in 1903, a fireboat was racing down the lakefront in response to a fire at a salt shed. The boat abruptly grounded, off 87th Street, on a reef not shown on government navigation charts, leaving the salt shed to burn down. Later, in the light of day, the crew determined that it "had run upon a lot of slag thrown into the lake by the Illinois Steel company." Though blameless, the crew was fined for failing to reach the fire. No action was taken against the steel company.[8]

Matters finally came to a head in 1905 in a political flap involving one Colonel Ricard O'Sullivan Burke, described as a "picturesque figure around the city hall" and "a leader among the agitators of freedom for Ireland." His city job at that time was as "engineer" in charge of harbors. During an investigatory tour of the Calumet River, which included Burke, Mayor Edward Fitzsimmons Dunne, and the commissioner of public works, the extensive made land in front of the Illinois Steel works was observed. When Burke could not explain how it had come about, the commissioner charged him with "gross neglect of duty and inefficiency" and suspended him from his position for thirty days. Other city officials predicted an "outburst of indignation from Irish catholics" against Mayor Dunne, who was already under attack as "a disloyal Irishman and a disloyal Roman catholic" for, among other derelictions, sending his son to the University of Michigan.[9]

FIGURE 8.1. Locations of public trust controversies on the South Side.

Rather than make a martyr of Burke, the mayor and his allies evidently decided that the wiser course was to go after Illinois Steel. In December 1905, the local state's attorney sought to enjoin the company from further landfilling and to force it to rent or purchase from the state the land it already occupied. He alleged that a total of two hundred acres had been made by dumping "ashes, slag, cinders, salamander, and other refuse matter into the waters of Lake Michigan." The company's general counsel responded with the implausible claim that although such material had been "dumped on the sand bordering the lake, . . . all accretions were natural."[10]

The matter came before a master in chancery, J. M. Holland, who proceeded at a leisurely pace. In June 1908, Holland finally released his report, finding that the steel company had illegally filled 92.79 acres. Interestingly, he found that the value of the unimproved submerged land was $6,747.73, whereas the value of the land after filling was $587,743.27. He recommended an injunction against further landfilling. Because a court could not decree the sale of state land, the next step would be for the General Assembly.[11]

In the next legislative session, the proposal of a sale of the land to Illinois Steel became entangled with the aggressive push, by Representative Burnett M. Chiperfield, to establish a joint legislative committee to launch a general investigation of unauthorized filling of Lake Michigan (discussed in chapter 4). The steel company responded that Chiperfield's investigation might cause it to abandon the South Works. The state representative from the steel mill's district, John Poulton, clashed with Chiperfield and made clear that the company was prepared to make a deal for the filled land. Meanwhile, the South Chicago Business Men's Association rallied support for the company. Speaking at the association's meeting, the city's commissioner of public works observed that "[t]here are 10,000 men employed in the mills and this means the livelihood of nearly 50,000 persons." Threats about relocating the steel mills to Indiana were made. A group called the East Side Improvement Association spoke somewhat more moderately, stating that the best use of the submerged land at the south end of the lake was industrial development, adding that Indiana permitted such reclaiming of submerged land, and pointing out the many advantages of greater employment.[12]

With remarkable speed and little dissent, the state legislature in 1909 authorized the sale of submerged land of Lake Michigan to the Illinois Steel Company and two manufacturers on the other side of the Calumet River. The price was one hundred dollars per acre. Illinois Steel lobbied successfully for a grant of 234 acres, more than what it had already taken. The Iroquois Steel Company secured 85 acres of new land, and the American Smelting and Refining Company got 16 acres. Chiperfield, seeing the writing on the wall, did not join with the majority but focused instead on keeping his proposed investigatory committee alive. A large delegation of businessmen who had traveled from the South Chicago neighborhood to Springfield was reportedly "wild with joy." In the characterization of one reporter, "[L]ittle 'Johnnie' Poulton has been made grand 'high mogul' of the South Chicago Hero club."[13]

Governor Charles S. Deneen had to decide whether to sign or veto the measure. Attorney General William H. Stead was consulted and opined that the legislation did not violate the trust obligation recognized in the *Lake Front Case*, since it appeared that the conveyance would "work no substantial impairment of the public interest in the lands and waters of Lake Michigan remaining." Although this was a paraphrase of a line in Justice Field's opinion, it was taken out of context. Whatever else the public trust may mean, surely the focus should be the effect on the public interest in the submerged lands *taken*, not those *remaining*. In any event, the governor signed the legislation.[14]

Informed observers probably drew a mixed message from the South Works episode. On the one hand, the public controversy over the company's landfilling, along with the decisions in *Kirk* and the *Lake Front Case*, undoubtedly solidified the understanding that riparian owners have no right to engage in artificial filling of Lake Michigan without prior governmental approval. The episode was immediately followed by Alderman Theodore K. Long's exposure of illegal landfilling on the lakefront, the Chiperfield Committee's denunciation of private landfilling, and the state attorney general's lawsuits challenging all artificial landfilling by riparian owners on the South Side (see chapter 7). A statute adopted by the Illinois legislature in 1911 codified the requirement of advance approval. Specifically, it created the Rivers and Lakes Commission and required its sign-off before any person could "make any improvements, or erect any work or structure," in any of the state's public bodies of water.[15]

On the other hand, the failure to mount a judicial challenge to the legislation ratifying the South Works landfilling probably underscored the understanding, reflected in the *Kirk* decision, that the courts would defer to judgments of the legislature as trustee. The stirring rhetoric of the *Lake Front Case* was largely forgotten. Attorney General Stead's superficial analysis of the massive land transfer seems to have been the only recorded reference to the public trust doctrine during the entire episode. As of 1910, preserving jobs in steel mills was a much stronger imperative than securing the right of the public to boat and fish on the lake.

The Period of Dormancy

After the South Works episode, the public trust idea entered a period of decline—or, more accurately, dormancy. Significant landfilling occurred in the ensuing decades, but it was done by, or under the active supervision of, public institutions, most notably the park districts. The only other major intrusion into the lake was the construction in 1914 of what is now known as Navy Pier. This encountered no objection based on the public trust doctrine, both because it was a public project and, more importantly, because it was designed to promote access to the lake for purposes of navigation.

It should also be noted that a number of significant public structures were built on filled land controlled by the park districts during the first half of the twentieth century. These included the Field Museum, the Shedd Aquarium, the Adler Planetarium, Soldier Field, and the air terminal, known as Meigs Field, on the manmade Northerly Island (which, in fact, was transformed into a peninsula in the late 1930s).

One park project, begun in the 1920s, triggered litigation. The South Park Commission decided to restore the Fine Arts Building, also known as the Palace of Fine Arts, in Jackson Park—the sole surviving Chicago building constructed for the World's Columbian Exposition of 1893. After the fair, the structure had housed a collection of artifacts of natural history before they were moved to the newly built Field Museum on what we now know as the Museum Campus. The purpose of the restoration was vague; promoters said initially that the building would be a museum devoted to fine arts such as architecture and sculpture, "also the liberal arts in the broadest scope," and later that it would be an industrial museum. (Today it is the home of the Museum of Science and Industry.) The project was expensive, and it elicited a taxpayer challenge as being beyond the park district's mandate. In 1926, the Illinois Supreme Court emphatically rejected the claim: it held that "[p]ark purposes are not confined to a tract of land with trees, grass and seats," but could also include "museums, art galleries, botanical and zoological gardens, and many other purposes, for the public benefit." This seemingly settled the question, at least for the balance of the century, whether the park districts could create museums, zoos, or stadiums on parkland—presumably including parks made from filled land—without violating the public trust doctrine.[16]

The Great Depression and World War II slowed the pace of landfilling, eliminating any reason to revisit the meaning of the *Lake Front Case*. This changed with the war's end and the prosperity of the 1950s. The public trust doctrine made an appearance in the postwar years in litigation involving two projects that entailed landfilling in the lake. Neither case provided any reason to think that the doctrine posed a significant impediment to landfilling that had the blessing of the legislature.

The first postwar project involved Chicago's construction of a huge water filtration plant in Lake Michigan. As shown in figure 8.2, the proposed plant would sit on more than sixty acres of landfill four hundred feet north of Navy

FIGURE 8.2. Locations of public trust controversies on the North Side.

Pier and, at its longer end, nearer the shore, five hundred feet east of Lake Shore Drive. A sort of spit of filled land at its southwest corner was to connect the plant to the shore.[17]

Two groups of plaintiffs were held to have standing to challenge the project. One, consisting of taxpayers, voiced concerns about the plant's cost and its effect on property taxes. A second group, consisting of original riparian landowners in Streeterville or their successors, argued that the plan violated covenants they had received when it was decided to extend Lake Shore Drive around the perimeter of the area pursuant to the state legislation in 1889 (see chapter 4).[18]

One of the claims advanced by the taxpayer group was that the proposed landfill violated the public trust recognized in the *Lake Front Case*. Ruling in 1954, the Illinois Supreme Court had little difficulty rejecting the claim. It was unnecessary to decide exactly what public interests are protected by the doctrine, the court said, because the plaintiffs' principal contention was that the filtration plant would interfere with navigation. The answer was that the Army Corps of Engineers had examined the plan in detail and, after public hearings, had concluded that the portion of the lake to be filled was little used for navigation. The court dismissed as speculative the plaintiffs' argument that the landfill would eliminate a potential site of a future harbor, observing that a harbor could be "constructed along any part of the Chicago lake front." As for the claims of plaintiffs invoking the original Streeterville riparian rights, the court concluded that the covenants granted by the Lincoln Park Commissioners at the end of the nineteenth century did not restrict this particular sort of development in the lake, east of Lake Shore Drive. Finally, returning to various claims of the taxpayers, but making an apparently broader contextual point, the court noted that the state legislature in 1949 had specifically authorized reclamation of submerged land for the filtration plant.[19]

The second project was a major convention center located in Burnham Park at 23rd Street, as shown in figure 8.1. Construction of the project, to be named McCormick Place, was to occupy 32.37 acres, of which 6.49 acres would come from new landfill. In 1958, this, too, was attacked by taxpayers, primarily with the claim that the state treasurer had acted improperly in agreeing to purchase bonds. But the public trust doctrine also appeared.[20]

The main argument regarding the taking of submerged lands for the convention center was that, while the statute authorized the park district to fill land, the district's plan was to have an independent convention center authority do the actual landfilling. The court was unmoved; it found nothing "to indicate a legislative intent that submerged land become a part of the Park District only if it is reclaimed by the district itself rather than through a lessee." The court recognized "that submerged lands reclaimed are impressed with a trust in the public interest," but held that "the facility here contemplated is in the public interest and has been approved by the proper authorities." End of matter.[21]

The Northwestern Campus Expansion

With the decisions approving the water filtration plant and the convention center, the public trust doctrine was reduced to little more than a requirement of prior legislative approval of any landfilling in Lake Michigan. The most striking illustration of the state of the doctrine in the early 1960s is provided by Northwestern University's project to expand its campus into the lake in the suburb of Evanston, just north of the Chicago city limits. The project—announced in 1960, approved by the state legislature and the Army Corps of Engineers in 1961, and completed in 1964—unfolded with remarkable dispatch and general goodwill. There was no public discussion of the public trust doctrine and no lawsuit.

We will tell the story briefly. By the 1950s, Northwestern University had outgrown its original Evanston campus, located between Sheridan Road and the shore of Lake Michigan. Community opposition made expansion to the west of Sheridan Road difficult. Any such expansion threatened to undermine the city's tax base (given the university's exemption from property taxes), made it harder for residents to find places to park their cars, and encountered resistance from homeowners who wanted to keep their houses. So university officials revived the idea, which had been bruited about many years earlier, of expanding the campus to the east, by filling the lake.

The university's lawyers were well aware of the *Lake Front Case* and the potential obstacle it presented. They also learned that the Chicago Title & Trust Company had refused to issue title insurance for the filled land occupied by the Illinois Steel Company on the far South Side, notwithstanding the grant from the state legislature. Even so, the lawyers signed off on the project. They regarded the *Lake Front Case* as "very old" and "obsolete." If litigation became necessary, they counseled, "the quasi-public nature of the University and the growing importance of higher education in this country would seem to provide adequate public justification for the transfer of submerged lands to an educational institution as a matter of public policy." Hence, Northwestern's lawyers concluded, the transfer of submerged land would "not be violative of the spirit of the *Illinois Central* decision." Indeed, they concluded that, legally speaking, the project depended on "only two *required* approvals": (1) a grant of the submerged land by the legislature, and (2) the approval of the Army Corps of Engineers with respect to federal law concerning navigation and navigability.[22]

Publicly announced in 1960, the plan called for the transfer of 152 acres of submerged land to the university. The price was one hundred dollars per acre, the same as had been set for the Illinois Steel Company in 1909. Only 74 acres were designated for immediate filling, which nevertheless would nearly double the size of the campus between Sheridan Road and the lakeshore. The lakeward addition would include open space, several new buildings, and a lagoon.[23]

Perhaps most impressive was the public relations campaign. The university engaged in a carefully orchestrated process of consultation with a wide range of political actors, including the mayor and city manager of Evanston, the Evanston City Council, Chicago's Mayor Richard J. Daley, the president of the Cook County Board of Commissioners, and the local congressional representative, among others. As the university's attorney, Alban Weber, later recounted, this was based on "the principle of 'recognition,' in effect a salute to the political status of the individuals consulted, and a recognition of their power, should they choose to do so, to create substantial difficulty if not make impossible, the project under consideration." It also had "another important aspect, [which] can best be summed up as the 'bandwagon psychology.'"[24]

The plan was remarkably effective. The announcement of the project featured maps and descriptions, including an artist's conception of the new lakefront campus, all featured in local newspapers. Local officials were feted at a breakfast where further details were disclosed. In a matter of weeks, Evanston's city council passed an enthusiastic resolution of approval. Bipartisan sponsors of the state legislation were lined up. Meetings were scheduled with elected officials. The legislative hearings went smoothly, and by the end of May 1961, legislation transferring title to the land to Northwestern, for a total of $15,200, had been enacted with no opposition in either legislative chamber.[25]

The process before the Army Corps of Engineers also encountered no resistance. Notice of a hearing was sent to 435 agencies and individuals, yet not a single objector appeared. The hearing itself lasted only forty minutes. The permit was issued in September 1961.[26]

An unexpected controversy emerged in 1962 over the source of the fill. The project involved a contract to take sand that the Bethlehem Steel Company was dredging in northern Indiana to enlarge a harbor for a steel complex there. At the time, Paul H. Douglas, senior US senator from Illinois, was actively promoting federal legislation to create a national lakeshore protecting the Indiana dunes. Although the area being dredged represented a tiny fraction of the dunes area, and was not an auspicious spot to include in a national lakeshore, Douglas and other supporters of the idea viewed the removal of 2.5 million cubic yards of sand from the dunes as an unwanted precedent. Northwestern soon found itself under public pressure to find an alternative source of fill in order to "save" the dunes. The university asked Bethlehem to release the contractors from their obligation. But when the company, backed by officials in Indiana, refused, the

FIGURE 8.3. Northwestern University landfilling in progress for Evanston campus expansion, 1963. Courtesy of McCormick Library of Special Collections and Northwestern University Archives.

university took the position that it had "no alternative but to proceed with the present arrangement." In fact, the university always had the option of asking its contractors to breach the agreement with Bethlehem and indemnifying them for any damages. But its argument quieted critics, and the dunes controversy faded away. Northwestern's newly created land was officially dedicated in 1964.[27]

The remarkable thing about the Northwestern campus expansion is that no one voiced any opposition based on the public trust doctrine. In part, this was attributable to the doctrine's evisceration by the Illinois Supreme Court. The university lawyers could fairly persuade themselves that the *Lake Front Case* was "obsolete." It was also in part because organized environmental groups had not yet emerged on the scene. But the most important explanation is that, in the public opinion of the early 1960s, the plan seemed entirely reasonable. Expansion of universities was regarded as a good thing. Avoiding the displacement of the local tax base and local homeowners was regarded as a good thing. The project was engineered in such a way that any impact on the Evanston water supply and existing city beaches would be minimal. And everyone seemed to agree, at least implicitly, that the substitution of seventy-four acres of solid land for shallow lake waters would have no appreciable effect on the use of the lake for navigation, fishing, or recreation. After all, the lake was vast in comparison to the relatively small addition to the campus. What was there to oppose?

The South Works—Part II

At the same time as sand was being deposited in the Northwestern University landfill, the US Steel Corporation decided to try its hand at securing a further augmentation of its South Works. Northwestern's easy success may have inspired the steel company; that much is speculation, but it seems telling both that the company did not have immediate plans for the new land and that, in announcing the effort, as the *Chicago Tribune* reported, it carefully "emphasized that no sand from the Lake Michigan shore will be used." US Steel argued that the lakefront facility, even as augmented by the landfilling authorized in 1909, would have to grow in order to compete effectively with other mills. Noting that expansion was blocked to the south (by the Calumet River), west (by a neighborhood), and north (by a water filtration plant), the company pitched the case for expansion through additional landfilling in the lake. Since the submerged land in question already belonged to the Chicago Park District, the plan called for the park district to retransfer the land to the state, which then would transfer title to US Steel. The legislature readily agreed, enacting a statute in 1963 that authorized US Steel to fill an additional 194.6 acres. The price, as in 1909 and for Northwestern University, was $100 per acre, or $19,460.[28]

The South Works plan encountered a new source of opposition beginning to emerge in the 1960s: the environmental movement. In Chicago, the first stirrings appeared in Hyde Park, the South Side enclave where the University of Chicago is located. The catalyzing episode was a proposal, pushed by Mayor Richard J. Daley, to rebuild south Lake Shore Drive from 47th Street to 67th Street, including the portion on the east side of Jackson Park. Some members of the Hyde Park–Kenwood community voiced strong opposition, as did the local alderman, Leon Despres, who was frequently at odds with Daley. The focal point of opposition was the need to cut down some eight hundred trees in Jackson Park. Daley insisted that the trees should be sacrificed for the greater public good of widening the roadway. When work crews arrived on September 9, 1965, fifteen members of an activist group called the Daniel Burnham Committee wrapped their arms and legs around trees in what the *Tribune* characterized as "a desperate but futile effort to keep workmen from felling the trees." There followed a "wild melee," as depicted by a reporter for the *Chicago Daily News*, in which the work

FIGURE 8.4. South Works in operation, ca. 1970. Courtesy of the Southeast Chicago Historical Society.

crews managed to fell a number of trees by cutting just over the heads of the protesters, one of whom was injured and several of whom were arrested. Public sympathy for the opposition ran high, with the columnist Mike Royko, a reliable barometer of popular sentiment, satirizing the Daley administration's commitment to roads over parks with a bit of doggerel, which began, "I think that I have never knowed / A sight as lovely as a road." Mayor Daley beat a tactical retreat, appointing a study commission and then announcing in November an indefinite delay of part of the project.[29]

The Hyde Parkers soon had another city project to fuel their ire: Daley's proposal to create a third Chicago airport by building an island three and a half miles offshore in Lake Michigan. As proposed in 1967, the island would cover eight thousand to fourteen thousand acres—a larger area than Chicago's O'Hare Airport and big enough to accommodate the supersonic planes then on the drawing board. There were plenty of grounds to question the wisdom of such a plan, and by 1968, the Hyde Park–Kenwood Community Conference and a new group called the Federation for an Open Lakefront were in vocal opposition. There is no indication that the public trust doctrine was cited as a reason for challenging the plan. The project was dropped in the early 1970s for other reasons, primarily an economic downturn and changes in air traffic projections.[30]

Given the emergence of environmental activism, it is not surprising that the 1963 sale of additional submerged land to US Steel for the South Works plant attracted a legal challenge and that it came from a member of the Hyde Park community. Two lawsuits, eventually consolidated, were filed in the name of one Albert C. Droste, an insurance broker living in Hyde Park, who described himself as "a private citizen trying to combat special-interest legislation at the expense of future public recreational facilities." Droste alleged that the sale of submerged land violated the Public Moneys Act, a statute permitting taxpayers to challenge the "disbursement" of "public funds" or "public moneys" by state officials. He also argued that the sale violated the Illinois Constitution's prohibitions against special legislation and the public trust doctrine.[31]

Droste lost in the circuit court and appealed directly to the Illinois Supreme Court. The high court had a great deal of difficulty making up its mind about the case, releasing three different majority opinions, only the last of which found its way into the official reports. In its first decision, the court held that Droste did not have standing as a citizen or taxpayer. Then, on the plaintiff's petition for rehearing, the court reversed itself, holding that Droste had standing and that the statute was unconstitutional special legislation. Now the defendants petitioned for rehearing, supported by friend-of-the-court briefs from the South Works steelworkers' union and the Illinois Manufacturers' Association. The court reversed itself again, finally ruling against Droste.[32]

These unseemly gyrations no doubt account for what the dissenting opinion in the final decision correctly characterized as a "curious inversion" of issues, in which the majority first addressed the merits of Droste's claims and then explained why he did not have standing to bring them in court. With respect to the Public Moneys Act claim, the court held that the act applied only to public funds, not land. On the public trust claim, the court seemingly held that the 1896 decision in *Kirk* foreclosed Droste's claim. As in *Kirk*, the legislature had specifically authorized the proposed transfer of submerged land to private hands for what lawmakers regarded as the public interest. The court wrote, "The *Kirk* case, sustaining grants to specified grantees, has never been overruled but has been relied upon by the public and property owners in Illinois over a period of almost 70 years. It has become a rule of property and should not now be overturned."[33]

Almost as an afterthought, or perhaps an alternative basis for the decision, the court reaffirmed the position taken in its initial decision that Droste had no standing to bring the various challenges. With respect to the public trust claim, the court regarded it as dispositive that he could not show that he had suffered "special damage" distinct from that allegedly suffered by other citizens.[34]

A long dissent by the respected jurist Walter V. Schaefer argued against the ruling, starting with standing. With respect to the public trust claim, our primary interest here, the majority had applied standing rules from cases complaining that certain uses of public property constituted a public nuisance, the dissent maintained; it should have followed cases granting broad rights of standing to any taxpayer complaining about the disposition of public funds. On the merits, Schaefer argued that the conveyance represented impermissible special legislation. In his view, the legislature could determine that a particular parcel of submerged land should be filled and devoted to some other purpose, with the land then being auctioned off "to the highest and best bidder." But "a legislative conveyance to a particular grantee for an unspecified use," he wrote, was "exactly what the constitutional provision against special legislation vacating public grounds was designed to prevent." Schaefer criticized the majority for "a surprising misreading" of the *Kirk* case, where the legislature had not itself specified that the submerged land should be conveyed to the various riparian owners, even as he acknowledged that the subsequent action of the park district in that previous situation had accomplished precisely that result.[35]

On its face, *Droste* represents the low point of the public trust doctrine in Illinois: even a transfer of 194 acres of submerged land to a private corporation is permissible, so long as it is authorized by the legislature. In hindsight, one can see stirrings of change. Both Droste and his lawyer, Calvin Sawyier, were from Hyde Park, where the nascent environmental movement dedicated to preservation of public parks was forming. Sawyier also served as counsel in the earlier McCormick Place convention center litigation and in the next decision we will consider. And the flip-flopping by the court suggested that it was open to a more aggressive protection of submerged lands, at least in a case where political forces were not clearly aligned in support of the project.

The Environmental Revolution and the Critical Pivot

Just as it seemed that the public trust doctrine had hit bottom, the Illinois Supreme Court suddenly revived it. The pivotal case, *Paepcke v. Public Building Commission*, was decided in 1970. The specific outcome was another defeat for the Hyde Park activists, but the opinion launched the public trust doctrine on a new career in Illinois.

The issue was whether the Chicago Park District could transfer a corner of Washington Park, just west of the Hyde Park neighborhood, to the city's Public Building Commission for the construction of a new public school (this can be seen in figure 8.1). The plaintiffs, described as "citizens, residents, taxpayers and property owners" of Chicago, were again represented by Calvin Sawyier. The lead plaintiff, Elizabeth Nitze Paepcke, was the daughter of a prominent University of Chicago professor. She and her husband, Walter Paepcke, a wealthy Chicago

FIGURE 8.5. Elizabeth Paepcke, 1980. © Aspen Historical Society; Cassatt Collection. All rights reserved.

industrialist, were prime movers behind the development of the ski resorts in Aspen, Colorado, and the creation of many of the cultural institutions there, including the Aspen Center for Environmental Studies, which she founded in 1968, after his death. It is likely that she helped underwrite the costs of the litigation.[36]

The plaintiffs' complaint alleged that the school construction project violated the public dedication doctrine, which Montgomery Ward had used to great effect in saving Grant Park from development. It also invoked the Public Building Commission Act and the public trust doctrine.[37]

The Illinois Supreme Court was unanimous in rejecting the challenge on all counts. But in one of those fortuities that divert the path of the law in a new direction, the assignment to write for the court was given to Justice Marvin F. Burt. Essentially forgotten today, Burt served on the court for barely more than a year, completing the term of a justice who had resigned in the wake of a scandal. Burt had been a circuit court judge in Freeport, nearing retirement, and earlier was a Republican politician. Among the causes he had promoted during his career was the preservation of public parks. The assignment to write the *Paepcke* opinion gave Justice Burt a unique opportunity to fortify the legal protection enjoyed by public parks in Illinois.[38]

There were a number of grounds available to reject the plaintiffs' challenge, but Burt's opinion, surprisingly, renounced the common-law doctrine that allowed private property owners to sue to enforce dedications of adjacent public land. The *Ward* cases were distinguished on the grounds that the dedication of Grant Park had been included in the Chicago city charter, and so the public dedication there had a statutory rather than a common-law basis. It is unclear why Burt was hostile to the common-law public dedication doctrine; perhaps he did not like giving private property owners special rights to control the fate of public parks. The challenge based on the Public Building Commission Act was rejected on the authority of an earlier decision.[39]

Turning to the public trust doctrine, Burt's opinion did three important things, two explicitly and one implicitly. First, the opinion overruled the standing portion of *Droste*, decided a mere four years earlier, and adopted Justice Schaefer's dissent as the better-reasoned position. "If the 'public trust' doctrine is to have any meaning or vitality at all, the members of the public, at least taxpayers who are the beneficiaries of that trust, must have the right and standing to enforce it," Burt wrote. "To tell them that they must wait upon governmental action is often an effectual denial of the right for all time." The decision to allow any taxpayer to sue to enforce the public trust doctrine dramatically expanded the potential for judicial enforcement of the doctrine.[40]

Second, Burt's opinion re-described the purposes served by the public trust doctrine. He wrote that the public trust obligation was not just concerned

FIGURE 8.6. Justice Marvin F. Burt (undated, likely ca. 1970). Abraham Lincoln Presidential Library and Museum.

with preserving navigation, commerce, and fishing, but applied much more broadly to any decision to reallocate public resources "'to more restricted uses *or* to subject public uses to the self interest of private parties.'" With this language, including the emphasis, the opinion quoted liberally from a law review article recently published by Professor Joseph L. Sax, of the University of Michigan Law School, urging that the public trust doctrine be applied as a general administrative law remedy for challenging privatization of public resources. Burt agreed with Sax that it would be unwise to freeze public resources in any particular use, as such an approach "strikes at the very essence of governmental power." At the same time, he also implicitly agreed with the professor's call for close judicial scrutiny of such proposals, using the public trust doctrine as a vehicle. By expanding the doctrine from one narrowly concerned with preserving public access to navigable waters to one designed to restrict any transfer of public resources to serve private "'self interest,'" the opinion again dramatically extended the scope of the doctrine.[41]

Third, Burt's opinion implicitly broke new ground by applying the public trust doctrine to public land having no connection to navigable waters. Washington Park did not abut any navigable water, nor was it built on any landfill of navigable water. In this respect the case was different from all public trust decisions of the Illinois Supreme Court before or, arguably, since. The opinion did not remark on this feature of the controversy, but simply assumed that the public trust was applicable to an inland park.[42]

The specific result was another defeat for the Hyde Parkers. The court rejected the contention that the diversion of parkland for a school was flawed because there was no statement from the legislature recognizing an awareness

FIGURE 8.7. Professor Joseph L. Sax, ca. 1967. Courtesy of the University of Michigan Law School.

of the existing public use. It found in the Public Building Commission Act and other statutes sufficient authority to support the change in use. It cited with approval some Wisconsin decisions laying out criteria for determining whether there has been a violation of the public trust doctrine, and commended them "as a useful guide for future administrative action." But without further analysis, it found that all of the Wisconsin criteria supported the "present plans for Washington Park."[43]

It is no coincidence that *Paepcke* was decided in the midst of what has been described as a national environmental revolution, which erupted in 1970. President Richard M. Nixon signed the National Environmental Policy Act into law on the first day of that year and the Clean Air Act on the last. In between, the first Earth Day, on April 22, witnessed widespread rallies and demonstrations in support of greater protection of the environment, and the Environmental Protection Agency was created by executive order. Courts got into the action, applying a "hard look" to governmental decisions affecting the environment, implicitly assuming that government agencies were captured by business groups and could not be trusted to give adequate weight to the public interest in environmental quality.[44]

Sax's attempt to transform the public trust doctrine into a general vehicle for securing judicial review of decisions privatizing public resources was very much in keeping with the tenor of the times. His January 1970 article portrayed the facts of the *Lake Front Case*, which Sax called the "lodestar" of the American public trust doctrine, as a sort of parable illustrating the dangers of capture of weak governmental institutions by corporate interests eager to seize, for private gain, resources belonging to the public. He suggested, as a solution, more demanding judicial review of any decisions that privatize public property or even just "infringe broad public uses in favor of narrower ones." Toward that end, he recommended, courts could reformulate the public trust doctrine.[45]

Viewed in light of the contemporaneous agitation for enhanced environmental protection, *Paepcke* has all the earmarks of an opinion eager to advance a popular cause but constrained by a lack of votes from reaching that result directly. At least with respect to the public trust doctrine, the opinion took its cues more from Sax's law review article than from Illinois precedent. Before *Paepcke*, Illinois decisional law reflected a powerful public dedication doctrine and a weak public trust doctrine. *Paepcke*, tracking Sax's proposal, turned this on its head. Yet notwithstanding its enlarged scope, it was not clear how powerful the new version of the public trust doctrine would be in practice. No clear principles emerged from the opinion about what sorts of public resources the doctrine protected, what sorts of public values the doctrine promoted, or how intensively courts should scrutinize decisions by political institutions to allow changes in existing uses of resources protected by the doctrine. In terms of exposition of the law, the decision was boldly revisionist. In terms of outcome, the court endorsed what the dominant political forces wanted to do in Washington Park.

The South Works—Part III

The reorientation of the public trust doctrine in *Paepcke* soon bore fruit, in what can be called the third installment of the South Works saga. This would generate the only Illinois Supreme Court decision invalidating a state statute on public trust grounds.

For reasons not entirely clear, though presumably related to its lack of clear plans for the additional land, US Steel did not promptly move to acquire the 194 acres in the lake offered by the Illinois legislature in 1963 and seemingly blessed by the Illinois Supreme Court in *Droste* in 1966. When the company in 1973 finally got around to tendering to the state the less than $20,000 required for the conveyance of the submerged land, in order to fill it, the political climate had shifted significantly.[46]

It is difficult today to grasp the politics of environmental protection as they existed in the early 1970s. The sudden emergence of widespread support for greater environmental protection caused both major political parties to try to capitalize on this sentiment. In Illinois, William J. Scott, a Republican, was young, handsome, and politically ambitious. First elected attorney general in 1968, he made several moves to establish a reputation as an environmental champion. In 1973, Scott sued to block the sale of submerged land to US Steel, alleging that this violated the public trust doctrine. Not to be outflanked, Governor Dan Walker, a Democrat who was named as a defendant in the suit, realigned as a plaintiff. A state legislator also had sued, and a bill was introduced in the legislature to repeal the 1963 grant.[47]

Scott won. The main issue in the Illinois Supreme Court was whether his challenge was foreclosed by the court's decision in *Droste* ten years earlier, in 1966. By a one-vote margin, the court said no. *Droste,* the court concluded, had rejected the public trust action on the grounds that the plaintiff, a private citizen, did not have standing—a ruling subsequently rejected in *Paepcke.* Although the earlier decision also contained language that seemed to uphold the 1963 act as consistent with the public trust doctrine, such parts of the decision were characterized as "*dicta.*"[48]

On the merits, the *Scott* court acknowledged there to be scant evidence that the projected landfilling would interfere with the rights enumerated in the *Lake Front Case*—navigation, commerce, and fishing. But the interests protected by the public trust doctrine, it held, were "not bound by inflexible standards." In

FIGURE 8.8. Attorney General William J. Scott. Illinois Blue Book Collection, 1971–72, Illinois Digital Archives, Illinois State Library–Office of the Illinois Secretary of State and State Librarian.

particular, "[T]here has developed a strong, though belated, interest in conserving natural resources and in protecting and improving our physical environment. The public has become increasingly concerned with dangers to health and life from environmental sources and more sensitive to the value and, frequently, the irreplaceability of natural resources." The court noted the then-recent 1970 state constitution, quoting its declaration that "[e]ach person has the right to a healthful environment."[49]

Citing and quoting Professor Sax as in *Paepcke*, the court suggested that the public trust doctrine was intended to prevent the conveyance of public lands for private purposes. The court acknowledged upholding landfilling in the lake for the water filtration plant and McCormick Place, but those were public projects. In the present case, the court said, "[W]e can perceive only a private purpose for the grant." Moreover, the court announced that any conveyance of trust lands "in favor of a private interest has to withstand a most critical examination." This was a new element. The deference given the legislature in *Kirk* was replaced by an unspecified standard of review that seemed to invite the court's complete substitution of its own judgment.[50]

Applying this new scrutiny, the court acknowledged the legislature's declaration that the filling would "result in the conversion of otherwise useless and unproductive submerged land into an important commercial development to the benefit of the people of the State of Illinois." But it "judge[d] these arguments to be unpersuasive." Although it would "consider" the legislature's description of a public purpose and its declaration that a statute serves the purpose, the court concluded that "[t]he claimed benefit here to the public through additional employment and economic improvement is too indirect, intangible and elusive to satisfy the requirement of a public purpose."[51]

Scott would prove to be the only Illinois Supreme Court decision to invalidate a duly enacted Illinois statute under the public trust doctrine. From the perspective of general norms of American public law, the most puzzling thing about the decision is the source of the court's authority to do this. Although the court cited the state constitution, it did not suggest that the public trust doctrine was grounded in state constitutional law. Nor was there any suggestion that federal law prohibited the conveyance of submerged land.[52]

The mystery is solved only by going back to the *Lake Front Case* and its theory that the state's title to certain land is qualified by a trust obligation. The idea advanced by Justice Field was that the United States, when it granted statehood to Illinois in 1818, conveyed title to the state to the submerged land beneath the navigable waters in the state. Such land, like the submerged lands of the original colonies created by grants from the king of England, was impressed by a trust protecting certain rights of the people. Because title to the land is impressed with this trust obligation, it can never be conveyed free of the trust. Under this theory, there is nothing the state can do to free itself from the trust. Not even a state constitutional amendment will do the trick. The trust lasts forever.[53]

As we have seen, the idea that the submerged lands are impressed with an indelible trust does not necessarily tie the hands of the state. The Illinois Supreme Court had held in *Kirk* that the state legislature is the trustee of these lands and, in that capacity, can decide that achieving certain purposes in the public interest requires the conveyance of submerged lands to private parties. The crucial question then became how much deference the courts would give to these legislative judgments. The general thrust of Illinois decisions up to *Scott* was to give significant deference to the legislature. What then accounts for the sudden move toward strict judicial review in *Scott*?

A number of plausible factors can be cited. The project involved the filling of a large amount of open water (194 acres), more than had been at issue in any of the previous public trust cases, other than the *Lake Front Case* itself. The consideration given the state for the grant (one hundred dollars per acre) seemed nominal at best, even if it was the same amount paid by the steel company in 1909 and by Northwestern in 1961. Title to the land would pass to a private, for-profit corporation, as opposed to a government agency or nonprofit entity. The proposed use of the land was for the expansion of a steel mill, the kind of highly polluting heavy industry that was the particular target of the burgeoning environmental movement. And the public benefits were what economists would call pecuniary externalities—more jobs and tax revenues—rather than any kind of infrastructural improvement or facility open to the general public.

Some or all of these factors no doubt influenced the Illinois Supreme Court in *Scott*. Another factor that may have been highly influential was that the political establishment, or at least a significant subset of it, had turned against the project. It is true that the legislature had approved the transfer of submerged land. But the approval had come many years before, in 1963, during the antediluvian era before the environmental revolution. In all previous cases, elected officials either were solidly supportive of the landfilling project or were at worst divided about its merits (*Kirk*). By the time *Scott* was decided, both the Democratic governor and the Republican attorney general opposed the project, as did a significant segment of the state legislature.

In terms of clarification of the law, *Scott* did little to resolve the questions raised by *Paepcke*. The resource in question was submerged land under Lake Michigan, which had been understood since the original decision in the *Lake Front Case* to be subject to the public trust. So the question about what other resources are covered by the doctrine remained unresolved. The proposed sale was a transfer in fee simple to a private, for-profit corporation. But, again, the *Lake Front Case* seemingly established that this kind of conveyance was subject to invalidation as a breach of trust, so other questions regarding potential transferees, such as a private university, were not addressed. And although the court gave little or no deference to the legislative judgment that the transfer of the submerged land was in the public interest, it failed to spell out exactly what standard of review courts should apply in determining whether there has been a breach of trust.

US Steel closed the South Works in 1992, selling or scrapping its blast furnaces, rolling mills, and other facilities. As discussed in chapter 9, the site has remained vacant ever since, and the South Chicago neighborhood surrounding the empty plant site remains economically depressed. It is impossible to attribute the closing of the plant solely to the *Scott* decision a decade and a half earlier. US Steel's president, who himself had worked at the South Works in the 1970s (in a white-collar job), pointed to "weak demand from high-rise construction, depressed market prices and competition from non-union, low-cost mini-mills." And given the consolidation of the steel industry in recent decades, the plant probably would have closed in any event. But one cannot be sure, especially given that the 1976 decision denied US Steel the economies of scale available from a larger plant. Some larger steel mills in nearby northern Indiana have remained open for decades since the South Works closed in Chicago.[54]

As for Attorney General Scott, his attempt to advance his political ambitions by taking up the environmental mantle did not succeed. Before he and his wife were divorced in 1970, she discovered that Scott had multiple safe-deposit boxes containing envelopes filled with cash—unspent and unreported campaign contributions; this came out years later, during a dispute between them over child support. Indicted for tax evasion, Scott lost the 1980 primary election for the US Senate seat that he coveted and was found guilty by a federal jury the next day. Released after seven months in prison, Scott sought to rehabilitate his legal career but died of a heart attack in 1986, at age fifty-nine, while washing his car outside his home in south suburban Chicago.[55]

The Loyola Campus Expansion

The next public trust controversy arose in the late 1980s, when Loyola University announced plans to expand its lakeshore campus in the Rogers Park neighborhood on the far North Side of Chicago (shown in figure 8.2). Like Northwestern in Evanston some four miles farther north, Loyola was essentially landlocked. The local alderman had told Loyola in no uncertain terms that any effort to expand north, west, or south would be opposed because of the "major disruption" it would cause to existing communities. Taking its cue from Northwestern, Loyola decided that the logical path was to fill part of the lake to the east.[56]

Loyola's plan, in comparison to Northwestern's, was modest, calling for the transfer of between 20 and 30 acres of submerged land to the university. A total of 18.5 acres would be filled. The outer perimeter of 2.1 acres would be subject to an easement given to the Chicago Park District, affording unrestricted public access. This public-use area would include a pedestrian walkway and bike path, as well as a plaza and a place for anyone to fish. The interior of the landfill, which would be owned by Loyola and include athletic fields, would have public access, subject to Loyola's rights. The provisions for public access represented a major change by the university, which had previously given the public no right of access to the lake from its campus. The project, depicted in figure 8.9, would also result in an expansion of Hartigan Beach, a Chicago park to the immediate north of the campus. There were no immediate plans to erect buildings on the new land.[57]

Like Northwestern before it, Loyola did everything one would expect by way of securing approval of the plan by politically accountable or representative institutions. Loyola consulted with, and gained the support of, the Rogers Park Community Council, the Southeast Rogers Park Neighbors Association, the Edgewater Community Council, the Association of Sheridan Condo-Coop Owners, the Open Lands Project, and the Metropolitan Planning Council. In 1988, the state legislature approved the conveyance of the submerged land for $10,000. The statute acknowledged that the land was impressed with a public trust, but found that the plan would advance the public interest, including the interests of the residents of Rogers Park, who would gain new access to the lake. The statute provided that if the property ever ceased to be used for university purposes, the state could retake it. City, state, and federal entities all duly reviewed and blessed the plan.[58]

Obtaining the approval of the Army Corps of Engineers seemed to be the highest hurdle. In the years since the Northwestern expansion in the early 1960s, major permitting decisions by the Army Corps had become subject to the requirements of the National Environmental Policy Act (NEPA), made law on January 1, 1970. For all "major Federal actions significantly affecting the quality of the human environment," the NEPA process requires a consideration of environmental impacts, potential alternatives to the project, and potential mitigation measures. Federal courts have jurisdiction to review the adequacy of these evaluations. Courts are not supposed to review the substantive merits of a federal agency's decision to grant or deny a permit as being in the public interest or not, but can enjoin a project for process failures such as not giving adequate consideration to one or more relevant environmental variables. As had become common practice, Loyola hired consulting firms to prepare an elaborate (four-volume) "environmental impact assessment" considering the various environmental

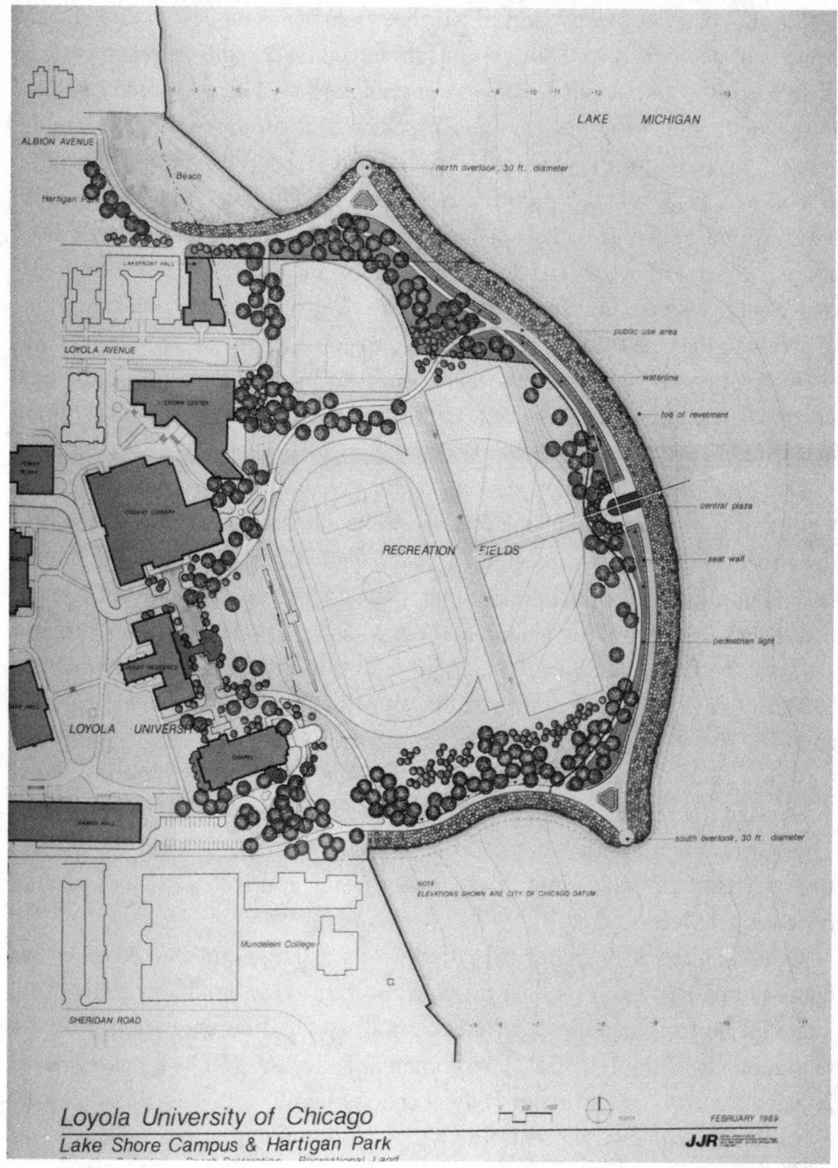

FIGURE 8.9. Loyola University with existing buildings and planned landfill for campus expansion, 1988. Courtesy of Loyola University Chicago Archives and Special Collections and of SmithGroup.

issues associated with the project; the Army Corps then reviewed the study in making its own evaluation. The evolution of the NEPA process had also established that other federal agencies and the Illinois Environmental Protection

Agency had authority to comment on the permit application, as did interested members of the public and environmental groups.[59]

To all appearances, the environmental impact assessment was quite rigorous—nothing remotely like it had occurred in connection with previous landfilling projects. The regional office of the federal Fish and Wildlife Service of the Department of the Interior negotiated for modifications to the plan before it would drop its opposition. The Illinois agency was not satisfied until further testing established that the fill material proposed for the site would not contribute to water pollution of the lake. The federal Environmental Protection Agency withdrew its own objections only after Loyola was able to satisfy the agency on a variety of specific points. Loyola commissioned an additional report to address the concern of the Army Corps about the project's impact on aquatic habitat in the lake. The army issued the requested permit on April 16, 1990.[60]

By the time Loyola revealed its plan, the environmental movement in Chicago had spread far beyond Hyde Park and had become institutionalized. For example, Friends of the Parks, which we encountered briefly in chapter 3, was formally organized in 1975 and had a full-time executive director. The local environmental community was divided about the Loyola initiative. Several groups came around to supporting the plan, including the Open Lands Project and the Metropolitan Planning Council, as did the local alderman, David D. Orr, and the local state senator, Arthur L. Berman, both of whom had strong credentials with environmental groups. But others voiced adamant opposition. The copresidents of Chicago's League of Women Voters denounced the project as "offensive." The state field representative of the Sierra Club labeled it a "moral outrage!" The gist of the argument against the project, as in the arguments against any further diversion of the waters of Lake Michigan (see chapter 5), was the slippery slope. The Loyola project would create "a decisive precedent: public trust land going to a private institution," the Sierra Club representative maintained. "A door that's ajar is easier to open." The executive director of Friends of the Parks put it this way: "The lakefront is priceless, and we're starting to nibble away."[61]

As Loyola issued construction contracts, a local environmental group called the Lake Michigan Federation filed suit in federal district court, seeking an injunction against the project. Federal jurisdiction was based on a challenge to the adequacy under NEPA of the consideration by the Army Corps of environmental impacts. The plaintiffs also attacked the plan as violating the public trust doctrine, arguing that the federal court could consider such a challenge—a state-law issue—under what the federal courts now call supplemental jurisdiction. This was potentially significant. As suggested by our account to this point, there is reason to believe that the state courts are sensitive to the level of political support for or opposition to landfill projects. Federal judges have life tenure and are generally regarded as being less susceptible to such influences. In the hands of a federal judge, the state public trust doctrine, in its dramatically expanded but vague reformulation after the decisions in *Paepcke* and *Scott*, would afford virtually unfettered discretion to approve or disapprove any lakefill decision incidentally involving the need for a federal permit.[62]

The case was assigned to Judge Marvin E. Aspen. He found it unnecessary to consider the challenge to the adequacy of the Army Corps's consideration of environmental factors under NEPA—the indispensable basis for his jurisdiction. Instead he ruled that the project was a "transparent giveaway of public property to a private entity," and hence violated the Illinois public trust doctrine.[63]

Reviewing the various Illinois precedents, Judge Aspen discerned that the public trust doctrine strongly disfavors any attempt by the state to "surrender valuable public resources to a private entity," "benefit a private interest," or relinquish the state's "power over a public resource." Although the Loyola project entailed filling 18.5 acres of the lake, Aspen mentioned no linkage to navigable waters as part of the public trust analysis. The fact that the project would entail benefits to the community, and indeed would improve access to the lake, was irrelevant. The facts of a public easement to the outer perimeter and of Loyola's commitment to allowing public access to various parts were irrelevant. The fact that Loyola was a nonprofit educational institution was irrelevant. The fact that all levels of government—federal, state, and local—had approved the project was irrelevant. Indeed, the judge read the Illinois cases as allowing no deference to any public-to-private transfer of public trust property. This was a remarkable decision.[64]

In a curious coda, Loyola filed a motion for reconsideration but then announced in a press conference that it had decided to abandon the project because of the mounting expense of litigation. Aspen took notice of the press conference but proceeded nonetheless to write an opinion formally denying reconsideration. One issue that he reached out to address, even though the parties had not raised it, was the apparent inequity of Northwestern's having been able to expand its campus by extensive landfilling while Loyola was denied any right to engage in a far more modest project a few miles away. The judge correctly noted that the Northwestern project had never been challenged under the public trust doctrine, although the oddity of this apparently did not shake his conviction that such projects were flatly prohibited by Illinois law. Even more curious was a concluding passage in which the judge virtually pleaded with—specifically, "urge[d]"—Loyola University to file an appeal. Whether he harbored last-minute doubts about his decision, or simply wanted responsibility for killing the project to be shared with a higher court, we will never know. Loyola declined to appeal. It would focus its future efforts on rearranging the limited space available.[65]

The Loyola campus decision marks the most extreme application of the public trust doctrine in Illinois. From a utilitarian or social-welfare perspective, the decision is hard to defend. There is no evidence that the Northwestern campus expansion has produced any significant harm to the lake, to its aquatic environment, or to any public interest in navigation, commerce, fishing, or even recreation. And the project has yielded major benefits to Northwestern and the Evanston community, both in terms of limiting university encroachment on the surrounding neighborhoods and in providing additional opportunities for the local community to enjoy the lakefront. The far more modest Loyola expansion presumably would have produced similarly salutary results.

The decision is explicable only as a reflection of a kind of preservationist creed that opposes any change in the "natural" environment. Yet nature is always changing and mankind is part of nature. It makes no sense to freeze one element of the natural environment—the submerged land under an enormous inland lake—while all other features of the environment undergo continual evolution, including pressure from growing human population and associated human needs, such as the need for expanded facilities for higher education and public recreation.

That the decision was rendered by a single federal judge, purporting to interpret Illinois law, limits its precedential significance. But this also makes it problematic on the grounds of democratic legitimacy. The Loyola campus expansion was considered from all angles by a wide range of community groups, local and state political institutions, and state and federal agencies responsible for protecting different aspects of the environment. After extensive deliberation and negotiation, nearly all affected interests reached a consensus that the project should go forward. It was blocked at the behest of an environmental advocacy group by one unelected judge. Loyola conceivably would have prevailed on appeal. But it had exhausted its available resources on consulting reports and legal fees. The result was to thwart the will of the community, in the name of an abstract ideal.

Nor does the decision make sense from the perspective of the role of the public trust doctrine that Professor Sax envisioned. Sax was concerned about the absence of any administrative forum in which the diffuse interests of the public could be raised in opposition to a "giveaway" of public resources, and about the lack of judicial review to provide a check against the capture of political institutions by profit-seeking developers. At least with respect to the filling of lands under navigable waters, however, the authority given the Army Corps of Engineers, as augmented by NEPA, provides just the kind of forum demanded by Sax. It also affords ample opportunity for judicial review. In this context at least, the problem identified by Sax had been solved, rendering any additional oversight by courts in the name of the public trust doctrine superfluous.[66]

The Soldier Field Case

The Illinois Supreme Court's most recent word on the public trust doctrine came in 2003. It involved a legal challenge, brought by Friends of the Parks and others, seeking to block the proposed reconstruction of Soldier Field that would add a new superstructure resembling a spaceship on top of the original colonnaded stadium. Soldier Field was originally opened in 1924 by the South Park Commission on landfill made in constructing south Lake Shore Drive and Burnham Park (see chapter 7). No one suggested in 1924 that building a sports stadium on previously filled land raised any issue under the public trust doctrine. Nor would any challenge to the reconstruction of the stadium be plausible under the pre-1970 version of the public trust doctrine: the project had the blessing of both the park district and the state legislature.

The contention that the public trust doctrine barred the remodeling of the stadium was based on the language in *Paepcke* and *Scott* that any transfer of public lands to "private" interests was barred by the doctrine. Specifically, the plaintiffs claimed that the reconstruction of the stadium, following a similar public-private undertaking to build a ballpark to keep the Chicago White Sox in town, was designed to enhance the revenues of the Chicago Bears, the principal tenant of Soldier Field.

The court in the *Soldier Field Case* devoted the bulk of its analysis to the claim that the project violated the Illinois constitutional provision that public funds may be used only for public purposes. In rejecting this claim, the Illinois Supreme Court quoted at length the legislative findings that the project would serve multiple public purposes, and it reaffirmed precedent setting forth a highly deferential standard of review in considering judicial challenges to such findings. The only question, the court said, was whether, "after according great deference to the legislative declaration of a public purpose, the stated public purpose is but an evasion." Not surprisingly, the constitutional challenge was rejected.[67]

The court then turned to the public trust claim, which received a more cursory treatment. Interestingly, the court began by noting that all parties agreed that Soldier Field "is public trust property." The court did not clarify whether this was because the stadium sits on land reclaimed from the lake or because it was sited in a public park. Quoting the *Lake Front Case*, the court seemed to suggest that once property is deemed public trust land, it remains public trust land for all time.[68]

Turning to the merits, the court sharply distinguished the Soldier Field makeover from the landfilling disapproved in the *Lake Front Case* and in *Scott*. The earlier cases involved a transfer of public trust property "to a private party." In the present case, the park district would remain "the owner" of Soldier Field. Notwithstanding the long-term lease to the Bears, running to the end of the 2033 season and renewable at the team's option for twenty additional years, there was no "conveyance" to the Bears, and the park district retained "control" over the property as landlord. The court also noted that *Paepcke* had upheld the changed use of public trust land from one public use to another and had said that the resolution of such conflicts "is for the legislature and not the courts."[69]

The court concluded that the public would benefit in several ways from the project, including having a better stadium for a variety of events, even beyond football and other sports, and better parking for access to museums and the lakefront. "These results," it said, "do not violate the public trust doctrine even though the Bears will also benefit from the completed project." The court said nothing specifically about the standard of review to be applied in public trust cases, although the highly deferential standard it applied to the separate challenge in the case based on

FIGURE 8.10. Soldier Field, ca. 1984. Chicago Public Library, Special Collections, Chicago Park District Photos, box 9, folder 16, image 1.

FIGURE 8.11. Soldier Field, 2012. Tom Regan, photographer.

the state constitution's "public purpose" requirement seemed to spill over to and at least color the discussion of the public trust claim.[70]

It is possible to read the *Soldier Field Case* as holding that long-term leases to private entities do not violate the public trust doctrine, so long as the fee remains with a public institution. This would render the doctrine largely meaningless, or at least would permit ready evasion. We think it rather more significant that the court did not invoke pecuniary externalities—higher taxes, more jobs—in rejecting the public trust challenge. Use by the public and retention of public control seemed to be critical in the court's mind, not benefits of an economic-development type.

What can be said by way of summary about the 125-year odyssey of the public trust doctrine in Illinois?

One thing is clear: the purpose of the doctrine has changed dramatically. Originally it was to preserve public access to navigable waters, in order to allow the public to engage in commerce or fishing. The focus changed with the environmental revolution in the 1970s. Today, the purpose is understood to be the preservation of public resources in the hands of public institutions. The doctrine has become an antiprivatization doctrine for certain select categories of public property.

Other things are very unclear. First, what sorts of lands are subject to the public trust doctrine? If the doctrine applies to all land reclaimed from Lake Michigan, then this has radical implications. All of the filled area east of Michigan Avenue between Randolph Street and the Chicago River, and much of Streeterville, would be subject to the public trust—not to mention all the private land up and down the lakefront transferred to private owners under the boundary-line agreements used in constructing Lake Shore Drive. Perhaps the doctrine applies to any public park, but then it is odd that only one Illinois Supreme Court decision—*Paepcke*—clearly applies the doctrine to land that was never under Lake Michigan, and the challenge was rejected in that case.

Second, it is extremely unclear what weight courts are to give findings by the Illinois legislature that the transfer of public lands, including submerged lands, is in the public interest. Some decisions, such as *Kirk*, give such findings virtually conclusive weight. Others, such as *Scott*, seem to give them no weight at all. Still others, such as the *Soldier Field Case*, seem to apply an unarticulated intermediate standard.

It is possible, looking at the broad run of decisions, to identify some factors that seem to predict the success or failure of a public trust challenge to a project in Illinois. Factors that point toward disapproval of a project include a large number of acres, filling open waters as opposed to building on existing land, transfer to a private entity, legislative approval of the project only in general legislation or with a long time lag before actual construction, and disagreement among politically accountable institutions about the merits of the project. Factors pointing to a project's passing muster under the doctrine include a small number of acres, development of filled or solid land as opposed to the filling of open waters, a change in public uses rather than a public-to-private transfer, specific and recent legislative approval, and a general concurrence among politically accountable institutions about the merits of the project.

Whether these predictive factors make sense as a normative matter is another question. In our view, a sensible public trust doctrine would return to the basic proposition that the legislature is the trustee of public trust resources and the courts should give considerable deference to legislative determinations about the proper disposition of those resources. Adherence to these principles would cause the Illinois doctrine to converge with that of other states, such as New York, where the public trust doctrine is used to force the legislature to take what we might term a "second look" at decisions to sell or otherwise transform lands open to the general public. This helps ensure that such matters are carefully deliberated, while preserving the authority of democratic institutions, accountable to the people, to make the final decision.[71]

If final responsibility were given to the legislature, rather than the courts, this would allow the set of resources protected by the doctrine to expand beyond navigable waters to include parks, wildlife preserves, and recreation areas. Similarly, it would allow the purposes furthered by the doctrine to expand beyond protecting access to navigable waters, so as to include the preservation of publicly owned natural resources more broadly and the promotion of values such as public recreation. The Illinois doctrine, grounded in the title theory associated with the bed of navigable waters, makes these expanded uses of the doctrine inherently problematic and unlikely, and complicates the capacity of the doctrine to evolve into a more useful form.

9

THE LAKEFRONT TODAY

The political settlements and legal understandings we have canvassed in our account continue to affect the Chicago lakefront today. In this final chapter, we offer brief snapshots of five more recent developments on the lakefront that reflect the influence of the past—and that may be indicative of the future.

The Illinois Central Disappears

From the middle of the nineteenth century until well into the twentieth, the Illinois Central Railroad was the most visible presence on the lakefront. The conflicts created by its dominating presence, and the aggressive landfilling it pursued, are significantly responsible for the contemporary appearance of the lakefront. Yet today the railroad has largely disappeared from the lakefront, in both name and fact.

The boundary-line agreement of 1912 planted the seeds of the Illinois Central's demise on the lakefront. As we have seen in chapter 7, the railroad agreed to vacate much of its filled land between 12th and 16th Streets, in return for augmented rights farther south. Its ambiguous commitment to electrifying its lines in Grant Park became a legal mandate with the Lake Front Ordinance of 1919. Pursuant to a series of legislated mileposts over the next two decades, only electric locomotives were supposed to operate along the lakefront in the city center. The process of electrification did not fully comply with the timetable contemplated in 1919, as the railroad repeatedly sought to delay the conversion process. Eventually, however, the Illinois Central eliminated all freight operations along the lakefront, leaving only commuter trains, which were operated by electrical motive power. After Amtrak was created in 1970, intercity rail passenger service to and from Chicago was consolidated at Union Station. Central Station, having lost its primary rationale, was demolished in 1974.[1]

Meanwhile, the Illinois Central's litigation victory in the *Hickey* case in 1966 (see chapter 7) allowed what had been a massive freight yard north of Randolph Street to be transformed into prime commercial real estate. The company used this windfall to transform itself from a railroad into an entirely different kind of entity.

The same year the railroad won the *Hickey* case, it hired an aggressive new chief executive officer, William B. Johnson. In keeping with the business fashions of the day, Johnson transformed what had been a railroad into a conglomerate. Johnson would dispose of most of the railroad's mileage in order to concentrate on the main line running from Chicago to New Orleans. More immediately, in 1969, he created an entity, called Illinois Center Plaza Venture, to develop the real estate holdings on the former peninsula north of Randolph Street. Johnson acted as CEO and chairman of both the carrier, known for a time as the Illinois Central Gulf Railroad, and a holding company, IC Industries. He added a hodgepodge of firms, ranging from the Midas muffler and automotive company to a Pepsi-Cola bottling company. Shortly after Johnson retired in 1987, the company sold its rail commuter service on Chicago's lakefront to the regional rail transit company, popularly known as Metra. The remaining rail assets were spun off as a separate company. After being acquired by a New York private equity firm, those railroad assets became part of the Canadian National Railway as the 1990s closed. Other conglomerate assets became Whitman Corp., then PepsiAmericas, which in turn was purchased by PepsiCo in 2009, with various spinoffs along the way.[2]

Today, one can still see the name "Illinois Central" on some railroad equipment in the Mississippi River Valley. But CN, or the Canadian National Railway, is the operator and prominent name. One has to look hard for the railroad itself near downtown Chicago. In Grant Park, electric commuter trains, not visible from ground level at Randolph, run south quietly on a depressed track in Grant Park and continue, always west of Lake Shore Drive, south of 12th Street (now Roosevelt Road). They bear names such as "Metra" and "South Shore Line."

The recent history of the Illinois Central is not atypical of America's major railroads. In the 1960s and subsequent decades, many railroads formed holding companies, partly in order to exploit real estate assets acquired in the days of land-grant subsidies in the nineteenth century, and then consolidated their freight operations through abandonments and mergers. The main significance of the disappearance of the Illinois Central, from the perspective of the lakefront, is its effect on the collective memory of the citizens of Chicago. Today, the miles of well-tended greenery and sandy beaches are taken to be part of the natural order persisting from time immemorial. The physical landscape betrays little clue as to how the Illinois Central Railroad and its many antagonists brought all of this about.[3]

Millennium Park

The *Ward* cases, the subject of chapter 3, continue to affect the shape of the lakefront. Although the Illinois Supreme Court disavowed the common-law public dedication doctrine in 1970, as discussed in chapter 8, it did not overrule the *Ward* cases, which had been based on that doctrine. The court regrounded the decisions in the Chicago city charter, thus giving the public dedication doctrine a statutory foundation in the city center. The court's revisionism nevertheless eliminated the doctrine's potential usefulness for the rest of the state, including the lakefront outside Grant Park. Chicago's Lakefront Protection Ordinance, enacted in 1973, is a late entry into regulating lakefront development, but it is enforced by a public entity, the Chicago Plan Commission, not by private landowners.[4]

Whatever its legal foundation, the public dedication doctrine in Grant Park was tested in a major way by a project undertaken at the dawn of the twenty-first century. As first conceived, the project—called Millennium Park—posed no particular challenge to the precedents restricting the construction of "buildings" in Grant Park. The idea was to make the northwest corner of the park a place that would attract people, to construct a new underground parking garage, and to use the revenues from the parking fees to fund landscaping and the construction of a new band shell. Figure 9.1 shows how the area had appeared at midcentury.[5]

As the project progressed, cost estimates soared. To cover the shortfall, charitable donations were sought from wealthy Chicago corporations and families. Many responded positively, but often—in a fashion reminiscent of proponents of the Field Museum and the Crerar Library—on the condition that their largesse be reflected in some permanent way in the park. Thus, the Pritzker family agreed to fund a new band shell, but effectively made it a condition that it be designed by the architect Frank Gehry. Plans for this "music pavilion," as it would be termed, became more and more expensive and elaborate, until it could scarcely be described as a "band stand." Similarly, the Harris Theater, a venue for music and dance, would be constructed mostly beneath Randolph Street at park

FIGURE 9.1. The rectangle in the center of this 1952 photograph is the area that a half century later would become Millennium Park: the borders are Monroe Street to the south (top), Michigan Avenue to the west, Randolph Street at the north, and Lake Shore Drive on the east, with Columbus Drive visible up to Monroe but not yet extended here. The open-air parking lot was replaced by an underground garage in the 1970s, well before the Millennium Park project was conceived. Chicago Public Library, Special Collections, Chicago Park District Photos, box 153, folder 8, image 10; Aerial Photograph Co.

level, but with entrances, lobbies, and the like rising the equivalent of three stories above the street.[6]

Were these various structures "buildings" within the meaning of the public dedication? The Illinois Supreme Court's 1952 decision involving the construction of underground parking garages seemed to suggest that, in cases of doubt, "building" should be construed to mean a structure that impairs access to light, air, and view for property owners abutting the park (see chapter 3). Under such a test, many of the structures proposed for Millennium Park would have to be regarded as buildings. The Jay Pritzker Pavilion—though perhaps in some extended sense a "band stand" and thus under a dictum in *Ward III* not a building—is so massive that it completely obscures the views toward the lake from Washington Street (see figure 9.2). The polished bean-shaped "Cloud Gate" weighs 110 tons, is sixty-six feet long, and stands thirty-three feet high. And the

Crown Fountain consists of two towers twenty-three feet wide, sixteen feet thick, and fifty feet tall. Millennium Park as finally conceived also included several structures that would be regarded as buildings under the dictionary definition of the term, including the Harris Theater, the Exelon Pavilions, and the McDonald's Cycle Center or bicycle station.[7]

Attorneys advising the proponents of Millennium Park accordingly concluded that the Harris Theater would certainly be regarded as a building, and possibly other structures would as well. Following the precedent established by the construction of the Art Institute (discussed in chapter 3), they advised that abutting landowners would have to give their consent to erecting these structures, in order to head off a challenge under the *Ward* precedents.[8]

The question was this: Who qualifies as an abutting owner? Based on the consent form found in the archives of the Art Institute and the discussion of the consents to that building in *Ward I*, the attorneys concluded that consents were required only from those who owned property directly opposite or diagonally across from the project. Consents were thus solicited and obtained from this group.[9]

In order to satisfy the underwriters of bonds to fund the project, something more than the opinion of the attorneys was needed. Accordingly, a test case, called *Boaz v. City of Chicago*, was filed on behalf of the owners of a condominium on Randolph Street east of Millennium Park. The plaintiffs duly claimed that their

FIGURE 9.2. Jay Pritzker Pavilion in Millennium Park, as viewed from the Loop (looking east on Washington Street), 2013. Richard Ellis/Alamy Stock Photo.

consent was also required. The city argued the opposite, maintaining that only those living immediately opposite or diagonally across from the project had to consent. In January 2000, Judge Albert Green of the Cook County Circuit Court ruled for the city, thus establishing that the consents obtained were legally sufficient. There was no appeal.[10]

The *Boaz* ruling may not be legally correct. As discussed in chapter 3, precedents subsequent to the Art Institute episode and *Ward I*—namely, the decisions in *Ward III* and the *Stevens Hotel* case—suggest that a much larger number of consents was required. The first of those decisions upheld Montgomery Ward's right to enjoin the construction of the Field Museum: it was to be located in Grant Park at Congress Street (as it then was called), a full five blocks south of Ward's property at Madison Street, and thus was neither opposite nor diagonally across from the proposed location. If Ward had a right to object, then his consent would be required under any use of the consent mechanism. Similarly, when the Stevens Hotel sought to block construction of the Chicago Yacht Club and an addition to the Art Institute, the courts did not suggest that the hotel lacked standing because it was not located directly opposite or diagonally across from these structures. Given its standing to object, its consent would also be required.

The *Boaz* consent theory is thus in tension with Illinois Supreme Court precedent, making Millennium Park, at least in theory, vulnerable to a legal challenge by one or more nonconsenting owners abutting other parts of the park. This does not mean that such an enlarged scope of required consents would be desirable. The history of the public dedication doctrine in Grant Park, as previously detailed, suggests that the doctrine is prone to overprotecting parkland, insofar as the preferences of adjoining property owners diverge from those of the public at large. Grant Park would be a less valuable public resource today without the Art Institute, which was made possible only because it was feasible to obtain the consent of directly abutting owners. Likewise, Grant Park would be less valuable without Millennium Park, also made possible by the narrower understanding of the consent mechanism. This in turn suggests that the number of abutting owners who may wield the veto should not be so numerous as to foreclose the prospect of securing unanimous consent for major modifications of the public space.[11]

If this conclusion is sound, then the understanding of the relevant universe of parties who must consent that was followed for the Art Institute and Millennium Park—immediately opposite plus diagonally situated owners—may be a better rule than the broader universe of needed consents implicitly reflected in decisions such as *Ward III* and the *Stevens Hotel* case. Today, with commercial real estate located on more sides of the park than just Michigan Avenue, and many of the structures organized as condominiums, securing unanimous consent of all abutting owners would be virtually impossible. History suggests that this is too inflexible. The precedent embedded in practice, at least in this context, is superior to the one embodied in *Ward III* and *Stevens Hotel*.

Whatever its aesthetic merits, Millennium Park created what is known as a "Bilbao effect," in the characterization of Blair Kamin, the *Tribune*'s longtime architecture critic. The former rail yard, for the first time in Grant Park's history, has drawn consistently large crowds, seeking to experience the "joyful postindustrial playground." Its success undoubtedly means that city planners will be tempted to fill the empty spaces of Grant Park with other constructions testing the limits of the *Ward* precedents. One such proposal emerged in 2006, when the city proposed to relocate a children's museum to the park. This immediately elicited objections from Michigan Avenue property owners, who no doubt could foresee phalanxes of school buses depositing rowdy children on field trips. The plan was shelved. Montgomery Ward, who disliked circuses, bicycle tracks, and political rallies, would have smiled.[12]

Nevertheless, the success of Millennium Park, combined with the Illinois Supreme Court's demotion of the public dedication doctrine to a statutory right limited to Grant Park, suggests that the *Ward* precedents have been weakened, perhaps fatally. If one trusts the city and the park district to correctly balance the competing public interests in open space and monumental structures, this might be a good thing. Being cautious incrementalists, we would prefer to see the *Ward* precedents preserved, subject to the narrower form of the consent mechanism.

The Deep Tunnel

Chicago has not finished with supersized engineering projects designed to protect the lakefront from pollution, such as those discussed in chapter 5. As is common in older US cities, Chicago's sanitary and storm sewers are connected. Consequently—even after the reversal of the river and the installation of wastewater treatment plants to capture the discharge from the Chicago-area sewer system—heavy rainstorms frequently caused storm sewers to overflow into wastewater sewers. When this happened, raw sewage was discharged into the lake from points such as the canal in Wilmette. By the 1970s, closings of public beaches on the lake off Chicago and the north shore during parts of the summer season became common. In addition, many residents of Chicago and surrounding suburbs suffered from flooded basements after rainstorms.[13]

To remedy the problem, the sanitary district determined in the early 1970s to embark on what became known as the Deep Tunnel project.* The basic concept entailed drilling shafts and tunnels deep underground, which would collect high volumes of stormwater and wastewater overflow and funnel it to reservoirs where it could be stored until properly treated and then discharged into the Chicago River or other waterways.[14]

Like the public-works projects undertaken in the nineteenth century for sewer, water, and river-flow purposes, the Deep Tunnel project required some innovative engineering. This included the creation of huge boring machinery, which cut tunnels as wide as thirty-five feet in diameter through rock hundreds of feet below the surface. As the tunnels were mined, they were lined with concrete by special apparatus. Just as the original Sanitary and Ship Canal helped develop technology used in digging the Panama Canal, the Deep Tunnel provided a model for aspects of the "Chunnel" project under the English Channel.[15]

The project was divided into two phases: phase one was designed primarily to eliminate overflows of polluted water, phase two to eliminate flooding. The cost has been enormous: the price tag for the project will come to nearly $4 billion. The sanitary district could not begin to fund such a project on its own. Phase one, begun in the mid-1970s, depended on generous federal appropriations secured by one of Chicago's congressional representatives, Dan Rostenkowski, then a member of the House Ways and Means Committee and, beginning in 1981, the committee's chair for more than thirteen years.[16]

Phase one was plagued by cost overruns and awards of no-bid contracts to politically connected construction firms. The sanitary district came in for broader scrutiny as well. In 1998, a federal jury found a past president of the district guilty of racketeering and other crimes for accepting bribes during his tenure in office earlier in the decade. Still, the Deep Tunnel work bore on. Phase one was completed in 2006 at a total cost of $2.33 billion. Its tunnels are capable of drawing water from a 375-square-mile combined sewer area, including Chicago and fifty-one suburbs. It can capture 2.3 billion gallons of combined sewer overflow.[17]

Phase two consists primarily of the construction of three massive reservoirs to capture water from combined storm and waste sewers during times of potential flooding. The first two reservoirs were completed on a permanent basis in 1998 and 2015. The third is being built on the site of a limestone quarry and is scheduled to be completed in 2029.[18]

The benefits have been significant. Today, the Chicago River is visibly less polluted. It is filled with excursion boats and boasts a river walk lined with

* Although its official name is now the Metropolitan Water Reclamation District of Greater Chicago, we continue to refer to it as the sanitary district.

condominiums and riverside cafes. Beach closings on Lake Michigan are unusual. If the sole benefit from the Deep Tunnel project were these recreational amenities, it might not pass a rigorous cost-benefit test, given the enormous cost. When the reduction of flood damage is factored in, the calculation becomes closer. In any event, the Deep Tunnel puts the final touches on a series of engineering feats that have secured, along the shore of Lake Michigan in Chicago, a water quality second to none. This is a vital element in the making of the specular lakefront that exists today.[19]

South Works Site

Although most of the Chicago lakefront today is a glamorous spectacle of greenery backdropped (or punctuated) with walls of brick, steel, and glass, there is one notable exception. The far south side of the Chicago lakefront, from 79th Street to the Calumet River, is a desolate wasteland. This was the location of US Steel's South Works complex. As described in chapter 8, the complex was largely created by landfilling, much of it illegal until ratified by the legislature in 1909. When the legislature authorized the filling of an additional 194 acres in 1963, the Illinois Supreme Court first upheld the grant but then, in a suit filed by the Illinois attorney general a decade later, held that it violated the public trust doctrine. US Steel closed the plant in 1992. Initially the company sought to sell the unwanted facility to another industrial concern. Finding no takers, the company demolished all structures and cleared the site.[20]

From that time to the present, US Steel has sought to sell the almost six-hundred-acre site for other uses. The company spent $10 million on environmental remediation in the 1990s, making the site useable for residential development. The property was put up for sale as a single tract for $85 million, but again there were no takers. In 1999, the Solo Cup Company offered to buy about one hundred acres to construct a new factory. City and state officials and community groups pressured US Steel to agree to the partial sale, and the state kicked in a subsidy as part of Governor George H. Ryan's $12 billion public-works spending program. But after breaking ground in 2002, Solo withdrew from the project in favor of focusing on an acquisition of a Maryland-based cup company.[21]

In 2004, state and local officials used barges to transport, from the dredging of Peoria Lake in downstate Illinois, large amounts of fill to cover the remaining slag, thus allowing vegetation to grow. The development firm McCaffery Interests joined forces with US Steel and announced an ambitious plan that envisioned a walkable neighborhood with shopping complexes, upscale condos, wind turbines, and a canal and boat marina. "Chicago Lakeside," as it was envisioned, would feature thirteen thousand homes and 17.5 million square feet of retail space. The total cost of the project was estimated to be $4 billion.[22]

The city and state both pitched in to facilitate the scheme, including establishing a tax incremental financing district to promote road construction and other public infrastructure. In order to help overcome the perceived isolation of the site, the state constructed a new segment of Lake Shore Drive along the western edge (i.e., not abutting the lake itself), from 79th to 92nd Streets, with city streets at either end (as well as the Calumet River to the south). This project, completed in 2013 at a cost of $64 million, featured a divided highway with two lanes in each direction, attractive landscaping, and a bicycle path. US Steel also donated one hundred acres of land to the park district to be used as a new park on part of the site. By July 2014, it appeared that the plan might succeed.[23]

Alas, it was not to be. Only one retailer committed to the site; then it dropped out. In 2016, McCaffery confirmed that it had terminated the Chicago Lakeside development, giving as a reason US Steel's precarious financial position. Some effort was made to convince the Lucas Museum of Narrative Arts, which was hoping to find a site on the lakefront for a new museum (see below), to choose the South Works site. But this, too, went nowhere.[24]

In August 2016, US Steel announced that it had retained a broker to try to sell the remaining 430 acres, either in parcels or to a single buyer. The land, rechristened 8080 Lakeshore, was touted as offering "three miles of pristine Lake Michigan shoreline," "unparalleled views of downtown Chicago," and the recently completed two-mile Lake Shore Drive segment. In 2017, Emerald Living, an Irish developer, and Barcelona Housing Systems, a Spanish company, teamed up to announce an agreement to buy the site, calling it "New SouthWorks." They intended to construct twenty thousand modular homes on the property. The closing was delayed, ostensibly because soil testing revealed potential contamination. The stated reason is questionable, the government having cleared the site as requiring no further remediation some years before. In any event, Barcelona soon dropped out, followed shortly by Emerald Living. As of this writing, the property is back on the market once again.[25]

How is it that the South Works site, with its miles of unobstructed shoreline and spectacular views, has remained an empty field of weeds for more than twenty-five years? The challenges are daunting. One impediment is the site's isolation. The new two-mile segment of Lake Shore Drive hardly solved the problem, given that the new drive simply funnels into city streets at its north and south ends. Even with the road addition, the site has no easy access either to the Chicago Loop, a dozen miles to the north, or to the interstate highways leading to Indiana, to the south and east. Another part of the answer is the depressed condition of the neighborhood surrounding the site. The area is filled with small homes built to house the steelworkers and their families who worked at the steel mill. With no such jobs for a quarter century, the housing stock is understandably badly deteriorated, as are the few remaining commercial establishments.

FIGURE 9.3. South Works site, 2016. Curtis Waltz, photographer.

Yet a further hurdle is the sheer size of the site, and the magnitude of the investment that would be needed to construct the streets, sewers, utilities, schools, and parks required to attract a viable mixed-use development.

In published reporting on the various plans for the South Works site, we have seen no reference to the public trust doctrine. But it would not take much research for a mortgage lender or title insurance company to discover that this was the very land at issue when the Illinois Supreme Court rendered its only decision declaring that the public trust doctrine forever bars any use of submerged land for a "private purpose." There is nothing to stop Friends of the Parks—or any other environmental group, or indeed any Illinois taxpayer—from suing in an effort to block a mixed-use development of the site as a violation of the public trust doctrine. So the doctrine hangs like a silent cloud over the title to the site, providing yet another reason why this extraordinary land remains barren.[26]

The Lucas Museum and Obama Presidential Center

The public trust doctrine recently made much more prominent and highly consequential appearances on the lakefront, being invoked by preservationist groups to challenge both a new museum and the construction of President Barack Obama's presidential library (called the Obama Presidential Center). Lawsuits invoking the public trust doctrine were filed against both projects in federal court. The litigation succeeded in killing off the Lucas Museum of the Narrative Arts, but not the Obama Presidential Center.

First, the museum. George Lucas, creator of the *Star Wars* and Indiana Jones films, wanted to establish a museum to house narrative art, film artifacts, and a display of digital art—the "orphaned arts," Lucas called them. After failing to gain a site in San Francisco, he turned to Chicago, his wife's hometown. In 2014, the political establishment—Mayor Rahm Emanuel and the city council—responded enthusiastically to the idea of putting the museum on the lakefront on the near South Side. The structure would be built without any taxpayer funding, would create jobs, and would draw additional tourists to the city. A task force recommended a site between Soldier Field and McCormick Place, then used as a parking lot.[27]

Lucas wanted an avant-garde design for his museum. Early depictions were reproduced in the newspapers. Lucas described it as "organic architecture," resembling "maybe a living thing like a sponge." Others thought it looked like a giant marshmallow dropped from the sky. Whether because of the controversial design or because of the precedent that it might set for filling up the lakefront parks and parking lots with (more) museums, Friends of the Parks announced its opposition to the plan. The *Chicago Tribune* joined in the opposition. In November 2014, Friends of the Parks went to federal court, asking for an injunction blocking the construction at the designated site, described as "land recovered from the navigable waters of Lake Michigan." The gist of the complaint was that the project violated the public trust doctrine because the state legislature had not specifically approved it.[28]

FIGURE 9.4. Unrealized concept design for the Lucas Museum of Narrative Art in Chicago by MAD Architects, 2016.

Given that the public trust doctrine is a matter of state law, how could a federal district court have jurisdiction over the issue? No federal permit was required for landfilling, as the museum would be built on land originally made in the 1920s as part of the construction of south Lake Shore Drive. Friends of the Parks nevertheless argued that a federal question was presented because the construction of the museum on the lakefront would violate its members' federal constitutional right to due process of law. The basis of the claim was that, under Illinois law, every taxpayer has standing to bring a public trust challenge. Therefore, the argument went, every taxpayer has a "property" interest in preserving lands subject to the public trust. The park district, by proposing to allow the museum to be built on public trust land without express legislative approval, was depriving every taxpayer in Illinois of property without due process of law.[29]

The argument was far-fetched. Property, for due process purposes, has always been limited to entitlements attached to particular persons, not interests shared in equal measure by all taxpayers in a state. The plaintiffs' argument would allow every public trust claim to be advanced in federal court, in the guise of a due process claim.[30]

Nevertheless, Judge John W. Darrah, ruling on the park district and city's motion to dismiss the lawsuit, held that the plaintiffs' complaint advanced a valid due process claim, because the defendants were proposing to transfer control of the lakefront property "without first obtaining authorization from the Illinois General Assembly." So the city promptly secured state legislation authorizing the park district to lease parkland, even if formerly submerged, for a museum or presidential library (the Obama presidential library then also being proposed for construction on parkland near the lakefront).[31]

With the required legislative mandate seemingly in hand, the park district and the Lucas Museum proceeded to hammer out a lease that would permit construction of the museum at the chosen location. Acting with extraordinary dispatch, in two weeks in October 2015, the park district board approved the lease; the Chicago Plan Commission endorsed the needed zoning changes; the museum and the Chicago Bears finalized a long-term agreement on parking and the like; and, in what the *Tribune* characterized as "the final vote by a public body needed to greenlight the museum going in south of Soldier Field," the required zoning was approved by the city council.[32]

Friends of the Parks went back to federal court, promptly amending the group's complaint to reflect the new legislation and the approvals. The defendants again moved to dismiss the lawsuit. In early 2016, Judge Darrah ruled once more that the complaint had stated a valid claim that the museum would violate the public trust doctrine and, derivatively, due process of law. The gist of his ruling was that the legislature, by passing a law that did not mention the Lucas

Museum by name, had failed to provide the necessary specific authorization to satisfy the public trust doctrine.[33]

Sensing that Lucas had run out of patience, the city sought extraordinary relief—a writ of mandamus—from the US Court of Appeals for the Seventh Circuit, asking the court to direct Darrah to dismiss the lawsuit for lack of federal jurisdiction. The appellate court seemed interested, ordering a response from the plaintiffs. But before it ruled on the merits of the mandamus request, George Lucas announced, on June 24, 2016, that he was abandoning any attempt to build the Lucas Museum in Chicago. He would subsequently reach an agreement to build it in Los Angeles.[34]

The Lucas Museum episode epitomizes the predominant version of today's disputes over the fate of the lakefront. On the one side, the politicians and city planners who worry about jobs and tax revenues were all in favor of the project, notwithstanding the quirky tastes of the donor in terms of both the architecture and subject matter of the museum. On the other side, the preservationists were put off by the commercial and self-referential overtones of the project, and worried about the precedent of filling more open spaces on the lakefront with permanent structures. Both sides claimed to speak for the general public. The project, at least in this case, was killed off by the uncertainty and delay associated with public trust litigation.

This brings us to the Obama Presidential Center. Its appearance on the lakefront scene was the result of a national invitation for proposals for the location of a center honoring the nation's first African American president. In an echo of the competition for the World's Columbian Exposition in the nineteenth century (see chapter 2), Chicago won the competition in 2016, barely a month after the loss of the Lucas Museum. And the site ultimately selected, as some 125 years earlier, was land in Jackson Park. As the arrangement involving twenty acres was ultimately hashed out between the city, the park district, and the charitable foundation supporting the Obama Presidential Center (OPC), the city would hold title to the land, while the OPC would build and operate the center under a ninety-nine-year use agreement, paying the city a nominal ten dollars. The center would contain a number of buildings, a public garden, and an underground parking garage. A museum would house artifacts from the Obama administration, but, in a departure from past practice, the voluminous presidential papers would be kept elsewhere, with digital copies accessible on computer terminals in the OPC.[35]

Friends of the Parks, after extensive but unsuccessful lobbying for a different site, ultimately decided not to sue. But a new environmental group, Protect Our Parks, soon popped up; joined by a small number of taxpayers, it filed suit claiming that the Obama Presidential Center violated the public trust doctrine.

FIGURE 9.5. Proposed Obama Presidential Center, with a view northward, toward the public plaza and the museum building, 2019. The Obama Foundation.

Protect Our Parks followed the lead of Friends of the Parks in the Lucas Museum case by suing in federal court. It advanced the same argument that every Illinois taxpayer has a right to enforce the public trust doctrine and thus has fractional "rights in . . . property" sufficient to claim a deprivation of due process whenever he or she feels that the doctrine has been violated. The city and park district, as in the Lucas case, moved to dismiss. A federal district judge, John Robert Blakey, rejected the city's motion, following the lead of Judge Darrah in finding that the universal-property-right theory was sufficient to support federal jurisdiction over a state-law public trust claim.[36]

The litigation generated numerous friend-of-the-court briefs and considerable media attention. The court moved quickly to resolve the merits. It ordered a short discovery period and briefing schedule, after which the parties filed motions for summary judgment. In June 2019, the court issued a substantial opinion granting the city's motion for summary judgment, and ordered the litigation "terminated."[37]

In resolving the public trust claim, Blakey was faced with the formidable task of trying to reconcile the numerous decisions of the Illinois courts responding to public trust controversies on the lakefront. He divided the cases into three categories: those that involved the filling of submerged land, those that involved the use of previously filled land, and those that involved land that had never been submerged.[38]

The judge found it incontestable that the site of the proposed OPC was in the "never-submerged land" category. The relevant date was 1818, when Illinois became a state and thus succeeded to title to the land under Lake Michigan.

The city produced an 1822 map showing as solid land what would become the west side of Jackson Park. Since no apparent change had occurred between 1818 and 1822, this provided decisive evidence about the status of the land in 1818. The plaintiffs had countered only with a study by the Illinois State Archeological Survey suggesting that the area may have been underwater during the "[l]ate Pleistocene and early Holocene" eras, roughly eleven thousand years ago.[39]

As to the appropriate legal standard for assessing a public trust challenge to land that had never been submerged, Blakey concluded that the relevant precedent was *Paepcke v. Public Building Commission*, which had applied the public trust doctrine to a park that had never been submerged. As discussed in chapter 8, *Paepcke*, the 1970 case involving Washington Park, is the only Illinois Supreme Court case to apply the doctrine, in any substantial way, outside the context of submerged or previously submerged land, and it was far from clear about the standard of review in such circumstances. Blakey concluded that the relevant standard was "whether sufficient legislative intent exists for a given land reallocation or diversion." He did not clarify whether this standard applies only to parks or, instead, to any publicly owned land (presumably, he was not suggesting that privately owned and never-submerged land requires previous legislative authorization for development). In any event, the required authorization was readily found for the OPC, since the state legislation authorizing the city to secure the Lucas Museum for the lakefront included a reference to "presidential libraries, centers, and museums."[40]

Blakey might well have stopped the discussion at this point, and arguably he should have. Yet he plunged ahead, offering his views as to how to interpret the Illinois precedents in the context of both changed uses of previously filled land and the filling of submerged land, in an effort to demonstrate that the OPC also would have passed muster under more exacting standards. As to previously submerged land, Blakey thought that the precedents required, in addition to legislative authorization, a finding that the proposed use did not "primarily benefi[t] a private entity, with no corresponding public benefit." As to the new filling of submerged land, he discerned that the relevant standard was whether the "primary purpose" of a legislative grant was "to benefit a private interest."[41]

These dicta may well represent the best reconciliation of the Illinois judicial precedents. Unfortunately, they do not jibe with the reality on the ground. As documented throughout this book, much private land along or near the Chicago lakefront sits on what was once submerged land. Just about all of the land between Randolph and the Chicago River, east of Michigan Avenue, was once under Lake Michigan—as is true of all of the land of Streeterville, all of the property transferred to riparian owners through boundary agreements to secure the construction of Lake Shore Drive, and much of the land constituting the site of the South Works. To open any changed use of this land to judicial challenge on the grounds that the new use would benefit a private entity, with no corresponding public benefit, would be utterly destabilizing of billions of dollars of private property. Public trust challenges should be limited to publicly owned land in this context, or cut off by some kind of statute or period of limitations. To cite only the most obvious example, subjecting any development of the South Works land on the far South Side to Blakey's proposed standard for previously filled land would discourage even further any attempt to use the site for a mixed-use development, which by general consensus is the best outcome for the area.

Protect Our Parks appealed Blakey's decision to the US Court of Appeals for the Seventh Circuit. The city and the park district, in a change of position, agreed that the case was properly in federal court—coming off a victory below, they wanted a definitive ruling on the merits of the challenges to the Obama Presidential Center. But the appeals court, in an opinion by Judge Amy Coney Barrett, held that there was no federal court jurisdiction over the public trust doctrine claim. Although the Illinois Supreme Court in *Paepcke* had held, as a matter of state law, that any taxpayer could bring a public trust action, standing to sue in federal court is stricter—requiring a plaintiff to allege injury in a "'personal and individual way,'" the Seventh Circuit explained. In particular, plaintiffs had not alleged that they "'use the affected area'" of Jackson Park to be taken for the OPC, the court noted, as is ordinarily required to support standing to bring environmental claims in federal court. It rejected as well the idea that the interest of an ordinary taxpayer is sufficient to establish a property right cognizable for federal constitutional purposes. These rulings closed the door to future use of Judge Darrah's universal-property-rights theory, from the Lucas Museum case, as a pathway for public trust claims to make their way into federal court. The ruling on standing would also make it more difficult to get such claims into federal court under a theory of supplemental jurisdiction, as in the Loyola case considered in chapter 8. More immediately, the court's decision terminated the federal case against the Obama Presidential Center, but required that Judge Blakey's rejection of the public trust challenge be vacated, leaving the plaintiffs or some other individual or group free to sue in state court. The merits of the public trust doctrine challenge to the Obama Presidential Center remained unadjudicated.[42]

The Lucas Museum and Obama Presidential Center cases confirm—if further confirmation is needed—that the public trust doctrine serves as a kind of wild card in determining how development of the Chicago lakefront can proceed. It is unpredictable whether advocacy groups will sue to enforce the doctrine. It is unpredictable how the courts will respond. The Lucas Museum case and the Loyola case years earlier show that one need not secure a final judgment in order to affect the outcome. Rulings by trial courts refusing to dismiss a case or ordering the parties to engage in lengthy discovery can cause enough delay and impose enough cost to cause the cancellation of projects. These concerns are magnified by allowing any citizen or group to sue to claim a violation of the public trust doctrine, and by the prospect that the issue will be heard by a single trial judge insulated from the ordinary political process.

The best explanation for the divergent outcomes of the Lucas Museum and Obama Presidential Center cases may not be that the former was to be located on land filled a century before and the latter was to be located on land that had never been submerged. More realistically, it may be that elite opinion was sharply divided about the merits of the former, whereas opposition to the OPC was perceived to be a fringe position. There are a variety of mechanisms for trying to discern consensus or dissensus and for reconciling conflicts in cases of the latter. But it is doubtful that putting the matter in the hands of a single trial judge, with the outcome determined in significant part by the judge's docket-management decisions, is either the most accurate or the most democratic way to resolve such questions. The Illinois Supreme Court would be well advised to limit the public trust doctrine to the filling of open navigable waters or proposals to sell off public parks, as opposed to changes in the use of any land previously filled. It should also reaffirm that the state legislature has the last word, or at least gets significant deference, in determining whether the public trust is satisfied.[43]

CONCLUSION

We return to the beginning: what explains how Chicago came to have the glorious lakefront we see today, with its parks, its Lake Shore Drive, its clean shoreline free of rotting docks and industrial facilities? Riparian land is commonly vexed by conflict between public and private rights. What caused Chicago, a city long dominated by private enterprise, to end up with such a relatively large quotient of public rights on its lakefront?

It would be presumptuous to offer a definitive answer to the question of how Chicago, of all places, came to have such a splendid, publicly accessible, and uncluttered lakefront, relative to other cities. Nevertheless, we venture to offer some thoughts. Some factors are unique to Chicago, and hence are not replicable elsewhere. And of course, certain individuals had a decisive impact on how the Chicago experience unfolded; by their very nature the idiosyncrasies of individuals cannot be foreseen or planned. Other forces, including the law, are more general, and hence provide some basis for influencing the fate of waterfront land beyond Chicago.

Chicago-Specific Factors

First: Chicago never got an outer harbor. In the second half of the nineteenth century, there was virtually unanimous consensus in Chicago that such a harbor was vital to relieve the congested state of the Chicago River. But the entity in the best position to construct such a harbor, the Illinois Central Railroad, was bitterly opposed by the property owners on Michigan Avenue. After the Illinois Central lost the *Lake Front Case*, attention shifted to the prospect of a public harbor. Yet public officials could never agree on a site—first it was to be in the center of the city, then variously in Streeterville or on the South Side—and even if they could have agreed, they did not have the revenue to build it. Eventually the Calumet River emerged as a substitute commercial harbor, rail and truck transportation became increasingly preferred relative to water, and the case for building an outer harbor faded away. The long-term result was that Chicago was spared the burden of having to deal with rotting piers and wharves associated with an outer harbor built in front of the city.

Second: the successful campaign of the Michigan Avenue property owners, led by Montgomery Ward, to keep Grant Park largely free of buildings. A key development here was the willingness of the courts to extend the public dedication doctrine, which originally applied only to a narrow strip of land running along Michigan Avenue, to all of the newly filled land east of the original Lake Park. The end result was a massive 319-acre lakefront park in the center of the city, which became the anchor of a system of parks and a parkway running up and down the lakefront.

Third: the decision of the Illinois Supreme Court in the *Revell* cases to eliminate the common-law right of riparian owners to wharf out into the lake. The immediate effect of this legal change was to reduce the cost of constructing parks along the lakefront. A more important consequence was that privately owned piers and docks disappeared from the lakefront. Since only one public pier was ever constructed—Navy Pier—the elimination of private docks and piers meant that the shoreline became uncluttered by artificial intrusions into the lake.

Fourth: the creation of park districts as semiautonomous local government entities. The rapid growth of Chicago in the nineteenth century made little provision for parks, and the park districts naturally looked to the lakeshore as a logical site to compensate for the deficit. The state obliged by giving the districts free submerged land, and everyone looked the other way as the districts swapped some of the submerged land for riparian rights. Fortunately, the acquisition of rights largely took place before high-rise apartments were built along the lakefront, which would have created too much political resistance to the project. Popular support for the parks also grew after the flow of the Chicago River was reversed, greatly improving the quality of the water along the lakefront.

The Influence of Individuals

It is also important not to overlook particular individuals and their importance, whether through their special skill, perseverance, or simply being in the right place at the right time. The Chicago lakefront would undoubtedly look different today without the efforts of certain critical actors. Without offering an exhaustive list, we would single out seven for special mention, some well known, others obscure.

Alonzo Mack. Without Mack's extraordinary ability to manipulate the Illinois legislature, it is far from clear that the Illinois Central Railroad would have obtained a grant of one thousand acres to develop an outer harbor in 1869. The railroad's tenacious effort to retain this bounty, even after it was repealed in 1873, stymied efforts to build an outer harbor for the balance of the century. Although the result was the opposite of what Mack sought to accomplish, the conflict unleashed by the Lake Front Act of 1869 helped assure that the outer harbor was never built.

Ellis Chesbrough. Chesbrough was the master engineer responsible for major projects that eventually solved the severe pollution problem affecting the Chicago River. He conceived and supervised construction of the comprehensive sewerage system, the construction of water-intake cribs in Lake Michigan, and the initial attempt to reverse the flow of the Chicago River. His leadership led to greatly improved water quality along the lakefront several decades before the development of wastewater treatment plants; this was instrumental in building public support for a system of lakefront parks.

Stephen Field. Field had only a glancing relationship with the Chicago lakefront, but he authored the judicial decision that effectively settled a multisided dispute over property rights on the lakefront and launched the American public trust doctrine. Field's formulation of the doctrine was affected by his unique Jacksonian-Democrat dislike of government-sponsored monopolies; this gave the doctrine its strong antiprivatization flavor, which came to resonate with twentieth-century environmentalists.

Montgomery Ward. Though Ward was not the first or last property owner on Michigan Avenue to invoke the public dedication doctrine to block construction of buildings in Grant Park, his persistence and willingness to fund litigation all the way to the Illinois Supreme Court created a body of precedent that preserved the massive park in the center of the city as an open space for more than a century. He deserved the title "watchdog of the lakefront."

Daniel Burnham. Burnham's organizational skills allowed the World's Fair of 1893 to be built in Jackson Park rather than on the lakefront; his *Plan of Chicago* promoted the idea of parkland, pleasure drives, and yacht harbors up and down the lakefront; and his preference for neoclassicism permanently affected the landscaping of Grant Park and various cultural institutions such as the Field Museum located along the lakefront.

Edward Brown. A little-known lawyer working for the Lincoln Park Commission in the early years of the twentieth century, Brown devised the boundary-line mechanism and engineered the judicial repeal of the common-law right to wharf out. Boundary-line agreements allowed the park districts to acquire the riparian rights needed to construct Lake Shore Drive without any out-of-pocket cost, and judicial abolition of the right to wharf out eliminated private wharves and piers on Lake Michigan, creating the clean line between parkland and water we see today.

Marvin Burt. Although he served on the Illinois Supreme Court for barely a year, Burt drew the assignment to write for the court in the *Paepcke* case in 1970. A longtime proponent of public parks, Burt through his opinion gave all taxpayers in Illinois standing to assert public trust claims and reformulated the doctrine in terms of privatization of public resources, rather than protection of public rights of navigation. This became the foundation of the principal legal doctrine used to mediate disputes between public and private rights on the lakefront today.

More-General Factors

In emphasizing these Chicago-specific factors and the role of particular individuals, we do not mean to suggest that broader social forces were not also at work. Since these forces are not unique to Chicago, they provide some basis for generalization beyond the Chicago experience. We would point to four broad categories of influence. With an eye toward the future in other cities, we would note that some of these are not subject to human control, but others are.

One influence that should not be overlooked is the magnetic attraction of a large body of water such as Lake Michigan. From the founding of Chicago to the present, real estate that enjoys direct exposure to the lake has commanded a substantial premium relative to property farther inland. This is due at least as much to aesthetics as to utility. Thus, we have seen how the wealthy residents of Michigan Avenue continually fought the Illinois Central, opposed putting the World's Columbian Exposition on the lakefront, and sued to block the erection of buildings in what became Grant Park. The upscale residents of Prairie Avenue on the South Side and of Lake Shore Drive on the North Side were equally adamant about preserving their views of the lake. Reflecting the same preferences, but generalizing it to the public as a whole, the park districts worked assiduously to extend public parks along the lakefront, so that more than just the wealthy could enjoy those vistas. Property owners cut off from the lake by the expanding parks pushed back; they, too, wanted to see the lake. And modern advocacy groups, such as Friends of the Parks, continue to this day to file lawsuits seeking to block projects on the lakefront. Similar innate preferences presumably exist wherever land borders on a substantial body of water.

Another powerful factor has been the changing state of technology. Water transport was vital to the founding of Chicago and was responsible for the building of the piers at the mouth of the Chicago River that allowed the river to be used as a harbor. Growth meant that the river became inadequate for this purpose, which helped drive the futile quest for an outer harbor and eventually the displacement of the Chicago River by the Calumet River as a commercial harbor for the city. The emergence of the railroads was obviously responsible for the presence of the Illinois Central on the lakefront and all the antagonism this produced. The railroads, and later interstate trucking, further diminished the importance of commercial water navigation over time. The demise of water transportation allowed the lakefront to be used for other purposes, particularly parks. As detailed in chapter 5, technological advances were also responsible for improving Chicago's sewers, securing a safe source of drinking water in the lake, and reversing the flow of the river. Ultimately these innovations greatly improved the quality of the waters along the lakefront so that they could be enjoyed more freely for swimming and other recreational activities.

Collectively, these technological changes helped unleash a transformation of public values associated with the lakefront. In the nineteenth century, Lake Michigan and the Chicago River were valued largely for narrow utilitarian ends—as a conduit for transportation of goods and people by water and as a repository for sewage and industrial waste. With changes in technology diminishing the importance of water as a mode of transportation and introducing alternative methods of reducing waste, the waters of the lake and river came to be valued increasingly for recreational and environmental ends—or simply for their magnetic attraction. The change in public values is seen most dramatically in the transformation of the public trust doctrine. Originally designed to preserve public access to the waters of the lake for navigation and fishing, it became in the late twentieth century a vague mandate to preserve the lake from further landfilling—and, at least aspirationally, to prevent further development of lands previously reclaimed from the lake. Indeed, by the end of the twentieth century, a significant segment of public opinion came to oppose any further filling or diversion of the waters of Lake Michigan, on the grounds that this would be a desecration of the lake's "natural" condition. This segment of public opinion was responsible for the undoing of the Loyola campus expansion and the resistance to the Lucas Museum, and also probably means that no major diversion of the waters of the lake will be permitted under the Great Lakes Compact in the foreseeable future.

A third important factor has been the growth in the size and effectiveness of government institutions. In the early decades of our story, government at all levels was poorly funded, understaffed, and consequently relatively weak. It was necessary to turn to the Illinois Central Railroad to build a breakwater protecting the lakefront from erosion, to rely on private riparian owners to build docks and piers in the Chicago River, to use nuisance suits to control interferences with navigation, and to rely on private landowners to preserve public parks by using the public dedication doctrine. Toward the end of the nineteenth century, government institutions gradually became better funded, better staffed, and endowed with greater legal authority. The federal government, through the Army Corps of Engineers, eliminated the sandbar at the mouth of the Chicago River, built an outer breakwater, dredged the Chicago and Calumet Rivers, monitored the diversion of water from Lake Michigan, and obtained general regulatory authority to prohibit any interference with the right of public navigation. Eventually the federal government largely paid for the construction of the Deep Tunnel project, which protected the lakefront from sewage overflows after storms.

In the nineteenth century, traditional state institutions—the state legislature and the city council—were easily captured by special interests and did little to advance broader public aspirations. But toward the end of that century, the state was prevailed on to create new forms of local government, which proved to be far more effective in supplying public goods. The park districts expanded Grant Park, acquired the riparian rights of landowners up and down the lake, and built Lake Shore Drive and associated parkland covering the better part of the lakefront. The sanitary district reversed the flow of the Chicago River, built wastewater treatment plants, and helped give Chicago a healthy water supply and a largely pollution-free lakefront. The growth in efficacy of government institutions both was facilitated by and, in turn, itself facilitated a decline in common-law riparian rights. Gradually, private law has been supplanted by administrative law.

A final factor—and the one most obviously subject to human control—is the law. We have relied extensively on legal sources and have discussed the law in some detail, regarding it, at least implicitly, as an important causal force. Broadly speaking, we think this to be correct. We are impressed by the willingness of the contending factions in the battles over the lakefront to submit their disputes to courts for resolution and to conform their behavior to the requirements of the law. There are exceptions, of course. George Wellington Streeter's gang used violence and intimidation—and his principal adversaries, the riparian owners, responded in kind with their private detectives and police raids. Other claimants for the formed land north of the river were guilty of fraud. Many up and down the lakefront engaged in landfilling that, at least once the state's title to the lakebed became clear, was unlawful. All this is true. But the large number of statutes and ordinances cataloged in this book, and the dozens of judicial decisions, are a testament to the general respect for law that has prevailed on the Chicago lakefront, as in American life more generally.

That said, we have uncovered few legal understandings of enduring permanence. A number of legal doctrines emerged to resolve conflicts between public and private rights on the lakefront, only to be forgotten or repudiated. When the city was founded, riparian owners thought they had title to the submerged land under the lake; then courts decided that it belonged to the state. The judiciary initially indicated that riparian owners had the right to wharf out into the lake, then decided they did not. The public trust doctrine burst onto the scene in the *Lake Front Case*, then entered a period of dormancy, then was reborn in the 1970s with a new scope and rationale.

Still, some legal doctrines have had a pronounced influence. The Illinois Central's vested-rights argument tied up the lakefront for a quarter century, before it was rejected by the Supreme Court. The public dedication doctrine succeeded for over a hundred years in keeping Grant Park free of major building projects. The ease with which the doctrine was circumvented for Millennium Park suggests that its days may be numbered, but the fact that it constrained public authorities for a century is impressive. The repudiation of the right to wharf out in Lake Michigan has had an equally impressive, if unintended, impact on the appearance of the lakefront.

By far the most enduring contribution of the law has been the protection afforded to those in active possession of filled land on the lakefront. Once submerged land has been filled—whether legally or illegally—and once that land has been developed with structures or is otherwise in active use, the law has protected the possessor against any claim based on public rights. Thus, the Illinois Central was allowed to keep—and develop at great profit—all of the lands it filled along the lakefront and used as railroad facilities. The riparian owners in Streeterville were allowed to keep—and develop at great profit—all of the reclaimed land up to the drive. The riparian owners up and down the lakefront who exchanged their riparian rights for submerged land in deals to facilitate the construction of Lake Shore Drive and Lincoln Park have never been asked to return the lands they filled and occupied. Courts have occasionally blocked grants of rights to engage in future landfilling, most consequentially in upholding the repeal of the Lake Front Act in the face of the Illinois Central's vested rights argument. But with the minor exception of the 1884 order to remove the baseball grounds, existing fills and structures have been allowed to stand. Whether this pattern reflects a special judicial solicitude for possession, or a more general sympathy for reliance interests associated with the status quo, is debatable. Whatever its source, the law has consistently lent its force to those in possession of resources, which has put a limit on claims of public right. This suggests that, for those interested in public control of a waterfront, it is vital that such control be established before private possession becomes entrenched.

By contrast, the public trust doctrine, even upon emerging reformulated in the later decades of the twentieth century, has played relatively little role in creating the Chicago lakefront celebrated today. The reformulated doctrine was used to block landfilling to expand the South Works plant on the far South Side and the Loyola campus on the far North Side. And delays associated with public trust litigation ran the proposed Lucas Museum out of town. Yet these are details in the larger scheme of things. In fact, if the public trust doctrine had been invoked with the rigidity demanded by its most ardent proponents today, most of Grant Park and all of the lakefront parks on the North and South Sides would not exist. Perhaps in the future the doctrine will be clarified and reformulated in a way that will make it a useful legal tool for enhancing the public value of waterfront land. If so, it will have to be a different doctrine.

Notes

Our research drew on materials in Chicago and across the country, as suggested in the introduction and reflected by our sources in the notes. The collections of two institutions appear frequently enough that we use the following abbreviations throughout the notes, without reintroducing them in each chapter:

CHM: Chicago History Museum
IC Papers: Illinois Central Railroad Company Archives, Newberry Library, Chicago

Both have extensive online finding guides that will enable an interested researcher to request on-site the specific materials that we cite.

1. THE LAKE FRONT STEAL

1. Bessie Louise Pierce, *A History of Chicago* (New York: Alfred A. Knopf, 1937), 1:6–9, describes the explorations by various seventeenth-century French missionaries and others of what we know as northeastern Illinois, including the potential for a link between the Chicago River and the Mississippi basin. A. T. Andreas, *History of Chicago* (Chicago: A. T. Andreas, 1884), 1:45, recounts different opinions of that earlier era on a canal's feasibility.

2. Douglas Schroeder, *The Issue of the Lakefront: An Historical Critical Survey* (Chicago: Chicago Heritage Committee, 1964), 2; John W. Larson, *Those Army Engineers: A History of the Chicago District U.S. Army Corps of Engineers* (Chicago: US Army Corps of Engineers, 1979), 3.

3. Libby Hill, *The Chicago River: A Natural and Unnatural History*, rev. ed. (Carbondale: Southern Illinois University Press, 2019), 56–58; Schroeder, *Issue of the Lakefront*, 2.

4. Record, 239–40, 246 (testimony of Jonathan Young Scammon), Illinois Central Railroad Co. v. Illinois, 146 U.S. 387 (1892), Nos. 14,135, 14,414, 14,415, and 14,416 (filed Sept. 6, 1890) (hereafter Lake Front Case Record); John N. Jewett, "The Lake Front Litigation—Part I," *John Marshall Law Quarterly* 3 (1937): 30; Robin L. Einhorn, "A Taxing Dilemma: Early Lake Shore Protection," *Chicago History* 18 (Fall 1989): 41, 46.

5. Einhorn, "Taxing Dilemma," 35–49; Robin L. Einhorn, *Property Rules: Political Economy in Chicago, 1833–1872* (Chicago: University of Chicago Press, 1991), 21–22, 91–94.

6. 9 Stat. 466 (1850); John F. Stover, *History of the Illinois Central Railroad* (New York: Macmillan, 1975), 15–30; 1851 Ill. Private Laws 61–62. See Paul Wallace Gates, *The Illinois Central Railroad and Its Colonization Work* (Cambridge, MA: Harvard University Press, 1934), 23–43, for historical background to the federal enactment.

7. 1851 Ill. Private Laws 61–62, 64.

8. Carlton J. Corliss, *Main Line of Mid-America: The Story of the Illinois Central* (New York: Creative Age, 1950), 46–49.

9. Einhorn, "Taxing Dilemma," 49. The appeal of lake views and lake breezes has been a constant throughout Chicago history. In the late 1830s, undeveloped lots fronting

on Michigan Avenue with direct views of the lake "sold for two or three, perhaps four, times as much" as lots one block to the west. Lake Front Case Record, 248 (testimony of Scammon). For the ordinance and its passage, see George W. Thompson and John A. Thompson, eds., *The Charter and Ordinances of the City of Chicago* (D.B. Cooke, 1856), 348–53; Stover, *History of the Illinois Central*, 43–44.

10. *Charter and Ordinances*, 348–49, §§ 1–2.

11. *Charter and Ordinances*, 349, §§ 2–3. The reporter's statement of the case in *Lake Front Case*, 146 U.S. 387, 403 (1892), describes Lake Park's shoreline relative to Michigan Avenue at this time.

12. *Charter and Ordinances*, 349, §§ 1, 3.

13. *Charter and Ordinances*, 351–52, §§ 7, 9.

14. Stover, *History of the Illinois Central*, 44–45, briefly describes the construction; Schroeder, *Issue of the Lakefront*, 4, notes the double line of track as well as the railroad's filling of the lake between Randolph and the river, to a point more than one thousand feet east of the track. B. F. Ayer, "Rights of the Illinois Central Railroad Company on the Lake Front," Dec. 1884, 5, 8, 17, IC Papers, recounts the use of two hundred feet and certain filling and construction in the lake between 12th and 16th Streets. Not until 1881 did the railroad seek to occupy the additional one hundred feet allowed under the 1852 ordinance; this, in fact, was the action that precipitated the *Lake Front Case*, as chronicled in chapter 2. For Great Central Station, see Alan R. Lind, *Limiteds along the Lakefront: The Illinois Central in Chicago* (Park Forest, IL: Transport History Press, 1986), 4–5.

15. An Ordinance Granting Right of Way for Approach to Passenger Depot (Sept. 10, 1855) is reprinted in *Encroachments upon the Harbor of Chicago, Ill.*, H.R. Exec. Doc. No. 95, 47th Cong., 1st Sess. (1882) (hereafter *1882 Encroachments Investigation*), 68–69, and An Ordinance concerning Additional Right of Way to the Illinois Central Railroad (Sept. 15, 1856) more formally appears in *Charter and Ordinances*, 539.

16. Joseph D. Kearney and Thomas W. Merrill, "The Origins of the American Public Trust Doctrine: What Really Happened in *Illinois Central*," *University of Chicago Law Review* 71 (2004): 823, 836–53.

17. Jewett, "Lake Front Litigation," 23, 25; James Kent, *Commentaries on American Law* (New York: O. Halsted, 1828), 3:344; James Kent, *Commentaries on American Law*, 9th ed. (New York: O. Halsted, 1858), 3:528–29; John M. Gould, *A Treatise on the Law of Waters* (Chicago: Callaghan, 1883), 15, 109–13.

18. See Martin v. Waddell, 41 U.S. (16 Pet.) 367, 410 (1842), arising from New Jersey, and Pollard v. Hagan, 44 U.S. (3 How.) 212, 223–24, 228–29 (1845), from Alabama. United States v. Alaska, 521 U.S. 1, 5, 33–36 (1997), provides a more recent statement of the equal-footing doctrine. For a survey of the doctrine's historical origins and the case law developing it, see James R. Rasband, "The Disregarded Common Parentage of the Equal Footing and Public Trust Doctrines," *University of Wyoming Land and Water Law Review* 32 (1997): 1–88.

19. Joseph K. Angell, *A Treatise on the Law of Watercourses*, 5th ed. (Boston: Little, Brown, 1854), 606–11, counted New York, Massachusetts, New Hampshire, Connecticut, Maine, Maryland, Virginia, Ohio, and Indiana as having adopted the English rule, and Pennsylvania, South Carolina, Tennessee, Alabama, and North Carolina as embracing the American view.

20. Middleton v. Pritchard, 4 Ill. 509 (3 Scam. 510), 519–22 (1842); City of Chicago v. Laflin, 49 Ill. 172, 176–77 (1868). The court also maintained this view in Board of Trustees of the Illinois and Michigan Canal v. Haven, 11 Ill. 554, 557 (1850), and rejected a request to overrule it in Ensminger v. People, 47 Ill. 384, 388–89 (1868).

21. For an example, when Senator Stephen A. Douglas granted the Illinois Central a right of way over riparian land he owned just south of the city, he specifically retained "all

title right and ownership to the land and water" to "the Centre of Lake Michigan." Article of Agreement between Stephen A. Douglas and the Illinois Central Railroad Co. (handwritten deed), July 27, 1852, IC Papers.

22. The Propeller Genesee Chief v. Fitzhugh, 53 U.S. (12 How.) 443, 453, 458–59 (1852), overruled The Thomas Jefferson, 23 U.S. (10 Wheat.) 428 (1825). Kearney and Merrill, "Origins," 831, discuss some subsequent nineteenth-century developments. For an instructive later Supreme Court opinion recognizing the evolution of the law in the direction of the American rule, and stressing the importance of *The Genesee Chief* in this process, see Packer v. Bird, 137 U.S. 661, 670–71 (1891), written by Justice Stephen J. Field, author of the *Lake Front Case*.

23. Joseph K. Angell, *A Treatise on the Common Law, in Relation to Watercourses*, 2nd ed. (Boston: Hilliard, Gray, 1833), 4; Joseph K. Angell, *A Treatise on the Law of Watercourses*, 3rd ed. (Boston: Charles C. Little and James Brown, 1840), 10–11; Joseph K. Angell, *A Treatise on the Law of Watercourses*, 4th ed. (Boston: Charles C. Little and James Brown, 1850), 35–38 (emphasis in original).

24. Seaman v. Smith, 24 Ill. 521, 524–25 (1860).

25. "Who Owns Lake Park?," *Chicago Tribune* (hereafter *Tribune*), June 23, 1867.

26. Letter to the editor, *Tribune*, June 27, 1867; see also letter to the editor, *Tribune*, June 25, 1867, arguing that the state "retains the title to the land [east of Michigan Avenue], but is [legally] pledged to maintain it as vacant ground."

27. Douglas to Osborn, Dec. 27, 1866, IC Papers.

28. "The Chicago Dock Bill," *Tribune*, Feb. 15, 1867, reproduced the bill. See 1867 Ill. House Journal, 1:705, for Shepard's sponsorship of the bill, and "Death Comes to Judge Shepard," *Tribune*, Oct. 17, 1904, on his career.

29. "A Magnificent Fraud," *Tribune*, Feb. 12, 1867; "The Great Harbor Swindle," *Chicago Times* (hereafter *Times*), Feb. 13, 1867.

30. "Another Attempted Swindle," *Tribune*, Feb. 12, 1867; "The Michigan Park Steal," *Times*, Feb. 13, 1867; Kearney and Merrill, "Origins," 850.

31. Douglas to C. C. P. Holden, telegram, Leland Hotel, Springfield, Feb. 16, 1867, IC Papers; see 1867 Ill. Senate Journal, 810 (noting introduction, on Feb. 18, 1867, of a bill to establish the city's rights over the harbor), and *Times*, Feb. 27, 1867 (decrying Shepard's efforts against the bill for city control of the harbor). See also Douglas to Holden, telegram, Leland Hotel, Springfield, Feb. 19, 1867, IC Papers (instructing the defeat of a bill for the Chicago Elevator Company "if it is to be located on the Lake").

32. Kearney and Merrill, "Origins," 842.

33. "The Future Harbor of Chicago," *Tribune*, Jan. 1, 1868.

34. "Important Park Project; Proposition to Sell a Portion of the Lake Park for Business Purposes," *Tribune*, Dec. 10, 1867; see also "The Park Question," *Tribune*, Dec. 4, 1868 (characterizing "the three blocks" as "almost useless as a pleasure-ground" and calling for the sale of the area, with the proceeds "applied strictly to park purposes").

35. Kearney and Merrill, "Origins," 846–47.

36. "Common Council; Proposition from H.M. Shepard, Esq., to Buy a Part of Lake Park for $1,000,000," *Tribune*, Feb. 11, 1868; "Another Proposition to Buy a Portion of Lake Park," *Tribune*, Feb. 25, 1868.

37. "Common Council," Feb. 11, 1868 (emphasis in original).

38. Kearney and Merrill, "Origins," 850–52.

39. "Lake Park," *Tribune*, Dec. 9, 1868.

40. "Springfield; . . . How Legislators Are Manipulated by the Lobby; A Powerful Combination to Defeat Anti-Monopoly Measures," *Tribune*, Feb. 7, 1867.

41. Newton Bateman and Paul Selby, eds., *Historical Encyclopedia of Illinois* (Chicago: Munsell, 1902), 348.

42. Bateman and Selby, *Encyclopedia*, 348; "Significant Indications," *Times*, Jan. 9, 1867. For a more nuanced view of Mack in the context of the proposed legislation regulating railroads in the 1867 session, see George H. Miller, *Railroads and the Granger Laws* (Madison: University of Wisconsin Press, 1971), 68–70.

43. "Springfield; Coy," *Tribune*, Mar. 10, 1869.

44. "Springfield; Coy."

45. The bill was introduced as "[a]n Act to enable the city of Chicago to enlarge its harbor, and to grant and to cede all the rights, title and interest in and to certain lands lying on and adjacent to the shore of Lake Michigan, on the eastern frontage of said city." 1869 Ill. House Journal, 1:239. The text appears in "The Lake Park," *Chicago Republican* (hereafter *Republican*), Jan. 14, 1869.

46. *Tribune*, Jan. 18, 1869; "The Lake Front, Chicago," *Daily State Journal* (Springfield), Jan. 26, 1869; Kearney and Merrill, "Origins," 861–62.

47. Douglas to Osborn, Jan. 4, 1869, IC Papers; "Springfield," *Republican*, Jan. 24, 1869.

48. HB 373, Amendment, 26th General Assembly (Ill. 1869), Illinois State Archives (Springfield), Record Series 600.001, §§ 3–6 (handwritten copy); 1851 Ill. Private Laws 72–73. See "The Lake Front Park Question; . . . Lake-Front Bill," *Times*, Jan. 27, 1869, setting forth reports of the contents of the Illinois Central's substitute bill, which as of the writing had not yet been submitted. See also "Municipal Park Bill," *Republican*, Jan. 27, 1869. That the substitute bill was prepared in great secrecy we know from the Illinois Central correspondence characterizing the work as being done in "as much silence" as possible. Douglas to Osborn, Jan. 30, 1869. The acreage is stated in *Lake Front Case*, 146 U.S. at 454. For the final Lake Front Act, which included further language on the applicability of the 7 percent tax to use of the lands in the new act, see 1869 Ill. Private Laws 245–48, or *Lake Front Case*, 146 U.S. at 405–8 (statement of the case).

49. Douglas to Osborn, Feb. 3, 1869, IC Papers. On public impressions of the upper hand, see Kearney and Merrill, "Origins," 864.

50. "The Lake Park Bill," *Chicago Evening Journal* (hereafter *Evening Journal*), Feb. 4, 1869; 1869 Ill. House Journal, 1:910–11; Kearney and Merrill, "Origins," 865. The *Tribune* printed Knickerbocker's minority report in full. "The Chicago Harbor Bill," *Tribune*, Feb. 10, 1869.

51. "Public Meeting; Great Mass Meeting!; Lake Shore Park!; The Great Swindle!; Confiscation of Public Property and Private Rights without Consideration!," *Times*, Feb. 16, 1869; "Our Lake Front," *Evening Journal*, Feb. 16, 1869. Signatories included a number of prominent citizens, such as John C. Haines, John Wentworth, Joseph Medill, M. D. Ogden, Samuel W. Fuller, and scores of other named individuals, along with "fifteen hundred [unnamed] others." On the reaction, see "Springfield; . . . Probability That the Chicago Lake-Front Bill Will Be Passed To-Day," *Times*, Feb. 20, 1869, and Kearney and Merrill, "Origins," 867.

52. Kearney and Merrill, "Origins," 867.

53. 1869 Ill. House Journal, 2:155.

54. "From Springfield; An Investigation Ordered into Alleged Bribery and Corruption in the Legislature," *Evening Journal*, Feb. 22, 1869; 1869 Ill. House Journal, 2:155.

55. Kearney and Merrill, "Origins," 868–69.

56. "Lake Park," *Tribune*, Feb. 23, 1869; 1869 Ill. Senate Journal, 1:736–37; Kearney and Merrill, "Origins," 869.

57. "The Chicago Harbor Bill," *Tribune*, Mar. 1, 1869; "Lake Front Bill," *Tribune*, Mar. 1, 1869.

58. 1869 Ill. Senate Journal, 2:345; "Passage of the Lake Front Bill in the Senate," *Tribune*, Mar. 9, 1869.

59. Letter to the editor, "Has the State the Right to Sell the Lake Front?," *Tribune*, Mar. 13, 1869; "The Lake Front; No Right in the State to Sell or Grant Away the Navigation," *Republican*, Mar. 14, 1869.

60. Letter to the editor, "The Lake Front; No Right in the State to Sell or Grant Away the Navigation," *Republican*, Mar. 15, 1869 (responding to the article of the day previous).

61. Palmer's veto message was reprinted in 1869 Ill. House Journal, 3:517–28, and in various newspapers. See, e.g., "The Lake Front; Gov. Palmer's Veto Message of the Lake Front Bill; He Objects to the Bill on the Ground of Expediency," *Republican*, Apr. 15, 1869.

62. "The Friends of the Bill," *Tribune*, Apr. 14, 1869; "Lake Front Bill," *Tribune*, Apr. 15, 1869.

63. See Ill. Const. of 1848, art. IV, § 21 (superseded 1870); 1869 Ill. Senate Journal, 2:922; "Final Passage of the Tax-Stealing and Lake Front Bills," *Tribune*, Apr. 17, 1869.

64. Osborn to Douglas, Apr. 19, 1869; Douglas to Osborn, Apr. 20, 1869; Osborn to Douglas, Apr. 23, 1869, IC Papers.

65. "The Title to the Chicago Lake-Front," *Times*, Jan. 15, 1869; "The Chicago Lake-Front—Bill to Be Reported in the House; The Fee of All the Submerged Lands Outside of the Track to Be Vested in the Illinois Central Railroad Company," *Times*, Jan. 26, 1869.

66. Osborn to Cunningham Borthwick (London), Apr. 20, 1869, IC Papers. Stover describes the importance of European investors to the Illinois Central, noting, for example, an estimate from this same era "that over half of the stock was held by Englishmen, more than a quarter by Dutch investors, and perhaps less than 15 percent by Americans." Stover, *History of the Illinois Central*, 32–38.

67. Osborn to Borthwick (London), June 9, 1869, IC Papers.

68. For the leading modern characterization of the Illinois Central's motives and actions, see Joseph L. Sax, "The Public Trust Doctrine in Natural Resource Law: Effective Judicial Intervention," *Michigan Law Review* 68 (1970): 490, 495, 496, 542–43 (describing the grant as "egregious," a "case in which the impropriety is so patent," an infringement on public uses to promote "private profits," and marred by "blatant evidence of corruption").

69. 1869 Ill. Private Laws 246 (the quoted material being in section 3 of the Lake Front Act, which is also reprinted in the reporter's statement in *Lake Front Case*, 146 U.S. at 406). Daniel R. Fischel and Alan O. Sykes, "Governmental Liability for Breach of Contract," *American Law and Economics Review* 1 (1999): 340–42, are an example of the assumption of the creation of a monopoly. For the right to wharf out, subject to public navigation, see the discussion earlier in this chapter of *Laflin*, 49 Ill. 172; chapter 6 of this book takes up the fate of this right.

70. The later commentator quoted is Sax, "Public Trust Doctrine," 490. We discuss the subsequent federal appropriations later in this chapter and in chapter 2. For an example of the universal assumption of the role of private enterprise in building dockage and the like, see *Report of Army Board of Engineers* (Aug. 3, 1871), in Lake Front Case Record, 643–46.

71. "The Lake Front," *Daily State Journal* (Springfield), Feb. 10, 1869.

72. The voting is analyzed in Kearney and Merrill, "Origins," 885–87.

73. "Lake Front Bill Again," *Daily State Journal* (Springfield), Feb. 10, 1869; "Another Railroad Bill by Senator Fuller," *Republican*, Feb. 10, 1869.

74. "Alleged Legislative Corruption," *Tribune*, Feb. 22, 1869.

75. "The Corruption Investigation Committee," *Times*, Feb. 23, 1869. The *Chicago Tribune* quoted the statement from the *Times* and said, "We should like to see a photograph of the countenances of Dr. Mack and E. S. Taylor, of Cook, while reading this paragraph." *Tribune*, Feb. 24, 1869. The *Tribune* agreed that legislators had yet received little: "Liquors and cigars, and perhaps a few advances on account, are all that members have received." But it reiterated its statement that payoffs would come later. Kearney and Merrill, "Origins," 890–91.

76. Douglas to Osborn, Jan. 14, 1869, IC Papers.

77. Douglas to Osborn, Feb. 3, 1869, IC Papers.

78. Osborn to Douglas, Apr. 23, 1869; Douglas to Osborn, May 31, 1869, IC Papers. Several sources indicate that the Illinois Central prepared a formal plan for development of the outer harbor, but if that plan was embodied in a written document, we have not found a copy of it. This is a description of the plan from an opinion letter written by the Illinois Central's general solicitor in 1884:

> In 1869, soon after the passage of the Lake Front act, a plan was prepared by the railroad company for the construction of an outer harbor within the limits specified in the grant. It was proposed to construct a series of piers six hundred feet wide, separated by intervening slips one hundred and fifty feet wide, to be thrown out into the lake from the company's breakwater as a base, to the distance of about 3,225 feet from the west line of Michigan avenue, and extending from the river on the north to the southern limit of the grant. Four hundred feet beyond the ends of the piers, an exterior breakwater was to be constructed in front of the whole work, sufficient to make a secure harbor in any state of the weather for vessels lying inside. (Ayer, "Rights of the Illinois Central," 13)

79. Douglas to Osborn, July 1, 1869, IC Papers.

80. 1869 Ill. Private Laws 248; *Lake Front Case*, 146 U.S. at 407–8 (statement of the case).

81. Douglas to Osborn, July 17, 1869; Osborn to Douglas, July 19, 1869; Douglas to Osborn, July 26, 1869, IC Papers.

82. United States v. Illinois Cent. R. Co., 26 F. Cas. 461, 461–62 (C.C.N.D. Ill. 1869). A political pamphlet circulated in 1881 stated that the suit was filed after Thomas Hoyne, a prominent citizen and himself a former US attorney, "having exhausted every other means of prevention and redress of this gigantic villainy, as a last resort, applied to the United States Government." A. S. Bradley, *Report of the Present Status of the Claims of the Illinois Central Railroad to the Lake Front, and Submerged Lands Adjoining, under the "Lake Front Steal" of 1869* (Chicago: Illinois Anti-Monopoly League, 1881), Illinois Historical Survey, University of Illinois at Urbana-Champaign, 5–6.

83. *Illinois Cent. R. Co.*, 26 F. Cas. at 462.

84. Kearney and Merrill, "Origins," 1455–56; Osborn to Borthwick, June 9, 1869.

85. See Kearney and Merrill, "Origins," 900–901, concerning Osborn. On the vested-rights doctrine, see especially Fletcher v. Peck, 10 U.S. (6 Cranch) 87, 135–37 (1810). *Fletcher* also involved a state land grant followed by a repeal when the original grant was discredited by allegations of corruption. Although exceptions to contracts-clause protection were increasingly recognized as the nineteenth century advanced—see generally Benjamin Fletcher Wright Jr., "Powers Which the States May Not Contract Away," chap. 8 in *The Contract Clause of the Constitution* (Cambridge, MA: Harvard University Press, 1938)—the Illinois Central could take comfort that the core holding of *Fletcher* seemed secure. See, e.g., Davis v. Gray, 83 U.S. (16 Wall.) 203, 232 (1873) (citing *Fletcher* and holding that the contracts clause prevented Texas from rescinding the grant of public land to a railroad).

86. Douglas to Osborn, July 26, 1869; Douglas to Osborn, July 17, 1869; Kearney and Merrill, "Origins," 901–2. Some of the railroad's political opponents, looking back on its behavior during this era, perceived things similarly. See Bradley, *Report of the Present Status*, 8, noting that the Illinois Central for ten years had borne "the risk and inconvenience of the slab shanties which have sufficed for its main depot . . . rather than waive its claim to the submerged lands."

87. See Ayer, "Rights of the Illinois Central," 13–14, concerning the Illinois Central's actions in 1869–71. The first quotation is from Douglas to Osborn, Apr. 20, 1870, which

noted, "It is the hardest time in traffic I have ever seen. There has probably never been in this state, according to the area planted, such an entire failure in the corn crops. I am myself alarmed for our own affairs." The second is from Osborn to Douglas, Apr. 14, 1870, IC Papers.

88. The resolution is described in the statement of the case in *Lake Front Case*, 146 U.S. at 408–9. The quotation is from Ayer, "Rights of the Illinois Central," 12. The provision in the 1870 constitution stated, "All existing charters or grants of special or exclusive privileges, under which organization shall not have taken place, or which shall not have been in operation within ten days from the time this constitution takes effect, shall thereafter have no validity or effect whatever." Ill. Const. of 1870, art. XI, § 2. The constitution took effect on August 8, 1870, so any grant that could be characterized as a "special or exclusive privilege" had to be "in operation" by August 18, 1870, or risk forfeiture. The State of Illinois, in its brief in the Supreme Court, would argue that the board's 1870 resolution was inadequate for technical reasons to place the grant in the Lake Front Act "in operation." See Brief on Behalf of the State of Illinois, 78–93, *Lake Front Case*, 146 U.S. 387 (1892). The court did not address this argument.

89. The bill is predicted in "State Legislatures; . . . Lake Front Bill," *Tribune*, Feb. 10, 1871; quoted in full in "Springfield; . . . The Chicago Lake Front," *Times*, Feb. 13, 1871; noted as referred to the Judiciary Committee in 1871 Ill. Senate Journal, 211; and reported as indefinitely postponed on the committee's recommendation in 1871 Ill. Senate Journal, 498. The bill is also mentioned in Osborn to John Newell (president, Illinois Central Railroad), Feb. 13, 1871, IC Papers. See "State Legislatures; . . . The Lake Front Bill Tabled in the Senate," *Tribune*, Apr. 6, 1871, for the quotation.

90. 16 Stat. 223, 226 (1870); Information, United States v. Illinois Central Railroad Co. (filed July 3, 1871), in *1882 Encroachments Investigation*, 22–23; Ayer, "Rights of the Illinois Central," 14–15.

2. THE LAKE FRONT CASE

1. Bessie Louise Pierce, *A History of Chicago* (New York: Alfred A. Knopf, 1937), 3:3–6; Carl Smith, *Urban Disorder and the Shape of Belief: The Great Chicago Fire, the Haymarket Bomb, and the Model Town of Pullman*, 2nd ed. (Chicago: University of Chicago Press, 2007), 19–22; John F. Stover, *History of the Illinois Central Railroad* (New York: Macmillan, 1975), 181–83.

2. Stover, *History of the Illinois Central*, 184; Howard Gray Brownson, *History of the Illinois Central Railroad to 1870* (Urbana: University of Illinois, 1915), 43; William K. Ackerman, *Historical Sketch of the Illinois-Central Railroad* (Chicago: Fergus, 1890), 81–83, 88.

3. In "Statement and Argument Addressed to the Attorney General in Reference to Dismissal of the Bill in Case of the United States vs. The Illinois Central Railroad Co. and Others," undated (ca. 1872), 5, IC Papers, the railroads argued that, after the "great fire of October last," a "new passenger depot is now absolutely required."

4. Illinois v. Illinois Central Railroad Co., 33 F. 730 (C.C.N.D. Ill. 1888), Evidence on Behalf of the Complainant and of Each of Said Defendants, Taken before E. B. Sherman, Master in Chancery of Said Court (hereafter Lake Front Case Cir. Ct. Record), 468; Alan R. Lind, *Limiteds along the Lakefront: The Illinois Central in Chicago* (Park Forest, IL: Transport History Press, 1986), 5–6; *Proceedings of the City Council of the City of Chicago, for Municipal Year 1878–9* (1880), 284–85, 294.

5. *Encroachments upon the Harbor of Chicago, Ill.*, H.R. Exec. Doc. No. 95, 47th Cong., 1st Sess. (1882) (hereafter *1882 Encroachments Investigation*), 19–24.

6. *1882 Encroachments Investigation*, 23.

7. Record, 349–50, 355–56 (testimony of L. P. Morehouse), Illinois Central Railroad Co. v. Illinois, 146 U.S. 387 (1892), Nos. 14,135, 14,414, 14,415, and 14,416 (filed Sept. 6, 1890) (hereafter Lake Front Case Record).

8. George H. Miller, *Railroads and the Granger Laws* (Madison: University of Wisconsin Press, 1971), an excellent study of the Granger Movement and the conditions inspiring it, includes a lengthy chapter on Illinois. The state's new constitution contained a separate section specifically forbidding diminution or impairment of any obligation of the Illinois Central—"ever." Ill. Const. of 1870, sections separately submitted.

9. Stover, *History of the Illinois Central*, 175; "Dr. A. W. Mack," *Chicago Tribune* (hereafter *Tribune*), Jan. 5, 1871.

10. Joseph D. Kearney and Thomas W. Merrill, "The Origins of the American Public Trust Doctrine: What Really Happened in *Illinois Central*," *University of Chicago Law Review* 71 (2004): 906.

11. "Lake Front," *Chicago Times* (hereafter *Times*), Mar. 13, 1873; "The Railroad Bills—Passage of the Lake Front Repeal Bill Very Doubtful," *Tribune*, Mar. 10, 1873. The reference in the text is to the famous decision holding that corporate charters are contracts protected by the contracts clause of the US Constitution against legislative impairment. Trustees of Dartmouth College v. Woodward, 17 U.S. (4 Wheat.) 518 (1819). A "pillar of the Chicago legal community," Jewett would help found the Chicago Bar Association and serve as dean of the John Marshall Law School from 1899 to 1904; for some further background on him, see Joshua A. T. Salzmann, *Liquid Capital: Making the Chicago Waterfront* (Philadelphia: University of Pennsylvania Press, 2018), 54–55.

12. Kearney and Merrill, "Origins," 907–8; 1873 Ill. Senate Journal, 307–8; 1873 Ill. House Journal, 341; "Lake Front," *Times*, Mar. 13, 1873; "The Lake Front Steal," *Inter Ocean* (Chicago), Mar. 17, 1873.

13. "The State Capital," *Tribune*, Mar. 19, 1873; 1873 Ill. House Journal, 402; "The Lake Front Bill," *Chicago Evening Journal* (hereafter *Evening Journal*), Mar. 24, 1873; Kearney and Merrill, "Origins," 908–9.

14. "Lake Front," *Tribune*, Mar. 21, 1873; George W. Wall to John Newell, Mar. 23, 1873, IC Papers (emphasis in original).

15. "Lake Front," *Tribune*, Mar. 21, 1873; "The Lake Front Bill," *Evening Journal*, Mar. 24, 1873.

16. 1873 Ill. House Journal, 440–41, 445–46; "The Lake Front Repeal Bill Passed in the House, 127 to 5," *Tribune*, Mar. 28, 1873; 1873 Ill. Senate Journal, 448–49; "The State Capital; Exciting Debate on the Lake-Front Repeal Bill in the Senate," *Tribune*, Mar. 29, 1873.

17. "The Lake-Front Investigation Bill Ordered to a Third Reading in the House," *Tribune*, Apr. 1, 1873.

18. "The Lake-Front Investigation Bill," *Tribune*, Apr. 1, 1873; 1873 Ill. House Journal, 477–78.

19. Kearney and Merrill, "Origins," 911–12; 1873 Ill. Senate Journal, 505; 1873 Ill. House Journal, 570.

20. For details about the alleged bribery, see Kearney and Merrill, "Origins," 887–94, 907, 927.

21. John W. Larson, *Those Army Engineers: A History of the Chicago District U.S. Army Corps of Engineers* (Chicago: US Army Corps of Engineers, 1979), 107; 16 Stat. 223, 226 (1870); 16 Stat. 538, 539 (1871); 17 Stat. 370 (1872); 17 Stat. 560 (1873); 18 Stat. 237 (1874); 18 Stat. 456 (1875); Kearney and Merrill, "Origins," 882.

22. Stover, *History of the Illinois Central*, 190 (table), reflects the railroad's struggles during the first half of the 1870s.

23. Stover, *History of the Illinois Central*, 190 (table), shows large increases in miles of line, freight traffic, and revenues between 1875 and 1885.

24. For roughly contemporaneous characterizations, see "The Railroads," *Tribune*, July 8, 1882, referring to the depot as a "miserable ruin," and "Railroads," *Tribune*, May 6, 1884, terming it a "dilapidated affair." For visual evidence, if of a slightly later period, see figure 2.1 in the text, a photo from 1893; and David Lowe, *Lost Chicago* (Boston: Houghton Mifflin, 1975), 54, a photo giving a view of the depot in 1895 (as correctly attributed).

25. Resolution from Meeting of the Board of the Michigan Central Railroad, May 6, 1880, IC Papers; 11 Cong. Rec. 80, Index, "Illinois" (Washington, DC, 1881); "The Council; The Mayor Submits the Railroad's Lake-Front Ordinance, and Some Amendments of His Own Which the Company Does Not Want," *Tribune*, Nov. 26, 1880.

26. "That Lake-Front Committee Report," *Tribune*, Dec. 18, 1885; Frederick S. Winston (Chicago Corporation Counsel), "Opinion upon the Lake Front Question," Jan. 23, 1886, 21, CHM; Stuyvesant Fish (president, Illinois Central Railroad) to Sidney Webster (director), June 28, 1889, IC Papers.

27. *Lake Front Case*, 146 U.S. 387, 410–11 (1892) (statement of the case).

28. William Ackerman (president, Illinois Central Railroad) to Board of Directors, Jan. 30, 1880, IC Papers, describes the advantages; William Cronon, "The Wealth of Nature: Lumber," chap. 4 in *Nature's Metropolis: Chicago and the Great West* (New York: W.W. Norton, 1991), discusses the Chicago lumber trade generally.

29. Egbert Jamieson and Francis Adams, *The Municipal Code of Chicago* (1881), 624–25. The city's ordinance was enacted on July 12, 1880. The Harlan opinion incorrectly gives the date as 1881. *Lake Front Case*, 33 F. 730, 749 (C.C.N.D. Ill. 1888). For the Illinois Central's arguments as to why the new piers and the viaduct were in the public interest, see "Rail Interesting; The Illinois Central's Viaduct Is Not Intended to Obstruct the Lake Front," *Times*, Feb. 18, 1880. Even while coming to an agreement on this development, the railroad and the city continued to dispute the railroad's claims to the lakefront under the 1869 Act. "The Lake Front," *Times*, Feb. 23, 1880.

30. 1851 Ill. Private Laws 61. The two lawyers for the Illinois Central most closely involved with advising the company in the 1880s—B. F. Ayer and John Jewett—both wrote legal opinions for the railroad confidently asserting that the 1873 repeal was an unconstitutional impairment of vested rights conferred by the Lake Front Act. B. F. Ayer, "Rights of the Illinois Central Railroad Company on the Lake Front," Dec. 1884, 43–44, IC Papers; John N. Jewett, "Illinois Central Railroad Company, Opinion as to Rights on the Lake Front, Chicago," Dec. 10, 1884, 13–15, 22, IC Papers. Ayer also publicly maintained the railroad's rights under the act. See, e.g., *Evening Journal*, Feb. 18, 1880.

31. Wilbert Jones, Kathleen Willis Morton, and Maureen O'Brien, *Chicago's Gold Coast* (Charleston, SC: Arcadia, 2012), 9; William H. Tyre, *Chicago's Historic Prairie Avenue* (Charleston, SC: Arcadia, 2008), 7; Robert Sharoff, "Restoring the Legacy of a Historic Chicago Neighborhood," *New York Times*, Sept. 4, 2005 (attributing the quoted phrase to an unnamed 1893 guidebook).

32. *Lake Front Case*, 33 F. at 749, 757–58; Lake Front Case Record, 374–75 (quoted material being testimony of E. T. Jeffery, general manager of the Illinois Central). Illinois Central Railroad Co. v. City of Chicago, 173 Ill. 471, 476–77, 50 N.E. 1104, 1106 (1898), aff'd, 176 U.S. 646 (1900), describes the breakwater south of 25th Street.

33. *1882 Encroachments Investigation*, 18; Lake Front Case Record, 369–70; Lind, *Limiteds*, 6.

34. *1882 Encroachments Investigation*, 2–4; Ayer, "Rights of the Illinois Central," 17; Carlton J. Corliss, *Main Line of Mid-America: The Story of the Illinois Central* (New York: Creative Age, 1950), 165–66.

35. *1882 Encroachments Investigation*, 71, gives Brewster's advice. Brewster's predecessor, the acting attorney general, had referred the matter to Joseph B. Leake, the US attorney for the Northern District of Illinois, for his opinion. Writing before Brewster, Leake

concluded that the question of title did matter, and drafted one of the more penetrating analyses of the vexing property-rights problem. His opinion was that only the state, not the city, had authority to grant the Illinois Central property rights in the bed of Lake Michigan. Given that the state had granted the railroad only a two-hundred-foot right of way in its charter, the city's attempt to authorize a three-hundred-foot right of way in 1852 was ultra vires. *1882 Encroachments Investigation*, 25–32. The documents from Major Lydecker's June 1881 stop order to the February 1882 opinion of the attorney general and Lincoln's letter transmitting the latter to the Illinois Central are collected in *1882 Encroachments Investigation*. Ayer, "Rights of the Illinois Central," 18–21, summarizes the subsequent board of inquiry report and Lincoln's June 1882 decision rejecting it.

36. Corliss, *Main Line of Mid-America*, 167.

37. The quotation in the section heading is from "The Lake Front Argument Ended," *Tribune*, July 15, 1887, which characterized the trial at the conclusion of oral argument. On the commencement of the suit and removal to federal court, see Illinois ex rel. McCartney v. Illinois Cent. R. Co., 16 F. 881 (C.C.N.D. Ill. 1883). The "federal questions" related to possible issues of construction of the act of cession creating the Northwest Territory and the act admitting Illinois as a state in 1818—neither of which featured in the decision—together with the Illinois Central's vested-rights argument grounded in the federal Constitution, which was a defense. *Id.* at 886–87. This was before the court's decision in Louisville & Nashville Railroad Co. v. Mottley, 211 U.S. 149 (1908), announcing that statutory federal-question jurisdiction of this sort (including for removal purposes) exists "only when the plaintiff's statement of his own cause of action shows that it is based upon [federal] laws or th[e] Constitution." *Id.* at 152. It is a near certainty that federal court jurisdiction would not be proper today.

38. "The Lake Front; . . . The Attorney General Requested to Look after the Interests of the United States," *Inter Ocean*, Feb. 9, 1887; *Inter Ocean*, June 3, 1887; "The Lake Front Steal; . . . United States Attorney Ewing to File a Bill for the United States," *Inter Ocean*, June 7, 1887. The lengthy delay before the trial allowed the parties to commission legal opinions sorting through the issues. We uncovered a number of such opinion letters dating from about this time: Ayer, "Rights of the Illinois Central," by the general solicitor of the Illinois Central; Jewett, "Illinois Central Railroad Company," by the railroad's longtime outside counsel; Lyman Trumbull, "Rights of Illinois Central Railroad Company on Shore Waters of Lake Michigan," Dec. 12, 1884, IC Papers, commissioned by the Illinois Central; Winston, "Opinion upon the Lake Front Question," addressed to Chicago's mayor by its corporation counsel; and Richard S. Tuthill, "Opinion and Suggestions to the Secretary of the Treasury, Touching Alleged Encroachments by the Illinois Central Railroad upon the Lake Front at Chicago," Apr. 3, 1886, IC Papers, by the local US attorney. Previously, the Board of Canal Commissioners had commissioned an opinion of its own: "Opinion of Lawrence, Campbell & Lawrence upon the Title to That Part of Fractional Section 15, 39, 14, Lying East of the East Line of Michigan Avenue," Dec. 10, 1879, CHM.

39. "The First Gun," *Inter Ocean*, Feb. 13, 1886; "The Lake Front; An Important Meeting of Citizens Considers Its Absorption by the Illinois Central," *Times*, Mar. 18, 1887; "The Lake Front; Some Facts Not Generally Known Relative to the Disputed Tract," *Times*, June 20, 1886; "The Railroad's Plea," *Tribune*, July 9, 1887; "The Lake Front Steal; Meeting of Citizens at the Grand Pacific Hotel Yesterday," *Inter Ocean*, Mar. 18, 1887; "The Lake Front; Another Row between the City and the Illinois Central Railroad," *Times*, Apr. 18, 1887; "News around Town; Roche Orders the Illinois Central to Stop Work," *Times*, May 17, 1887; "Lake Front Revision," *Chicago Herald* (hereafter *Herald*), May 11, 1887; "The Lake Front," *Inter Ocean*, May 10, 1887; "Lake-Front Litigation," *Tribune*, May 17, 1887.

40. Lake Front Case Record, 230–31; Lake Front Case Cir. Ct. Record, 493, 517; "The Lake Front Fight," *Times*, Mar. 30, 1887; "The Lake Front Case," *Times*, Apr. 13, 1887.

Herman Kogan, *Traditions and Challenges: The Story of Sidley & Austin* (Chicago, 1983), 34–35, 48–51, describes the work of John Leverett Thompson on behalf of the Citizens Association supporting the state.

41. Lake Front Case Record, 232–58, 345–427.

42. *Lake Front Case*, 33 F. at 755.

43. *Lake Front Case*, 33 F. at 754, 759; *id.* at 777 (dissenting opinion).

44. *Lake Front Case*, 33 F. at 755–58. For discussion of three of the opinions cited by Harlan, including Yates v. Milwaukee, 77 U.S. (10 Wall.) 497 (1871), see chapter 6.

45. *Lake Front Case*, 33 F. at 756.

46. *Lake Front Case*, 33 F. at 759–71.

47. *Lake Front Case*, 33 F. at 771.

48. *Lake Front Case*, 33 F. at 746, 772–76. "Fee" is a shorthand reference for "fee simple absolute," the common-law expression used to indicate full ownership of land.

49. *Lake Front Case*, 33 F. at 747, 776.

50. Ayer to Fish, Feb. 25, 1888, IC Papers, gives an early reaction: "The general impression here is that the decision, on the whole, is more favorable to the Company than to the State or City. You will have observed by the decision that every material question but one raised in the case was determined in our favor." His bottom line: "I think we are better off with this decision than we would have been if the Lake Front case had never been brought."

51. Trumbull to Ayer, Feb. 13, 1890; Jewett to Ayer, Feb. 15, 1890; Ayer to the Board of Directors, Illinois Central Railroad Company, Feb. 25, 1890, IC Papers. The trial court judgment was not entered until more than six months after the decision was announced, so the subsequent appeal (within two years of the judgment) was timely under the statute of the time.

52. Pierce, *History of Chicago*, 3:501–3.

53. Rossiter Johnson, *A History of the World's Columbian Exposition Held in Chicago in 1893* (New York: D. Appleton, 1897), 1:15–16, 19–24, 33–34, 52.

54. "World's Fair News; Lake Front Bastioned," *Herald*, Sept. 18, 1890; *Report of the President to the Board of Directors of the World's Columbian Exposition* (Chicago, 1892–93), 19; "Lake Front Advocates," *Tribune*, Mar. 2, 1890; Salzmann, *Liquid Capital*, 126.

55. Ayer to Fish, Feb. 1887, IC Papers; Stover, *History of the Illinois Central*, 217; Johnson, *Columbian Exposition*, 1:22, 48–49; *The World's Columbian Exposition Illustrated* (Chicago: James P. Campbell, 1892), 1:20.

56. Johnson, *Columbian Exposition*, 1:34; "All about the Site," *Inter Ocean*, June 29, 1890. Telford Burnham and James F. Gookins, "The Lake Front Settlement," undated (but evidently summer 1890), IC Papers, describe the directory's proposal and urge the city on its basis to settle the lakefront litigation. "Can Take Your Choice of Two Widely Differing Opinions," *Herald*, Aug. 18, 1890, recounts interviews with two directors holding different opinions about the feasibility of coming to terms with the Illinois Central and thus about the site of the fair.

57. Johnson, *Columbian Exposition*, 1:34; "They Accept the Site," *Times*, July 3, 1890; "The Lake Front Wins," *Evening Journal*, July 2, 1890.

58. *Proceedings of the City Council of the City of Chicago for Municipal Year 1890–91* (1891), 694–95; Ayer to Fish, Nov. 17, 1890, IC Papers (enclosing *Report of the Committee of Lake Front Property Owners on the Lake Front Question* of same date).

59. Johnson, *Columbian Exposition*, 37; "Settled It at Last," *Times*, Aug. 2, 1890; 1890 Ill. Laws 5–7.

60. Elizabeth Stevenson, *Park Maker: A Life of Frederick Law Olmsted* (New York: Macmillan, 1977), 395–97; Johnson, *Columbian Exposition*, 1:35–36, 42; "They Are Out of Site," *Evening Journal*, Aug. 13, 1890; "Black Eyes for the Sites," *Tribune*, Aug. 13, 1890;

see also Justin Martin, "A White City Dreamscape," chap. 30 in *Genius of Place: The Life of Frederick Law Olmsted* (Philadelphia: Da Capo, 2011).

61. Ayer to Fish, Aug. 26, 1890, IC Papers (conveying letter from Ayer to Telford Burnham of same date); "The Tender Not Good," *Evening Journal*, Sept. 4, 1890.

62. Johnson, *Columbian Exposition*, 1:37–38. In creating it, the Illinois General Assembly had provided that the "board of public park commissioners for the towns of South Chicago, Hyde Park, and Lake [would] be known under the name of the 'South Park Commissioners.'" 1869 Ill. Private Laws 358. It was often called the South Park Commission, and we follow that popular convention when we are not simply abbreviating it. A similar thing was true of the North Side, where the legislature created a board to "be named and styled the Commissioners of Lincoln Park," 1869 Ill. Private Laws 368, and we proceed similarly, calling it the Lincoln Park Commission. The West Side, which had its own commission, is, for better or worse, no part of our story, given its distance from the lake.

63. Johnson, *Columbian Exposition*, 1:41–43.

64. "Here Is a High Trump," *Herald*, Jan. 15, 1891.

65. Ayer to Fish, Nov. 17, 1890 (with aforementioned enclosure).

66. "World's Fair Work," *Times*, Nov. 29, 1890.

67. "Can't Settle the Row," *Herald*, Jan. 10, 1891; "World Fair's Work; The Lake-Front Site Question Has Again Stirred Up a Great Deal of Bad Feeling," *Times*, Jan. 11, 1891.

68. "Will This One Suit?," *Times*, Jan. 13, 1891; "It Isn't Settled Yet," *Herald*, Jan. 14, 1891.

69. "Will Sink the Tracks," *Tribune*, Jan. 14, 1891; "Abandons the Lake-Front," *Tribune*, Jan. 13, 1891.

70. "Will Try It Once More," *Tribune*, Jan. 14, 1891; "Lifted a Heavy Load," *Herald*, Jan. 20, 1891.

71. "Lifted a Heavy Load"; "Clinching the Bargain," *Tribune*, Jan. 21, 1891; "Waterside Domes; At Least Five Buildings Will Rise on the Lakefront, West of the Tracks," *Inter Ocean*, Jan. 20, 1891; "Lake Front Question Settled at Last," *Herald*, Jan. 21, 1891; "Down to Hard Work," *Herald*, Jan. 27, 1891.

72. "Down to Hard Work."

73. "No Nearer to the End," *Herald*, Jan. 28, 1891.

74. John Dunn (assistant to the president) to Fish, Feb. 16, 1891, IC Papers.

75. "Bad for Lake Front," *Herald*, Feb. 3, 1891; "The Lake Front Only to Be a Gate Way," *Tribune*, Feb. 22, 1891; "World's Fair Doings," *Herald*, Jan. 17, 1891.

76. "It Surprises Them All," *Tribune*, Jan. 10, 1891; Johnson, *Columbian Exposition*, 1:46–47.

77. "Give Up the Lake-Front," *Tribune*, Feb. 21, 1891; "Mr. Gage on the Lake Front," *Herald*, Feb. 28, 1891; "Leland's Expansive Smile," *Herald*, Feb. 22, 1891. The directory would vote, later and more narrowly (fifteen to twelve), to place the fine arts exhibit, the last remaining lakefront possibility, in Jackson Park. "Settled for All Time; No Art Exhibit on the Lake Front," *Herald*, June 20, 1891.

78. "Directors in Doubt," *Herald*, Jan. 13, 1891; "New Plans for Docks and Piers," *Tribune*, Dec. 10, 1891; "Guide for Visitors," *Tribune*, Apr. 30, 1893. Johnson, *Columbian Exposition*, 1:92–99, characterizes "[t]he transportation question" as "the stone of Sisyphus" and provides considerable detail about transportation plans and infrastructure, with particular emphasis on the area near Jackson Park.

79. "Planned a Compromise," *Tribune*, Mar. 5, 1891; James Fentress (general solicitor) to Fish, Apr. 7, 1891; Fentress to Fish, Apr. 15, 1891, IC Papers; *Proceedings of the City Council of the City of Chicago for Municipal Year 1890–91*, 1831–44.

80. "On the Railroad's Side," *Tribune*, Apr. 29, 1891.

81. "The Unfair Lake-Front Ordinance," *Tribune*, Apr. 24, 1891; "The Lake Front Grab," *Herald*, Apr. 30, 1891; "The Illinois Central Does Not Need the Four Blocks," *Tribune*, Apr. 26, 1891.

82. "Denounces the Steal," *Times*, May 19, 1891; "Nor Will This Do," *Times*, May 21, 1891; "The All Gall Lake Front Deal," *Herald*, May 18, 1891.

83. Stover, *History of the Illinois Central*, 217–18; Lind, *Limiteds*, 6.

84. "Favor Lake-Front Docks," *Tribune*, Sept. 6, 1891; Fish to J.F. Wallace (railroad's engineer of construction), Jan. 22, 1892; W.T. Baker (president of the World's Fair directory) to Fish, June 9, 1892; Fish to Baker, June 10, 1892, IC Papers; "Fish Shows His Hand," *Herald*, Dec. 8, 1891.

85. "To Settle the Lake Front Fight," *Herald*, Dec. 10, 1891; "To Advance Lake Front Cases," *Herald*, Dec. 15, 1891; "Advances the Cases," *Tribune*, Dec. 21, 1891.

86. Fish to Dunn, May 27, 1892; Fish to Baker, June 10, 1892, IC Papers; "Guide for Visitors"; "Haul Over a Million; Great Capacity of the Illinois Central's Fair System," *Tribune*, May 3, 1893.

87. "Fair Directors Win," *Tribune*, May 24, 1892; "Lake Front Work," *Tribune*, July 14, 1892; Johnson, *Columbian Exposition*, 1:96.

88. Stover, *History of the Illinois Central*, 217–20.

89. *Lake Front Case*, 146 U.S. at 476. Harlan would not have participated either early in the court's history or today. David P. Currie, *The Constitution in the Supreme Court: The First Hundred Years, 1789–1888* (Chicago: University of Chicago Press, 1985), 76, relates that in the nineteenth century, "[t]he Justices were soon to abandon their early practice (now required by [statute]) of refusing to review their own decisions," although he also observes that "in England judges habitually sat in review of their own decisions."

90. *Lake Front Case*, 146 U.S. at 434–37. With respect to the previous decisions: Barney v. Keokuk, 94 U.S. 324 (1877), had opined that the American rule of state ownership of nontidal submerged land was "sound" but that whether to abandon the English rule was "for the several States themselves to determine." *Id.* at 338. In Hardin v. Jordan, 140 U.S. 371 (1891), involving a small lake, the court split six to three over the question whether Illinois was still committed to the English rule with respect to navigable ponds and lakes. Justice Joseph Bradley concluded for the court that Illinois remained among the common-law faithful as to lakes as well as rivers. But twice in dicta he suggested that Lake Michigan should be regarded as being in a special category as "one of the internal seas of the country," *id.* at 386–87, 391, thereby clearly anticipating the *Lake Front Case*. Packer v. Bird, 137 U.S. 661 (1891), authored by Justice Field, held that the "courts of Illinois" had adopted the English view "to its fullest extent." *Id.* at 669.

91. *Lake Front Case*, 146 U.S. at 437–48, 464.

92. *Lake Front Case*, 146 U.S. at 448.

93. *Lake Front Case*, 146 U.S. at 448–55.

94. Winston, "Opinion upon the Lake Front Question," 18–19, is the pretrial allusion, and "The Lake Front Grab," *Inter Ocean*, July 7, 1887, reflects the repetition of the concept at trial. The city made its argument in the Supreme Court in two briefs: see Argument for the City of Chicago, 42–67 (filed by S. S. Gregory), and Brief and Argument for the City of Chicago (filed by John S. Miller), 52–60, variously relying on decisions such as Martin v. Waddell, 41 U.S. (16 Pet.) 367 (1842), and Arnold v. Mundy, 6 N.J.L. 1, 10 (1821), a case involving rights to dig for shellfish in the tidal waters of New Jersey, on which the court had relied in *Waddell*. Simply to give a flavor of it: "The rule is well settled in this country that the bed or soil of navigable waters is held by the people of the state in trust for the public uses for which it is adapted." Brief and Argument, 53 (Miller); see also *Lake Front Case*, 146 U.S. at 421–22 (reporter's summary of Miller's argument in this respect). The state attorney general's brief also included a version of the public trust argument, but it was buried near

the end of the brief and less well developed. Brief on Behalf of the State of Illinois, 130–54, *Lake Front Case*. For scholarship exploring the origins of the doctrine or analogues, see J.B. Ruhl and Thomas McGinn, "The Roman Public Trust Doctrine: What Was It, and Does It Support an Atmospheric Trust?," *Ecology Law Quarterly* 47 (2020): 117–78.

95. *Lake Front Case*, 146 U.S. at 440–45, 448–52. Concerning Field's philosophy generally, see Kearney and Merrill, "Origins," 806.

96. *Lake Front Case*, 146 U.S. at 452–55.

97. *Lake Front Case*, 146 U.S. at 455–60.

98. *Lake Front Case*, 146 U.S. at 460–62.

99. *Lake Front Case*, 146 U.S. at 462–63. Kearney and Merrill, "Origins," 921, elaborate briefly on this.

100. *Lake Front Case*, 146 U.S. at 467, 474 (Shiras, J., dissenting).

101. Fletcher v. Peck, 10 U.S. (6 Cranch) 87, 137 (1810); *Lake Front Case*, 33 F. at 774–75.

102. Fentress to Fish, Dec. 12, 1892; Fish to Ayer, Mar. 7, 1893; Fish to Guthrie, Mar. 18, 1893; Guthrie to Fish, Apr. 12, 1893, IC Papers; "Brings Glad Tidings; . . . Petition for Rehearing Ignored," *Tribune*, April 11, 1893. Guthrie would later serve as Ruggles Professor of Constitutional Law at Columbia University. "W. D. Guthrie Dies Suddenly at 76," *New York Times*, Dec. 9, 1935.

103. United States v. Illinois Central Railroad Co., 154 U.S. 225, 236–39, 241–42 (1894).

104. *Illinois Central*, 154 U.S. at 238–39.

105. Illinois ex rel. Hunt v. Illinois Cent. R. Co., 91 F. 955, 957 (7th Cir. 1899) (quoting the circuit court's decree).

106. Illinois v. Illinois Central Railroad Co., 184 U.S. 77, 98 (1902).

107. *Illinois Central*, 184 U.S. at 98.

3. THE WATCHDOG OF THE LAKEFRONT

1. City of Chicago v. Ward, 169 Ill. 392, 48 N.E. 927 (1897) (hereafter *Ward I*); Bliss v. Ward, 198 Ill. 104, 64 N.E. 705 (1902) (hereafter *Ward II*); Ward v. Field Museum of Natural History, 241 Ill. 496, 89 N.E. 731 (1909) (hereafter *Ward III*); South Park Commissioners v. Montgomery Ward & Co., 248 Ill. 299, 93 N.E. 910 (1910) (hereafter *Ward IV*).

2. Joseph D. Kearney and Thomas W. Merrill, "Private Rights in Public Lands: The Chicago Lakefront, Montgomery Ward, and the Public Dedication Doctrine," *Northwestern University Law Review* 105 (2011): 1444, 1449–50, discuss the various precedents of both the US and Illinois Supreme Courts.

3. On the original provenance of this land within the United States and the grid system, see Paul W. Gates, *History of Public Land Law Development* (Washington, DC: Public Land Law Review Commission, 1968), 49–55, 68; Payson Jackson Treat, *The National Land System: 1785–1820* (New York: E.B. Treat, 1910), 179–97; Bill Hubbard Jr., *American Boundaries: The Nation, the States, the Rectangular Survey* (Chicago: University of Chicago Press, 2009), 49–53, 183–214. Kearney and Merrill, "Private Rights," 1423; *Lake Front Case*, 146 U.S. 387, 394–98 (1892) (statement of the case); Gates, *Public Land Law Development*, 346–47, 350–51; and Dennis H. Cremin, *Grant Park: The Evolution of Chicago's Front Yard* (Carbondale: Southern Illinois University Press, 2013), 2, all concern the canal legislation and project. Concerning fractional section 15, see *Lake Front Case*, 146 U.S. at 394, 398 (statement of the case), and 437.

4. Kearney and Merrill, "Private Rights," 1424–25, set forth the commercial map. Concerning the higher land values, see Transcript of Record, 244–46, *Ward I*; *Ward I*, 169 Ill. at 401, 48 N.E. at 930; *Ward II*, 198 Ill. at 110, 64 N.E. at 706; Cremin, *Grant Park*, 4.

5. The original recorded copy of Birchard's map was destroyed in the Chicago fire of 1871, and it is unknown whether the original document containing Birchard's comment still exists. Kearney and Merrill, "Private Rights," 1426. The first quotations are notations in figure 3.2 itself; the last can be found in *Lake Front Case*, 33 F. 730, 733–34 (C.C.N.D. Ill. 1888). There is evidence that the restriction of land as "public ground" was demanded by local residents, with that area to revert to the federal government in the event of its being built upon. Kearney and Merrill, "Private Rights," 1426. The map restriction contains no language of reversion, and the Supreme Court later held, in resolving the United States' appeal in the *Lake Front Case*, that the federal government retained no property rights in section 10. United States v. Illinois Central Railroad Co., 154 U.S. 225, 236–39, 241–42 (1894).

6. Kearney and Merrill, "Private Rights," 1428.

7. Harold M. Mayer and Richard C. Wade, *Chicago: Growth of a Metropolis* (Chicago: University of Chicago Press, 1969), 56–61; Kearney and Merrill, "Private Rights," 1428.

8. 1861 Ill. Private Laws 136. 1863 Ill. Private Laws 96 is essentially identical.

9. Cremin, *Grant Park*, 17–18; "The Copperhead Amphitheater," *Chicago Tribune* (hereafter *Tribune*), May 31, 1864.

10. Kearney and Merrill, "Private Rights," 1453–54. For the subsequent removal, see Cremin, *Grant Park*, 19.

11. United States v. Illinois Cent. R. Co., 26 F. Cas. 461, 464 (C.C.N.D. Ill. 1869).

12. Cremin, *Grant Park*, 28–30.

13. "Our Exposition," *Tribune*, Mar. 21, 1873; "The Council," *Tribune*, Apr. 29, 1873; Cremin, *Grant Park*, 31–40; Kearney and Merrill, "Private Rights," 1432; R. Craig Sautter and Edward M. Burke, *Inside the Wigwam: Chicago Presidential Conventions, 1860–1996* (Chicago: Wild Onion Books, 1996), 47, 57. The Interstate Exposition Building was originally designed by William W. Boyington, who had designed Chicago's Water Tower, which still stands. Renovations by 1885 enabled the structure to accommodate musical offerings with the creation of a six-thousand-seat auditorium designed by the famed engineer-architect Dankmar Adler. Cremin, *Grant Park*, 32, 38.

14. Kearney and Merrill, "Private Rights," 1433; Cremin, *Grant Park*, 30–34.

15. Kearney and Merrill, "Private Rights," 1433; Cremin, *Grant Park*, 44; "Given Notice to Move; The Baltimore and Ohio Depot Ordered Off the Lake-Front," *Tribune*, Sept. 19, 1891; J. Seymour Currey, *Chicago: Its History and Its Builders* (Chicago: S. J. Clark, 1912), 3:859; Bill of Complaint, 7–8, United States v. Chicago Base Ball Club, No. 19026 (C.C.N.D. Ill. May 27, 1884); C. H. Mottier, "History of Chicago Passenger Stations: Central Station Group," *Journal of the Western Society of Engineers* 42 (Oct. 1937): 254.

16. Kearney and Merrill, "Private Rights," 1458; "The Baltimore & Ohio and the Litigation about the Lake-Front," *Tribune*, Nov. 4, 1882; "The Lake-Front; Judge Drummond Decides a Point in Favor of the Railroads," *Tribune*, Nov. 8, 1882. Previously, since about 1875, the B&O had been using part of the Interstate Exposition Building for depot purposes. "Baltimore & Ohio Depot," *Tribune*, Dec. 16, 1874; "The Railroads; A Brand-New Depot for the Baltimore & Ohio on the Lake Front," *Tribune*, Aug. 18, 1882.

17. Myra Bradwell, ed., "The Lake Front; A Temporary Injunction Granted Restraining the Erection of Any More Buildings on the Lake Park," *Chicago Legal News* 15 (1883): 290; Bill of Complaint, 1, 13–14, Stafford v. City of Chicago, No. 83C44290 (Cook Cnty. Cir. Ct., Ill., Mar. 23, 1883).

18. Bill of Complaint, 6, 8–9, 13, *Chicago Base Ball Club*.

19. "The Lake-Front; No More Trespassers Allowed to Occupy the Ground," *Tribune*, July 18, 1884.

20. Kearney and Merrill, "Private Rights," 1463; Andreas, *History of Chicago*, 3:358.

21. Kearney and Merrill, "Private Rights," 1464–65.

22. Kearney and Merrill, "Private Rights," 1465.
23. Kearney and Merrill, "Private Rights," 1466.
24. Kearney and Merrill, "Private Rights," 1467.
25. Kearney and Merrill, "Private Rights," 1467.
26. Kearney and Merrill, "Private Rights," 1467–68.
27. Transcript of Record, 312, *Ward I*; Frank B. Latham, *A Century of Serving Customers: The Story of Montgomery Ward*, 2nd ed. (Chicago: Montgomery Ward, 1972), 29–30; Kearney and Merrill, "Private Rights," 1468.
28. Transcript of Record, 312–15, *Ward I.*
29. Kearney and Merrill, "Private Rights," 1470.
30. Kearney and Merrill, "Private Rights," 1470; Latham, *Century of Serving Customers*, 51; Gene Morgan, "How Grant Park Was Saved for People; Ward's Great Fight Waged 21 Years," *Chicago Daily News*, June 8, 1935.
31. *Ward I*, 169 Ill. at 393, 48 N.E. at 928; Transcript of Record, 17–19, *Ward I.*
32. Cremin, *Grant Park*, 52–55.
33. Affidavit of Caryl Young, 1–3, Daggett v. City of Chicago, No. 89C74794, 3 Ill. Cir. Ct. Rep. 79 (Cook Cnty. Cir. Ct., Ill., 1892). Later authors have stated, erroneously, that Ward gave his consent to the Art Institute. See, e.g., Allison Dunham, "The Chicago Lake Front and A. Montgomery Ward," 95 (app. B), in *Preservation of Open Space Areas: A Study of the Non-Governmental Role* (Chicago: Welfare Council of Metropolitan Chicago, 1966), later reprinted in *Land-Use Controls: A Quarterly Review* 1 (1967): 15, and *University of Chicago Law School Record* 25 (Winter 1979): 15. There is no documentary evidence supporting this claim, and it is inconsistent with the list of consenting owners in the *Daggett* case file.
34. Affidavit of Caryl Young, 1–3; Kearney and Merrill, "Private Rights," 1471–72. Stafford also opposed the Art Institute, but he had entered into a long-term lease of his property, which raised (legitimate) doubts about his standing to object or consent. "Alone in the Fight," *Tribune*, June 2, 1892.
35. *Daggett*, 3 Ill. Cir. Ct. Rep. at 86–87; "Gives Its Reasons," *Tribune*, May 21, 1892; Kearney and Merrill, "Private Rights," 1472.
36. "Against the Art Institute," *Tribune*, June 1, 1892; "Oppose Mrs. Daggett," *Tribune*, June 21, 1892; "For an Institute," *Tribune*, June 22, 1892; "For the Institute," *Tribune*, June 24, 1892.
37. *Daggett*, 3 Ill. Cir. Ct. Rep. at 81, 87–88.
38. *Daggett*, 3 Ill. Cir. Ct. Rep. at 92; Cremin, *Grant Park*, 61.
39. "Notes: Montgomery Ward," *Bulletin of the Art Institute of Chicago* 7 (Jan. 1914): 47; Kearney and Merrill, "Private Rights," 1474.
40. Kearney and Merrill, "Private Rights," 1435. No property owners south of Washington Street objected to this procedure, even though under the logic informing the Illinois Supreme Court's subsequent decisions in *Ward III* and *Ward IV* the library arguably should have obtained the consent of all property owners on the surrounding streets, including Michigan Avenue, not just those abutting the dedicated block.
41. Transcript of Record, 484–88 (petition of Adam Forepaugh Shows), *Ward I*; "Small Boys Are Happy," *Tribune*, May 12, 1891; *Ward I*, 169 Ill. at 394, 48 N.E. at 928.
42. "Against the Democratic Wigwam," *Tribune*, Apr. 3, 1892; *Ward I*, 169 Ill. at 420, 48 N.E. at 936; A. Montgomery Ward, "Mr. Ward Explains," letter to the editor, *Tribune*, Nov. 2, 1900.
43. Transcript of Record, 33–34, 39–54, 57–59, *Ward I.*
44. Kearney and Merrill, "Private Rights," 1476; Ward v. Congress Const. Co., 99 F. 598, 600 (7th Cir. 1900).

45. Rossiter Johnson, *A History of the World's Columbian Exposition Held in Chicago in 1893* (New York: D. Appleton, 1897), 1:134–80, generally details the fair's construction. Erik Larson, *The Devil in the White City* (New York: Crown, 2003), gives a popular account of the fair and its impact on the city, emphasizing Burnham's role. Cremin, *Grant Park*, 68–75, 89–90, concerns the plans for Lake Park.

46. Daniel H. Burnham and Edward H. Bennett, *Plan of Chicago Prepared under the Direction of the Commercial Club during the Years MCMVI, MCMVII, and MCMVIII*, ed. Charles Moore (Chicago: Commercial Club, 1909). See generally Carl Smith, *The Plan of Chicago: Daniel Burnham and the Remaking of the American City* (Chicago: University of Chicago Press, 2006). For the various proposals for the Field Museum and Crerar Library, see Timothy J. Gilfoyle, *Millennium Park: Creating a Chicago Landmark* (Chicago: University of Chicago Press, 2006), 21–30, 45.

47. Kearney and Merrill, "Private Rights," 1437–38.

48. Cremin, *Grant Park*, 77–78; Dennis H. Cremin, "Building Chicago's Front Yard: Grant Park 1836 to 1936" (PhD diss., Loyola University Chicago, 1999), 249.

49. Transcript of Record, 68–69, *Ward I*; *Ward I*, 169 Ill. at 393–96, 48 N.E. at 928; "One Year to Take Park," *Tribune*, Sept. 15, 1896; "Death Takes Ward, Lake 'Watchdog,' Following Fall," *Tribune*, Dec. 8, 1913. The newspaper had previously thus characterized Warren Leland, in particular, and Sarah Daggett. "Music on the Lakefront," *Tribune*, July 22, 1891; "Alone in the Fight," *Tribune*, June 2, 1892; "Watchdogs of the Lake-Front," *Tribune*, Dec. 6, 1892.

50. *Ward I*, 169 Ill. at 400–406, 416–17, 422, 48 N.E. at 927–31, 935, 937.

51. *Ward I*, 169 Ill. at 418, 48 N.E. at 935.

52. *Ward I*, 169 Ill. at 418–22, 48 N.E. at 935–37.

53. *Encyclopedia Britannica Online*, s.v. "Pullman Strike," by Melvin I. Urofsky, last updated May 4, 2020, https://www.britannica.com/event/Pullman-Strike; Richard Schneirov, "'To the Ragged Edge of Anarchy': The 1894 Pullman Boycott," *Organization of American Historians Magazine of History*, 13 (Spring 1999): 27–28; Harry Barnard, *Eagle Forgotten: The Life of John Peter Altgeld* (New York: Duell, Sloan, & Pearce, 1938), 151, 286–98; Almont Lindsey, *The Pullman Strike: The Story of a Unique Experiment and of a Great Labor Upheaval* (Chicago: University of Chicago Press, 1942), 207–8; David Ray Papke, "The Strike and Boycott," chap. 2 in *The Pullman Case: The Clash of Labor and Capital in Industrial America* (Lawrence: University Press of Kansas, 1999).

54. "Park in the Lake," *Tribune*, Jan. 14, 1894.

55. "Wants Armory Work Stopped," *Tribune*, June 20, 1900.

56. *Ward II*, 198 Ill. at 112–14, 121, 64 N.E. at 706–7, 709.

57. *Ward II*, 198 Ill. at 115–16, 64 N.E. at 707.

58. Kearney and Merrill, "Private Rights," 1481.

59. Kearney and Merrill, "Private Rights," 1483.

60. "Court May Pick Crerar Site," *Tribune*, Apr. 12, 1901; 1903 Ill. Laws 262–64; South Park Commissioners, meeting minutes, Dec. 15, 1909, Chicago Park District Archives, 160–62 (quoting 1905 proceedings); "To Start Crerar Library," *Chicago Record-Herald* (hereafter *Record-Herald*), June 22, 1906.

61. "'Watchdog' Given Contempt Order," *Tribune*, June 26, 1906; "Library Board Firm," *Record-Herald*, June 28, 1906; "Must Take Workmen's Sheds from Crerar Library Site," *Tribune*, June 30, 1906; "Library without a Home," *Tribune*, July 3, 1906.

62. "Given to Chicago: Means to Establish a Great Columbian Museum," *Tribune*, Oct. 28, 1893; "Funds to Buy Curios," *Tribune*, Nov. 4, 1893; Kearney and Merrill, "Private Rights," 1437–38, 1484–85; "Field Museum History," Field Museum, accessed Aug. 3, 2020, https://www.fieldmuseum.org/about/history.

63. "Will Watch Dog Be Manger Dog?," *Tribune*, Feb. 20, 1903; South Park Commissioners, meeting minutes, Aug. 6, 1909, Chicago Park District Archives, 7.

64. "Death Comes to Marshall Field," *Tribune*, Jan. 17, 1906; "Museum Loss Feared," *Record-Herald*, Nov. 21, 1908; Marshall Field, will dated Sept. 5, 1905, 35, 39–40, CHM; "Fight on Museum Starts in Court," *Tribune*, Feb. 24, 1907.

65. "Field Museum Gets Site," *Tribune*, Jan. 22, 1907; Kearney and Merrill, "Private Rights," 1486–87, include some further information concerning Higinbotham, a strong-willed character who had previously served as president of the Columbian Exposition.

66. Kearney and Merrill, "Private Rights," 1487.

67. "Lake Front Suit Hits Snag in Court Order," *Record-Herald*, Nov. 20, 1908; "No Gain to Ward in Museum Ruling," *Tribune*, Nov. 24, 1908; Myra Bradwell, ed., "The Recent Elections: Judge George A. Dupuy," *Chicago Legal News* 37 (1905): 103; "Lake Front Open to Park Houses," *Tribune*, Jan. 25, 1908.

68. "Ward Explains War on Museum," *Tribune*, Nov. 26, 1908; "Offer Spurned by Park Board," *Tribune*, Nov. 27, 1908; Kearney and Merrill, "Private Rights," 1487.

69. "Site for Museum Seems Assured," *Tribune*, Dec. 10, 1908; "Field Museum Wins; Ward Fight Delayed," *Record-Herald*, Dec. 10, 1908.

70. *Ward III*, 241 Ill. at 506–10, 89 N.E. at 735–37.

71. *Ward III*, 241 Ill. at 510, 89 N.E. at 736.

72. "Moving to Block Victory of Ward," *Tribune*, Oct. 27, 1909.

73. "Mr. Ward and the Field Museum," *Tribune*, Oct. 28, 1909.

74. "Moving to Block Victory of Ward"; "Fight on Museum Starts in Court"; South Park Commissioners, meeting minutes, Dec. 15, 1909, 160, 163.

75. Kearney and Merrill, "Private Rights," 1489–90.

76. "Dismisses Suits of Field Museum," *Tribune*, Mar. 15, 1910.

77. *Ward IV*, 248 Ill. at 301–6, 312–13, 93 N.E. at 911–13, 915; *id.* at 322–23, 93 N.E. at 918 (Dunn, J., dissenting); *id.* at 337–38, 93 N.E. at 924 (O. Carter, J., dissenting).

78. For a more modern sensibility, see "Comment: The Status of Dedicated Land in Illinois," *DePaul Law Review* 11 (1961–62): 61–76. The US Supreme Court has held that eminent domain can be used for memorial grounds and parks. United States v. Gettysburg Electric Railway Co., 160 U.S. 668 (1896), upheld the use of eminent domain to acquire part of Gettysburg battlefield for a memorial park, and Shoemaker v. United States, 147 U.S. 282 (1893), upheld its use to acquire land for Rock Creek Park in Washington, DC.

79. "$6,750,000 New Field Museum to Open Tomorrow," *Tribune*, May 2, 1921.

80. "Ward Stops Bryan Tent," *Tribune*, Nov. 1, 1900; "Jones Cries 'Boycott Ward,'" *Tribune*, Nov. 2, 1900; "Mr. Ward Explains."

81. "City Prevents Uncle Sam from Building a Fence," *Tribune*, Oct. 25, 1901.

82. Kearney and Merrill, "Private Rights," 1483, 1495. For a suggestion of animus on Ward's part against Field, see Lois Wille, *Forever Open, Clear, and Free: The Struggle for Chicago's Lakefront*, 2nd ed. (Chicago: University of Chicago Press, 1991), 78 (quoting Higinbotham).

83. Latham, *Story of Montgomery Ward*, 32; Kearney and Merrill, "Private Rights," 1495–96.

84. Kearney and Merrill, "Private Rights," 1439–40. The City Beautiful movement stressed an integrated plan of buildings, parks, and walks, typically in a neoclassical style, as a corrective for haphazard urbanization. Concerning its connection with the Columbian Exposition and Chicago, see William H. Wilson, *The City Beautiful Movement* (Baltimore: Johns Hopkins University Press, 1989), 53–74. The Chicago Commercial Club and other Chicago elites actively promoted the movement. J. Theodore Fink, *Grant Park Tomorrow: Future of Chicago's Front Yard* (Chicago: Open Lands Project, 1979), 74–79; Gilfoyle, *Millennium Park*, 43; Smith, *Plan of Chicago*, 14–15, 66–67, 154.

85. Gilfoyle, *Millennium Park*, 26–27, 47–48.

86. Gilfoyle, *Millennium Park*, 32–42, 369; "Garages," Millennium Garages, accessed Aug. 3, 2020, http://www.millenniumgarages.com/, provides a map of the current layout.

87. Kearney and Merrill, "Private Rights," 1468, 1496.

88. Kearney and Merrill, "Private Rights," 1497. It is true that Merrick filed suit on behalf of Ward challenging an expansion of the temporary post office in 1899. But this legal action may have been motivated more by Merrick's concern about defeating any estoppel argument, as had been advanced by the city in *Ward I*, than by Ward's hostility to having a post office opposite his property.

89. Dunham, "Chicago Lake Front," 19, estimates Ward's litigation costs.

90. See Wille, *Forever Open*, 71–72, for the populist hypothesis.

91. "To Be a Fine Park," *Tribune*, Jan. 24, 1893.

92. On Ward's attention to detail in his business, see Daniel J. Boorstin, "A. Montgomery Ward's Mail-Order Business," *Chicago History* 2 (1973): 147–49.

93. "Bar for the Wires," *Tribune*, Mar. 31, 1898; "Ban on Loop to Stand," *Tribune*, Apr. 14, 1898; Chicago City Ry. Co. v. Montgomery Ward & Co., 76 Ill. App. 536, 542, 544 (1898).

94. Kearney and Merrill, "Private Rights," 1501–2; "Rules Against Ward & Co.," *Tribune*, Dec. 19, 1899.

95. Kearney and Merrill, "Private Rights," 1502–3; "Have Right to View of Lake," *Tribune*, June 21, 1901. Ward would purchase Marks's property the next year, as reflected in figure 3.11. "For $600,000; Southwest Corner of Michigan Avenue and Washington Street Sold to Montgomery Ward & Co.," *Economist* (Chicago), Feb. 1, 1902, 135–36.

96. Chicago Yacht Club v. Marks, 97 Ill. App. 406, 410–11 (1901).

97. "Defends Lake Front Too," *Tribune*, May 22, 1901; *Marks*, 97 Ill. App. at 411–13.

98. McCormick v. Chicago Yacht Club, 331 Ill. 514, 163 N.E. 418 (1928); Stevens Hotel Co. v. Chicago Yacht Club, 339 Ill. 463, 171 N.E. 550 (1930). The McCormick who sued the yacht club was not Colonel Robert R. McCormick, the publisher of the *Chicago Tribune*, but Robert H. McCormick. Kearney and Merrill, "Private Rights," 1504.

99. Concerning agitation for an outer harbor, see chapter 7.

100. Neither the denotation nor the connotation of "building" appears to have changed much over the centuries. For example, a dictionary close in time to the public dedication of the lakefront area defined "building" as a "fabric or edifice constructed for use or convenience, as a house." Noah Webster, *An American Dictionary of the English Language*, 5th ed. (New York: S. Converse, 1830), s.v. "building." Around the time of the *Ward* cases, a dictionary gave this more elaborately stated but essentially identical definition: "[t]hat which is built; specif.: . . . As now generally used, a fabric or edifice, framed or constructed, designed to stand more or less permanently, and covering a space of land, for use as a dwelling, storehouse, factory, shelter for beasts, or some other useful purpose. *Building* in this sense does not include a mere wall, fence, monument, hoarding, or similar structure, though designed for permanent use where it stands; nor a steamboat, ship, or other vessel of navigation." *Webster's New International Dictionary of the English Language* (Springfield, MA: G. & C. Merriam, 1909), s.v. "building."

101. Michigan Boulevard Building Co. v. Chicago Park District, 412 Ill. 350, 352, 361–62, 106 N.E.2d 359, 361, 365–66 (1952); "Pouting Pigeons Hamper Razing of Colonnade; Peristyle Wrecked for Grant Park Garage," *Tribune*, Feb. 21, 1953.

102. *Michigan Boulevard Building Co.*, 412 Ill. at 361–62, 106 N.E.2d at 365–66.

103. *Michigan Boulevard Building Co.*, 412 Ill. at 362–63, 106 N.E.2d at 366.

104. Cremin, *Grant Park*, 102–4; Gilfoyle, *Millennium Park*, 47, 59.

105. Gilfoyle, *Millennium Park*, 50–63; Kearney and Merrill, "Private Rights," 1509.

106. Robert Davis and Stanley Ziemba, "Compromise Reached on New Band Shell," *Tribune*, Nov. 11, 1977; "Bandshell Won't Be Removed," *Tribune*, Oct. 25, 1978; Gilfoyle, *Millennium Park*, 63–69.

107. *Ward III*, 241 Ill. at 510, 89 N.E. at 736 (emphasis added). The *Ward* cases were frequently alluded to as legal impediments to a new band shell, but we have discovered only one instance (in 1977) in which a lawsuit was seriously threatened. Kearney and Merrill, "Private Rights," 1510–11.

108. The park district also faced obstacles from the Chicago Plan Commission, which had to approve all designs for new structures in the park. Paul Gapp, "Grant Park Band Shell Back to Drawing Board," *Tribune*, Mar. 14, 1977; Paul Gapp, "Park District Seeks Bids on Disputed Band Shell," *Tribune*, Mar. 18, 1977.

109. Stevens Hotel Co. v. Art Institute of Chicago, 260 Ill. App. 555, 570 (1931); Kearney and Merrill, "Private Rights," 1512–13.

110. Stevens Hotel Co. v. Art Institute of Chicago, 342 Ill. 180, 180–81, 185, 173 N.E. 761, 762–63 (1930); *Stevens Hotel Co.*, 260 Ill. App. at 557, 559–61, 569–70; Cremin, *Grant Park*, 119.

111. *Stevens Hotel Co.*, 260 Ill. App. at 561–63, 565–67, 575–77 (emphasis omitted). The court took the language of "*necessary enlargement of the building* known as the Art Institute" from the superior court decree in *Ward I*, where that building had not been challenged. For the text of the original consents for the Art Institute, which we uncovered in the court records for the *Daggett* case, see Kearney and Merrill, "Private Rights," 1514–15.

112. *Stevens Hotel Co.*, 260 Ill. App. at 570, 575–78. Property rights in the nature of easements can be extinguished by prescription. Jon W. Bruce and James W. Ely Jr., "Termination by Prescription," in *The Law of Easements and Licenses in Land* (Egan, MN: Thomson Reuters, 2019), § 10.25.

113. *Stevens Hotel Co.*, 260 Ill. App. at 577–78; Decree, 3–4, Stevens Hotel Co. v. Art Institute of Chicago, Gen. No. 176132 (Cook Cnty. Cir. Ct., Ill., July 9, 1931).

114. For a general explanation of how neighborhood amenities are capitalized in land values, see William A. Fischel, *The Homevoter Hypothesis: How Home Values Influence Local Government Taxation, School Finance, and Land-Use Policies* (Cambridge, MA: Harvard University Press, 2001).

115. On the general difficulties of collective action, see Mancur Olson, *The Logic of Collective Action: Public Goods and the Theory of Groups* (Cambridge, MA: Harvard University Press, 1965).

4. THE STRUGGLE FOR STREETERVILLE

1. On the accretion/avulsion distinction, see generally Henry P. Farnham, *The Law of Waters and Water Rights* (Rochester, NY: Lawyers Cooperative, 1904), 3:2192–94, 2485–86, 2492; Joseph K. Angell, *A Treatise on the Common Law, in Relation to Water-Courses* (Boston: Wells & Lilly, 1824), 92–96. Joseph L. Sax, "The Accretion/Avulsion Puzzle: Its Past Revealed, Its Future Proposed," *Tulane Environmental Law Journal* 23 (2010): 305–67, traces the history of the distinction and its reception in American law. On the ownership of land affected by accretion or avulsion, see Nebraska v. Iowa, 143 U.S. 359, 360–63 (1892).

2. An example is Lovingston v. County of St. Clair, 64 Ill. 56, 64–65 (1872), aff'd, 90 U.S. (23 Wall.) 46 (1874), which concluded that a riparian owner can claim accretions caused by the erection of an artificial structure only if the structure was made by some third party on other land. Brundage v. Knox, 279 Ill. 450, 465–67, 117 N.E. 123, 128–29 (1917), is to similar effect.

3. Stop the Beach Renourishment, Inc. v. Florida Department of Environmental Protection, 560 U.S. 702, 731–32 (2010).

4. On such permission or encouragement (and for an example), see Hendrik Hartog, *Public Property and Private Power: The Corporation of the City of New York in American Law, 1730–1870* (Chapel Hill: University of North Carolina Press, 1983), 44–68. See also Jason Anthony Robison and Anthony Dan Tarlock, *Law of Water Rights and Resources* (Toronto: Thomson Reuters, 2020), § 8:25 (discussing restrictions under the public trust doctrine on filling navigable waters).

5. In addition to chapter 1 and the discussion in this chapter of the 1896 *Kirk* case, Fuller v. Shedd, 161 Ill. 462, 474–87, 44 N.E. 286, 290–95 (1896), reviews the evolving jurisprudence on the ownership of lakebeds.

6. Jon C. Teaford, *The Rise of the States: Evolution of American State Government* (Baltimore: Johns Hopkins University Press, 2002), 5, 111, depicts state government of the time as "spare, with little administrative muscle," and notes, for example, the nonexistence of any statewide park systems during the nineteenth century. Lawrence M. Friedman, *A History of American Law*, 4th ed. (New York: Oxford University Press, 2019), 156–58, also describes the weakness of state institutions during this time.

7. Ann Durkin Keating, *Rising Up from Indian Country: The Battle of Fort Dearborn and the Birth of Chicago* (Chicago: University of Chicago Press, 2012), 68–70, 146–50, 170–72, 187–88, 191–92, 209–22, recounts Kinzie's story in detail. For the federal survey system, see the beginning of chapter 3. Concerning Wall (whom some sources call "Walls") and his survey, see Edward O. Brown, "The Shore of Lake Michigan: A Paper Read before the Law Club of the City of Chicago," Apr. 25, 1902, 7–8, CHM; Ulrich Danckers and Jane Meredith, *Early History of Chicago* (River Forest, IL: Early Chicago, 1999), 53, 350.

8. In re Harvey M. La Follette et al., 26 Pub. Lands Dec. 453, 457 (1898); Kinzie v. Winston, 56 Ill. 56, 59–60 (1870); Joseph D. Kearney and Thomas W. Merrill, "Contested Shore: Property Rights in Reclaimed Land and the Battle for Streeterville," *Northwestern University Law Review* 107 (2013): 1070–72; Homer Hoyt, *One Hundred Years of Land Values in Chicago* (Washington, DC: Beard Books, 2000), 33–37.

9. Libby Hill, *The Chicago River: A Natural and Unnatural History*, rev. ed. (Carbondale: Southern Illinois University Press, 2019), 57–59; Harold M. Mayer and Richard C. Wade, *Chicago: Growth of a Metropolis* (Chicago: University of Chicago Press, 1969), 16–17; A. T. Andreas, *History of Chicago* (Chicago: A. T. Andreas, 1884), 2:234–35; John W. Larson, *Those Army Engineers: A History of the Chicago District U.S. Army Corps of Engineers* (Chicago: US Army Corps of Engineers, 1979), 59, 62–64; Jones v. Johnston, 59 U.S. (18 How.) 150, 152 (1855).

10. "The Dens in the Sands Broken Up," *Chicago Tribune* (hereafter *Tribune*), Apr. 21, 1857.

11. 1857 Ill. Private Laws 499–502; Chicago Dock and Canal Co. v. Kinzie, 93 Ill. 415, 426–28 (1879); Harold M. Mayer, *The Port of Chicago and the St. Lawrence Seaway* (Chicago: University of Chicago Press, 1957), 11–12; *Report of the Submerged and Shore Lands Legislative Investigating Committee* (Springfield, IL, 1911) (hereafter *Chiperfield Committee Report*), 2:201–5.

12. Jones v. Johnston, 59 U.S. (18 How.) 150 (1855); Bates v. Illinois Central Railroad Co., 66 U.S. (1 Black) 204 (1861); Johnston v. Jones, 66 U.S. (1 Black) 209 (1861); Banks v. Ogden, 69 U.S. (2 Wall.) 57 (1864); Kinzie v. Winston, 14 F. Cas. 649 (Cook Cnty. Cir. Ct., Ill.) (No. 7,835), aff'd, 56 Ill. 56 (1870); Chicago Dock Co. v. Kinzie, 49 Ill. 289 (1868); Lombard v. Kinzie, 73 Ill. 446 (1874); Chicago Dock and Canal Co. v. Kinzie, 93 Ill. 415 (1879).

13. *Banks*, 69 U.S. (2 Wall.) at 67–69.

14. *Chicago Dock and Canal Co.*, 93 Ill. at 427–28; *La Follette*, 26 Pub. Lands Dec. at 458.

15. See Mayer and Wade, *Chicago*, 108, for a map showing the area destroyed by the 1871 fire. The Sands served as a refuge for thousands of Chicagoans fleeing the flames

of the city and carrying whatever possessions they could hold. Andreas, *History of Chicago*, 2:744, 754–55, and H.A. Musham, "The Great Chicago Fire, October 8–10, 1871," in *Papers in Illinois History and Transactions for the Year 1940* (Springfield: Illinois State Historical Society, 1941), 130–31, describe how, as the fire raged on and the heat became unbearable, many of those taking refuge had to go into the waters of the lake, up to their necks. On the augmentation, looking back just after the end of the nineteenth century, an especially close student of the Chicago lakefront (whom we meet at length in chapter 6) would say this of Kinzie's Addition in the period from 1886 to 1889: "This accretion had been in the main natural, but at various points had been undoubtedly artificially aided by the shore owners who (some of them at least) thought and had been advised that they were entitled to reclaim land from the lake without limit, save as to the risk of interfering with navigable water." Brown, "Shore of Lake Michigan," 10.

16. Kearney and Merrill, "Contested Shore," 1081, discuss the acreage.

17. Brown, "Shore of Lake Michigan," 19. Brown came to Chicago in 1872, where he established the law firm Peckham & Brown with a former Harvard Law School classmate. Later he was appointed attorney for the Lincoln Park Commission, where he had extensive involvement in lakefront matters. His lengthy address to the Law Club of the City of Chicago in 1902, recounting his version of these events, is an invaluable source. In 1903, he was elected a state court judge and was then appointed by the Illinois Supreme Court to the appellate division. Walter Nugent, "A Catholic Progressive? The Case of Judge E.O. Brown," *Journal of the Gilded Age and Progressive Era* 2 (2003): 12–13, 16–17, 33–34. Chapter 6 further discusses Brown and the lakefront.

18. A recent retelling, which helps sort out fact from fiction, is Wayne Klatt, *King of the Gold Coast: Cap'n Streeter, the Millionaires, and the Story of Lake Shore Drive* (Charleston, SC: History Press, 2011). See also Kearney and Merrill, "Contested Shore," 1082–90.

19. Everett Guy Ballard, *Captain Streeter: Pioneer* (Chicago: Emery, 1914), 214–15; Joshua Salzmann, "The Chicago Lakefront's Last Frontier: The Turnerian Mythology of Streeterville, 1886–1891," *Journal of Illinois History* 9 (2006): 204–6; Bill of Complaint of George Wellington Streeter, 8–12, Streeter v. Healy, No. 217933 (Cook Cnty. Super. Ct., Ill., Oct. 21, 1901); K.C. Tessendorf, "Captain Streeter's District of Lake Michigan," *Chicago History* 5 (1976): 157–58; Klatt, *King of the Gold Coast*, 75–76.

20. Salzmann, "Chicago Lakefront's Last Frontier," 207–8.

21. Klatt, *King of the Gold Coast*, 45–46; Brown, "Shore of Lake Michigan," 32–33; Salzmann, "Chicago Lakefront's Last Frontier," 208; "True Bills for Capt. Streeter," *Tribune*, Feb. 1, 1902. The versions vary somewhat.

22. For Streeter's claim, see John N. Low, "The Legacies of Turner, Cody, Streeter, and the Pokagon Potawatomi," in *Imprints: The Pokagon Band of Potawatomi Indians and the City of Chicago* (East Lansing: Michigan State University Press, 2016), 116; Bill of Complaint of George Wellington Streeter, 8, Streeter v. Healy, No. 217933 (Cook Cnty. Super. Ct., Ill., Oct. 21, 1901). On meander lines (and boundaries) generally, see Railroad Co. v. Schurmeir, 74 U.S. (7 Wall.) 272 (1869); Hardin v. Jordan, 140 U.S. 371 (1891); Walter G. Robillard and Donald A. Wilson, *Brown's Boundary Control and Legal Principles*, 7th ed. (Hoboken, NJ: John Wiley & Sons, 2014), § 9.8, 264–66.

23. In re George W. Streeter et al., 21 Pub. Lands Dec. 131, 133 (1895); Klatt, *King of the Gold Coast*, 31. Paul W. Gates, *History of Public Land Law Development* (Washington, DC: Public Land Law Review Commission, 1968), 281–83, provides an overview of the system in which, after the Civil War, Congress awarded certain homestead rights involving public lands to veterans.

24. For photographs of some of the structures, see Klatt, *King of the Gold Coast*, 26, 34, 59, 114; Tessendorf, "Captain Streeter's District," 153–54, 156; "Saga of Streeterville—A Forty Year Real Estate War," *Tribune*, Sept. 5, 1937.

25. Klatt, *King of the Gold Coast*, 58–59; Salzmann, "Chicago Lakefront's Last Frontier," 206–7; "He Stands by the Ship," *Tribune*, Sept. 10, 1890; "He Is a Modern Crusoe," *Tribune*, Nov. 7, 1891; Fairbank v. Streeter, 142 Ill. 226, 31 N.E. 494 (1892); Tessendorf, "Captain Streeter's District," 157–58; "The Fall of Streeterville," *Tribune*, Nov. 15, 1915; "'Ma' Streeter Fights On as the 'Cap'n' Dies," *Tribune*, Jan. 25, 1921. There is significant confusion about Streeter's various marriages, apparently four in number, and their status. Klatt seems to have sorted most of it out, and it is summarized in Kearney and Merrill, "Contested Shore," 1088.

26. "District Battle Ends in Murder," *Tribune*, Feb. 12, 1902; "Lay Murder to Streeter," *Tribune*, Feb. 28, 1902; Klatt, *King of the Gold Coast*, 100–103.

27. Salzmann, "Chicago Lakefront's Last Frontier," 207–8; "Chicago's 'Oasis' Raided by Police," *New York Times*, Nov. 15, 1915.

28. The first forcible-entry-and-detainer suit was the one brought by Fairbank, described above. Kearney and Merrill, "Contested Shore," 1089, describe the second, brought by Louisa Healy, the widow of the portrait artist George Healy. For other legal actions involving Streeter, see Klatt, *King of the Gold Coast*, 94, 99–102, 115.

29. 10 Stat. 745 (1853); 25 Stat. 1307 (1889); "To End M'Kee Scrip Case," *Tribune*, Nov. 22, 1896; "Plan to Secure Lake Front Acres," *Tribune*, Sep. 20, 1896; Brown, "Shore of Lake Michigan," 20. This was not the first time the McKee scrip had been mentioned with respect to the lakefront. After Congress's revision, "The M'kee Scrip," *Inter Ocean*, Aug. 25, 1889, maintained (quite vaguely) that the Illinois Central was negotiating to purchase the rights to the scrip and to use them with respect to the Chicago lakefront, presumably somewhere south of the river.

30. Brown, "Shore of Lake Michigan," 20–22; "One More on Lamoreux," *Tribune*, Mar. 11, 1897; *La Follette*, 26 Pub. Lands Dec. at 454–55; "Lake-Front Arguments Closed," *Tribune*, Nov. 26, 1896. Some renderings of Lamoreaux's name omit the second *a*.

31. Brown, "Shore of Lake Michigan," 22–23; "Says Benner Has Won," *Tribune*, Mar. 7, 1897; "May Be a Scandal," *Tribune*, Mar. 9, 1897.

32. On the general difficulty of securing judicial reversal of a Land Office decision, see Murray's Lessee v. Hoboken Land and Improvement Co., 59 U.S. (18 How.) 272, 284 (1856), noting that it had been "repeatedly decided" that the resolutions of claims to public lands by officers of the Land Office were "conclusive, either upon particular facts involved . . . or upon the whole title." Jerry L. Mashaw, "Reluctant Nationalists: Federal Administration and Administrative Law in the Republican Era, 1801–1829," *Yale Law Journal* 116 (2007): 1636–740, discusses the development of the General Land Office and the limited role of courts in adjudicating public land disputes in the nineteenth century. Courts began offering limited review later in the nineteenth century in cases alleging fraud or forgery, and even later for alleged errors of law. But whether such review would lie in any particular case continued to be a matter of uncertainty. Jerry L. Mashaw, "Federal Administration and Administrative Law in the Gilded Age," *Yale Law Journal*, 119 (2010): 1408–11.

33. Brown, "Shore of Lake Michigan," 23–24.

34. Brown, "Shore of Lake Michigan," 24–28.

35. Brown, "Shore of Lake Michigan," 27; "May Be a Scandal."

36. Brown, "Shore of Lake Michigan," 27–28; "A Land Office Scandal," *New York Times*, Mar. 14, 1897; "Lamoreux's Resignation Accepted," *Tribune*, Mar. 20, 1897.

37. "Decision against M'Kee Scrip Holders," *Tribune*, May 22, 1897; "Scrip Claim Thrown Out," *Chicago Daily News* (hereafter *Daily News*), May 26, 1897; *La Follette*, 26 Pub. Lands Dec. at 464–65, 474.

38. *La Follette*, 26 Pub. Lands Dec. at 473–74.

39. "In Real Estate Circles," *Tribune*, Oct. 13, 1901; "Deed Filed to Shore Land Held under a Scrip Claim," *Tribune*, July 25, 1902.

40. On the Potawatomi's inhabitation of the area, see Keating, *Rising Up from Indian Country*, 12–14. For the treaties, see Treaty with "United Nation of Chippewa, Ottowa, and Potawatamie Indians," Sept. 26, 1833, 7 Stat. 431; "Treaty with the Pottowautomie Nation," June 5 and 17, 1846, 9 Stat. 853. For background on the Indians' right of occupancy and, in particular, its extinguishment by the treaties under Johnson v. M'Intosh, 21 U.S. (8 Wheat.) 543 (1823), see Stuart Banner, *How the Indians Lost Their Land: Law and Power on the Frontier* (Cambridge, MA: Belknap Press of Harvard University Press, 2005), 178–88.

41. For background on the Catholic Potawatomi and specific details of Simon Pokagon and the Streeterville claim, see James A. Clifton, "Simon Pokagon's Sandbar," *Michigan History* 71 (Sept./Oct. 1987): 12–17. This is a "much revised excerpt" of a more accessible (but less detailed) account in James A. Clifton, *The Pokagons, 1683–1983: Catholic Potawatomi Indians of the St. Joseph River Valley* (Lanham, MD: University Press of America, 1984), 112–16. Cox may have assisted in forging the patent that Streeter used to dupe investors into buying lots in Streeter's "District." Brown, "Shore of Lake Michigan," 35–36.

42. Clifton, "Simon Pokagon's Sandbar," 16; Brown, "Shore of Lake Michigan," 35; "End of Pottawatomie Claims," *Tribune*, Mar. 9, 1900; "Indians' Claim to Lake Front," *Tribune*, Mar. 27, 1900; "End of Po-ka-gon Claim," *Tribune*, June 1, 1900.

43. Clifton, "Simon Pokagon's Sandbar," 16–17; "Cash or the Tomahawk; Red Men Prepare to Collect a Bill in Chicago," *Tribune*, Apr. 28, 1901; "Train to Fight Red Men," *Tribune*, Apr. 29, 1901; "Indian Invasion a Dream," *Tribune*, May 30, 1901.

44. "Indians Have No Title to Sell," *Tribune*, Jan. 21, 1902.

45. For the investigations, see *Chiperfield Committee Report*; *Report of Special Senate Committee*, 38th General Assembly (Ill. 1893), Illinois State Archives, Record Series 600.001 (hereafter *Bartling Committee Report*); "Lincoln Park Investigation," *Daily News*, May 13, 1893 (concerning Bartling Committee); *Biennial Report of the Attorney General to the Governor of Illinois* (1895) (hereafter *1895 Biennial Report*); "Mr. Moloney Smells a Land Grab," *Tribune*, Feb. 21, 1894 (attorney general investigation). Once the matter entered litigation in 1894 (in the *Kirk* case discussed later in this section), all riparian owners were represented by the Chicago Title & Trust Company, with the result that the precise identities of the owners were obscured from public view.

The riparian owners formed two associations. Henry N. Cooper appears to have had a role in each. In a biographical sketch, Cooper was said to have "formed the North Side Land Association, and the Pine Street Land Association, both of which have proved eminently successful." "Henry N. Cooper," in *The Biographical Dictionary and Portrait Gallery of Representative Men of Chicago, St. Louis and the World's Columbian Exposition* (Chicago: American Biographical, 1893), 675–76. A brief account of a land transaction on Chestnut Street in 1900 says that Cooper transferred the property to Louisa Healy through a court of equity based on a "decree of foreclosure against the North Side Land association," which would suggest that the association had legal title to land as far north as Chestnut Street. "Chicago Real Estate," *Tribune*, July 29, 1900. In his obituary, Cooper was identified as having been vice president and treasurer of "Fitzsimmons & Connell Co., contractors for public works." "Death Takes H.N. Cooper, Long in Realty Business," *Tribune*, Apr. 5, 1920. The preferred spelling of the company's leading principal appears to have been (Charles) Fitz Simons, although the last name even contemporaneously was rendered variously: as quoted in the foregoing newspaper piece, or as restated here but sometimes with a hyphen or without a space. Fitz Simons owned land in the Streeterville area and was the primary contractor for the Streeterville extension of Lake Shore Drive. John W. Stamper, "Shaping Chicago's Shoreline," *Chicago History* 14 (Winter 1985): 46–51.

46. 1869 Ill. Private Laws 1:368–79; I. J. Bryan, comp., *Report of the Commissioners and a History of Lincoln Park* (Chicago: Commissioners of Lincoln Park, 1899), 20–24.

47. Bryan, *History of Lincoln Park*, 13, 26–28, 60–64, 74–76; "The North Side; The Lake Shore Drive," *Tribune*, Sept. 26, 1870; 1869 Ill. Private Laws 1:372; Kearney and Merrill, "Contested Shore," 1097–98.

48. Thomas E. Tallmadge, *Architecture in Old Chicago* (Chicago: University of Chicago Press, 1941), 184–85; Paul Gilbert and Charles Lee Bryson, *Chicago and Its Makers* (Chicago: Felix Mendelsohn, 1929), 197–98; Bryan, *History of Lincoln Park*, 76; Bessie Louise Pierce, *A History of Chicago* (New York: Alfred A. Knopf, 1937), 3:59–60.

49. Klatt, *King of the Gold Coast*, 61–62.

50. Kearney and Merrill, "Contested Shore," 1099; Bryan, *History of Lincoln Park*, 90–91; "Many Piers on Shore," *Tribune*, Dec. 1, 1894.

51. *Bartling Committee Report*, 8.

52. *1895 Biennial Report*, 121–22; 1889 Ill. Laws 212–13.

53. Brown, "Shore of Lake Michigan," 12.

54. Brown, "Shore of Lake Michigan," 12–13; "Mr. Moloney Smells a Land Grab." Richard B. Fizdale, *999: A History of Chicago in Ten Stories* (Chicago: Ampersand, 2014), 51, discusses the three members of the commission.

55. Brown, "Shore of Lake Michigan," 14–16; Kearney and Merrill, "Contested Shore," 1103.

56. *Bartling Committee Report*, 7–9.

57. *1895 Biennial Report*, 122–23; Brown, "Shore of Lake Michigan," 16–18; Kearney and Merrill, "Contested Shore," 1104.

58. *Lake Front Case*, 146 U.S. 387, 455–56 (1892). For the acreage, see People ex rel. Moloney v. Kirk, 162 Ill. 138, 148, 45 N.E. 830, 833 (1896).

59. "May Push the Drive; Judge Windes Dismisses Moloney's North Shore Suit," *Tribune*, Jan. 31, 1895. In an aspect that would not be challenged on appeal, the judge also upheld the Lincoln Park Commissioners' plan to devote the land between Chicago Avenue and Pearson Street outside the city's water-pumping station for a public park, even though the city had not given its consent. The state was not required to compensate the city for this use of the land because, the judge said, "[p]ublic property belonging to a city not appropriated, used, or needed for any purpose may be devoted by the Legislature to some other public purpose within the city." This land today includes Seneca Park, a small playground to the immediate east of the pumping station, and the larger Lake Shore Park, farther to the east and abutting Lake Shore Drive. This was originally envisioned as one park, Chicago Avenue Park, but in 1926, in the area in between today's two parks, the state completed an armory, which in modern times has given way to the Museum of Contemporary Art (opened in 1996). Bryan, *History of Lincoln Park*, 13; Frank R. Schwengel, "The New Armory of the 122nd Field Artillery in Chicago," *Field Artillery Journal* 16 (Jan.–Feb. 1926): 1–6; "Art for Armory on Michigan Avenue," *Tribune*, May 12, 1988.

60. *Kirk*, 162 Ill. at 151, 45 N.E. at 834–35.

61. *Kirk*, 162 Ill. at 156–57, 45 N.E. at 836–37.

62. The north segment of the new drive (essentially Oak Street extended) was the last segment to be completed. The commissioners had agreed to fund this segment themselves, and it proved to be more expensive than contemplated. General Charles Fitz Simons, the contractor, also made a purported error resulting in the reclamation of more land there than the plan contemplated; in light of his owning land in the area, this generated more fodder for the legislative and judicial investigations. Klatt, *King of the Gold Coast*, 55, 60–64. The last small piece of the legal puzzle, involving a piece of land north of Oak Street, fell into place in early 1903. It was thereupon announced that the Potter Palmer

estate and other Streeterville property owners would proceed with their improvements—i.e., filling the submerged lands. "Park Commission Wins Lake Shore Drive Suit; . . . Opens Way for Completion of Street and Improvements," *Tribune*, Jan. 7, 1903.

63. Frank A. Randall, *History of the Development of Building Construction in Chicago* (Urbana: University of Illinois Press, 1949), 244, 252, 255, 260, 270; Fizdale, *999: A History of Chicago*, 19; Charles E. Hayes, "Streeterville Building, 68, to Be Reborn," *Tribune*, Feb. 10, 1985.

64. Klatt, *King of the Gold Coast*, 104–7, 111–15.

65. Klatt, *King of the Gold Coast*, 115–19; "'Cap' Streeter Turns Lawyer in Own Behalf," *Tribune*, Nov. 22, 1916.

66. Klatt, *King of the Gold Coast*, 120–22.

67. "'Ma' Streeter Sues for Cool $100,000,000," *Tribune*, May 27, 1924; "Judge Rules against 'Ma' Streeter's Claims," *Tribune*, Apr. 21, 1925.

68. Kearney and Merrill, "Contested Shore," 1109.

69. "Indians' Suit for Strip on Lake Front Rejected," *Tribune*, Mar. 19, 1914; Williams v. City of Chicago, 242 U.S. 434, 437 (1917).

70. *Chiperfield Committee Report*, 1:1, 6–12, 18.

71. *Chiperfield Committee Report*, 2:207, 211.

72. Burnham, *Plan of Chicago*, 64 (fig. 71), 99, 114–15 (embracing fig. 137). The southern pier was projected to be at 22nd Street.

73. Kearney and Merrill, "Contested Shore," 1112.

74. *Kirk*, 162 Ill. at 151, 45 N.E. at 835.

75. Quiet-title actions had been recognized in Illinois. See, e.g., Hardin v. Jones, 86 Ill. 313, 315–16 (1877).

76. Something like this strategy would work for the Illinois Central Railroad a half century later when it sought to develop the air rights above its landfill south of the river. See chapter 7.

77. Kearney and Merrill, "Contested Shore," 1116–18.

78. Indenture between Arthur L. and Katherine I. Farwell and Northwestern University (recorded July 13, 1920); Northwestern University board of trustees, minutes, 1920–21, meeting of Oct. 26, 1920, 14–17, and meeting of Sept. 29, 1920, 23–24; Indenture from Newberry Library to Northwestern University, July 1, 1927, Northwestern University Archives, Evanston, IL (hereafter cited as NUA). On the legal significance of warranty and quitclaim deeds, see Waterman Hall v. Waterman, 220 Ill. 569, 574, 77 N.E. 142, 144 (1906).

79. "Resolutions on Proposed Chicago Campus of Northwestern University," North Central Association, Apr. 30, 1920; "North Central Bulletin, Northwestern University Chicago Campus, To the Members of the North Central Association and Its Friends," May 5, 1920, NUA. For a broader sense of the North Central Association's activities, see John W. Stamper, *Chicago's North Michigan Avenue: Planning and Development, 1900–1930* (Chicago: University of Chicago Press, 1991), 21–27.

80. William R. Roalfe, *John Henry Wigmore: Scholar and Reformer* (Evanston, IL: Northwestern University Press, 1977), 155–58, 174–75; Kevin Leonard, "The Origins of Northwestern University's Chicago Campus—1915–1926" (unpublished paper, Northwestern University, June 1, 1976), 3–4, 10–14, NUA; Joseph D. Kearney and Thomas W. Merrill, "Private Rights in Public Lands: The Chicago Lakefront, Montgomery Ward, and the Public Dedication Doctrine," *Northwestern University Law Review* 105 (2011): 1465; Harold F. Williamson and Payson S. Wild, *Northwestern University: A History, 1850–1975* (Evanston, IL: Northwestern University Press, 1976), 146–55. On Elbert Gary, see "Ex-Gov. Miller May Succeed Gary; Steel Leader's Funeral to Be Held Thursday," *Tribune*, Aug. 16, 1927.

81. Elizabeth McNulty, *Chicago: Then and Now* (San Diego: Thunder Bay, 2000), 58; "The Drake," *Tribune*, Nov. 30, 1920; "News of Society; New Year's Parties Will Mark Formal Opening of Drake," *Tribune*, Dec. 8, 1920.

5. REVERSING THE CHICAGO RIVER

1. Wisconsin v. Illinois, 278 U.S. 367, 402 (1929); Louis P. Cain, "A Canal and Its City: A Selective Business History of Chicago," *DePaul Business Law Journal* 11 (1998): 126–27; Bessie Louise Pierce, *A History of Chicago* (New York: Alfred A. Knopf, 1937), 1:6–9; Libby Hill, *The Chicago River: A Natural and Unnatural History*, rev. ed. (Carbondale: Southern Illinois University Press, 2019), 9–10.

2. 15 Annals of Cong. 1677–78 (1854) (reflecting 1818 amendment of statehood bill in House of Representatives); Hill, *Chicago River*, 47–50; James E. Davis, *Frontier Illinois* (Bloomington: Indiana University Press, 1998), 162; Caroline M. McIlvaine, introduction to *The Autobiography of Gurdon Saltonstall Hubbard* (Chicago: Lakeside, 1911), xix–xx. For the correct mileage, which is often understated, see David W. Scott, "Setting the Northern Border of Illinois," *Journal of the Illinois State Historical Society* 111 (Fall 2018): 9–11, 15–17, 31.

3. Cain, "Canal and Its City," 137, 142; Hill, *Chicago River*, 51–53; Joshua A.T. Salzmann, *Liquid Capital: Making the Chicago Waterfront* (Philadelphia: University of Pennsylvania Press, 2018), 39.

4. Peter L. Bernstein, *Wedding of the Waters: The Erie Canal and the Making of a Great Nation* (New York: W. W. Norton, 2005), 31, 327–28; William Cronon, *Nature's Metropolis: Chicago and the Great West* (New York: W.W. Norton, 1991), 60–61, 153–55, 320, 377.

5. Hill, *Chicago River*, 54, 59, 64–70, 100. Examples of adjudicated disputes of the sort mentioned in the text include City of Chicago v. Laflin, 49 Ill. 172 (1868); McClean v. Mathews, 7 Ill. App. 599 (1880); and City of Chicago v. Van Ingen, 152 Ill. 624, 38 N.E. 894 (1894).

6. A. T. Andreas, *History of Chicago* (Chicago: A. T. Andreas, 1884), 2:63; Hill, *Chicago River*, 68–69.

7. On the commerce clause, see Gibbons v. Ogden, 22 U.S. (9 Wheat) 1 (1824), and Pennsylvania v. Wheeling and Belmont Bridge Co., 54 U.S. (13 How.) 518 (1852); see generally Robert W. Adler, "The Ancient Mariner of Constitutional Law: The Historical, Yet Declining Role of Navigability," *Washington University Law Review* 90 (2013): 1643–706. The phrase "tragedy of the commons" was popularized by Garrett Hardin, "The Tragedy of the Commons," *Science* 162 (1968): 1243–48. Russell Hardin, *Collective Action* (Baltimore: Johns Hopkins University Press, 1982), 16–37, explains the tragedy of the commons as a prisoner's dilemma.

8. Hill, *Chicago River*, 64–65, 68–69; Salzmann, *Liquid Capital*, 21–22.

9. Pierce, *History of Chicago*, 3:155–60; Hill, *Chicago River*, 69; Salzmann, *Liquid Capital*, 92; Harold M. Mayer, "Current Trends in Great Lakes Shipping," *GeoJournal* 2 (1978): 118.

10. John W. Larson, *Those Army Engineers: A History of the Chicago District U.S. Army Corps of Engineers* (Chicago: US Army Corps of Engineers, 1979), 199; Elliott Flower, "Chicago's Great River-Harbor," *Century Magazine* 63 (1902): 487; Salzmann, *Liquid Capital*, 106–9; Hill, *Chicago River*, 226.

11. On the decomposition of organic matter and organic pollution in streams, see P. D. Abel, *Water Pollution Biology*, 2nd ed. (London: Taylor & Francis, 1996), 35–41.

12. "Cleaning the City—Cholera. &c.," *Gem of the Prairie*, Aug. 21, 1850; see Donald L. Miller, *City of the Century: The Epic of Chicago and the Making of America* (New York: Simon & Schuster, 1996), 122–24, for a discussion of the sewage and cholera and other

epidemics in Chicago and the reference to "death fogs." For the death toll statistic, see "Chicago's Quest for Pure Water," *Chicago Tribune* (hereafter *Tribune*), Jan. 2, 1900, and for a history of germ theory, Mervyn Susser and Zena Stein, "Germ Theory, Infection, and Bacteriology," chap. 10 in *Eras in Epidemiology: The Evolution of Ideas* (New York: Oxford University Press, 2009), 107–22.

13. 1855 Ill. Private Laws 93–108; Miller, *City of the Century*, 124–25; Louis P. Cain, "Raising and Watering a City: Ellis Sylvester Chesbrough and Chicago's First Sanitation System," *Technology and Culture* 13 (1972): 355–58.

14. Miller, *City of the Century*, 124; Board of Sewerage Commissioners, *Report and Plan of Sewerage for the City of Chicago* (1855), 15–17, 20; Louis P. Cain, *Sanitation Strategy for a Lakefront Metropolis: The Case of Chicago* (DeKalb: Northern Illinois University Press, 1978), 26–29; Robin L. Einhorn, *Property Rules: Political Economy in Chicago, 1833–1872* (Chicago: University of Chicago Press, 1991), 141.

15. Andreas, *History of Chicago*, 1:193; Cain, *Sanitation Strategy*, 29–30; Liston Edgington Leyendecker, *Palace Car Prince: A Biography of George Mortimer Pullman* (Niwot: University Press of Colorado, 1992), 31–35; Joseph Kirkland, *The Story of Chicago* (Chicago: Dibble, 1892), 231–33; Miller, *City of the Century*, 125–26.

16. Cain, *Sanitation Strategy*, 37–43; Carl Smith, *City Water, City Life* (Chicago: University of Chicago Press, 2013), 40.

17. Smith, *City Water*, 41–43.

18. Smith, *City Water*, 43–47; Cain, *Sanitation Strategy*, 46–47.

19. Andreas, *History of Chicago*, 2:68–69.

20. Smith, *City Water*, 50–51, 231. Most of the water-intake cribs had been built in Lake Michigan by 1915, and the most recent was constructed in 1935. See George A. Soper, John D. Watson, and Arthur J. Martin, *A Report to the Chicago Real Estate Board on the Disposal of the Sewage and Protection of the Water Supply of Chicago, Illinois* (1915), 52; John F. Hogan, "Carousels in the Lake," chap. 7 in *The Chicago Water Tower* (Charleston, SC: History Press, 2019), giving some history about each of the cribs and identifying the active two.

21. Concerning the stockyards and Bubbly Creek, see Upton Sinclair, *The Jungle* (New York: Doubleday, Page, 1906), 112; Miller, *City of the Century*, 116–17, 198–208; Patrick T. Reardon, "A Stagnant Symbol of the Stockyards Waits Its Turn for Revival," *Tribune*, June 27, 1999.

22. Cain, *Sanitation Strategy*, 26; Miller, *City of the Century*, 129–30; Smith, *City Water*, 236.

23. Miller, *City of the Century*, 131; Hill, *Chicago River*, 93–94; Andreas, *History of Chicago*, 3:135; Citizens' Association of Chicago, *Report of the Committee on the Main Drainage and Water Supply* (1885), 7, 10–11; Harold L. Platt, *Shock Cities: The Environmental Transformation and Reform of Manchester and Chicago* (Chicago: University of Chicago Press, 2005), 187.

24. Miller, *City of the Century*, 131; "Sanitary," *Tribune*, July 16, 1879; Louis P. Cain, "The Creation of Chicago's Sanitary District and Construction of the Sanitary and Ship Canal," *Chicago History* 8 (1979): 98; Ernest Bruncken, "The Chicago Water Diversion," *Marquette Law Review* 13 (1929): 191–92.

25. For original accounts or references to the 1885 events, see "And a Flood Came," *Tribune*, Aug. 3, 1885, and Cain, "Creation of Chicago's Sanitary District," 98–99. For recent revisionism, see Libby Hill, "The Making of an Urban Legend," *Tribune*, July 29, 2007, and "Chicago's Legendary Epidemic," *Tribune*, Aug. 22, 2007, calling the story of an 1885 epidemic "a fiction" that was "concocted [in the twentieth century] to sell the public on a Chicago-area flood control scheme." For the growing acceptance of the germ theory in Chicago, see Platt, *Shock Cities*, 381–89. Richard Shelton Kirby, Sidney Withington,

Arthur Burr Darling, and Frederick Gridley Kilgour, *Engineering in History* (New York: McGraw-Hill, 1956), 429–30, summarize the more general acceptance of germ theory and bacteriology and their use in sanitation from the late 1850s to the 1880s and into the early twentieth century.

26. *Report of the Committee on the Main Drainage and Water Supply*, 12–17; Richard Lanyon, *Building the Canal to Save Chicago* (Chicago: Lake Claremont, 2016), 4–9; Cain, "Creation of Chicago's Sanitary District," 99–102; 1887 Ill. Laws 314–15; Hill, *Chicago River*, 96–98.

27. 1889 Ill. Laws 125–137; Cain, "Creation of Chicago's Sanitary District," 102; Hill, *Chicago River*, 99. Lanyon, *Building the Canal*, 15–17, summarizes a number of the act's details.

28. Ill. Const. of 1870, art. IX, § 12; 1889 Ill. Laws 130; Cain, "Creation of Chicago's Sanitary District," 102.

29. J. Seymour Currey, *Chicago: Its History and Its Builders* (Chicago: S.J. Clarke, 1912), 3:113.

30. Cain, "Creation of Chicago's Sanitary District," 102–3; State of Illinois, Department of Public Works and Buildings, Division of Waterways, *Documentary History of the Illinois and Michigan Canal: Legislation, Litigation and Titles* (1956), 152; Hill, *Chicago River*, 104; Lanyon, *Building the Canal*, 19–36.

31. Cain, "Creation of Chicago's Sanitary District," 103–5; Lanyon, *Building the Canal*, 39–219.

32. Department of Commerce and Labor, Bureau of Statistics, *Monthly Summary of Commerce and Finance of the United States* (Washington, DC: Department of Commerce and Labor, 1905), 7:2379. "Turn the River into Big Canal," *Tribune*, Jan. 3, 1900, similarly noted that "the people of Chicago have expended upwards of $33,000,000."

33. House Committee on Foreign Affairs, *Diversion of Water from the Great Lakes and Niagara River: Letter from the Secretary of War* (Washington, DC, 1921), 180; Cain, *Sanitation Strategy*, 73–80; 26 Stat. 426, 454 (1890).

34. Cain, *Sanitation Strategy*, 76–80. For the text of the secretary of war's permit, see Lyman E. Cooley, *The Diversion of the Waters of the Great Lakes by Way of Chicago: A Brief of the Facts and Issues* (Chicago: Sanitary District of Chicago, 1913), 210–11, collecting a number of other primary documents as well.

35. Cain, "Creation of Chicago's Sanitary District," 108–9.

36. Wyatt Winton Belcher, *The Economic Rivalry between St. Louis and Chicago, 1850–1880* (New York: Columbia University Press, 1947), provides a general economic history of earlier years. From the beginning, the canal had been promoted for its ability to handle large boats. Wisconsin v. Illinois, 278 U.S. 367, 403 (1929).

37. "New War on Drainage Canal; City of St. Louis Now Seeking to Prevent the Operation of the Chicago Enterprise," *Tribune*, Oct. 29, 1898; Louis P. Cain, "Unfouling the Public's Nest: Chicago's Sanitary Diversion of Lake Michigan Water," *Technology and Culture* 15 (1974): 602; "The Report of the St. Louis Commission on the Chicago Drainage Canal," *Engineering News and American Railway Journal* 41 (1899): 270–73; Cain, "Creation of Chicago's Sanitary District," 109.

38. H.G. Wood, *A Treatise on the Limitation of Actions at Law and in Equity* (Boston: Soule & Bugbee, 1883), 1:121–25.

39. "Turn the River into Big Canal"; Lanyon, *Building the Canal*, 335.

40. 1889 Ill. Laws 136–37; Hill, *Chicago River*, 111–12; Cain, "Creation of Chicago's Sanitary District," 110; Lanyon, *Building the Canal*, 329–38.

41. On the economics of competitions to capture open-access resources, see Dean Lueck, "The Rule of First Possession and the Design of the Law," *Journal of Law & Economics* 38 (1995): 393–436. For the possibility that even the winner will spend more than

the prize is worth, see Gordon Tullock, "Efficient Rent Seeking," in *Toward a Theory of the Rent-Seeking Society*, ed. James M. Buchanan, Robert D. Tollison, and Gordon Tullock (College Station: Texas A&M University Press, 1980), 97–112.

42. Missouri v. Illinois, 180 U.S. 208, 209–16 (1901) (statement of the case) (hereafter *Missouri Jurisdictional Decision*).

43. *Missouri Jurisdictional Decision*, 180 U.S. at 216–18 (statement of the case). Article III, section 2, is the relevant provision of the US Constitution.

44. *Missouri Jurisdictional Decision*, 180 U.S. at 218–41.

45. *Missouri Jurisdictional Decision*, 180 U.S. at 241.

46. *Missouri Jurisdictional Decision*, 180 U.S. at 242. See Thomas W. Merrill, "Golden Rules for Transboundary Pollution," *Duke Law Journal* 46 (1997): 937–41, concerning the *Missouri v. Illinois* decision and the principle of attribution. The court's determination that both Missouri and Illinois were proper parties meant not only that it could hear the case but also that no other court could do so. Congress always has provided, from section 13 of the Judiciary Act of 1789 to the current statute at 28 U.S.C. § 1251, that the Supreme Court's original jurisdiction involving states is of two types: suits involving a state and a nonstate party from elsewhere fall within the court's original jurisdiction that is concurrent with that of other courts, but suits between two or more states fall within the court's exclusive original jurisdiction.

47. *Missouri Jurisdictional Decision*, 180 U.S. at 245–49; Steven J. Burian, Stephan J. Nix, Robert E. Pitt, and S. Rocky Durrans, "Urban Wastewater Management in the United States: Past, Present, and Future," *Journal of Urban Technology* 7, no. 3 (2000): 46–51.

48. *Missouri Jurisdictional Decision*, 180 U.S. at 249–50 (Fuller, C.J., dissenting).

49. Robert V. Percival, "The Clean Water Act and the Demise of the Federal Common Law of Interstate Nuisance," *Alabama Law Review* 55 (2004): 724.

50. Richard Craswell, "When Nicknames Were Crowdsourced: Or, How to Change a Team's Mascot," *Stanford Law Review* 67 (2015): 1249–50.

51. Percival, "Clean Water Act," 724.

52. Missouri v. Illinois, 200 U.S. 496, 503, 510 (1906) (argument for complainant) (hereafter *Missouri Merits Decision*). For a contemporaneous account of some of the scientific examination, largely supporting Illinois's position, see "Chicago Drainage Canal and the City of St. Louis," *Scientific American* 88 (1903): 464.

53. *Missouri Merits Decision*, 200 U.S. at 510, 513 (argument for defendants); *id.* at 525–26 (decision of the court).

54. *Missouri Jurisdictional Decision*, 180 U.S. at 248; *Missouri Merits Decision*, 200 U.S. at 518, 522–24.

55. *Missouri Merits Decision*, 200 U.S. at 518, 524–25. Given the speed with which it rendered a decision, it is doubtful that the justices delved deeply into the voluminous record. Indeed, his evident fascination notwithstanding, Holmes seemed to say as much: "We have studied the plaintiff's statement of the facts in detail and have perused the evidence, but it is unnecessary for the purposes of decision to do more than give the general result in a simple way." *Id.* at 522.

56. *Missouri Merits Decision*, 200 U.S. at 521–22, 526.

57. *Missouri Merits Decision*, 200 U.S. at 515 (argument for defendants, stating these maxims); Merrill, "Golden Rules," 998, 1004. In New York v. New Jersey, 256 U.S. 296, 309–10, 313 (1921), the court held that New York had failed to meet its burden of showing that New Jersey's discharge of sewage into New York Bay was a public nuisance, in part because New York City for many years had been discharging raw sewage into the bay.

58. Cain, "Unfouling the Public's Nest," 602–3. Chicago, by contrast, experimented with water filtration only in the late 1920s, and its first major plant opened after World War II. Oscar Hewitt, "Test Filtration to Give South Side Pure Water," *Tribune*, Feb. 20,

1928; Louis P. Cain, "Sanitation in Chicago: A Strategy for a Lakefront Metropolis," Encyclopedia of Chicago, accessed Aug. 3, 2020, http://www.encyclopedia.chicagohistory.org/pages/300017.html. Chapter 8 takes up the legal challenge to the large filtration plant that Chicago built on landfill in Lake Michigan just north of Navy Pier in the 1950s.

59. Jon C. Teaford, *The Unheralded Triumph: City Government in America, 1870–1900* (Baltimore: Johns Hopkins University Press, 1984), 2–3, 66–80, 217.

60. "Water in Chicago River; Since the Canal Was Opened the Stream Begins to Move," *New York Times*, Jan. 14, 1900; Cain, "Creation of Chicago's Sanitary District," 110. Platt, *Shock Cities*, 377, gives an 1885–1914 table showing typhoid fever in Chicago and the drop in the number of deaths and in the mortality rate after 1903.

61. For a look at this general time period, see Virginia M. Harding, "Burnham, Water, and the *Plan of Chicago*: A Historical Explanation of Why Water Was Ignored and the Consequences of Ignoring Water," *John Marshall Law Review* 43 (2010): 413–37.

62. Cain, "Creation of Chicago's Sanitary District," 105–6; Herbert H. Naujoks, "The Chicago Water Diversion Controversy" (pt. 3), *Marquette Law Review* 31 (1947): 49; Cain, *Sanitation Strategy*, 87–88; Frank Millerd, "Global Climate Change and Great Lakes International Shipping" (prepared for the Committee on the St. Lawrence Seaway: Options to Eliminate Introduction of Nonindigenous Species into the Great Lakes, Phase 2, May 2007), 2–11 (section titled "The Impact of Lower Water Levels on Commercial Navigation").

63. Sanitary District of Chicago v. United States, 266 U.S. 405, 429–32 (1925) (Holmes, J., for the court); Wisconsin v. Illinois, 278 U.S. 367, 399–400, 409, 419–21 (1929) (Taft, C.J., for the court), and 281 U.S. 179, 199, 201 (1930) (Holmes, J., for the court).

64. Wisconsin v. Illinois, 289 U.S. 395, 398–99 (1933), and 388 U.S. 426, 427, 430 (1967); Martin Doyle, *The Source: How Rivers Made America and America Remade Its Rivers* (New York: W. W. Norton, 2018), 193. The court also ordered modifications in 1956, on an emergency basis (a diversion up to 8,500 CFS as determined by the Army Corps of Engineers), 352 U.S. 945, 946 (1956), and in 1980, with respect to the procedure for determining whether Illinois was diverting more or less water than allowed by the 1967 modification. 449 U.S. 48 (1980). Bruce Barker, "Lake Diversion at Chicago," *Case Western Reserve Journal of International Law* 18 (1986): 203–18, provides a helpful discussion of the physical and operational aspects of the diversion as it then existed under the court's decrees.

65. "The Great Lakes Charter: Principles for the Management of Great Lakes Water Resources," Council of Great Lakes Governors, Feb. 11, 1985, https://digitalcommons.unl.edu/cgi/viewcontent.cgi?article=1000&context=lawwater; Water Resources Development Act of 1986, § 1109(d), 100 Stat. 4231 (codified as amended at 42 U.S.C. § 1962d-20(d) (2018)).

66. Peter Annin, *The Great Lakes Water Wars*, rev. ed. (Washington, DC: Island, 2018), 63, 74–83.

67. Annin, *Great Lakes Water Wars*, 78, 82, 221–43; Daniel A. Injerd, "Managing Great Lakes Water Diversions: A Diversion Manager's Viewpoint," *Buffalo Environmental Law Journal* 1 (1993): 299. Kenneth Kilbert, Aubrey Merkle, and Forrest Miller, *An Assessment of the Great Lakes States' Implementation of the Water Management and Conservation Provisions of the Great Lakes–St. Lawrence River Basin Water Resources Compact* (University of Toledo College of Law's Legal Institute of the Great Lakes, Oct. 2019), 7–87 and appendix, reproduce the 2005 compact and summarize each state's implementing legislation (with citations) and its subsequent implementation progress. The individual statutory enactments by the states followed their own various numbering conventions and have included minor substantive variations. The federal approval was the Great Lakes–St. Lawrence River Basin Water Resources Compact, Pub. L. No. 110–342, 122 Stat. 3739 (2008).

68. Annin, *Great Lakes Water Wars*, 223–24. In the federal approval cited above, this provision can be found in section 4.14, 122 Stat. 3757–58.

69. Elinor Ostrom, *Governing the Commons: The Evolution of Institutions for Collective Action* (Cambridge: Cambridge University Press, 1990), 15–21. Adopting a unanimous-consent requirement to permit diversion of a resource such as the Great Lakes effectively creates what Michael Heller calls an "anticommons," in which anyone can block anyone else from engaging in a use of the resource. The predictable result is underconsumption. Michael Heller, "The Tragedy of the Anticommons," chap. 1 in *The Gridlock Economy: How Too Much Ownership Wrecks Markets, Stops Innovation, and Costs Lives* (New York: Basic Books, 2008).

70. The Clean Water Act was first enacted as the Federal Water Pollution Control Act Amendments of 1972, Pub. L. 92–500, 86 Stat. 816.

71. Dan Egan, *The Death and Life of the Great Lakes* (New York: W.W. Norton, 2017), 164–81.

72. Annin, *Great Lakes Water Wars*, 99. In the two editions of his book, the author tells the long saga of a proposed diversion by Waukesha, Wisconsin, and notes that its effect on the level of the lakes would be "imperceptible," as it would take one hundred such diversions to equal the volume of the Chicago diversion. "As with prior diversion controversies," he notes in the first edition, "what Waukesha's critics worried about was precedent." Peter Annin, *Great Lakes Water Wars* (Washington, DC: Island, 2006), 240–55; see also Annin, *Great Lakes Water Wars*, 288–95. The Great Lakes–St. Lawrence River Basin Water Resources Council (commonly known as the Compact Council) approved Waukesha's diversion request in 2016. Great Lakes–St. Lawrence River Basin Water Resources Council, *Final Decision in the Application by the City of Waukesha, Wisconsin, for a Diversion of Great Lakes Water from Lake Michigan and an Exception to Allow the Diversion* (June 21, 2016); Egan, *Great Lakes*, 275–76.

73. It has been suggested that if the Asian carp should succeed in breaching the electronic barrier and colonizing the Great Lakes via the Chicago diversion, public pressure to re-reverse the Chicago River could mount. A 2014 study by the Army Corps of Engineers estimated that doing so—including modifying Chicago's sewer system, constructing new wastewater treatment plants, and enhancing capacity to collect stormwater runoff—would require $18 billion and many years to complete. Egan, *Great Lakes*, 309. Without federal funding, it is inconceivable that Illinois would agree to take on this burden.

6. NORTH LAKE SHORE DRIVE

1. Joseph W. Dellapenna, "The Scope of Riparian Rights," § 6.01 in *Waters and Water Rights*, ed. Amy L. Kelly, 3rd ed. (New Providence, NJ: LexisNexis/Matthew Bender, 2011), 1:6-4 to 6-7, 6-63; Frank Emerson Clark, "Riparian Rights a Valuable Appurtenant," chap. 14, § 314, in *A Treatise on the Law of Surveying and Boundaries* (Indianapolis: Bobbs-Merrill, 1922), 334; Stop the Beach Renourishment, Inc. v. Florida Department of Environmental Protection, 560 U.S. 702, 713 (2010); Leitch v. Sanitary District of Chicago, 369 Ill. 469, 475, 17 N.E.2d 34, 36–37 (1938).

2. I. J. Bryan, comp., *Report of the Commissioners and a History of Lincoln Park* (Chicago: Commissioners of Lincoln Park, 1899), 13, 26–28, 74–76, discusses the creation of the park district, the construction of the original Lake Shore Drive inside the park, and the opening of the original extension of the drive to the south, and chapter 4 of this book notes the last of these, including the 1869 enabling statute. The 1889 legislation authorizing extensions of the drive and conveyance of submerged land west of the drive, also discussed in chapter 4, was one act. 1889 Ill. Laws 212–13. Another act, passed at the same time, transferred to the Lincoln Park Commission submerged land to be used for

constructing the drive, such land "to be held for the use and benefit of the public as a part of said park and for no other purpose whatever." 1889 Ill. Laws 214.

3. 1895 Ill. Laws 282–84.

4. 1895 Ill. Laws 284. See Robin L. Einhorn, *Property Rules: Political Economy in Chicago, 1833–1872* (Chicago: University of Chicago Press, 1991), 91–94, for a general introduction to opposition in Chicago to special assessments, and *Report of the Commissioners of Lincoln Park from April 1, 1896, to March 31, 1897* (1897), 7–9, for a more specific, nearer-in-time sense, in the context of the Streeterville extension of Lake Shore Drive. Examples of the later legislation concerning bond issuances can be found at 1911 Ill. Laws 433–34; 1915 Ill. Laws 537–38; 1925 Ill. Laws 485–87; and 1929 Ill. Laws 567–69.

5. *Report of the Submerged and Shore Lands Legislative Investigating Committee* (Springfield, IL, 1911) (hereafter *Chiperfield Committee Report*), 2:212–13, 220.

6. 1903 Ill. Laws 260–61 (emphasis added); *Chiperfield Committee Report*, 2:213, 220–28.

7. *Chiperfield Committee Report*, 2:212–28.

8. Atlee v. Packet Co., 88 U.S. (21 Wall.) 389, 393 (1875).

9. See generally Henry P. Farnham, *The Law of Waters and Water Rights* (Rochester, NY: Lawyers Cooperative, 1904), 1:525–26, 533–34.

10. The three decisions and discussions are reported, respectively, at 66 U.S. (1 Black) 23, 32–33 (1861); 74 U.S. (7 Wall.) 272, 289 (1869); and 77 U.S. (10 Wall.) 497, 503–4 (1871).

11. Ensminger v. People ex rel. Trover, 47 Ill. 384, 392 (1868); City of Chicago v. Laflin, 49 Ill. 172, 176–77 (1868). For such later decisions, see City of Chicago v. Reed, 27 Ill. App. 482, 486 (1888), and City of Chicago v. Van Ingen, 152 Ill. 624, 631–35, 38 N.E. 894, 895–97 (1894).

12. *Lake Front Case*, 33 F. 730, 755–58 (C.C.N.D. Ill. 1888). As discussed in chapter 2, Harlan also relied on provisions of the Illinois Central's original 1851 charter, allowing it to use, among other things, all "lands" and "streams" of the state to build any ancillary facilities necessary for railroad operations. This interpretation of the charter was soon rejected by the Illinois Supreme Court in the 1898 *IC Charter Case*, described in chapter 8.

13. *Lake Front Case*, 146 U.S. 387, 445–46 (1892) (citation omitted).

14. Recall Middleton v. Pritchard, 4 Ill. 509 (3 Scam. 510), 519–22 (1842), discussed in chapter 1, for riparian ownership of the riverbed. On the revocability of licenses, see, e.g., Marrone v. Washington Jockey Club, 227 U.S. 633, 636–37 (1913); Wood v. Leadbitter, 153 Eng. Rep. (Exch.) 351, 354–55, 13 M. & W. 838, 844–45 (1845); and Brooks v. Chicago Downs Association, Inc., 791 F.2d 512 (7th Cir. 1986), which interprets Illinois law. Alfred E. McCordic and Wilson G. Crosby, "The Right of Access and the Right to Wharf Out to Navigable Water," *Harvard Law Review* 4 (1890): 21, note disagreement among courts, when riparian ownership extends only to the edge of the water, as to whether the right to wharf out is a license, a means of exercising the right of access, or an independent right of property.

15. Edward O. Brown, "The Shore of Lake Michigan, A Paper Read before the Law Club of the City of Chicago," Apr. 25, 1902, 40–41, CHM. See also Edward Osgood Brown, "Chicago's Lake Shore," *Chicago Tribune* (hereafter *Tribune*), Oct. 1, 1909.

16. Shively v. Bowlby, 152 U.S. 1, 18–28, 36–37, 46–47, 57–58 (1894).

17. The 1890 act provided that "the creation of any obstruction, not affirmatively authorized by law, to the navigable capacity of any waters, in respect of which the United States has jurisdiction, is hereby prohibited." 26 Stat. 426, 454 (1890).

18. Brown, "Shore of Lake Michigan," 40–41; Information, People v. Revell, No. 145480 (Cook Cnty. Cir. Ct., Ill., summons issued July 23, 1895); Revell v. People, 177 Ill. 468, 469–70, 52 N.E. 1052, 1053 (1898); Gordon v. Winston, 181 Ill. 338, 54 N.E. 1095

(1899). From the beginning of the *Revell* case to the end, Brown was listed as co-counsel along with the attorney general and unquestionably led the development of the arguments presented. By the time of *Gordon* and subsequent cases, title to the submerged land had passed from the state to the Lincoln Park Commissioners under the terms of the 1895 legislation authorizing the extension of Lake Shore Drive. So the lawsuit could be brought in the names of the commissioners (Frederick H. Winston et al.). See 1895 Ill. Laws 283 for the condition of the passage of title and *Revell*, 177 Ill. at 471–72, 52 N.E. at 1054, for its satisfaction in late 1895 by the promulgation of a park plan.

19. Gordon's brief did little more than argue that the state's demand to tear down his wharf was unreasonable in the absence of any showing that it was a public nuisance. See Brief and Argument for Appellant, 8–9, *Gordon*. The Lincoln Park Commissioners filed two briefs in response, one of them by Brown. The list of authorities in this filing and its references to and extensive quotations from Brown's joint brief with the attorney general in *Revell* suggest that that earlier brief (now lost) was an impressive effort. See Brief and Argument for Appellees, 3–15 (the one filed by Brown), *Gordon*. Brown and his partner had previously authored several exhaustive research memoranda for the Lincoln Park Commission discussing title to the lakebed and riparian rights and published them as a monograph. Edward O. Brown and George Packard, *Rights of the State and of Shore Owners in, to and over the Submerged Lands of Lake Michigan in Illinois* (1896). This research undoubtedly provided the foundation for the brief in *Revell*.

20. *Revell*, 177 Ill. at 478–83, 52 N.E. at 1055–57.

21. Matthew Hale, who wrote in the seventeenth century but whose work was published only in the eighteenth, is commonly credited with legitimizing the theory that the king held prima facie title to lands overflowed by the tides. Lord Matthew Hale, "De Jure Maris et Brachiorum Ejusdem," in *A Collection of Tracts Relative to the Law of England, from Manuscripts*, vol. 1, ed. Francis Hargrave (Dublin: E. Lynch et al., 1787), 5–6. Later research by Stuart A. Moore, *A History of the Foreshore and the Law Relating Thereto* [. . .], 3rd ed. (London: Stevens & Haynes, 1888), called Hale's account into question. Farnham, *Law of Waters*, 1:182–86, 209–10, and William R. Tillinghast, "Tide-Flowed Lands and Riparian Rights in the United States," *Harvard Law Review* 18 (1905): 345–50, lay out these matters. While both were published (shortly) after *Revell*, the more careful treatises among those cited by the court pointed toward arrentment, not abatement, unless the wharf was a nuisance. See, for example, the very quotation by *Revell*, 177 Ill. at 480–81, 52 N.E. at 1056, of Robert Henley Eden, *A Compendium of the Law and Practice of Injunctions, and of Interlocutory Orders in the Nature of Injunctions*, 3rd ed. (New York: Banks, Gould, 1852), chap. 11, 2:259-1 to 260-1. Finally, on advance approval: generally, see Farnham, *Law of Waters*, 1:528, 532; and for documentation of the process, in the treatises cited by *Revell*, see H. J. W. Coulson and Urquhart A. Forbes, *The Law Relating to Waters, Sea, Tidal, and Inland* (London: Henry Sweet, 1880), 421–22; John M. Gould, *A Treatise on the Law of Waters*, 2nd ed. (Chicago: Callaghan, 1891), 47–48.

22. We discuss the first premise's underlying concepts—the English common-law rule concerning title to submerged land and its modification in the United States, including Illinois—in chapter 1. The basis of *Revell*'s second premise was an enactment by the first Illinois legislature, in 1819, generally declaring that the common law of England as of 1606 governed "until repealed by legislative authority." The current version, scarcely changed, can be found at 5 Ill. Comp. Stat. Ann. 50/1 (West 2013). See generally Ford W. Hall, "The Common Law: An Account of Its Reception in the United States," *Vanderbilt Law Review* 4 (1951): 791–825.

23. *Revell*, 177 Ill. at 484–89, 52 N.E. at 1057–59.

24. *Revell*, 177 Ill. at 486, 52 N.E. at 1058; *Gordon*, 181 Ill. at 340, 54 N.E. at 1095.

25. *Revell*, 177 Ill. at 479, 488–89, 52 N.E. at 1056, 1059.

26. "Cobb to Fight to Build Pier," *Tribune*, Feb. 18, 1900; Cobb v. Commissioners of Lincoln Park, 202 Ill. 427, 427–28, 67 N.E. 5, 6 (1903). The Lincoln Park Commission maintained that the effect of Cobb's piers had been to induce accretion. Brief and Argument for Appellee, 19, *Cobb*.

27. Brief and Argument for Appellant, 13–112, and Brief and Argument for Appellee, Lincoln Park Commissioners, 13–71, *Cobb*; *Cobb*, 202 Ill. at 435–37, 67 N.E. at 8.

28. Concerning judicial takings in this context, see the opinions of various justices, none commanding a majority of the court in this regard, in Stop the Beach Renourishment, Inc. v. Florida Department of Environmental Protection, 560 U.S. 702 (2010). Barton H. Thompson Jr., "Judicial Takings," *Virginia Law Review* 76 (1990): 1449–1544, gives an introduction and overview, and D. Benjamin Barros, "The Complexities of Judicial Takings," *University of Richmond Law Review* 45 (2011): 903–60, and Laura S. Underkuffler, "Judicial Takings: A Medley of Misconceptions," *Syracuse Law Review* 61 (2011): 203–12, are among those providing commentary after *Stop the Beach Renourishment*.

29. Justice Field's opinion in the *Lake Front Case* distinguished between small grants of submerged lands for purposes of constructing wharves, piers, and other aids to navigation, which he indicated were permissible, and large grants of an entire harbor, which were inconsistent with the trust with which title to the submerged lands was held. *Lake Front Case*, 146 U.S. at 452–56. The line between small and large obviously is highly imprecise, and would likely deter anyone from building a substantial wharf or dock for commercial navigation purposes in Lake Michigan. An example of this is provided by the fate of the 1908 proposal (first mentioned in chapter 4) of the Pugh Terminal Company to construct a system of docks in the lake north of the Chicago River. Pugh held a long-term lease on the lands granted by the state in 1857 to the Chicago Dock and Canal Company for the construction of a dock and slip. The grant included lands "on the shore and in the navigable waters of Lake Michigan." 1857 Ill. Private Laws 499–500. Pugh's lawyers advised that, given the express grant of submerged land from the state, the only thing needed to proceed with the construction was the approval of the War Department certifying that the project would not interfere with public rights of navigation. "Shore Right of City Disputed," *Tribune*, May 24, 1910. The city corporation counsel disagreed, maintaining that the 1857 charter was invalid under the public trust doctrine recognized in the *Lake Front Case*. "City Will Fight the Pugh Plans," *Tribune*, June 7, 1910. The War Department granted a permit in 1910, but Pugh dropped the project in 1913 given the city's continued hostility and the threat of litigation. "Pugh Has Permit; City Will Fight," *Tribune*, June 21, 1910; "Pugh Drops Fight on City Harbor; Rumors of Break," *Tribune*, Feb. 9, 1913. After the Pugh plan collapsed, the city proceeded to build Navy Pier in the area.

30. For discussions of a public outer harbor, see Chicago Harbor Commission, *Report to the Mayor and Aldermen of the City of Chicago* (1909), 6, 11–19, 280, which also details how the Calumet River had become the region's largest port, surpassing the Chicago River by 1906, and Committee on Harbors, Wharves and Bridges of the City Council of the City of Chicago, *Report of the Sub-Committee on Harbor Development* (1911). For the plans for the Calumet Harbor and its development as Chicago's principal port, see John W. Larson, *Those Army Engineers: A History of the Chicago District U.S. Army Corps of Engineers* (Chicago: US Army Corps of Engineers, 1979), 118–22, and Harold M. Mayer, *The Port of Chicago and the St. Lawrence Seaway* (Chicago: University of Chicago Press, 1957), 12–13. See also United States Army Corps of Engineers, *Annual Report of the Chief of Engineers to the Secretary of War for the Year 1870* (Washington, DC, 1870), 104–7, reflecting the

initial proposal by J. B. Wheeler, major of engineers, for the improvement of the Calumet Harbor and estimating the cost at $695,000, just over half being for dredging. On the construction and use of Navy Pier, see Bernard R. Kogan, "Chicago's Pier," *Chicago History* 5 (Spring 1976): 28–38.

31. Illinois ex rel. Hunt v. Illinois Cent. R. Co., 91 F. 955, 957, 962 (7th Cir. 1899); Brief and Argument for Appellant at 50–60, 72–80, *Hunt.*

32. *Illinois ex rel. Hunt,* 91 F. at 957; Illinois v. Illinois Central Railroad Co., 184 U.S. 77, 84–93 (1902).

33. Illinois Central Railroad Co. v. City of Chicago, 173 Ill. 471, 483–87, 50 N.E. 1104, 1107–9 (1898), aff'd, 176 U.S. 646 (1900), discussed in chapter 8; *Chiperfield Committee Report,* 1:6–7.

34. *Report of the Commissioners of Lincoln Park for the Year 1908* (1908), 67–69; see also *Chiperfield Committee Report,* 2:219–21.

35. With respect to the original plan, see Robbins v. Commissioners of Lincoln Park, 332 Ill. 571, 572–73, 164 N.E. 10, 11 (1928), for a description of the more northern segment, and Wall v. Chicago Park District, 378 Ill. 81, 85–86, 37 N.E.2d 752, 755 (1941), concerning initial development of the more southern one. For a possible reason for the gap in between, see *Chiperfield Committee Report,* 2:223, stating that the southern part of the intermediate section "is occupied by many attractive and valuable residences, the location being considered one of the best on the North Side of Chicago." The Lincoln Park Commission closed the gap between the segments by completing the drive in this area in October 1923. "Open New Drive on North Side with Big Parade; Throngs Attend Breaking of One 'Bottle Neck,'" *Tribune,* Oct. 21, 1923.

36. *Wall,* 378 Ill. at 85–86, 37 N.E.2d at 755.

37. James O'Donnell Bennett, "Greater Lincoln Park Will Have Wonder Drives," *Tribune,* Sept. 14, 1923; Eugene R. Pike, "More Than 5,000 Cars Each Hour in Lincoln Park," *Tribune,* Jan. 25, 1925.

38. *Wall,* 378 Ill. at 86, 37 N.E.2d at 755; Ernst Schroeder, the Commissioners of Lincoln Park, *General Plan of Proposed Extension to Lincoln Park in Connection with Existing Conditions,* June 3, 1926 (map), Chicago Public Library, Special Collections, Chicago Park District Archives, Drawing CPD4361.

39. *Robbins,* 332 Ill. at 572–75, 164 N.E. at 11–12.

40. "Court Upholds North Extension of Outer Drive," *Tribune,* July 6, 1927; "New Lincoln Drive Extension Ready for Traffic Dec. 1," *Tribune,* Nov. 27, 1927.

41. *Robbins,* 332 Ill. at 577–82, 164 N.E. at 13–14.

42. *Wall,* 378 Ill. at 89–90, 37 N.E.2d at 756–57; "32 Suits Filed in Extension of North Drive; Park Board Is Forced to Condemn Land," *Tribune,* Oct. 7, 1928. See Commissioners of Lincoln Park v. Schmidt, 395 Ill. 316, 317–19, 69 N.E.2d 869, 871–72 (1946), for the case's procedural history, and Commissioners of Lincoln Park v. Schmidt, 375 Ill. 474, 474–77, 31 N.E.2d 969, 969–71 (1941), for the arguments and the trial.

43. 1927 Ill. Laws 684–85; 1931 Ill. Laws 689–92; *Wall,* 378 Ill. at 87–88, 37 N.E.2d at 755–56.

44. *Wall,* 378 Ill. at 87–89, 37 N.E.2d at 755–56.

45. *Wall,* 378 Ill. at 83–85, 90, 37 N.E.2d at 754–55, 757.

46. *Wall,* 378 Ill. at 88–89, 91, 37 N.E.2d at 756–57.

47. *Wall,* 378 Ill. at 83, 86–87, 37 N.E.2d at 754, 755.

48. *Wall,* 378 Ill. at 89, 37 N.E.2d at 756.

49. "Open Extension of Outer Drive to Foster Today," *Tribune,* Sept. 23, 1933.

50. Frank Sturdy, "Parks to Speed Buying of Land for Boulevard," *Tribune,* Apr. 16, 1947; "Beaches along Extended Drive Will Be Public," *Tribune,* July 5, 1954; "Pact with Club to Extend Lake Drive Approved," *Tribune,* Apr. 9, 1947; Al Chase, "Saddle Club to

Sell Land on Sheridan Rd.," *Tribune*, Aug. 19, 1950. The park district already owned the riparian rights immediately north of this area, east of the Edgewater Beach hotel and apartments.

51. Hal Foust, "Hollywood Av. Extension of Drive Opened," *Tribune*, Nov. 28, 1954; see Alvin Nagelberg, "Building Pace Quickens in Sheridan Road with Construction of New Apartments," *Tribune*, Nov. 4, 1965, noting the opening of a high-rise apartment on Sheridan Road north of Hollywood as early as 1954.

7. SOUTH LAKE SHORE DRIVE AND BRIDGING THE RIVER

1. "Planned a Compromise," *Chicago Tribune* (hereafter *Tribune*), Mar. 2, 1891; "The Lake Front," *Chicago Globe*, Apr. 26, 1891; "The Caton Boulevard," *Chicago Times*, Apr. 30, 1891.

2. Daniel H. Burnham, "Speech on Lakefront Plans, [1896]," 6, Ryerson and Burnham Archives, Art Institute of Chicago, accessed Aug. 3, 2020, http://digital-libraries.saic.edu/cdm/compoundobject/collection/mqc/id/3741/rec/24. See Robert A. Holland, *Chicago in Maps: 1612 to 2002* (New York: Rizzoli International, 2005), 133–35, for the so-called "Wüllweber map" mentioned in the text (correctly attributed to 1896).

3. 1903 Ill. Laws 256–58. Other 1903 legislation, enacted at the same time, involved authorizing the SPC to condemn public dedication rights in order to build the Crerar Library (see chapter 3) and the LPC to use boundary-line agreements to extend north Lake Shore Drive (see chapter 6). Local taxation in Illinois (and especially in Chicago) was a most complex matter in this era. See generally Thomas R. Pegram, *Partisans and Progressives: Private Interest and Public Policy in Illinois, 1870–1922* (Urbana: University of Illinois Press, 1992), 91–95.

There are two points of particular interest. One is that while the legislature acted at various times to give the park boards authority to issue bonds upon approval by voters, the LPC had no general authority to impose taxes but rather required the action of elected officials, unlike the SPC. See "Will Have Cash for Lake Front," *Tribune*, Feb. 22, 1905; 1911 Ill. Sen. J. 1007–12 (opinion of the attorney general discussing the longtime situation of the LPC with respect to taxing authority); "Lincoln Park Taxes," *Tribune*, Jan. 24, 1899. The discrepancy went all the way back to 1869. While the Lincoln Park Commission was authorized first in that legislative session, the South Park Commission went to the necessary popular referendum more promptly. Its approval only after considerable opposition from heavier taxpayers prompted the General Assembly to make a late-session amendment, reducing the LPC's taxing authority in an effort to help ensure its approval by voters. I. J. Bryan, comp., *Report of the Commissioners and a History of Lincoln Park* (Chicago: Commissioners of Lincoln Park, 1899), 14, 22.

The other relevant point of distinction is that downtown was part of the SPC's jurisdiction. "The value of the property, therefore, against which [the South Park] commission has authority to issue bonds and levy taxes far exceeds the combined value of the property over which the West and Lincoln Park commissions have similar powers." Graham Romeyn Taylor, "Recreation Developments in Chicago Parks," *Annals of the American Academy of Political and Social Science* 35 (March 1910): 91–92. Useful references to the various 1869 acts, together with amendments and cases and other information, can be found in George Allen Mason and Frederic Beecher Fuller, "Park Acts," chap. 4 in *The Law of Special Assessment and Special Taxation for Local Improvements in the State of Illinois* (Chicago: Callaghan, 1898), and Louis W. Mack, "History of the Development of the Park Systems of the City of Chicago" (bachelor's thesis, University of Illinois, 1906), https://core.ac.uk/download/pdf/158314678.pdf.

4. 1907 Ill. Laws 433–36; see Lake Shore Reclamation Commission, *Report to the Mayor and the City Council of the City of Chicago* (1912) (hereafter *1912 Lake Shore Report*), 64, 113, for some sense of the Commercial Club's extensive lobbying for the 1907 act.

5. *1912 Lake Shore Report*, 304.

6. *1912 Lake Shore Report*, 311–12; Susan O'Connor Davis, *Chicago's Historic Hyde Park* (Chicago: University of Chicago Press, 2013), 124–25. *Chicago City Manual* (Chicago: Bureau of Statistics and Municipal Library, 1912), 32–33, gives background on Long.

7. *1912 Lake Shore Report*, 11–20, 33–39.

8. *1912 Lake Shore Report*, 33–39, 74–76, 315, 318–30.

9. *1912 Lake Shore Report*, 74–76, 122–23, 128, 224, 320, 322–26. The figure of 162 acres appears to have been the city's official estimate, with 120 being submerged land and 42 being existing land, while the SPC put the total at 108 acres. Central Station is discussed in chapter 2; for its demolition, see Clifford J. Downey, *Chicago and the Illinois Central Railroad* (Charleston, SC: Arcadia, 2007), 127. The Illinois Central was careful not to explicitly commit to electrifying its tracks. The president confidentially assured the chairman that "[t]here is no foundation whatever" for any "private assurances" attributed to him concerning electrification, but that "it is only natural that the thought would suggest itself to the newspaper people." Charles H. Markham to Charles A. Peabody, Dec. 13, 1911, IC Papers. The railroad seems to have found it advantageous to maintain the impression. See "I. C. Will Electrify Soon," *Tribune*, Nov. 23, 1912 (attributing a statement concerning electrification's being "a matter of the not distant future" to a company official wishing to remain anonymous).

10. *1912 Lake Shore Report*, 56–57, 63, 75, 87, 90–93, 100, 144–45, 157, 223–25.

11. *1912 Lake Shore Report*, 110–12.

12. *1912 Lake Shore Report*, 285–86, 314; 1912 Ill. Laws 51–57.

13. Lake Shore Reclamation Commission, *Report to the Mayor and the City Council of the City of Chicago* (1915) (hereafter *1915 Lake Shore Report*), 10. Agreement over the Morgan lands involving the Chicago Beach Hotel took slightly longer. "Rights of Chicago Beach Hotel," *Tribune*, July 22, 1915.

14. *1912 Lake Shore Report*, 345–55.

15. *1912 Lake Shore Report*, 340–45, 355–65. The Illinois Supreme Court decree in South Park Commissioners v. Van Vlissingen, No. 8807 (Apr. 15, 1913), is unpublished but reproduced in the *1915 Lake Shore Report*, 14–16.

16. The railroad's president changed his tune about the condemnation bill as it made its way through the legislature. Though not favoring it, he initially had little concern about its possible effect. Markham to the Executive Committee, New York City, Mar. 26, 1912. But he soon confided that lobbying to defeat the bill was "receiving our very best attention as the passage of such a bill at this time would seriously embarrass us in the carrying out of the present agreement [of March 30, 1912]." Markham to A. G. Hackstaff, vice president, New York City, Apr. 23, 1912, IC Papers.

17. The papers of the Illinois Central, especially correspondence between its officials, reveal substantial landfilling south of 16th Street but also suggest that this became much harder to accomplish as time went on. See John Dunn to Stuyvesant Fish, Aug. 14, 1891, describing 750 lineal feet of filling between 18th and 20th Streets "beyond the limits of what is called for by the deeds we hold" and reporting Ayer's advice to lay tracks "thereon at once, so as to appropriate this land for railroad purposes"; James Fentress to Fish, Nov. 3, 1897, relating that the company had begun filling between 25th and 27th Streets and was positioning itself to be able to "allege and prove that it was absolutely necessary for the uses of the Railroad that this land should be filled in where it is covered by water"; Fish to J. T. Harahan, Oct. 4, 1899, relating the belief that the city would not object to the railroad's filling in gaps south of 16th Street, between the tracks and the breakwater, and

instructing that the company so proceed immediately, during the favorable political climate, with slag from the Illinois Steel Company; Fish to J. C. Welling, Jan. 12, 1900, noting Fish's authorization to Harahan to spend $13,000 to fill the lakefront from 30th to 39th Streets with slag; Fish to Harahan, Feb. 28, 1900, asking Harahan to "push this work more rapidly" and authorizing him to spend more than $13,000 if necessary; Harahan to Fish, Mar. 26, 1900, indicating that the filling in with slag between the tracks and the breakwater near 39th Street was stopped by the city when the US Supreme Court announced its decision in the *IC Charter Case* two weeks earlier but that "the matter has been fixed, and the work of filling has been resumed, within the 200 feet right of way" but not otherwise; and Illinois Central Railroad Company, "Supporting Papers," in minutes of meeting of the board of directors, Nov. 21, 1900, IC Papers, reporting the near completion of the filling between 30th and 39th Streets for two additional tracks at a cost (through midsummer) of $16,555.14.

18. Markham to the Executive Committee, Mar. 26, 1912.

19. *1915 Lake Shore Report*, 21–26, 66 (emphasis in original); 37 Stat. 595, 626 (1912).

20. "City May Force Action by Road," *Tribune*, Jan. 18, 1917; Arthur M. Evans, "Peace Revives Vision of Lake Parkway Plan," *Tribune*, Nov. 15, 1918; Oscar Hewitt, "I.C. to Spend $88,523,890 on Shore Plan," *Tribune*, July 5, 1919; An Ordinance for the Establishment of Harbor District Number Three; the Construction by the Illinois Central Railroad Company of a New Passenger Station; Electrification of Certain of the Lines of the Illinois Central and Michigan Central Railroad Companies within the City; and the Development of the Lake Front (July 19, 1919) (hereafter 1919 Lake Front Ordinance), *Journal of the Proceedings of the City Council of the City of Chicago*, 978–79 (art. III, § 10(c)), 980–81 (art. V, § 14), 995 (Specifications D); "U.S. Approves South Shore Improvement," *Tribune*, Jan. 9, 1920; *Hearings before the Select Committee on Nine-Foot Channel from the Great Lakes to the Gulf, United States Senate, on a Bill for the Improvement of Commerce and Navigation, and for Other Purposes*, 67th Cong. 222 (1923); "Park Bonds Win; Great Projects for South Side Get Voters' O.K.," *Tribune*, Feb. 25, 1920.

21. "$20,000,000 Bond Issues on Park Projects Carry," *Tribune*, Apr. 4, 1923; "Outer Drive on South Side Will Be Opened Today," *Tribune*, July 15, 1925; "Two More Miles of Outer Drive Opened," *Tribune*, Sept. 8, 1928; "Link Opening Gives 9-Mile No-Stop Drive," *Tribune*, Dec. 18, 1929; "South Side Outer Drive Opened to Traffic," *Tribune*, May 4, 1930; "Viaduct Sought at 47th Street and Outer Drive," *Tribune*, Mar. 17, 1935; Lisa D. Schrenk, *Building a Century of Progress: The Architecture of Chicago's 1933–34 World's Fair* (Minneapolis: University of Minnesota Press, 2007), 1–5.

22. Clayton Kirkpatrick, "Sidewalk Poll Favors 1 Name for Lake Drive," *Tribune*, Apr. 18, 1946; "Lake Highway Now Becomes Lake Shore Dr.," *Tribune*, June 19, 1946.

23. For the filling between 1921 and 1924, see Abstract of Record, 9, and Brief for the Appellants, 27, Hickey v. Illinois Central Railroad Co., 35 Ill. 2d 427, 220 N.E.2d 415 (1966) (No. 39772) (hereafter *Hickey*). Chapter 9 gives a sense of how the electrification project actually unfolded.

24. Chicago Plan Commission, *The Outer Drive along the Lake Front Chicago* (1929) (hereafter *1929 Bridge Report*), 5–7, 10–13.

25. *1929 Bridge Report*, 16–17, 26–27, 51, 63–71, 83–87, 108–20, and Drawing No. 150, between pp. 54 and 55.

26. In *1929 Bridge Report*, see Drawing No. 182, showing comparative lengths and heights of three ways of crossing the Chicago River (specifically, a tunnel, high bridge, and moveable bridge); pp. 10–35, describing the bridges and alternatives; the several renderings and illustrations in Study No. 2, especially Drawings Nos. 102–3, 105, 110, 162–65, 167–71, 177–81, 184–96, between pp. 48 and 49. The acceptances or the like came from the Chicago Plan Commission on June 27, 1927; the LPC on April 11, 1928; the SPC on

May 16, 1928; and the city on January 10, 1929. *1929 Bridge Report*, 18, 63, 69, 109. For the general references to the area east of Michigan Avenue, both north and south of the river, as becoming intensively developed, see *1929 Bridge Report*, 11, 29, 34–35, 61. See also *1929 Bridge Report*, 43, referring to the importance of "promot[ing] the highest and best use of . . . the Illinois Central property," and the rendering after p. 60, viz., Drawing No. 201, which shows the wall of skyscrapers (reproduced as our figure 7.8).

27. Chicago City Council, *Journal of the Proceedings of the City Council of the City of Chicago* (1929), 1321–50. At the time, Columbus Drive (running north) ended south of the Illinois Central property, at Monroe Street. The extension connecting Columbus Drive with Fairbanks Court across the river by bridge was not built until much later in the twentieth century. For basic illustrations and comment on this later extension, see Timothy J. Gilfoyle, *Millennium Park: Creating a Chicago Landmark* (Chicago: University of Chicago Press, 2006), 58, fig. 3.26; Paul Gapp, "A Sign of Things to Come," *Tribune*, Mar. 10, 1974; Stanley Ziemba, "At Last—Columbus Drive Bridge," *Tribune*, Jan. 2, 1979. For the final completion of the bridge linking Columbus Drive to Fairbanks Court, see "Columbus Drive Bridge Opens," *Tribune*, Nov. 1, 1982.

28. Abstract of Record, 94–95, 97–99, 116, and Brief for Appellants, Exhibit S-IV, *Hickey*; *Hickey*, 35 Ill. 2d at 436, 220 N.E.2d at 420.

29. See *1929 Bridge Report*, 19, 27–29 (Drawing No. 200), for the plan, including the S-curve; Brief for Appellants, 108–10, *Hickey*, for the location of the drive north of Randolph and west of the new boundary line. Some evidence of the last point in the text is that one of the plans submitted in the 1930 boundary-line proceeding showed "proposed railroad connections (never built) to a proposed harbor district outside the boundary line." Brief for Appellants, 108, *Hickey*.

30. Abstract of Record, 19, 65–116, *Hickey*.

31. "Argue Granting Delay for Work on Lake Front," *Tribune*, July 14, 1932; Robert J. Dunham, "Outer Drive to Be Ready for Trafic [*sic*] Sept. 1," *Tribune*, Nov. 15, 1936; "Vintage: The Outer Drive Bridge," *Tribune*, Sept. 13, 2013, https://www.chicagotribune.com/news/chi-130912-vintage-outer-drive-bridge-roosevelt-pictures-photogallery.html.

32. Abstract of Record, 475, 477–83, 509–11, *Hickey*; James N. Adams, "Illinois in 1955," *Journal of the Illinois State Historical Society* 49 (Spring 1956): 89; Ernest Fuller, "Dedicate New Prudential 41 Story Building," *Tribune*, Dec. 9, 1955; "Set Dedication for Outer Drive Apartment Bldg.," *Tribune*, June 15, 1964; "S-curve Blues to End on Monday . . . for the Northbound," *Tribune*, Oct. 6, 1985. Once the project to eliminate the S-curve was completed in 1986, Outer Drive East (now known as 400 East Randolph) found itself situated *west* of the drive. Two large plinths marking the point where the drive originally crossed Randolph Street still stand on the south side of the street near the entrance to Millennium Park.

33. Ernest Fuller, "Texas Group Bidding for I.C. Air Rights; Seek Portion of Lake Front Site," *Tribune*, May 12, 1959, and "Air Rights Worth 150 Millions to I.C.," *Tribune*, Mar. 1, 1967, give rough estimates of the values of the projects, the latter also speaking to land south of Grant Park. For the suit and the description of the relief sought, see Hickey v. Illinois Central Railroad, 278 F.2d 529, 530–31 (7th Cir. 1960).

34. Concerning the father, in addition to the discussion in chapter 6, see "Hugh E. Young, 68, Former City Engineer, Dies," *Tribune*, Nov. 30, 1951. Burton Young himself died before the briefs on the merits were filed in the Illinois Supreme Court in the subsequent state court litigation. The consolidated brief of the appellants includes the unusual memorial statement "that the State's case rests, in large part, on the insights of a man whose signature does not appear on its final page." This individual, the statement continues, "was one of the original taxpayer-plaintiffs, and as counsel he most conscientiously gave of his time and skill to this case from its inception until his untimely death. If, as we

shall show, the State is still entitled to the benefits from these immensely valuable lands, the credit is significantly Burton H. Young's." Brief for Appellants, 35, *Hickey*.

35. *Hickey*, 278 F.2d at 531–32; Hickey v. Illinois Central Railroad Co., 30 Ill. 2d 163, 164–65, 195 N.E.2d 716, 717 (1964); *Hickey*, 35 Ill. 2d at 429–30, 220 N.E.2d at 416, 417. To judge from a later procedural move and reportage of the time, it is possible that the reason for the Illinois attorney general's change of mind and intervention included an interest on the part of the state and city in having a final decision on the ownership of the Illinois Central land. See "Ask Rehearing on Air Rights," *Tribune*, Oct. 7, 1966, suggesting that this may have been the purpose of the state and city's request for rehearing of the state supreme court's subsequent 1966 ruling: "Such a final decision in favor of the railroad would clear the way once and for all for the redevelopment of 184 acres of I. C. air rights. Three development firms have been making preparations for some time for redeveloping the 16 blocks of air rights between Randolph street and the river."

36. *Hickey*, 35 Ill. 2d at 430, 220 N.E.2d at 417.

37. *Hickey*, 35 Ill. 2d at 428, 430, 220 N.E. 2d at 416, 417.

38. See Brief for Appellees, 47–48, *Hickey*, and Harlan's decree, entered Sept. 24, 1888, which can be found both in Abstract of Record, 425–26, *Hickey*, and in the Record, 222–23, Illinois Central Railroad Co. v. Illinois, 146 U.S. 387 (1892), Nos. 14,135, 14,414, 14,415, and 14,416 (filed Sept. 6, 1890) (emphasis added).

39. Brief for Appellants, 21–23, 42–63, 89, *Hickey*.

40. Brief for Appellants, 23–31, 36–41, 78–79, 82–111, *Hickey*. For the state constitutional principle, subsequently abolished in 1970, see Ill. Const. of 1870, art. IV, § 26.

41. Brief for Appellees, 21–29, 57–65, 68–76, *Hickey*.

42. *Hickey*, 35 Ill. 2d at 439–47, 220 N.E.2d at 421–25.

43. *Hickey*, 35 Ill. 2d at 447–50, 220 N.E.2d at 425–27.

44. For an assessment after *Hickey*, by a noted scholar of Chicago's built environment, of the coming opportunities and challenges in developing the former Illinois Central peninsula, see Harold M. Mayer, "Air-Rights Development on Downtown Chicago's Lakefront," *Land-Use Controls: A Quarterly Review* 1 (1967): 1–10.

8. THE TRANSFORMATION OF THE PUBLIC TRUST DOCTRINE

1. *Lake Front Case*, 146 U.S. 387, 452–53 (1892), discussed in chapter 2.

2. Shively v. Bowlby, 152 U.S. 1 (1894), discussed in chapter 6.

3. People ex rel. Moloney v. Kirk, 162 Ill. 138, 45 N.E. 830 (1896), discussed in chapter 4.

4. 1851 Ill. Priv. Laws 61; see Brief on Behalf of Plaintiff in Error at 6, Illinois Central Railroad Co. v. City of Chicago, 176 U.S. 646 (1900), for the army's approval.

5. Illinois Central Railroad Co. v. City of Chicago, 173 Ill. 471, 483–87, 50 N.E. 1104, 1107–9 (1898), aff'd, 176 U.S. 646 (1900). The quoted section of the charter went on to state that "[a]ll such lands, waters, materials and privileges belonging to the state, are hereby granted to said corporation for said purposes," but the court regarded the phrase "such . . . waters" as not expanding the reference to "streams" and thus as not including lakes.

6. See Victor Windett, "The South Works of the Illinois Steel Company," *Journal of the Western Society of Engineers* 3 (1898): 789–814, for the background and operation of the South Works, and Arundel Cotter, *The Authentic History of the United States Steel Corporation* (New York: Moody Magazine and Book Company, 1916), 9–16, 24, for an update of the more general corporate story into the early twentieth century.

7. "Shore Land Is Untaxed," *Chicago Tribune* (hereafter *Tribune*), Apr. 14, 1900; "Shore Lands for City," *Tribune*, Apr. 15, 1900; "Plans to Eject Illinois Steel," *Tribune*, Apr. 19, 1901;

"Blocks Big Land Grab," *Chicago Journal* (hereafter *Journal*), Apr. 19, 1901; "'Making' Land in Lake," *Tribune*, Sept. 21, 1905.

8. "City May Seize New Shore Land," *Tribune*, Sept. 21, 1905.

9. "Fights $4,000,000 Lake Land Grab," *Tribune*, Sept. 20, 1905; "City May Seize New Shore Land"; "Bolt Hits Dunne Man," *Chicago Daily News* (hereafter *Daily News*), Sept. 19, 1905.

10. "State Sues Steel Co.," *Daily News*, Dec. 6, 1905; "'Made' Land Suit Begun," *Tribune*, Dec. 7, 1905.

11. "Builds on Illegal Acres," *Tribune*, June 5, 1908.

12. "Stir in Steel Circles over Chiperfield Act," *Daily News*, Feb. 24, 1909; "Ready to Dicker for State Lands," *Tribune*, Mar. 10, 1909; "Rush to Buy 'Made' Land," *Journal*, Mar. 9, 1909; "Offers to Buy Lake Lands," *Tribune*, Mar. 11, 1909; "Would Give Land to Big Steel Co.," *Tribune*, Apr. 7, 1909.

13. "Steel Concerns Get Land Grant," *Tribune*, May 30, 1909; 1909 Ill. House Journal, 1226–27; 1909 Ill. Senate Journal, 1105–6; 1909 Ill. Laws 432–36; "Senate Puts O.K. on Sale of Land," *Tribune*, May 14, 1909. Chiperfield had enough challenges on his hands: the next year, for example, the governor, who had clashed with Chiperfield in the past, vetoed a measure appropriating $10,000 for Chiperfield's investigating committee, ostensibly on the grounds that it was not a proper subject for the special session then underway. Chiperfield responded that he was prepared to "go down into his own pockets" to continue the investigation. Whether this became necessary is not clear. "Deneen to Veto Lake Land Bill," *Tribune*, Feb. 8, 1910.

14. William H. Stead, *Biennial Report of the Attorney General of the State of Illinois* (Springfield, 1910), 102–4. The line from Field's opinion reads as follows: "The control of the State for the purposes of the trust can never be lost, except as to such parcels as are used in promoting the interests of the public therein, or can be disposed of without any substantial impairment of the public interest in the lands and waters remaining." *Lake Front Case*, 146 U.S. at 453. In context, Field was speaking of the grant of relatively small parcels for piers and wharves, which would not impair public access to navigable waters based on the "lands and waters remaining." Field had made this clear earlier in the same paragraph of his opinion, to which the already-quoted sentence was an allusion: "It is grants of parcels of lands under navigable waters, that may afford foundation for wharves, piers, docks and other structures in aid of commerce, and grants of parcels which, being occupied, do not substantially impair the public interest in the lands and waters remaining, that are chiefly considered and sustained in the adjudged cases as a valid exercise of legislative power consistently with the trust to the public upon which such lands are held by the State." More broadly, if the conveyance of one thousand acres to a railroad—for the purpose of constructing an outer harbor—violated the trust, then surely the conveyance of several hundred acres to private steel companies to expand steel mills was at least problematic without reference to what remained.

15. 1911 Ill. Laws 115–16, 119. The subsequent Civil Administrative Code abolished the Rivers and Lakes Commission and transferred the approval authority to the Department of Public Works and Buildings. 1917 Ill. Laws 4, 16, 24. The current statute vests the authority in the Office of Water Resources of the state's Department of Natural Resources. 20 Ill. Comp. Stat. Ann. 801/5-5(b) (West 2015).

16. "Move to Save Old Fine Arts Building Grows," *Tribune*, May 22, 1921; "New Bids to Be Opened for Fine Arts Building," *Tribune*, Aug. 11, 1928; Furlong v. South Park Commissioners, 320 Ill. 507, 508, 511, 151 N.E. 510, 510–11 (1926).

17. "N. Side Filter Plant Wins in Supreme Court," *Tribune*, May 25, 1954.

18. Bowes v. City of Chicago, 3 Ill. 2d 175, 179–85, 120 N.E.2d 15, 19–22 (1954).

19. *Bowes*, 3 Ill. 2d at 185–99, 205, 120 N.E.2d at 22–28, 31.

20. Fairbank v. Stratton, 14 Ill. 2d 307, 310–11, 316–19, 152 N.E.2d 569, 571, 574–75 (1958).

21. *Fairbank*, 14 Ill. 2d at 317–19, 152 N.E.2d at 574–75.

22. Alban Weber, *Legislative Grant for a Private University* (Evanston, IL, June 1962), 24–27, Northwestern University Archives (emphasis in original).

23. Harold F. Williamson and Payson S. Wild, *Northwestern University: A History, 1850–1975* (Evanston, IL: Northwestern University, 1976), 262; Weber, *Legislative Grant*, 55–56; "Evanston OK's N. U. Expansion by Lake Fill," *Tribune*, Mar. 20, 1962.

24. Weber, *Legislative Grant*, 69–71.

25. Weber, *Legislative Grant*, 36–47; "NU Expansion Plan: Fill in Lake," *Daily News*, Oct. 13, 1960; Richard Philbrick, "N.U. to Add 65 Acres to Campus by Lake Fill," *Tribune*, Oct. 14, 1960; 1961 Ill. Laws 1:566–68; Williamson and Wild, *Northwestern University*, 263.

26. Weber, *Legislative Grant*, 52; "N.U. Lake Expansion Wins Engineers' OK," *Evanston Review*, Sept. 14, 1961.

27. "Don't Use Sand from Dunes, N.U. Requests," *Tribune*, May 1, 1962; Mary Huff, "Winds of Controversy Whistle across Dunes as New Squall Nears," *Tribune*, July 15, 1962; "Sand Removal from Dunes Is Hit at Hearing," *Tribune*, July 27, 1962; Weber, *Legislative Grant*, 64–67; Williamson and Wild, *Northwestern University*, 278. Construction on the new land began shortly after the filling was completed. In 1968, Northwestern filled ten more acres of the lake (for an arts center), and several building projects occurred on the filled land in the 1970s. Williamson and Wild, *Northwestern University*, 278–81.

28. John McDonnell, "U.S. Steel Acts to Reclaim Land from Lake for Plant Growth," *Tribune*, Apr. 23, 1963; 1963 Ill. Laws 1:1229–31.

29. "Oppose Revised Lake Shore Plan," *Tribune*, Mar. 28, 1965; Jay McMullen, "Trees Must Go—Daley," *Daily News*, Sept. 7, 1965; "Fail to Save Jackson Pk. Trees," *Tribune*, Sept. 10, 1965; Paul Gapp, "Jackson Park Tree Battle!," *Daily News*, Sept. 9, 1965; "Nab Official's Wife in Park Tree Protest," *Tribune*, Sept. 11, 1965; Paul Gapp, "Why Did Daley Change His Mind?," *Daily News*, Nov. 16, 1965. Royko's riff on Joyce Kilmer was for a speech that he purported to propose for Daley to give; here it is in full:

> **A Road**
> I think that I have never knowed
> A sight as lovely as a road.
> A road upon whose concrete tops
> The flow of traffic never stops;
> A road that costs a lot to build
> Just as the city council willed;
> A road the planners say we need
> To get the cars to greater speed;
> We've let the contracts so dig in
> And let the chopping now begin;
> Somebody else can make a tree
> But roads are made by guys like me.

Mike Royko, "Here's a Script for Jackson Park Tree-Breaking Rite," *Daily News*, Sept. 7, 1965.

30. "Daley Seeks a Site for Third Airfield," *Tribune*, Jan. 21, 1967; "Air-Space for Our Third Airport," *Tribune*, June 26, 1967; "Urge 3d Airport within an Hour of Loop," *Tribune*, Oct. 12, 1967; "Group Fights Proposal for Lake Airport," *Tribune*, Feb. 7, 1968; Mary Ullrich, "Groups Back Lake Front Plan," *Tribune*, Mar. 17, 1968; "City Delays Planning on 3d Airport," *Tribune*, Nov. 18, 1971; "3d Airport Need Less Pressing," *Tribune*, Jan. 4, 1972.

31. "Block Sale of Park Land to U.S. Steel," *Tribune*, Nov. 20, 1965; Droste v. Kerner, 34 Ill. 2d 495, 497–502, 217 N.E.2d 73, 75–78 (1966).

32. The jurisdictional statement filed by Droste in the US Supreme Court, available at Droste v. Kerner, No. 671, 1966 WL 115317, at *2, *11–12 (filed Oct. 13, 1966), briefly summarizes the two unpublished decisions; its appendix reprinting them is not available online. The US Supreme Court declined this request to review the Illinois Supreme Court's final decision. Droste v. Kerner, 385 U.S. 456 (1967).

33. *Droste*, 34 Ill. 2d at 499–504, 217 N.E.2d at 76–79; *id.* at 505, 217 N.E.2d at 79 (Schaefer, J., dissenting).

34. *Droste*, 34 Ill. 2d at 504–5, 217 N.E.2d at 79.

35. *Droste*, 34 Ill. 2d at 505–16, 217 N.E.2d at 79–85 (Schaefer, J. dissenting).

36. Paepcke v. Public Building Commission of Chicago, 46 Ill. 2d 330, 331, 263 N.E.2d 11, 13 (1970); "Eve in the Garden of Aspen," *New York Times*, Jan. 1, 1995; Richard B. Fizdale, *999: A History of Chicago in Ten Stories* (Chicago: Ampersand, 2014), 152–55.

37. *Paepcke*, 46 Ill. 2d at 335, 263 N.E.2d at 15.

38. Robert Howard, "2 Join State High Court until '70 Vote," *Tribune*, Oct. 10, 1969; Kenan Heise, "Marvin Burt, Former Judge, State Legislator," *Tribune*, Oct. 22, 1983. Burt was a twenty-five-year member of the Illinois Association of Park Districts and served a term as president; he also would help establish the Jane Addamsland Park Foundation and the Pecatonica Prairie Path. For background on the scandal, see Kenneth A. Manaster, *Illinois Justice: The Scandal of 1969 and the Rise of John Paul Stevens* (Chicago: University of Chicago Press, 2001).

39. *Paepcke*, 46 Ill. 2d at 338–40, 342–43, 263 N.E.2d at 16–19. This was a questionable distinction of the *Ward* cases. The *Paepcke* court pointed "especially" to *Ward I* (46 Ill. 2d at 339, 263 N.E.2d at 17), but in fact that case had stated that "the legislation of 1861 and 1863 [i.e., the city charters] added nothing to its trust, and can only be looked upon as confirmatory of the same." City of Chicago v. Ward, 169 Ill. 392, 408, 48 N.E. 927, 932 (1897).

40. *Paepcke*, 46 Ill. 2d at 341, 263 N.E.2d at 18.

41. *Paepcke*, 46 Ill. 2d at 336–37, 263 N.E.2d at 15–16 (quoting Joseph L. Sax, "The Public Trust Doctrine in Natural Resource Law: Effective Judicial Intervention," *Michigan Law Review* 68 (1970): 482, 490).

42. Clement v. Chicago Park District, 96 Ill. 2d 26, 449 N.E.2d 81 (1983), would summarily reject a public trust challenge to the construction of a golf driving range in Jackson Park. The issue was a secondary one in the case, and the court did not consider whether the doctrine properly applied, but simply, in a single sentence, invoked the consideration of the *Paepcke* factors by the Illinois Appellate Court in reaching the judgment under review in that case. That court, too, did not consider the basis for the doctrine's application, simply relying on *Paepcke* for the "standards" applicable in "determin[ing] the validity of proposed changes in the use of public trust lands." Clement v. O'Malley, 95 Ill. App. 3d 824, 834, 420 N.E.2d 533, 540–41 (1981). Surveys of decisions enforcing the public trust doctrine throughout the United States reveal that nearly all of them have some connection with navigable waters. Robin Kundis Craig, "A Comparative Guide to the Eastern Public Trust Doctrines: Classifications of States, Property Rights, and State Summaries," *Penn State Environmental Law Review* 16 (2007): 1–113; Robin Kundis Craig, "A Comparative Guide to the Western States' Public Trust Doctrines: Public Values, Private Rights, and the Evolution toward an Ecological Public Trust," *Ecology Law Quarterly* 37 (2010): 53–197; David L. Callies, "The Public Trust Doctrine," *Brigham-Kanner Property Rights Journal* 8 (2019): 71–91.

43. *Paepcke*, 46 Ill. 2d at 343–44, 263 N.E.2d at 19.

44. Concerning the developments of 1970 and the environmental revolution more generally, see Philip Shabecoff, "The Environmental Revolution," chap. 6 in *A Fierce Green Fire: The American Environmental Movement* (New York: Hill & Wang, 1993); Richard J. Lazarus, "Building a Road: The 1970s," chap. 5 in *The Making of Environmental Law* (Chicago: University of Chicago Press, 2004); Michael J. Graetz, "The Environment Moves Front and Center," chap. 3 in *The End of Energy: The Unmaking of America's Environment, Security, and Independence* (Cambridge, MA: MIT Press, 2011). On the emergence of "hard look" review in environmental cases during this period, see Thomas W. Merrill, "Capture Theory and the Courts: 1967–1983," *Chicago Kent Law Review* 72 (1997): 1092–96.

45. Sax, "Public Trust Doctrine," 489–91.

46. "The U.S. Steel Lake Deal," *Tribune*, Aug. 23, 1973; Richard Philbrick and Stanley Ziemba, "Delay Land Sale, Park Board Told," *Tribune*, Oct. 24, 1973.

47. Robert Gottlieb, *Forcing the Spring: The Transformation of the American Environmental Movement* (Washington, DC: Island, 1993), 105–14, gives a sense of the shifting culture and politics with respect to environmentalism during this time. E. Donald Elliot, Bruce A. Ackerman, and John C. Millian, "Toward a Theory of Statutory Evolution: The Federalization of Environmental Law," *Journal of Law, Economics, and Organization* 1 (1985): 333–38, illustrate how environmentalists capitalized on this to pressure Nixon and Senator Edmund Muskie in a way that led to "some of the surprisingly stringent provisions of the Clean Air [Act] of 1970." For various other undertakings by Scott during this time, see Casey Bukro, "Scott to Sue Milwaukee over Dumping and Polluting Lake," *Tribune*, Apr. 23, 1970; James Kloss and Harlan Draeger, "Scott to Sue Several Indiana Cities to Halt Lake Pollution," *Daily News*, Apr. 23, 1970; "Scott Sues Two Indiana Steel Firms," *Tribune*, Jan. 18, 1972; see also Edward Baumann and Valerie J. Phillips, "Ex-Atty. Gen. William Scott Dead at 59," *Tribune*, June 23, 1986. Scott had previously sued US Steel over pollution from the South Works. "Air Pollution Suit by Scott Hits Steel Co.," *Tribune*, Oct. 16, 1969. Concerning the suit over the submerged land, see "Walker Joins Fight to Block Lake Land Sale to U.S. Steel," *Daily News*, Oct. 23, 1973; "Lake Land Project Faces Suit by Mann," *Daily News*, Aug. 21, 1973.

48. People ex rel. Scott v. Chicago Park District, 66 Ill. 2d 65, 67–68, 71–72, 360 N.E.2d 773, 775, 777 (1976).

49. *People ex rel. Scott*, 66 Ill. 2d at 78–79, 360 N.E.2d at 780; Ill. Const. of 1970, art. XI, § 2.

50. *People ex rel. Scott*, 66 Ill. 2d at 77–80, 360 N.E.2d at 779–81.

51. *People ex rel. Scott*, 66 Ill. 2d at 80–81, 360 N.E.2d at 781.

52. Only one other Illinois Supreme Court decision has invoked the public trust doctrine in invalidating what was claimed to have been state action: the *IC Charter Case* in 1898. That decision, discussed toward the beginning of this chapter, did not overturn a state statute but ruled that the original state charter of the Illinois Central did not authorize the carrier to engage in landfilling in the lake. It relied on the public trust doctrine as an alternative holding: "But even if the grant in the charter was broad enough to include the waters of Lake Michigan . . ." Illinois Central Railroad Co. v. City of Chicago, 173 Ill. at 485–87, 50 N.E. at 1108–9.

53. *Lake Front Case*, 146 U.S. at 452–54.

54. John N. Maclean, "USX Actions Point to Final Days for South Works," *Tribune*, Jan. 9, 1992; Frederick H. Lowe, "South Works to Close," *Chicago Sun-Times* (hereafter *Sun-Times*), Jan. 10, 1992; "South Works Demolition Approved by U.S. Steel," *Tribune*, Mar. 29, 1993; John W. Miller, "Remade in the USA: Indiana Steel Mill Revived with Lessons from Abroad," *Wall Street Journal*, May 21, 2012.

55. "Chronology of Probe—Divorce Case Set It Off," *Tribune*, Apr. 10, 1979; Maurice Possley, "'Stunned' by Cash Find: Scott Ex-Wife," *Sun-Times*, Jan. 23, 1980; Roger Flaherty, "William Scott Dies," *Sun-Times*, June 23, 1986.

56. Affidavit of Philip R. Kosiba in Opposition to Plaintiffs' Motion for Temporary Restraining Order, 5, Lake Michigan Federation v. United States Army Corps of Engineers, No. 90 C 2809, 742 F. Supp. 441 (N.D. Ill. 1990) (hereafter Kosiba Affidavit and *Loyola Case*, respectively).

57. The sources vary in their characterizations of the size of the entire area, with the low end in the Kosiba Affidavit, 2–3, 9–10, and *Loyola Case*, 742 F. Supp. at 443; the high end in Harold Henderson, "A Piece of Lakefront," *Chicago Reader*, Sept. 22, 1988; and numbers halfway in between in "State Bill Would Let Loyola Build Lakefill," *Tribune*, Mar. 25, 1988, and Casey Bukro, "Loyola's Lakefill Plan Is Running into Rough Water," *Tribune*, Apr. 10, 1988. These sources also include the other details.

58. Kosiba Affidavit, 8–11; *Loyola Case*, 742 F. Supp. at 443; 1988 Ill. Laws 1113–20 (Public Act 85-1145).

59. NEPA, § 102(2)(C), 83 Stat. 853 (1970) (codified at 42 U.S.C. § 4332(2)(C) (2018)); 40 C.F.R. § 6.203 (2019). For a general overview of the NEPA process in the context of Army Corps permitting decisions, see Van Abbema v. Fornell, 807 F.2d 633, 636–37 (7th Cir. 1986). Loyola's environmental impact assessment is included in the Exhibits of Defendant Loyola University of Chicago in Opposition to Plaintiffs' Motion for Preliminary Injunction, *Loyola Case*.

60. Kosiba Affidavit, 12–18.

61. Rudolph Unger, "'Friends of Parks' Offer 10 for Boards," *Tribune*, Mar. 27, 1975; Henderson, "Piece of Lakefront."

62. *Loyola Case*, 742 F. Supp. at 442–44.

63. *Loyola Case*, 742 F. Supp. at 444, 447.

64. *Loyola Case*, 742 F. Supp. at 445–47.

65. *Loyola Case*, 742 F. Supp. at 448–50.

66. Sax, "Public Trust Doctrine," 481, 491, 540, 559–61.

67. Friends of the Parks v. Chicago Park District, 203 Ill. 2d 312, 314–18, 321–25, 786 N.E.2d 161, 163–64, 166–69 (2003) (hereafter *Soldier Field Case*).

68. *Soldier Field Case*, 203 Ill. 2d at 325–26, 786 N.E.2d at 169.

69. *Soldier Field Case*, 203 Ill. 2d at 319, 325–28, 786 N.E.2d at 165, 169–70.

70. *Soldier Field Case*, 203 Ill. 2d at 320–25, 328, 786 N.E.2d at 166–70.

71. Friends of Van Cortlandt Park v. City of New York, 95 N.Y.2d 623, 750 N.E.2d 1050 (2001); Thomas W. Merrill, "The Public Trust Doctrine: Some Jurisprudential Variations and Their Implications," *University of Hawai'i Law Review* 38 (2016): 261, 272–76. For a variety of perspectives on the ultimate purpose of the public trust doctrine, see Michael C. Blumm and Aurora Paulsen Moses, "The Public Trust as an Antimonopoly Doctrine," *Boston College Environmental Affairs Law Review* 44 (2017): 1–54; Richard A. Epstein, "The Public Trust Doctrine," *Cato Journal* 7 (1987): 411–30; Carol Rose, "The Comedy of the Commons: Custom, Commerce, and Inherently Public Property," *University of Chicago Law Review* 53 (1986): 711–81.

9. THE LAKEFRONT TODAY

1. For a brief reference to a transition by the railroad in 1926 to electric locomotives for commuter trains, see John F. Stover, "The Management of the Illinois Central Railroad in the 20th Century," in *Business and Economic History*, ed. Paul Uselding (Cambridge: Cambridge University Press, 1979), 8:56. Yet various deadlines for eliminating use of the lakefront by steam engines were not met, and in 1942, the city council amended the 1919

Lake Front Ordinance to permit the use of diesel engines to satisfy what had been the electrification requirement; the city also dropped its plan for a terminal to replace Central Station. Philip Hampson, "Move to Amend City's Famous Lake Front Law," *Chicago Tribune* (hereafter *Tribune*), Aug. 20, 1941; Chicago City Council, *Journal of the Proceedings of the City Council of the City of Chicago, Illinois* (1942), 6849–50. Paul Gapp, "At the End of the Line: Towers to Surmount City's Last Great Rail Terminal," *Tribune*, Dec. 8, 1985, gives a good brief history of Chicago's railroad stations and their fates.

2. Graydon Megan, "Railroad Magnate Built Up Company," *Tribune*, May 3, 2013, https://www.chicagotribune.com/news/ct-xpm-2013-05-03-ct-met-william-johnson-obit-20130503-story.html; Alvin Nagelberg, "New Venture to Develop 83-Acre Site; Will Buy Land from I.C.," *Tribune*, Aug. 14, 1969; William B. Johnson, *IC Industries* (New York: Newcomen Society in North America, 1973), 8–9, 12–22; Mark R. Wilson, "IC Industries Inc.," in *Encyclopedia of Chicago*, ed. James R. Grossman, Ann Durkin Keating, and Janice L. Reiff (Chicago: University of Chicago Press, 2004), 929; Kenneth N. Gilpin and Todd S. Purdum, "Pet Inc. Chairman Gets Posts at IC," *New York Times*, Feb. 19, 1985; John P. Hankey, "Illinois Central Railroad," in Grossman, Keating, and Reiff, *Encyclopedia of Chicago*, 407; Steven Lipin and Christopher Chipello, "Canadian National Railway to Acquire Illinois Central in $2.4 Billion Accord," *Wall Street Journal*, Feb. 11, 1998; Michael J. de la Merced, "PepsiCo to Pay $7.8 Billion to Buy Its Two Top Bottlers," *New York Times*, Aug. 5, 2009.

3. On phenomena such as holding companies, mergers, and real estate development among railroads, see James Burns, "Railroad Holding Companies: Keys to Diversification," chap. 8 in *Railroad Mergers and the Language of Unification* (Westport, CT: Quorum Books, 1998); Robert E. Gallamore and John R. Meyer, "How Railroads Got Their Final Sizes and Shapes," chap. 10 in *American Railroads: Decline and Renaissance in the Twentieth Century* (Cambridge, MA: Harvard University Press, 2014). See also Interstate Commerce Commission, *Railroad Conglomerates & Other Corporate Structures: A Report to Congress* (Washington, DC, Feb. 5, 1977), 9, noting that "[b]efore the advent of the holding companies," "[m]uch of the land and other natural resources under railroad ownership remained undeveloped or minimally developed, although railroad managements' policies respecting development of land grant resources were virtually unrestricted by the land grant statutes."

4. The Lake Michigan and Chicago Lakefront Protection Ordinance, Chicago, Ill., Mun. Code, § 16-4. Clement v. O'Malley, 95 Ill. App. 3d 824, 828–31, 420 N.E.2d 533, 536–38 (1981), aff'd sub nom. Clement v. Chicago Park District, 96 Ill. 2d 26, 449 N.E.2d 81 (1983), gives an introduction to the ordinance.

5. Timothy J. Gilfoyle, *Millennium Park: Creating a Chicago Landmark* (Chicago: University of Chicago Press, 2006), 81–88.

6. Gilfoyle, *Millennium Park*, 117, 126–29, 147–51, 159–74, 193–95, 251–60.

7. Gilfoyle, *Millennium Park*, 261, 277, 320–23.

8. Gilfoyle, *Millennium Park*, 140–41.

9. Gilfoyle, *Millennium Park*, 140–41. In the case of Millennium Park, this conception of who had to consent meant every owner (and in some cases lessees) on the west side of Michigan Avenue from Monroe Street to Randolph Street and every owner on the north side of Randolph Street from Michigan Avenue to Columbus Drive, plus the diagonally situated property owners on Michigan just south of Monroe, on Michigan just north of Randolph, and on Randolph just east of Columbus. There were fifteen owners in all in this area. Motion to Dismiss Complaint, ¶¶ 4–6 (Nov. 12, 1999), Boaz v. City of Chicago, No. 99L-3804 (Cook Cnty. Cir. Ct., Ill.). The exhibits to the motion include maps showing the location of the various properties whose owners consented to the Art Institute construction.

10. Gilfoyle, *Millennium Park*, 141–43; Motion to Dismiss Complaint, ¶ 8, and Order (Jan. 14, 2000) granting the motion, *Boaz*, No. 99L-3804.

11. The consent procedure followed in obtaining approval for the Art Institute and Millennium Park is also inconsistent with the legislature's charters for Chicago in 1861 and 1863, which provided that no encroachments were to be permitted in the park "without the assent of *all* the persons owning lots or land on said street or avenue." 1861 Ill. Private Laws 136 and 1863 Ill. Private Laws 96 (emphasis added). The charters were an incidental part of the court's rationale in *Ward I* but promoted in importance by *Paepcke*, as discussed in chapter 8.

12. Blair Kamin, "The Millennium Park Effect," *Tribune*, June 26, 2005. Joseph D. Kearney and Thomas W. Merrill, "Private Rights in Public Lands: The Chicago Lakefront, Montgomery Ward, and the Public Dedication Doctrine," *Northwestern University Law Review* 105 (2011): 1443, give a brief history of an unsuccessful administrative law challenge to the approval of the children's museum. Museum opponents thereafter prevailed politically: the museum was located elsewhere. Dahleen Glanton, "Kids Museum Signs 90-Year Navy Pier Lease," *Tribune*, Oct. 30, 2012. This victory meant that property owners could forgo an otherwise likely lawsuit challenging the construction under the *Ward* precedents.

13. Environmental Protection Agency, *Report to Congress, Combined Sewer Overflows into the Great Lakes Basin*, Apr. 2016, EPA 833-R-16-006; Victor A. Koelzer, William J. Bauer, and Frank E. Dalton, "The Chicago Area Deep Tunnel Project—A Use of the Underground Storage Resource," *Journal of the Water Pollution Control Federation* 41 (1969): 517–18; David Thompson, "Health Board Urges Closing of Lake County [Ill.] Beaches," *Tribune*, July 29, 1969; "Rise in Bacteria Count Causes Closing of Waukegan's Beaches," *Tribune*, June 20, 1971; Lucia Mouat, "Chicago's 'Deep Tunnel' May Be in Deep Trouble," *Christian Science Monitor*, Dec. 22, 1980, https://www.csmonitor.com/1980/1222/122242.html.

14. Timothy B. Neary, "Chicago-Style Environmental Politics: Origins of the Deep Tunnel Project," *Journal of Illinois History* 4 (2001): 89–90.

15. Rita Robison, "The Tunnel That Cleaned Up Chicago," *Civil Engineering* 56 (July 1986): 34–37; Christopher Steiner, "Deep Tunnel Digging Finished," *Tribune*, Dec. 11, 2003.

16. Louis P. Cain, "Water," in Grossman, Keating, and Reiff, *Encyclopedia of Chicago*, 863; David L. Schein, "Deep Tunnel," in Grossman, Keating, and Reiff, *Encyclopedia of Chicago*, 230; Neary, "Chicago-Style Environmental Politics," 93–94; Steiner, "Deep Tunnel Digging Finished."

17. Neary, "Chicago-Style Environmental Politics," 99; United States v. Blassingame, 197 F.3d 271 (7th Cir. 1999); Metropolitan Water Reclamation District of Greater Chicago, *TARP Status Report as of December 31, 2018*, Dec. 2018, 1, 3, https://mwrd.org/sites/default/files/documents/June%202019%20Status%20Report.pdf.

18. Metropolitan Water Reclamation District of Greater Chicago, *TARP Status Report*, 1–3; Mike Nolan, "Applause for Area's 'Grand Canyon': Largest Stormwater Reservoir in World to Fill Part of Quarry," *Tribune*, Sept. 2, 2015; "Tunnel and Reservoir Plan Overview," Metropolitan Water Reclamation District of Greater Chicago, accessed Aug. 3, 2020, https://mwrd.org/tunnel-and-reservoir-plan.

19. Neary, "Chicago-Style Environmental Politics," 98–99, contrasts the Chicago River before 1985 and a decade and a half after. For a detailed description of the Deep Tunnel project, see Richard Lanyon, *West by Southwest to Stickney: Draining the Central Area of Chicago and Exorcising Clout* (Chicago: Lake Claremont, 2018), 293–318. To be sure, the project scarcely eliminated all residential flooding in the area. Michael Hawthorne, "Even with $1 Billion Upgrade, Deep Tunnel Swamped by Winter Storm as Streets and

Basements Flooded," *Tribune*, Mar. 15, 2018, https://www.chicagotribune.com/news/breaking/ct-met-deep-tunnel-swamped-20180307-story.html; Michael Hawthorne and Morgan Greene, "Flooding in the Chicago Area Has Been So Bad in the Last Decade That Only Places Ravaged by Hurricanes Sustain More Damage," *Tribune*, May 10, 2019, https://www.chicagotribune.com/news/breaking/ct-met-chicago-flooding-basement-sewage-20190506-story.html.

20. John N. Maclean, "U.S. Steel to Clear South Works Property for Sale," *Tribune*, Mar. 29, 1993.

21. J. Linn Allen, "Steel Mill Offered for Housing, Other Uses," *Tribune*, Sept. 26, 1997; Sallie L. Gaines, "South Works Deal Got Heavy Help," *Tribune*, June 11, 1999; Kelly Quigley, "Solo Cup Digs into South Side," *Crain's Chicago Business*, Oct. 11, 2002, https://www.chicagobusiness.com/article/20021011/NEWS12/20006820/solo-cup-digs-into-south-side; "Solo Cup: South Works Cancellation Downplayed," *Tribune*, June 15, 2005.

22. Liam Ford, "Peoria Mud Finds Home on Lakefront; Sludge Will Turn Mill Site into Park," *Tribune*, May 18, 2004; Jay Koziarz, "Chicago Lakeside Development Mega-Project Abandoned as Developer and US Steel Split," Curbed, Mar. 1, 2016, https://chicago.curbed.com/2016/3/1/11140996/chicago-lakeside-development-project-abandoned.

23. "Chicago Lakeside Phase 1 TIF," City of Chicago, accessed Aug. 3, 2020, http://www.cityofchicago.org/city/en/depts/dcd/supp_info/tif/chicago_lakesidephase1.html; Jon Hilkevitch, "S. Lake Shore Drive Extension to Open," *Tribune*, Oct. 25, 2013; Jessica Wohl, "Mariano's Plans New Store on Former Steel Mill Site in South Chicago," *Tribune*, July 9, 2014.

24. Sam Cholke, "Lakeside Development Dead After U.S. Steel and McCaffery Interests Split," DNAinfo, Feb. 29, 2016, https://www.dnainfo.com/chicago/20160229/south-chicago/lakeside-development-dead-after-us-steel-mccaffery-interests-split/; Joseph S. Pete, "South Works Site May Be Redeveloped More Modestly," *Times of Northwest Indiana*, Mar. 5, 2016, https://www.nwitimes.com/business/local/south-works-site-may-be-redeveloped-more-modestly/article_5d487f3e-a5b3-5653-9731-c8d85c3a127d.html; AJ LaTrace, "Developer Wanted Lucas Museum at Former US Steel South Works Site," Curbed, Dec. 22, 2016, https://chicago.curbed.com/2016/12/22/14051174/lucas-museum-us-steel-lakeside-development-mccaffery-emanuel.

25. Fran Spielman, "Former South Works Site Could Be Sold in Pieces or as a Whole," *Chicago Sun-Times*, Aug. 1, 2016, https://chicago.suntimes.com/2016/8/1/18370522/former-south-works-site-could-be-sold-in-pieces-or-as-a-whole; Office of the Mayor of the City of Chicago, "Mayor Emanuel, Emerald Living, and U.S. Steel Announce Purchase Agreement on South Works Property," press release, Aug. 1, 2017; Danny Ecker, "South Works Developer Says Project Is Still On," *Crain's Chicago Business*, Apr. 24, 2018, https://www.chicagobusiness.com/article/20180424/CRED03/180429956/developer-of-chicago-s-south-works-says-project-is-still-on; Ryan Ori, "Irish Developer Walks Away from Plan to Build 20,000 Homes on South Works Site," *Tribune*, May 24, 2018, https://www.chicagotribune.com/columns/ryan-ori/ct-biz-south-works-deal-ends-ryan-ori-20180524-story.html.

26. People ex rel. Scott v. Chicago Park District, 66 Ill. 2d 65, 80, 360 N.E.2d 773, 781 (1976).

27. Melissa Harris, "Lucas Lays Out Museum Vision," *Tribune*, Oct. 19, 2014; Melissa Harris, "A George Lucas Museum in Chicago?," *Tribune*, Apr. 10, 2014; Melissa Harris, "City Hopes Soldier Field Offering Scores with Lucas," *Tribune*, May 21, 2014.

28. Harris, "Lucas Lays Out Museum Vision"; Spencer Peterson, "MAD's Lucas Museum Is a Moon Mountain with a 'Floating' Halo," Curbed, Nov. 4, 2014, https://www.curbed.com/2014/11/4/10027916/mad-architects-lucas-museum-design; "Keep George Lucas' Museum off Chicago's Lakefront," editorial, *Tribune*, Nov. 7, 2014, https://www.chicagotribune.com/business/ct-lucas-museum-edit-1109-20141107-story.html; Friends

of the Parks v. Chicago Park District, No. 14-cv-09096, 2015 WL 1188615, at *1–2 (N.D. Ill. Mar. 12, 2015).

29. *Friends of the Parks*, 2015 WL 1188615, at *2–4, *9–10.

30. Londoner v. City & County of Denver, 210 U.S. 373 (1908), and Bi-Metallic Inv. Co. v. State Board of Equalization, 239 U.S. 441 (1915), remain the leading expositions of "property" in this legal context, modern developments being not to the contrary as relevant here. Thomas W. Merrill, "The Landscape of Constitutional Property," *Virginia Law Review* 86 (2000): 956–57.

31. *Friends of the Parks*, 2015 WL 1188615, at *10; Monique Garcia and Patrick M. O'Connell, "Rauner Sent Bill on Obama, Lucas Sites," *Tribune*, Apr. 24, 2015; "Obama's Presidential Library: A Once-in-a-Lifetime Exception," *Tribune*, May 5, 2015; 2015 Ill. Laws 238–39 (Public Act No. 99-003). The court was also mistaken in its conclusion that Friends of the Parks had standing to sue in federal court simply because any taxpayer in Illinois can bring a public trust claim. 2015 WL 1188615, at *3. It is well established that standing under state law does not automatically translate into standing under federal law. ASARCO Inc. v. Kadish, 490 U.S. 605, 617 (1989). And, in fact, the objection of a taxpayer to a project on the grounds that it violates the public trust doctrine would seem to be among the "generalized grievances" that do not create standing for federal purposes. Schlesinger v. Reservists Committee to Stop the War, 418 U.S. 208, 216–23 (1974).

32. Grace Wong, "Park District Clears Lease for Lucas Museum," *Tribune*, Oct. 15, 2015; John Byrne, "Lucas Museum Jumps Another Hurdle," *Tribune*, Oct. 16, 2015; John Byrne, "Bears Parking Deal in Place, Council Clears Lucas Museum," *Tribune*, Oct. 29, 2015.

33. Friends of the Parks v. Chicago Park District, 160 F. Supp. 3d 1060, 1062, 1064–65 (N.D. Ill. 2016).

34. Jason Meisner and Patrick M. O'Connell, "City Tries New Tactic for Museum," *Tribune*, May 5, 2016; Order, In re Chicago Park District, No. 16–2022 (7th Cir. May 5, 2016); Patrick M. O'Connell and Bill Ruthhart, "Chicago Loses Lucas Museum," *Tribune*, June 25, 2016; Deborah Vankin, "Los Angeles Will Be Home to George Lucas' $1-Billion Museum," *Los Angeles Times*, Jan. 10, 2017, https://www.latimes.com/entertainment/arts/la-et-cm-la-wins-lucas-museum-20170110-htmlstory.html.

35. Don Gonyea, "Bidding Starts Early for Site of Obama's Future Library," National Public Radio, Feb. 8, 2014, https://www.npr.org/2014/02/07/273056702/bidding-starts-early-for-site-of-obamas-future-library; "Obama Foundation Announces Jackson Park as Site of the Obama Presidential Center," Obama Foundation, July 29, 2016, https://www.obama.org/updates/obama-foundation-announces-jackson-park-site-obama-presidential-center/; Lolly Bowean, "Group Suing to Stop Obama Presidential Center Criticizes New Agreement over Use of Jackson Park," *Tribune*, Sep. 19, 2018, https://www.chicagotribune.com/news/obama-center/ct-met-environmentalists-push-against-obama-foundation-20180919-story.html; Angela Caputo, Katherine Skiba, and Blair Kamin, "Monument to the Future: Obamas Unveil Design for 'Transformational' Center in Jackson Park," *Tribune*, May 4, 2017; Lolly Bowean, "Obama Center Parking Buried: Community Opposition to Above-Ground Garage Alters Jackson Park Plan," *Tribune*, Jan. 9, 2018.

36. Protect Our Parks, Inc. v. Chicago Park District, 368 F. Supp. 3d 1184, 1188–1192, 1194–95 (N.D. Ill. 2019).

37. Protect Our Parks, Inc. v. Chicago Park District, 385 F. Supp. 3d 662, 667 (N.D. Ill. 2019); Aaron Gettinger, "Judge in OPC Lawsuit to 'Micromanage' Discovery, Sets May 30 for Hearing," *Hyde Park Herald*, Feb. 27, 2019. One of the authors of this book (Merrill) was among the law professors who submitted an amicus curiae brief in the case, maintaining that the plan did not violate the public trust doctrine, consistently with the views maintained here.

38. *Protect Our Parks*, 385 F. Supp. 3d at 676–83.

39. *Protect Our Parks*, 385 F. Supp. 3d at 676–77.

40. *Protect Our Parks*, 385 F. Supp. 3d at 677–79.

41. *Protect Our Parks*, 385 F. Supp. 3d at 681–82.

42. Protect Our Parks, Inc. v. Chicago Park District, 971 F.3d 722, 730–32, 737–38 (7th Cir. 2020) (quoting various Supreme Court decisions).

43. For critiques of the public trust doctrine based on its tensions with democratic norms, see, e.g., William D. Araiza, "Democracy, Distrust, and the Public Trust: Process-Based Constitutional Theory, the Public Trust Doctrine, and the Search for a Substantive Environmental Value," *UCLA Law Review* 45 (1997): 385–452; James L. Huffman, "A Fish Out of Water: The Public Trust Doctrine in a Constitutional Democracy," *Environmental Law* 19 (1989): 527–72; Richard J. Lazarus, "Changing Conceptions of Property and Sovereignty in Natural Resources: Questioning the Public Trust Doctrine," *Iowa Law Review* 71 (1986): 631–716.

Index of Published Decisions

Index of Subjects

Page numbers in *italics* indicate illustrations that are not otherwise part of the page range or reference.